The Bloomsbury Reader in Christian-Muslim Relations, 600–1500

ALSO AVAILABLE FROM BLOOMSBURY

The Bloomsbury Reader in the Study of Myth,
Edited by Jonathan Miles-Watson and Vivian Asimos

The Bloomsbury Reader in Cultural Approaches to the Study of Religion,
Edited by Sarah J. Bloesch and Meredith Minister

The Bloomsbury Reader in Religion, Sexuality, and Gender,
Edited by Donald L. Boisvert and Carly Daniel-Hughes

The Bloomsbury Reader in Christian-Muslim Relations, 600–1500

EDITED BY DAVID THOMAS

BLOOMSBURY ACADEMIC
LONDON • NEW YORK • OXFORD • NEW DELHI • SYDNEY

BLOOMSBURY ACADEMIC
Bloomsbury Publishing Plc
50 Bedford Square, London, WC1B 3DP, UK
1385 Broadway, New York, NY 10018, USA
29 Earlsfort Terrace, Dublin 2, Ireland

BLOOMSBURY, BLOOMSBURY ACADEMIC and the Diana logo
are trademarks of Bloomsbury Publishing Plc

First published in Great Britain 2022

Cover design: Toby Way
Cover image: *A Moor and a Christian playing the lute*, miniature in a book of music from the 'Cantigas' of Alfonso X 'the Wise' (1221-84)
© Index Fototeca/Bridgeman Images

A catalogue record for this book is available from the British Library.

A catalog record for this book is available from the Library of Congress.

ISBN: HB: 978-1-3502-1410-1
PB: 978-1-3502-1409-5
ePDF: 978-1-3502-1412-5
eBook: 978-1-3502-1411-8

Typeset by Integra Software Services Pvt. Ltd.

Contents

Introduction
David Thomas 1

Map of Western Europe and the Middle East 6

Muslim Arabic

Muslims encountering Christians in the Islamic Empire
David Thomas 9

1 Ibn al-Layth, *The letter of Ibn al-Layth*
Clint R. Hackenburg 12

2 *The Pact of ʿUmar*
Milka Levy-Rubin 16

3 Abū ʿUthmān al-Jāḥiẓ, *In rebuttal of the Christians*
James E. Montgomery 19

4 ʿAlī l-Ṭabarī, *The book of religion and empire*
David Thomas 23

5 Abū ʿĪsā l-Warrāq, *The refutation of the three sects of the Christians*
David Thomas 27

6 *Islamic Psalms of David*
David R. Vishanoff 30

7 Al-Shābushtī, *Book of monasteries*
Hilary Kilpatrick 34

8 ʿAbd al-Jabbār, *Confirmation of the signs of prophethood*
Gabriel Said Reynolds 37

9 Al-Juwaynī, *Assuaging thirst*
David Thomas 41

10 Abū l-Qāsim al-Anṣārī, *The indispensable, on theology*
Richard Todd 45

11 Ibn Jubayr, *Travels*
Alex Mallett 49

12 Usāma ibn Munqidh, *The book of instructions*
Alex Mallett 53

13 Najm al-Dīn al-Ṭūfī, *Critical commentary on the four Gospels*
Lejla Demiri 56

14 Ghāzī ibn al-Wāsiṭī, *Refutation of the* dhimmīs *and those who follow them*
Alex Mallett 59

15 Ibn Taymiyya, *The correct answer*
Jon Hoover 62

Christian Arabic

Arabic-speaking Christians in the Islamic Empire
David Thomas 67

16 Abū Rāʾiṭa l-Takrītī, *On the Incarnation*
Sandra Toenies Keating 70

17 Theodore Abū Qurra, *Some statements of Theodore, Bishop of Ḥarrān*
John Lamoreaux 73

18 ʿAbd al-Masīḥ al-Kindī, *Apology*
Sandra Toenies Keating 76

19 ʿAmmār al-Baṣrī, *Book of questions and answers*
Mark Beaumont 79

20 The Muqaṭṭam miracle, from the Copto-Arabic *Synaxarion*
Mark Swanson 83

21 Elias of Nisibis and Abū l-Qāsim, *An epistolary exchange*
Michael Kuhn 86

22 *The Apocalypse of Samuel*
Jos van Lent 90

23 Yaḥyā of Antioch on the Caliph al-Ḥākim
Paul Walker 93

24 *Letter from the people of Cyprus*
David Thomas 97

25 *The Martyrdom of Rizqallāh ibn Nabaʿ*
Mark Swanson 100

Iberian Arabic

Muslims and Christians in Islamic Spain
Juan Pedro Monferrer-Sala 105

26 Ibn Ḥazm, *Judgement regarding the religions, inclinations and sects*
Camilla Adang 107

27 Al-Ṭurṭūshī, *A lamp for rulers*
Maribel Fierro 111

28 *The Letter of al-Qūṭī*
Diego R. Sarrió Cucarella 115

29 *Trinitizing the unity of God*
Juan Pedro Monferrer-Sala 119

30 Al-Bājī, *Book against the Torah*
Camilla Adang 123

Greek

Greek authors responding to Islam
Johannes Pahlitzsch 129

31 John of Damascus, *On heresies*, chapter 100
Manolis Ulbricht 132

32 Theophanes the Confessor, *Chronographia*
Thomas Pratsch 136

33 Nicetas of Byzantium, *Refutation of the Qur'an*
Manolis Ulbricht 139

34 Euodios the Monk, *Martyrdom of the forty-two martyrs*
Athina Kolia-Dermitzaki 143

35 *Digenēs Akritēs*
Elizabeth Jeffreys 147

36 Nicetas Choniates, *History*
Niccolò Zorzi 152

37 Manuel II Palaeologus, *Dialogue with a Persian*
Miriam Salzmann and Tristan Schmidt 155

38 *The Life of George the Younger: An account of a martyr who was martyred in our time*
Mirela Ivanova 159

39 Gennadios Scholarios, *Questions and answers concerning our Lord Jesus Christ*
Klaus-Peter Todt 162

Armenian, Syriac and Other Languages

Syriac and Armenian Christians under Muslim rule
Thomas A. Carlson 169

40 Sebeos the Armenian, *History of Sebeos*
Rachel Claire Dryden 172

41 Giwargis I, *Synodal canons*
Lev Weitz 176

42 Theodore bar Koni, *Scholion*, chapter 10
Ryann Elizabeth Craig 179

43 Dionysius of Tell Maḥrē, *Chronicle*
Marianna Mazzola 183

44 Two excerpts from the *Life of Gabriel of Beth Qustan*
Jeanne-Nicole Mellon Saint-Laurent 187

45 *The History of the Anonymous Storyteller*
Tim Greenwood 190

46 Elias of Nisibis, *Chronography*
Anna Chrysostomides 194

47 Matthew of Edessa, *Chronicle*
Tara L. Andrews 198

48 Dionysius bar Ṣalībī, *Commentary on the Cross*
Kelli Bryant Gibson 201

49 Gregory Barhebraeus, *Candelabrum of the sanctuaries*
Salam Rassi 205

50 *The history of Mār Yahballāhā and Rabban Ṣawmā*
Thomas A. Carlson 209

51 Grigor Tat'ewac'i, 'Against the Tajiks', from the *Book of Questions*
Sergio La Porta 212

Latin and Romance Languages

Latin and Romance writings on Islam
Graham Barrett 217

Latin writings

52 *History or deeds of the Franks*
Roger Collins 221

53 *Book of Pontiffs*
Graham Barrett 224

54 Paschasius Radbertus, *Commentary on the Gospel of Matthew*
Charles West 228

55 Paul Alvarus, *Indiculus luminosus*
Kenneth Baxter Wolf 231

56 *Chronicle of Albelda*
Graham Barrett 235

57 *Passion of Pelagius*
Kati Ihnat 239

58 Gregory VII, *Register*
Guy Perry 242

59 Raymond of Aguilers, *History of the Franks who captured Jerusalem*
Susan B. Edgington 245

60 Guibert of Nogent, *Deeds of God through the Franks*
Beth Spacey 248

61 *Book of Testaments of Lorvão*
Graham Barrett 251

62 Robert of Ketton, *Prologue* and *Preface*
Robert Portass 255

63 Caffaro of Genoa, *History of the capture of Almería and Tortosa*
Rodrigo García-Velasco 259

64 William of Tyre, *Chronicle*
Andrew D. Buck 263

65 Peter the Chanter, *Summa on the sacraments and spiritual advice*
Emily Corran 267

66 Francis of Assisi, *Rules of the Friars Minor*
Graham Barrett 270

67 Roger Bacon, *The greater work*
Amanda Power 274

68 Riccoldo da Monte di Croce, *Letters to the Church triumphant*
Rita George-Tvrtković 278

69 Petrus Marsilius, *Letter to an apostate of the Order of Friars Minor*
Antoni Biosca i Bas 281

70 Juan de Segovia, *Letter to the Cardinal of Saint Peter (Nicholas of Cusa)*
Anne Marie Wolf 284

71 Diogo Gomes, *On the first discovery of Guinea*
Martha T. Frederiks 288

Romance writings

72 Old French epic poems and the *Song of Roland*
Carol Sweetenham 291

73 Ramon Llull, *The book of the Gentile and the three wise men*
Graham Barrett 295

74 Marco Polo, *Description of the world*
Sharon Kinoshita 299

75 Jean de Joinville, *Life of Saint Louis*
Huw Grange 302

76 John Mandeville, *Book of wonders*
Iain Macleod Higgins 305

77 Juan Manuel, *Book of estates*
Anita Savo 309

78 Bertrandon de la Broquière, *Voyage to the Middle East*
Attila Bárány 312

79 Hernando de Talavera, *Instruction from the Archbishop of Granada*
Anita Savo 316

Table of themes 320

Glossary 321

Index 326

Introduction

Christian-Muslim relations

David Thomas, University of Birmingham

This book is about relations between people of faith. It shows how their experiences of the other and stories they heard about them, together with their interpretations of their own scriptures, shaped their ideas of the other and their attitudes towards them. In the years 600–1500, these were crucial in determining the ways in which Christians and Muslims dealt with one another.

In the latter years of his life, as ruler of a powerful state in western Arabia, the Prophet Muḥammad sent armies into the borders of the Eastern Roman Empire. After his death in 632, his successors continued this policy, and within a few decades great tracts to the north, east and west had come under Islamic rule. Most of the people the armies encountered in these regions were Christians, speakers of Arabic, Greek, Syriac and other languages. On the basis of references in the Qur'an, Muslims classified them as parts of a distinct religious community with its own revelation brought by the prophet ʿĪsā (Jesus). Together with the Jews and others who had also received revelations, they gave them the qur'anic name People of the Book (*Ahl al-kitāb*). From an early date they imposed taxes on them, and within a short time they established rules to govern their conduct and their relations with themselves. These rules were gradually refined and particularized, and named the *Pact of ʿUmar*, conferring on them the authority of the second caliph ʿUmar ibn al-Khaṭṭāb (r. 634–44).

Muslim rule continued over the captured areas, roughly comprising present-day Jordan, Iraq, Syria, Palestine and Egypt, from the first century of Islam, and later extended further through North Africa and into the Iberian Peninsula, and moved into Iran and Central Asia, Anatolia and south-eastern Europe. The populations of many parts of them were predominantly Christian, and it is here that meetings led to familiarity and engendered attitudes that profoundly affected dealings between them.

Muslims and Christians rarely encountered one another as friends, either within the Islamic Empire, where the one was conspicuously superior to the other, or outside, where encounters regularly took the form of armed confrontations. And if experience taught that relations were hostile, the scriptures of the two faiths showed why there could be no alternative.

On the Christian side, the New Testament portrays Jesus Christ as the climax of God's relations with His creation. It suggests that the whole of history led up to his coming and that nothing after would change what he had been and done. In 1321, some Christians in Cyprus confidently explained this at the end of a letter they sent to Muḥammad ibn Abī Ṭālib al-Dimashqī (d. 1327), a leading Muslim scholar of the day:

> If the rank of the complete man born from Mary outstrips the ranks of all humans in exaltedness, including the prophets, the blessed and the angels, to the extent I have described of the creative Word of God and His Spirit uniting with him, then he must be perfection. And after this perfection there is nothing left to put in place, because everything that came before required it and there was no need for what came after it. For nothing can come after perfection and be superior, but must rather be inferior or derivative, and there is no need for what is derivative.[1]

They make it unmistakably clear that there is no place for Islam in the divine plan, and by implication that Islam cannot be of God.

The attitude on the Muslim side was analogous, though it differed in detail. The Qur'an, as God's direct word to humanity, taught that it itself was part of a succession of revelations brought by a line of prophetic messengers. These were all men (as it turned out) who had been chosen by God and sent to individual communities, and their messages were all essentially the same because they came from the one divine Source. The Qur'an was the culmination of this succession, and Muḥammad was the last in the line of messengers. Unlike his predecessors, he was sent to the whole world, and the Qur'an was universal in scope. This meant that Christianity, Judaism and other scriptural religions should yield to Islam, and their followers should become Muslims as they recognized its final authority. As al-Dimashqī writes at the end of his reply to the Cypriots:

> What a shame it is for you Christians, brothers in kind and in person! If only you would understand these words I have put before you, the things I have proved and made plain! But I hope, if God the exalted wills, that you will understand them, so that what is clear to us will become clear to you, and you will know that there is no god but God alone with no partner.[2]

For him, any claims that challenge the uniqueness of God are demonstrably wrong, so Christian teachings must be mistaken.

---

[1] R. Ebied and D. Thomas (eds and trans), *Muslim-Christian Polemic during the Crusades: The Letter from the People of Cyprus and Ibn Abī Ṭālib's Response*, Leiden, 2005, p. 144.
[2] Ebied and Thomas, *Muslim-Christian Polemic*, p. 494.

Christians maintain that the Bible says nothing about Islam or Muḥammad (though this would be hotly disputed by Muslims). All it does say is that Jesus is the final word from God. On the other hand, the Qur'an is very detailed in what it says about Jesus and Christianity. Its main theme is that God is one, so it follows that Christian claims that God is three and that Jesus is His Son are wrong. Messengers before Muḥammad attested to this, and so did the scriptures they brought. As one of these messengers, the human Jesus expressly denied being divine or Son of God, despite being born of a virgin or being raised to God instead of dying on the cross. The *Injīl* was a revelation in the form of a single scripture brought by Jesus, but the People of the Book (including Christians) concealed, substituted or corrupted their scriptures. In saying these things, it is as though the Qur'an is answering points made by Christians and correcting them.

Among Christians throughout the Islamic world knowledge about Islam must have increased quickly, and it would also have spread beyond. Within a century, exchanges between followers of the two faiths are recorded from both the Arab heartlands and the West, while works about and against Islam appeared in Greek, Syriac, Armenian and Latin. At the time of the Crusades in the eleventh to thirteenth centuries the number of works in Latin grew enormously, and at about the same time works in vernacular European languages also appeared. Nearly all of them exhibit a fascinating variety of argumentative strategies. A noticeable trait in works by both Muslims and Christians is that as they developed points introduced by earlier authors, they often reproduced the same arguments as them. In this way, traditions of polemic came into being and continued through the period of 600–1500 and well beyond, as far as the nineteenth century and to the present. It also suggests that these traditions frequently replaced live encounters and fresh direct information.

On the Muslim side, these arguments were inspired directly by the Qur'an. With regard to the being of God, theologians fashioned rational proofs that the doctrine of the Trinity could not be reconciled with monotheism because the three divine Persons could not be reduced to a single Being. They likewise showed that the Incarnation was illogical because it involved the infinite Divinity becoming limited within the body of Jesus. With regard to the Gospels and Torah, they found verses that could be interpreted to refer to Muḥammad – among the most frequently cited were the Paraclete verses in the Gospel of John – or they argued that the actual texts had been corrupted, either deliberately or through disasters, and were no longer reliable.

Demonstrations to prove the correctness of these claims were largely conducted with forensic thoroughness and decorum. But this was not the case with Christian polemics, where it was a matter of showing that Muḥammad could not be a true messenger from God or the Qur'an a revealed scripture. As Christian authors were able to learn more about Muḥammad, they found evidence to show his trances were really epileptic fits, his marriages were to satisfy his lust and his career was motivated by the cynical desire to gain power and wealth. He thus fell short of Jesus, and his prophetic claims failed. Christians found the Qur'an a jumble, attributing it to Muḥammad misunderstanding borrowed biblical passages and taking parts from a heretical or disillusioned monk. Criticisms of this kind were often unrestrained in their invective and sometimes included lurid descriptions of his activities. Of course, Muslim authors could not respond with personal insults against Jesus because he was one of their prophets.

These and similar arguments provided the ideological foundations for both scholarly disputes and armed clashes. Christians frequently saw Muslims as instruments of the devil because they regarded Islam as a temptation to diverge from true belief, while Muslims accused Christians of irresponsibility in corrupting their scripture to such a degree that the doctrines derived from it were bound to be confused and irrational. There are hardly any signs of wishing to understand the other or to find ways towards agreement. The problem was that both Christians and Muslims judged the other according to the principles of their own religion: Muḥammad should show the same virtues as Jesus; the trinitarian God should exhibit the pure simplicity of the qur'anic God. They nearly always missed the advantages in the other and were far too often speaking past them than with or to them.

It should be borne in mind that despite these opposing attitudes, Christians and Muslims did benefit one another immensely. Within the Islamic Empire, Christians functioned as doctors, bureaucrats and translators, in the latter role making accessible important Greek works and stimulating intellectual advances in the Islamic world. In turn, Muslims composed works of philosophy, medicine, mathematics and so on, that when they were translated into Latin stimulated European minds in unprecedented ways. There was undeniable indebtedness, and sometimes collaboration, though this did not stop general opposition and the abiding sense that the other was an adversary.

The passages presented here are examples of the ways in which Christians and Muslims showed their knowledge of the other and their attitudes towards them, as well as the strategies they employed to prove they were culpably wrong. Of course, the works from which they are taken were all composed by people who were literate, and thus the degree to which they represent general attitudes, rather than the poised positions of the study or debating hall, is open to question. But this is the nature of the material, and at least as far as can be seen the reports they provide suggest the attitudes were virtually endemic. Each passage has been taken from a significant work in the history of Christian-Muslim relations, and many have been translated for the first time. They are all kept relatively short in order to show one or a few significant features in the works from which they come, and each is preceded by a brief account of the work, its author, and its significance in Christian-Muslim relations.

Further details about the works from which the passages are taken can be found in one of the early volumes of *Christian-Muslim Relations: A Bibliographical History* (Leiden, 2009 continuing (*CMR*)), which is intended as a comprehensive history of relations as told through the writings of both faiths. Any studies that have appeared since the *CMR* entry was published are given at the end of the introduction to each passage.

This Reader was brought into being in the middle of the Covid-19 pandemic, amid the turmoil caused to family life and to teaching and research. The main editor is deeply thankful to the section editors, Graham Barrett, Thomas Carlson, Juan Pedro Monferrer

Sala and Johannes Pahlitszch, for selecting passages and translators, and generally keeping to schedules, and also to John Chesworth for coordinating the work and maintaining order. It is a pleasure to thank the Spalding Trust for a grant towards the work.

General reading

Robert Hoyland, *Seeing Islam as Others Saw It: A Survey and Evaluation of Christian, Jewish and Zoroastrian Writings on Early Islam*, Princeton, NJ, 2002.
John V. Tolan, *Saracens. Islam and the Medieval European Imagination*, New York, 2002.
John Renard, *Islam and Christianity: Theological Themes in Comparative Perspective*, Berkeley, CA, 2011.
David Cheetham, Douglas Pratt and David Thomas (eds), *Understanding Interreligious Relations*, Oxford, 2014.
Samuel Noble and Alexander Treiger (eds), *The Orthodox Church in the Arab World, 700–1700: An Anthology of Sources*, DeKalb, IL, 2014.
Jarbel Rodriguez, *Muslim and Christian Contact in the Middle Ages: A Reader*, Toronto, 2015.
Hugh Goddard, *A History of Christian-Muslim Relations*, 2nd edition, Edinburgh, 2020.
Luigi Andrea Berto, *Christians under the Crescent and Muslims under the Cross c.630–1923*, London, 2020.

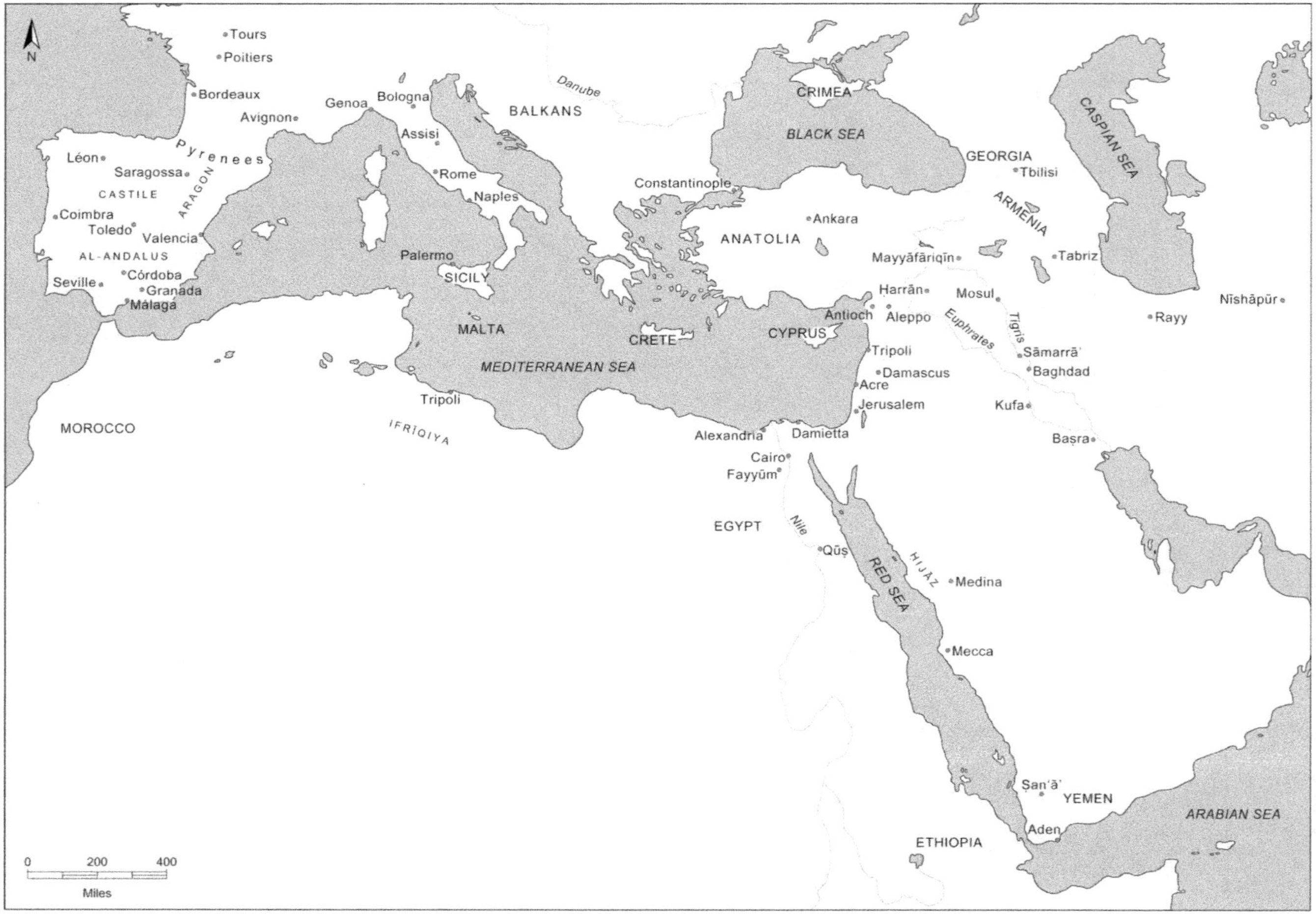

Western Europe and the Middle East

Muslim Arabic

Muslims encountering Christians in the Islamic Empire

David Thomas, University of Birmingham

From the earliest years of Islam, Muslims met with opposition from Christians both in armed clashes and in religious and philosophical debates. Muslim attitudes towards Christians that were formed through these experiences settled into patterns that were repeated and elaborated until, through long usage, they assumed a form of orthodoxy.

During Muḥammad's latter years in Medina (630–2) raiding parties were sent north into the margins of the Eastern Roman or Byzantine Empire. In the decades following his death, Palestine, Syria, Mesopotamia, Persia and Egypt came under Muslim control, and within a century the southern coasts of the Mediterranean and the Iberian Peninsula were added. The vast empire thus created included substantial Christian populations. Its first rulers were from the Umayyad dynasty (661–750), with its capital at Damascus in Syria. The dynasty was eliminated by the ʿAbbasids, though a surviving Umayyad descendant set up a state in the Iberian Peninsula, with its capital at Córdoba. The ʿAbbasids moved the capital east to the new city of Baghdad, from which they ruled until 1258, though increasingly in name only. When the Mongols assassinated the last Baghdad ʿAbbasid, a continuing line of figurehead caliphs was set up Cairo (1261–1517).

From the middle of the ninth century, Turkic tribes moved in from the east and took effective control in Baghdad, while at the same time the empire progressively split into independent regional states. Islam, however, remained the recognized religion, and Christians both within the empire and outside continued as religious and military competitors.

In the early centuries, the main external opponents were the Christian Byzantines. Muslim armies were sent against their capital Constantinople within decades of Muḥammad's death, and clashes between the two sides continued until the Ottoman Turks finally conquered the city in 1453. Western Europe was a major opponent through the eleventh to thirteenth centuries, when a succession of Crusading armies confronted Muslim forces in Syria, Palestine and Egypt. Jerusalem, their professed goal, was seized from the Muslims and later recovered, and for a time a series of

Christian states were established in Syria and Lebanon. Over roughly the same period, Islamic domains in Iberia were progressively seized by Christian armies until Granada, the last emirate, finally surrendered in 1492.

It was in these centuries that Islam developed as a political entity and distinctive religion, and the regulations governing the populations of Christians within the Islamic Empire were instituted. Together with Jews and other recipients of revealed scriptures, Christians were recognized as *Ahl al-kitāb* ('People of the book', see e.g. Q 2:105) and were accorded the status of *Ahl al-dhimma* or *dhimmī*s ('People of the Covenant'), giving them guarantees in law in exchange for compliance with certain regulations, which in reality served to ensure they remained subordinate. This body of regulations was known as the *Pact of ʿUmar*, after the second caliph, though it only settled into its complete form long after his time.

The Qur'an calls Christians *Naṣārā* ('Nazarenes') and sees them as a community to whom the messenger ʿĪsā (Jesus) was sent to give God's guidance in the form of the *Injīl* (Gospel). Like other revelations, such as the *Tawrāt* (Torah) revealed to Mūsā, the *Zabūr* (Psalms) revealed to Dāwūd, and the *Qur'an* (Recitation) revealed to Muḥammad, this was a single text, essentially identical to the Qur'an in its insistence on the oneness of God and foretelling the coming of Muḥammad (Q 7:157, 61:6). In consequence, Christians were worthy of respect as possessors of their own scripture. The Qur'an praises them as people who are closest in affection to the Muslims (5:82). However, the Qur'an also criticizes the *Naṣārā* for beliefs that defy monotheism, most seriously the claim that God is three (4:171, 5:73) and Jesus is His son (4:171) and shares in His divinity. It also denies that Jesus was crucified (4:157) and hints that Christians, as part of the *Ahl al-kitāb*, were guilty of concealing and distorting parts of their original scripture (2:75, 2:140, 3:78).

On the basis of the Qur'an, Muslim apologists in the early centuries accused Christians of either deleting references to Muḥammad from the *Injīl* or interpreting passages to conceal predictions of him. In the same period, rationalist or speculative theologians (*mutakallimūn*) developed demonstrations of the logical confusion of Christian doctrines in consequence of Christians ignoring the uniqueness and strict oneness of God. Some scholars also constructed defences of Muḥammad's prophetic status, often by interpreting biblical verses to support this. Generally, Muslims tended to regard Christians as having wasted what they had received from God, so that the whole edifice of their beliefs was askew. Since Christians refused to acknowledge this, they could only be pitied or despised and compelled by logic to see that they had abandoned the truth.

Even so, Muslims were greatly indebted to Christians living under their rule. At certain times, notably under the Umayyads, Christians made up the state bureaucracy because of the expertise they possessed, while under the early ʿAbbasids the leading medical experts were Christians, as were the best translators of Greek scientific and philosophical works. In certain circles in Baghdad, Christian and Muslim philosophers learned from one another and explored together scientific and philosophical issues.

It is evident that Muslim treatment of their Christian subjects varied greatly according to place, time and government, though the *Pact of ʿUmar* was rarely far from mind. While Christians might enjoy relative freedom at times, Muslims were seldom slow to remind them of their position, and rulers such as the Umayyad ʿUmar ibn ʿAbd al-ʿAzīz (r. 717–20), the ʿAbbasid al-Mutawakkil (r. 847–61), the Fāṭimid al-Hākim bi-Amr Allāh (r. 996–1021) and many Mamlūk sultans were known for their enforcement of the pact. There was unremitting pressure to convert to Islam, and Christians who resisted found it increasingly expedient to keep their faith to themselves.

Further reading

Richard Fletcher, *The Cross and the Crescent, Christianity and Islam from Muhammad to the Reformation*, London, 2003.

Hugh Goddard, *A History of Christian-Muslim Relations*, 2nd edition, Edinburgh, 2020.

Carole Hillenbrand, *The Crusades: Islamic Perspectives*, Edinburgh, 1999.

Zachary Karabell, *People of the Book. The Forgotten History of Islam and the West*, London, 2007.

Alex Mallett, *Popular Muslim Reactions to the Franks in the Levant, 1097–1291*, Farnham, 2014.

David Thomas (ed.), *Routledge Handbook on Christian-Muslim Relations*, London, 2018.

Arthur S. Tritton, *The Caliphs and Their Non-Muslim Subjects*, London, 1930 (reissued frequently).

Jacques Waardenburg, *Muslim Perceptions of Other Religions: A Historical Survey*, New York, 1999.

1

Ibn al-Layth, *The letter of Ibn al-Layth*

Clint R. Hackenburg

In the late eighth century, Abū l-Rabīʿ Muḥammad ibn al-Layth (d. *c.* 819), who was secretary to a succession of early ʿAbbāsid rulers, addressed a letter on behalf of the Caliph Hārūn al-Rashīd (r. 786–809) to the Byzantine Emperor Constantine VI (r. 780–97). This work, known as *Risālat Abī l-Rabīʿ Muḥammad ibn al-Layth allatī katabahā li-l-Rashīd ilā Qusṭanṭīn malik al-Rūm* ('The letter of Abū l-Rabīʿ Muḥammad ibn al-Layth which he wrote for al-Rashīd to the Byzantine emperor Constantine'), is in many ways the continuation of an earlier Islamic tradition, which claimed that Muḥammad had sent letters to various rulers inviting them to embrace Islam. Ibn al-Layth was maintaining this diplomatic convention, albeit from a position of far greater military strength.

In his letter, Ibn al-Layth not only reiterates the great points of religious controversy between Christians and Muslims that were prevalent during the early ʿAbbasid period, but also introduces several original apologetic and polemical strategies. First, he defends the absolute oneness of God, which he associates with the perfectly guided orderliness of the physical world. Second, he presents Muḥammad as the indisputable Seal of the Prophets sent by God (Q 33:40), maintaining that this position is supported by reason and miracles as well as by verses from the Bible and Qur'an, and discrediting well-established Christian objections to this claim by accentuating Muḥammad's message of respect, modesty and abstinence from worldly living. Moreover, he concludes that in order to obscure this evidence in the Bible, Jewish and Christian scholars changed its text (*taḥrīf al-naṣṣ*) and altered its meaning (*taḥrīf al-maʿnā*). Generally speaking, in this letter Ibn al-Layth greatly expands upon the limited exegesis of the Bible found in the Qur'an and *Sīra*. Furthermore, he stands out as one of the earliest Muslim apologists who sought to utilize the Bible and the Qur'an together not only to defend Islamic doctrine, but also to discredit Christian beliefs.

In the third and final section of his letter, Ibn al-Layth condemns the Christian doctrines of the Trinity and Incarnation as specious, illogical and absurd. With his closing remarks, he offers the Byzantines three choices: to convert to Islam, to pay the poll-tax (*jizya*) and demonstrate subservience, or to face destruction by armed force (*jihād*). Ibn al-Layth's final words are an early attestation to the volatile and hostile nature of ʿAbbasid–Byzantine relations. Moreover, the candour with which he addresses the Byzantine emperor on behalf of Hārūn al-Rashīd represents a self-assured ʿAbbasid caliph who clearly believed that he was dictating policy to a subordinate ruler.

CMR 1, pp. 347–53.

This translation is based on Hadi Eid (ed. and trans.), *Lettre du calife Hârûn al-Rashîd*, Paris, [1993], pp. 185–7.

[Ibn al-Layth and the threat of jihād*]*

The Commander of the Believers hopes that God will carry out his vengeance upon you through the hands of the Muslims, for after he had established a covenant with you and instituted a pact with sacred oaths and inviolable agreements, whose fulfilment was your burden and your responsibility, you brought God as a witness against yourself; those around you heard the oaths and agreements, and your patricians and bishops governed in accordance with them. However, by violating this covenant, by hating Muslims, by betraying loyalty, and by permitting the forbidden, you [have now demonstrated] that you no longer fear God, nor are you shamed by man. Therefore, anticipate punishment and expect dishonour. The Commander of the Believers trusts that divine punishment will not be withheld, if God wills.

Some of the ways in which God wants to take revenge on you involve the Commander of the Believers, who will become determined and resolved to do what God has cast into his heart – that is, the will, desire and hope to mount armies to overrun your country, to send fighters to capture your land, to free himself of any distraction apart from you and to wage *jihād* against you, preferring that over any other action, until you believe in God – whether you are willing or unwilling – or until you pay the *jizya* out of hand, as a subordinate. Therefore, be prepared to have the *jizya* imposed on you, and you can be certain that you have neither the power nor the fortitude to avoid it. The troops of the Commander of the Believers are abundant and available, his treasuries are full and abounding, his soul spends generously and his hand gives freely. The Muslims have actively turned against you, and God has prepared them to battle you; they lie in wait for such a battle and in fighting you they will inflict a punishment more grievous than any other, if God wills.

The letter of the Commander of the Believers is the forewarning that precedes his troops and his armies, if God wills. Unless you pay the *jizya*, which the Commander of the Believers invites and urges you and your people to embrace out of mercy for the weak, to whom you have not shown mercy, and out of sympathy for the poor, to whom you have not shown sympathy, they will face deportation, exile, slaughter, captivity, poverty and oppression because your selfishness and the hardness of your heart. You safeguard your elites and banish your common folk – that is, the weak, the poor and the impoverished, whom you do not adequately protect, whom you do not skilfully defend and whom you do not watch over with mercy and sympathy, despite the teaching of Christ and his word in the scripture, 'Blessed are those who show people mercy, for surely they will be shown mercy. Blessed are those who make peace among the people, for surely they are the pure ones of God and the light of the sons of Adam.'

By God, if the impoverished, the peasants, the poor, the weak and the manual labourers among you knew what the Commander of the Believers could provide for them, they would come to him and offer themselves to him, for he would shelter them, settle them in his vast land, grant them access to flowing waterways and treat them with a justice which you cannot reach or even approach, out of compassion, consideration and decency for them. Meanwhile, he would grant them freedom in their religious affairs, neither forcing a different religion upon them nor coercing them into another. [If they knew these benefits], they would choose the company of the Commander of the Believers over yours, as well as his companionship over yours, and in doing so, they would save themselves, their wealth, their children, their wives and their families from that which befalls them every year and what they experience every raiding season.

Therefore, fear God and accept that which the *jizya* offers you, and do not refuse the fortune it holds for you and the people of your kingdom. As for us, we hope that God neither delays this fortune nor drives it away from you. Rather, [we hope that] he will bring about this fortune through the hands of the people of the house of prophecy and mercy and the people who have inherited the scripture and wisdom. By complying with them and paying them the *jizya*, no sense of disdain, failure or shame should come upon you; they will fulfil that which they have pledged to you, and their actions will correspond to what they have said. The Commander of the Believers – out of consideration for his religion and out of fear for his Lord – will personally act accordingly: on account of what God has instilled in his judgement and his discernment with respect to bounty, mercy, equity, respect for treaties, pacts and stipulations; on account of what God has cast into his heart as well as the hearts of the Muslims with respect to love, obedience and zeal; on account of what God has impressed upon the Muslim community regarding the unanimity of their word, the harmony of their hearts and the sincerity of their advice in both private and public; and on account of the glorious victory, impending conquest and unmistakable triumph that God has customarily granted him against those who displayed enmity towards him, who bombarded him with plots and who harassed him with their schemes.

Therefore, pay what you will of the *jizya* and designate what you desire of it. Know that the Commander of the Believers does not urge you towards it on account of any need he or the Muslims might have; rather, [he does so] out of obedience to his Lord and out of diligence to his position so that matters between you and him will be conducted as he sees fit.

Moreover, know that al-Mahdī[1] (may God have mercy on him) had accepted the *fidya* from you on account of the demands placed upon him as the Commander of the Believers. He did not desire it, nor did he need it, nor did he hold it in high regard. In fact, during one meeting of the *majlis*, he would give many times such an amount. However, that was the opinion the Commander of the Believers had of you at that time. As for today, given that your betrayal, your reneging, your defaulting, your contempt for your religion and your insolence towards your Lord have become apparent to him, there is no alternative between the Commander of the Believers and you except conversion to Islam or all-out war, if God wills.

The Commander of the Believers has no power or strength without God, upon whom he relies, in whom he trusts and whom he asks for help. Peace be upon he who follows the right path.

[1] Father of Hārūn al-Rashīd and third ʿAbbasid caliph (r. 775–85).

2

The Pact of ʿUmar

Milka Levy-Rubin, National Library of Israel

The Pact of ʿUmar, or *Shurūṭ ʿUmar*, is the canonical document listing the rules and restrictions pertaining to non-Muslims living under Muslim rule. Containing a series of obligations supposedly undertaken by the conquered in return for the assurance of protection (*amān*) from the Muslims, it is allegedly a treaty signed between the Muslim conquerors and the Christians of one city following its defeat. In Islamic society, it was applied to all non-Muslims living under Muslim rule.

Traditionally attributed to the second caliph ʿUmar ibn al-Khaṭṭāb (r. 634–44), the document in its final form portrays a state of established co-existence between Muslims and non-Muslims that reflects a time later than the seventh century. According to most scholars, it was produced sometime around the end of the eighth and the beginning of the ninth centuries. Although it was not always systematically or strictly enforced between the ninth and eleventh centuries, it seems to have progressively become the accepted norm.

Opinions are divided as to the process of its formation. While some scholars regard the document as a product of jurists of the ninth century, others claim that the ʿUmar referred to in it is not ʿUmar ibn al-Khaṭṭāb but the Umayyad caliph ʿUmar ibn ʿAbd al-ʿAzīz (r. 717–20), in whose days the initial document was forged. Still others believe that many of the clauses in the document reflect the conditions of the immediate post-conquest period, although they all believe that it went through a process of development and stylization by later jurists.

The Pact reflects a change of attitude towards non-Muslims. While the initial conquest agreements represented a tolerant approach of 'live and let live', demanding in general only the payment of the *jizya* in return for protection (*amān*), the Pact replaces these with an intolerant and restrictive approach, reflecting the new social order according to which Muslims were the superior ruling class of society while non-Muslims were the inferior and humiliated class. This new order was entrenched in the ethos of pre-Islamic Persian Sasanian society, which was now turned to the advantage of the Muslim rulers. Like Sasanian society, Muslim society distinguished between the ruling class and the subjected class through distinguishing marks such as clothes and paraphernalia, riding habits and privileges in the public sphere.

CMR 1, pp. 360–4. See further:

M. Levy-Rubin, *Non-Muslims in the Early Islamic Empire – From Surrender to Coexistence*, Cambridge, 2011.

N. Berend, Y. Hameau-Masset, C. Nemo-Pekelman and J. Tolan (eds), *Religious Minorities in Christian, Jewish and Muslim Law (5th–15th centuries)*, Turnhout, 2017.

The translation below is taken from B. Lewis, *Islam from the Prophet Muḥammad to the Capture of Constantinople*, vol. 2, New York, 1974, pp. 217–19 (a translation of Abū Bakr Muḥammad ibn al-Walīd al-Ṭurṭūshī's [d. 1126] version of *Shurūṭ ʿUmar* in *Sirāj al-mulūk*. The division into clauses is made here for reference only and is not found in the original. Select additions from other versions of the Pact are given in parentheses: IM=Ibn al-Murajjā, *Faḍāʾil bayt al-maqdis*; IQ=Ibn Qayyim al-Jawziyya, *Aḥkām ahl al-dhimma*).

We heard from ʿAbd al-Raḥmān ibn Ghanam [d. 697] as follows: When ʿUmar ibn al-Khaṭṭāb (may God be pleased with him) accorded a peace to the Christians of Syria, we wrote to him as follows:

In the name of God, the Merciful and Compassionate. This is a letter to the servant of God ʿUmar, Commander of the Faithful, from the Christians of such-and-such a city. When you came against us we asked you for safe-conduct (*amān*) for ourselves, our descendants, our property and the people of our community, and we undertook the following obligations towards you:

1 We shall not build, in our cities or in their neighbourhood, new monasteries, churches, convents or monks' cells, nor shall we repair, by day or by night, such of them as fall in ruins or are situated in the quarters of the Muslims.

2 We shall keep our gates open wide for passers-by and travellers. We shall give board and lodging for three days to all Muslims who pass our way. We shall not give shelter in our churches or in our dwellings to any spy, nor hide him from the Muslims.

3 We shall not teach the Qur'an to our children.

4 We shall not manifest our religion publicly nor convert anyone to it. We shall not prevent any of our kin from entering Islam if they wish it.

5 We shall show respect towards the Muslims [IM: and we shall show them the way], and we shall rise from our seats when they wish to sit.

6 We shall not seek to resemble the Muslims by imitating any of their garments, the *qalansuwa*,[2] the turban, footwear or the parting of the hair. We shall not speak as they do, nor shall we adopt their *kunyas*.[3]

[2] A tall hat, originating in the Persian world, which indicated the high status of the wearer.

[3] A forename that precedes the personal name itself, usually in the form 'father of … ' or 'mother of … ', e.g. Abū Yūsuf, 'father of Joseph'. Arabs were often addressed by their *kunyas* instead of their names.

7 We shall not mount on saddles, nor shall we gird swords or bear any kind of arms or carry them on our persons.

8 We shall not engrave Arabic inscriptions on our seals.

9 We shall not sell fermented drinks [IM, IQ: nor shall we keep pigs in their (the Muslims') vicinity].

10 We shall clip the fronts of our heads.

11 We shall always dress in the same way wherever we may be, and we shall bind the *zunnār* round our waists.

12 We shall not display our crosses or our books in the roads or markets of the Muslims [IM, IQ: nor shall we conduct processions (lit. 'go out') on Palm Sunday and Easter].

We shall only use clappers in our churches very softly [IM, IQ: and we shall not display the cross on the churches].

We shall not raise our voices in our church services or in the presence of Muslims, nor shall we raise our voices when following our dead.

We shall not show lights on any of the roads of the Muslims or in their markets.

We shall not bury our dead near the Muslims.

13 We shall not take slaves who have been allotted to the Muslims.

14 We shall not build houses overtopping the houses of the Muslims.

When I brought this letter to ʿUmar (may God be pleased with him), he added: 'We shall not strike any Muslim.'

We accept these conditions for ourselves and for the people of our community, and in return we receive safe-conduct. If in any way we violate these undertakings for which we ourselves stand surety, we forfeit our covenant (*dhimma*) and we become liable to the penalties for contumacy and sedition.

3

Abū ʿUthmān al-Jāḥiẓ, *In rebuttal of the Christians*

James E. Montgomery, University of Cambridge

Abū ʿUthmān ʿAmr ibn Baḥr, known as al-Jāḥiẓ because he may have suffered from the eye condition exophthalmos, was born in about 776–7 and died in 868–9. During his early life in Baṣra he studied the scientific theories of Abī Isḥāq Ibrāhīm al-Naẓẓām (d. between 835 and 845) and the Arab linguistic and religious sciences. He moved to the court at Baghdad at the invitation of the Caliph al-Maʾmūn (r. 813–33), though a severe attack of paralysis down one side forced him from the new capital Sāmarrāʾ back to Baṣra, where he may have been crushed to death under a pile of books.

Al-Jāḥiẓ's career as a writer was prolific, and some 245 titles of works on most of the major issues of the day are recorded. These writings explore his version of the burgeoning theological system of Muʿtazilism: at a time when Greek scientific and philosophical texts were being translated into Arabic, he synthesized the spiritual and ethical universe of the Qur'an, the Arabic poetic and linguistic heritage, Aristotelian natural philosophy and scientific speculation (in the tradition of al-Naẓẓām).

Al-Jāḥiẓ's *Fī l-radd ʿalā l-Nasārā* ('In rebuttal of the Christians') has survived as a series of excerpts in a later anthology of his writings. Probably composed in the first decade of the caliphate of al-Mutawakkil (r. 847–61), it is framed as advice on how to refute some Christian thinkers who allege that accounts of Christianity and the Bible given in the Qur'an are inaccurate and inconsistent. By considering the status and history of Christians in Muslim society, the tract launches an excoriating attack on what are presented as the doctrinal and theological illogicalities of Christianity.

Fī l-radd ʿalā l-Nasārā, written by a highly perceptive intellectual who was skilled at documenting and analysing the contours of his society, offers insight into what in the ninth century al-Jāḥiẓ argued that the ruling Muslim elite ought to consider the weaknesses, threats and demerits of Christians and Christianity.

CMR 1, pp. 706–12.

The following passage is taken from al-Jāḥiẓ, *The Proofs of the Prophet and Other Epistles*, ed. and trans. J.E. Montgomery, New York (in preparation).

Among the uneducated members of our society, Christianity continues to enjoy a regal status, for they observed how the Christian community is able to attract many outsiders, how some Umayyad rulers had been born to Roman women and how there are Christians who are dialectical theologians, physicians and astrologers. In other words, these members of our society formed a view of the Christians as wise philosophers, as men of reason. But they could find no evidence of this among the Jews, for Jews consider philosophical speculation to be unbelief, opining that to subject religion to dialectical debate is a heretical innovation which leads to all sorts of doubts, that only the contents of the Torah and the books of the prophets count as knowledge, and that to place one's faith in medicine and to assent to astrologers leads to Manichaeism and to the materialism of those who argue that the universe has no Creator – in fact for the Jews, it is outright contradiction of their forefathers and the paragons whose behaviour they imitate. The Jews are so committed to this that they prohibit conversing with anyone who practises philosophical speculation and do not even seek retribution if someone who does so is killed.

If the uneducated members of our society realized that the Christians and the Romans have no real intelligence, no philosophical wisdom and no capacity for clear communication, except for a sort of clever dexterity with lathe and wood-chisel and a capacity for the figural arts and for weaving fine silk, then they would strike them from the register of philosophers and sages, no longer classifying them as men of culture and learning.

I say this because the *Book of Logic, On Generation and Corruption*, and the *Meteorology*, to name but a few, are by Aristotle, who was neither Roman nor Christian. The *Almagest* is by Ptolemy, who was neither Roman nor Christian. *The Book of Euclid* is by Euclid, and he was neither Roman nor a Christian, and the *Book of Medicine* is by Galen, and he was neither Roman nor Christian. The same holds true for the books of Democrates, Hippocrates, Plato and so on.

These thinkers were ancient Greeks – a community long gone, though the impress of their intellect remains – who followed a different religion from this current lot, and their learning differs too. The Greeks were scholars, whereas this lot are handymen who have appropriated their writings because they happen to be neighbours who live near where they did. They actually ascribe some ancient Greek writings to themselves, and alter others to share their confessional identity, with the exception, of course, of famous works and well-known philosophies. If they are unable to change their titles, they allege that the ancient Greeks were a Roman tribal unit. In this way, they use Greek religious systems to preen over the Jews, to wax arrogant over the Arabs and to treat the Indians with disdain. According to them, our wise thinkers are simply following in the footsteps of their wise men, our philosophers are merely imitating their example. And on and on they go.

Please pay close attention. Christianity is like Manichaeism; some of its features are cognate with the materialism of those who argue that the universe has no Creator. It gives rise to every aporetic doubt and specious argument conceivable. Out of all the confessional identities familiar to us, Christians are the most prone to Manichaeism.

They are also the most likely to reel about in a state of aporetic confusion, but then this is what happens to people who speculate on obscure subjects with weak intellects! Have you not noticed that by far the greatest number of those who publicly profess Islam but convert to Manichaeism are those whose fathers and mothers were Christians? For if you were to count today all the folk who profess suspect beliefs and were to list all their dubious notions, you would discover that the vast majority of them are Christian.

Now, some Christians are high-ranking bureaucrats, valets of kings, physicians to the aristocracy, perfumers and money-changers. In the hearts and minds of the common people, Christians are thus a people of power and charismatic influence. If you come across a Jew, he will be either a dyer, a tanner, a cupper, a butcher or a mender of broken pots. So the uneducated members of our society have come to imagine that, in terms of other religions, Judaism enjoyed the same low regard as Jewish occupations do in terms of other occupations, and have concluded that, since they are the filthiest and most impure community, their unbelief was the filthiest and most impure unbelief imaginable.

Christians suffer from many physical deformities. The only reason they suffer from fewer physical deformities than the Jews is that an Israelite will only marry his daughter to another Israelite: their womenfolk are reserved for them alone, no one else. As they do not mix with non-Jewish women, the virility of other races is not inseminated among them. In this way intellect, physique and cleverness all suffer. You can observe the self-same thing in horses, camels, asses and pigeons.

Please understand me. I do not disagree with our common people that Christians are very rich, that they continue to enjoy regal status, that their styles of dress and behaviour are cleaner, their occupations seemlier than those of the Jews. Where we do disagree is the difference between these two groups and their types of unbelief when we consider how ferociously and persistently they both oppose the message of Islam, constantly plotting and laying traps for Muslims, when considered in conjunction with their ignoble and vile origins.

Let us take the topics of regal status, occupation and appearance. As we know, the Christians ride about on decent horses and noble thoroughbreds,[4] they keep troops of attendants and they play polo. Their hair is cut in a short, fringed bob and they wear garments darned and stitched with pearls. They employ private militias and give themselves names such as al-Ḥasan and al-Ḥusayn, al-ʿAbbās, al-Faḍl and ʿAlī.[5] They also use these names for their children. They are but one step short of calling themselves Muḥammad and using the Prophet's patronym, Abū l-Qāsim! The Muslims like this and approve of it. Many Christians have even stopped tying the sash around their waist, while others have begun to wear it under their clothes. Many nobles have refused to pay the poll-tax, being too proud and self-important to hand it over. They

[4] This and most of the practices that follow are expressly forbidden in extant versions of the *Pact of ʿUmar*.

[5] Names of Muḥammad's close relatives, and too revered to be used by anyone other than Muslims.

exchange insult for insult and blow for blow. And what is to stop them going even further, when our qadis, or at least the less specialized ones, think that the blood of the Catholicos, the Metropolitan and the Bishop is equivalent to the blood of Jaʿfar, ʿAlī, al-ʿAbbās and Ḥamza,[6] and that a Christian should merit no more than the discretionary punishment for calumniating the mother of our blessed Prophet by saying that she lived in a state of religious error, arguing that Christians say this simply because the mother of the Prophet was not a Muslim?

[6] Early Muslims who died for the faith.

4

ʿAlī l-Ṭabarī, *The book of religion and empire*

David Thomas, University of Birmingham

Abū l-Ḥasan ʿAlī ibn Rabban Sahl al-Ṭabarī was born into a Nestorian family in Ṭabaristān in the northern Iranian region of the ʿAbbasid Empire, sometime in the later eighth century. Both his father Sahl, who was known as *rabban* ('our master') in recognition of his scholarly achievements, and his uncle were acknowledged Christian intellectuals. ʿAlī acquired a thorough grounding in the Bible and Christian doctrine, though he specialized in medicine and became famous for his expertise.

In the early 840s, ʿAlī was taken as a secretary into the service of the Caliph al-Muʿtaṣim (r. 833–42) in the capital Sāmarrāʾ, continuing under the Caliphs al-Wāthiq (r. 842–7) and al-Mutawakkil (r. 847–61). He was evidently very close to the latter, who made him a table companion. He wrote a number of medical works, among them the *Firdaws al-ḥikma* ('Paradise of wisdom'), which became a foundation text for medical practitioners in the Islamic world.

Sometime around 850 ʿAlī converted to Islam. In the years that followed he wrote two responses to Christianity, *Al-radd ʿalā l-Naṣārā* ('Refutation of the Christians'), written just after about 850, and *Kitāb al-dīn wa-l-dawla* ('The book of religion and empire'), written in about 855. In the latter he affirms (maybe with some exaggeration) that al-Mutawakkil was instrumental in this conversion.

In these two anti-Christian works, ʿAlī shows his deep knowledge of the Bible and Christian teachings, and his conviction that whereas Christianity is confused both rationally and biblically, Islam is based on firm foundations of scripture, reason and history. The *Kitāb al-dīn wa-l-dawla* brings together in ten chapters proofs that Muḥammad was a true prophet, making it one of the earliest surviving examples of the *dalāʾil al-nubuwwa* ('proofs of prophethood') genre. It begins with arguments that Muḥammad and his closest Companions were pious, abstemious and just, and that Muḥammad performed miracles and foretold events – all acknowledged qualifications of an authentic prophet and his community. To these it adds in chapter 10 a long and elaborate sequence of interpretations of verses from the Bible to show that Muḥammad and Islam were predicted in the scripture of the Jews and Christians. These apparently original interpretations, some based on words that are linguistically related to the name Muḥammad, demonstrate ʿAlī's ingenuity in finding in the passages pointers to the coming of Islam, and also the ease with which he seems to have abandoned traditional Christian interpretations for interpretations based on the teachings of Islam, even of Old Testament verses that would be familiar to any Christian as predictions of Jesus.

CMR 1, pp. 669–74.

This translation is taken from R. Ebied and D. Thomas (eds), *The Polemical Works of ʿAlī al-Ṭabarī*, Leiden, 2016, reprinted with permission.

I have already mentioned four prophecies about Ishmael (peace be upon him),[7] in which are testimonies to the true nature of the community of the Prophet (may God bless him and give him peace) that only an ignoramus would not recognize, only a fool would reject, and according to which the prophecies would be invalidated and proved impossible if the Prophet (may God bless him and give him peace) had not been sent. I will mention the rest of the prophecies of the prophets (peace be upon them) about him, which are like things that are familiar and obvious. Among them were those who described his time, his country, his mission, his followers and his helpers, and have given clear explanations of his name.[8]

The fifth prophecy that points to him and indicates his prophetic status and his truthfulness are the words of Moses (peace be upon him) in chapter 11 of the fifth book of the Torah, the last, to the People of Israel: 'The Lord your God will raise up a prophet like me from among you and from among your brothers, and you shall listen to him.'[9] In this same chapter the Torah says in confirmation and verification of these words, 'The Lord said to Moses (peace be upon him): I will raise up for them a prophet like you from among their brothers, and whichever man does not hear My words which this man will relay in my name, I will avenge myself upon him.'[10] God has never raised up a prophet from among the brothers of the People of Israel except Muḥammad (peace be upon him), and His words 'from among them' are a confirmation and specification that he was from the children of their father not from the children of his uncles. Now Christ (peace be upon him) and the other prophets (may God bless them) were from them themselves, and whoever thinks that God almighty has not distinguished between someone from the people themselves and someone from their brothers is deficient in thinking.

---

[7] ʿAlī discusses these four prophecies, Genesis 17:20, 16:7-12, 21:13 and 21:14-21, in the preceding chapter; Ebied and Thomas, *Kitāb al-dīn wa-l-dawla*, pp. 326–31.

[8] In total, in this chapter ʿAlī presents prophecies about Muḥammad from Genesis, Psalms, Isaiah, Hosea, Micah, Habakkuk, Zephaniah, Zechariah, Jeremiah, Ezekiel, Daniel and the Gospels.

[9] Deuteronomy 18:15.

[10] Deuteronomy 18:18-19.

Anyone who claims that this prophecy is about Christ (peace be upon him) is wrong on two counts, and apparently knows nothing in two respects. One of these is that Christ (peace be upon him) was from the children of David, and David was from among them themselves not from among their brothers. And the other is that for one who says at one time that Christ is Creator and not created and then claims that Christ is like Moses, his statement contradicts itself and his teaching wavers about. And one who claims that this prophecy concerns Joshua son of Nun is wrong because Joshua is not included among the prophets and did not convey anything about God almighty to the People of Israel except what Moses (peace be upon him) had conveyed, and because he was from the people themselves and not from their brothers. But the prophet whom God almighty raised up from the descendants of their brothers was Muḥammad (may God bless him and give him peace). He is the one against whose opponents God has vengeance, and you may indeed see the effects of vengeance clear on those who oppose him, and the signs of grace manifest on those who acknowledge him.

Moses said in this Book in chapter 20: 'The Lord came from Mount Sinai and appeared to us from Seir and became manifest from Mount Paran. With him on his right hand were myriads of the holy ones. To these he granted power and made them to be loved by the people, and he invoked blessing on all his saints.'[11] Now Paran is the area in which Ishmael (peace be upon him) dwelt, and for this reason God mentions it earlier in the Torah in his words: 'He learned archery in the desert of Paran.'[12] Everybody knows that Ishmael dwelt in Mecca, and his children and descendants there and around know the habitation of their ancestor and are not ignorant of his country and region. And 'the Lord appeared from Paran': if this is not as we have said, let them show us a lord who was manifest from Mount Paran, though they will not be able to. The word 'lord' here refers to the Prophet (may God bless him and give him peace). It is a word employed among Arabs and foreigners for God, great and mighty, and for his servants, such as your saying 'lord of the house'. Syriac-speakers' term for one whom they wish to honour is *mār*, which is 'my lord', 'my master', *mār* being 'lord' in Syriac. [pp. 341–3]

[...] The prophet David (peace be upon him) says in Psalm 45: Because of this, God has given you blessing for ever. So gird yourself with the sword, O great one, because your splendour and praise (*ḥamd*) are conquering splendour and praise (*al-ḥamd*).[13] Ride upon the word of truth and on the course of divinity, for your law and injunctions are at the leisure of your right hand. Your arrows are sharpened and the nations fall down beneath you.[14] We know of no one to whom these matters of girding on the

[11] Deuteronomy 33:2-3.
[12] Genesis 21:20-1.
[13] The derivation of the word *ḥamd* from *ḥ.m.d*, the same triliteral root from which Muḥammad is derived, allows ʿAlī to argue that this and the following verses refer to the Prophet.
[14] Psalm 45:2-5.

sword, sharpening arrows, leisure of right hand and nations falling down beneath him rightly refer except the Prophet (may God bless him and give him peace). For he rode upon the word of truth, humbled himself before God in faith and strove against the polytheists until religion was made manifest.

David (peace be upon him) says in Psalm 48: 'Our Lord is great and greatly praised (*maḥmūd*); in the city of our God and in his mountain there is a holy one and Muḥammad, and joy prevails through all the earth.'[15] This prophecy of David (peace be upon him) is clarity and explanation, and doubts cannot obscure it because he names the Prophet openly.

David (peace be upon him) says in Psalm 50: 'From Zion God caused to appear a crown greatly praised (*maḥmūd*). God will come and will not fail to see; fires will burn before him and will flare up in a blaze around him.'[16] Can you not see that the prophet David (peace be upon him) does not omit from his prophecies any mention of Muḥammad or Maḥmūd, as you can read yourselves? The meaning of his words 'a crown greatly praised' is 'a head and leader Muḥammad and greatly praised'. And the meaning of Muḥammad, *maḥmūd*, and *ḥamīd* is linguistically one, while he makes 'crown' an image of headship and leadership. [p. 345]

[15] Psalm 48:1-2.
[16] Psalm 50:2-3.

5

Abū ʿĪsā l-Warrāq, *The refutation of the three sects of the Christians*

David Thomas, University of Birmingham

Abū ʿĪsā Muḥammad ibn Hārūn ibn Muḥammad al-Warrāq composed works that remained influential for centuries after his death, which probably occurred just after about 860, although almost nothing definite is known about him, except that he was most likely active in Baghdad in the middle of the ninth century. Muslim biographers speak vaguely about him belonging to the rationalist theological school of the Muʿtazila but then abandoning them for a form of Shīʿism, while some later authors link him with individuals who were notorious for their heretical views, and one says he was a Zoroastrian, probably because he wrote a well-known account of Persian dualism that was impartial and even sympathetic towards them.

Abū ʿĪsā was commonly maligned after his death, even though his works were widely used for the information in them about religions of the day. Surviving fragments suggest that he showed objectivity in his religious writings and a disturbingly inquisitive approach to all religious claims. This evidently caused uncertainty in many Muslim minds about his own beliefs. He left what was probably a detailed account of the major religions, *Maqālāt al-nās wa-ikhtilāfihim* ('The opinions of people and the differences between them'), and a series of refutations of beliefs of the Jews, Christians, dualists and others, including Muslims. All these are now lost. They appear to have provoked widespread aversion which turned to personal condemnation as people mistook impartiality and critical keenness for irreverence and suspicion.

This approach is evident in the passages below. They come from the one work of Abū ʿĪsā that survives in anything more than short fragments, *Al-radd ʿalā l-thalāth firaq min al-Naṣārā* ('The refutation of the three sects of the Christians'). Directed against the denominations of Nestorians, Melkites and Jacobites in the Islamic Empire, it describes and refutes in fine detail the two major doctrines of the Trinity and Incarnation in the form that these Churches held them. The passages here occur at the end of the part on the Trinity, in a section against the evident attempt by Arabic-speaking Christians to formulate their doctrine in terms of Muslim explanations of the relationship between the essential being of God and the properties, or attributes, by which God's existence and activities can be known. A number of Christian theologians living under Muslim rule in the early ʿAbbasid era made use of this comparison, and Abū ʿĪsā was one of many Muslims who demonstrated its incongruity. His argument here is that if the Christian doctrine is set out according to the logic of the Muslim doctrine, it lacks coherence and any resemblance to what Christians have said, as the three Persons of the Godhead lose their traditional characteristics.

As in all other parts of the *Radd*, Abū ʿĪsā's detailed knowledge of Christian doctrine demonstrated here is unmistakable, and so is the logical rigour with which he analyses it in terms of the contemporary understanding of the relationship between a property and the being qualified by it.

CMR 1, pp. 695–701.

This translation is taken from Abū ʿĪsā l-Warrāq, *Al-radd ʿalā l-thalāth firaq min al-Naṣārā*, ed. and trans. D. Thomas, *Anti-Christian Polemic in Early Islam, Abū ʿĪsā al-Warrāq's 'Against the Trinity'*, Cambridge, 1992, with permission.

[The three Persons as properties or attributes of the Godhead]

If anyone among them [the Christians] claims that the hypostases[17] are properties,[18] we question them about this and ask: Properties of what, of themselves or of a fourth thing that is not them? If they say: 'Of a fourth thing that is not them', they exceed the bounds of the doctrine of the Trinity in affirming a fourth.[19]

If at this point one of the Melkites should raise an objection by saying: 'The hypostases are properties of the substance, and the substance is other than them although it is not a fourth to them in number,'[20] [...] say to him: If the hypostases are properties of the substance which is not them, then Speech will be a property of the substance, and it is this [the substance] that will be speaking because of it [Speech], not the Father or any other hypostasis. Similarly, Life will necessarily be a property of the substance not of the hypostases and this [the substance] will be living because of it [Life], not the Father or the Son. So, the Father, the Son and Life will not be living or speaking, because the property of Life and the property of Speech will belong to the substance which is not them, and therefore the properties will not be properties of them [the hypostases]. [...]

If those who are asked about the original question claim that the hypostases are properties of themselves, they make a thing a property of itself. According to their

---

[17] Entities that can exist autonomously.

[18] Entities that endow a being with qualities by adhering to it: thus, the property of power makes a being powerful by adhering in it. Properties cannot exist autonomously, but only by adhering to another being.

[19] Since properties did not exist independently of the being they qualified, the Christian analogy of the three divine hypostases with properties necessitates a fourth entity in the Godhead through which they must exist and which they endow with qualities.

[20] In the descriptive introduction to his refutation, Abū ʿĪsā describes how Melkites differ from the two other Christian groups by defining the divine substance as different from the hypostases but not distinct from them.

teaching this is the gravest error because, according to them, to say 'property' assumes a thing specified, and to say 'a thing specified' assumes a property, like saying 'living' and 'life' or 'speaking' and 'speech'. So, as long as they accept the existence of a thing specified that is itself a property, they are compelled to accept the existence of a being who is living to be itself life, and a being who is speaking to be itself speech. There is no difference, according to their principles, between any of this and between this person's meaning of a property. So, as long as it is acceptable for the property to be the hypostasis that is specified and nothing else, then it is acceptable for Life to be the hypostasis that is living and nothing else, and for Speech to be the hypostasis that is speaking and nothing else.[21]

If they claim that the hypostases are properties of one another, we say: Then the Son will be a property of the Father and the Father of the Son, so that a thing will be a property of its property and an attribute of its attribute. This is simple confusion. According to this statement, they have to accept that the Father is son of his Son and the Son father of his Father, and that the Son is speech of his speech and word of his word and life of his life. The same applies to the Spirit, and it is quite simply folly and confusion. [...]

If they claim that each of the hypostases is the property of one hypostasis alone, we say: If the Son is a property of the Father and not of the Spirit, and the Father is a property of the Son and not of the Spirit, the Spirit is left without a property, although it does not merit this any more than the other two hypostases, and neither of them merits a property any more than it does. The same applies to the Father and the Son: if either of them occupies the position of the Spirit, it remains without a property. [pp. 172–7]

As for those of them who claim that the hypostases are individuals, we shall ask them about the difference between their being individuals and being corporeal forms or bodies or the like.[22] And if they claim that the terms 'persons' and 'corporeal forms' contain overtones of contingency, we say: For your opponents who deny anthropomorphism the term 'individuals' suggests contingency in the same way. If they say that corporeal forms or bodies are combined, composite or limited, or anything such as this, say to them: But individuals are like this; and the [Christians] should be asked what is the difference. [pp. 180–1]

---

[21] Abū 'Īsā compels his Christian opponents to accept that if they define a hypostasis as a property, as they do at the beginning, and allow that properties can be properties of themselves and not of other entities, then only the hypostasis of Life (the Holy Spirit) can be living and none of the other Persons, and only the hypostasis of Speech (the Son = Word or Reason) can be speaking.

[22] The Christians evidently mean by the term 'individuals', *ashkhāṣ* (sing. *shakhṣ*), that the three hypostases are distinct beings. In Muslim understanding, however, this term cannot be used of God but only of beings which are physical. Hence, Abū 'Īsā is able to compare it with the similar terms *shabaḥ* ('corporeal form') and *jism* ('body'), which are only ever used of physical beings.

6

Islamic Psalms of David

David R. Vishanoff, University of Oklahoma

The *Zabūr* is mentioned a number of times in the Qur'an as a scripture revealed to the prophet David (e.g. Q 4:163, 17:55), who is also traditionally regarded as the author of the Psalms in the Bible. Sometime in the eighth or ninth century an unknown Muslim of moderately ascetic inclinations recreated this imagined *Zabūr* by compiling wise sayings and sermonic exhortations, which he framed as divine speech modelled on the Qur'an. Later editors rewrote and expanded this core text into at least seven recensions. These rewritten Psalms have a twofold significance: they contain explicit and implicit polemics against Christian doctrines, practices and scriptures, and they draw upon sayings, stories and forms of piety common to all three Abrahamic faiths, thus belying the very boundaries to which they refer.

CMR 3, pp. 724–30. See further:

David R. Vishanoff, 'Why Do the Nations Rage? Boundaries of Canon and Community in a Muslim's Rewriting of Psalm 2', *Comparative Islamic Studies* 6 (2010) 151–79.

[The Christology of Psalm 2]

Psalms 1 and 2 in the Islamic Psalms are the only ones that echo the biblical Psalms. Psalm 2 in what is known as the 'Pious' recension (MS Oxford, Bodleian – Hunt. 515, fol. 6r.9–v.4, dated 1356) pre-empts Christological interpretations of biblical Psalm 2, and alludes to a Qur'anic verse about extinguishing God's light.

In the name of God, the merciful, the compassionate.

O David, what are the nations and the peoples saying? They have joined together against the Lord and his army. They wish to extinguish God's light with their mouths, but God refuses that his light and his holiness should be extinguished.[23]

David, I made you my messiah and my prophet. But Jesus son of Mary will be taken as a god beside me on account of the power I vested in him, allowing him

---

[23] Q 9:32.

to resurrect the dead by my leave, and to heal the blind and the leper,[24] for I am continually generous and merciful to my creatures. I am mighty and wise.

[A prediction of Muḥammad erased from the Bible]

The Qur'an states that Muḥammad was foretold in earlier scriptures [7:157], and Psalm 107 in the 'Sufi' recension ends with just such a prediction, along with an explanation of its absence from the Christian Bible. In one manuscript (MS Florence, Laurenziana – Orient. Palat. 267, fol. 76r.1–8, dated 1262) the folio containing Muḥammad's name has gone missing, presumably because of its apologetic value, but the missing lines are supplied here thanks to Dennis Halft OP, who discovered another copy in Iran (MS Qom, Centre for the Revival of Islamic Heritage – Khūy Namāzī 77, fol. 68r.15–v.14, dated 1306).

O David, Muḥammad is the praiseworthy one, exalted, uppermost, and esteemed. He is the proof, the mighty one, the conclusive argument. He is praiseworthy, chosen, trustworthy, approved, truthful, and pure, created from a pure lineage. He is fervent in what pleases Me and vehement in what angers Me, devoted to Me, genuine, zealous for My religion. He is not bedazzled by the beauty and splendour of this world. In him resides the light of both sun and moon. He is the most perfect of the noble company of prophets. For his sake I unburden the clouds when they are overloaded with rain and beg me for relief. Were it not for him, I would not have put Adam on earth or filled the world with life.

Do you know who he is, O David? A chief among the descendants of Abraham (God's prayers be upon him). He has the noble standing of Abraham and Adam. Whoever disbelieves in him, my curse is upon him.

But there will come forth a people claiming to be monks who will erase his name from their scriptures.[25] Do you know, David, why those disbelievers concoct this in their minds? It is because Satan lay with their mothers alongside their fathers, so that his sperm mixed with theirs. So they erred and disbelieved, led many others astray, and wandered from the level path.

Whoever believes in Muḥammad has taken hold of faith, but whoever disbelieves in Muḥammad has disbelieved in Me and in My scriptures. Whoever believes in the Torah, the Gospel and the Psalms, and makes no distinction between any of My books, I will abundantly reward. For I am mighty and wise.

[True worship and the perils of this world]

Another prediction of Muḥammad appears at the beginning of Psalm 18 in the original core text of the Islamic Psalms, which is reconstructed here from several later

[24] Q 5:110.

[25] According to Q 57:27 monasticism is an invention of the Christians, though monks are not often identified by Muslim authors as the particular culprits who removed Muḥammad's name from the original Christian scriptures.

recensions, including MS Istanbul, Süleymaniye – Fatih 28, fols 20r.5–21r.3, dated 1229, and MS Istanbul, Süleymaniye – Ayasofya 30, fol. 9r.20–v.11. The prediction alludes to Q 21:105, which itself quotes biblical Psalm 37:29. Muslim worship is then contrasted with Christians' veneration of images and liturgical ringing of bells, but the text quickly shifts from interreligious polemic to exhortations and parables addressed to worldly people of all faiths, urging them to pursue a life of spiritual devotion.

In the name of God, the merciful, the compassionate.

O David, listen to what I say! Command Solomon to proclaim after you that I will give the earth as an inheritance to Muḥammad and his community.[26] They are [my true] worshippers, and they are not like you: they do not ring bells, nor do they worship idols. If you wish to worship me, then weep much! Every hour in which you do not invoke my name is an hour lost.

O David, the blind man is not he who does not see with his eye, but he who does not see with his heart.

O David, tell the Children of Israel not to drink water from the river or it will leave them short of breath, and not to accumulate wealth from what is forbidden or it will leave them in hell. I will not accept their prayer. So leave your father and brother to their forbidden things!

And recount to the Children of Israel the story of two men who lived at the time of Enoch. There arose for both a business opportunity just when an obligatory prayer had come due. Said the one: 'As for me, I will begin with the command of God.' Said the other: 'As for me, I will begin with my business, and then I will get around to God's command.' So the one went off to his business, and the other to his prayer. So I inspired some clouds and they set off towards the merchant, and I commanded a dragon of the sky and it breathed and lit a fire that enveloped the merchant; but he was preoccupied with the clouds and the darkness, and lost both his business and his prayer. So it was written above the door of his house: see what greed and the distractions of this world do to their patrons!

[Muslims fulfil the Sermon on the Mount]

The exhortation to spiritual perfection continues in Psalm 9 of the 'Moses' text, a collection of sayings originally ascribed to Moses that was also appended to some Islamic Psalm texts. One version, from MS Princeton – Garret 108B, fol. 98r.6–v.3, dated 1672 – addresses itself to the People of the Book, accusing Christians of failing to uphold the high standards of Jesus's Sermon on the Mount [Matthew 5:46–7].

O People of the Book! Your Lord has sent you a compelling proof and a cure for the heart, yet you do good only to those who do you good, you associate only with those who associate with you, you speak only to those who speak to you, you feed

[26] Q 21:105.

only those who feed you, and you honour only those who honour you; not one of you is gracious to another.[27]

But the Believers, who believe in God and his Prophet, they are the ones who do good to those who do them ill, who associate with those who snub them, who speak to those who avoid them, who feed those who deny them, who are God-fearing towards those who cheat them, who honour those who despise them, and who forgive those who wrong them. I am knowing and aware.

[27] See, e.g. Q 5:51.

7

Al-Shābushtī, *Book of monasteries*

Hilary Kilpatrick

This extract is taken from the *Kitāb al-diyārāt* ('Book of monasteries') by ʿAlī ibn Muḥammad al-Shābushtī (d. *c.* 998), a poet and man of letters probably of Iraqi origin, who served in Cairo as librarian to the Fāṭimid caliph al-ʿAzīz (r. 975–96). His is the only one of five compilations about monasteries written by Muslims in the tenth century to have survived.

Compilations were a very common form in medieval Arabic literature, and included anecdotes, verses and factual information from different periods. Al-Shābushtī's compilation is arranged in sections according to monastery. The majority of the fifty odd he mentions are in Iraq, with a few in Syria, Palestine and Egypt. He gives factual information about their location and feast days, lists their attractions for visitors, and quotes samples of poetry and anecdotes in which they figure. He traces the connections between monasteries and pre-Islamic and Islamic rulers, suggesting how these gradually loosened with the passage of time. He also affirms a link between monasteries and the humanistic literary culture of the secretaries (*kuttāb*), some of whom were Christians. Furthermore, anecdotes from different sections of the book, when taken together, encourage reflection on subjects such as the exercise of power.

As a Muslim, al-Shābushtī, as well as his sources, took Christian monasteries for granted as part of the landscape and society in which they lived, and evidently appreciated them for their beautiful surroundings, their wine, the opportunities they offered for innocent and not-so-innocent pleasures, and in some cases their miracle-working shrines and healing springs.

CMR 2, pp. 565–9. See further:

Al-Shābushtī, *The Book of Monasteries*, ed. and trans. Hilary Kilpatrick, New York (in preparation).

This translation is based on Abū l-Ḥasan ʿAlī ibn Muḥammad al-Shābushtī, *Al-diyārāt*, ed. Kūrkīs ʿAwwād, 2nd edition, Baghdad, 1966, pp. 163–5.

The monastery of Mār Mārī[28]

This monastery is in Samarra at the Waṣīf bridge. It is prosperous, has many monks and is surrounded by vineyards and orchards. People go there on outings, as it is a healthy and beautiful spot.

Al-Faḍl ibn al-ʿAbbās ibn al-Maʾmūn[29] composed a short poem on it:

I wore out the steeds of my pleasure in Samarra,
gaining there my wishes and my heart's desire,
bringing life to parks of pleasure, plunged into revelry
between rivers and gardens at Mār Mārī's monastery.
Then yet again we drank the morning draught
and in the evening passed the cup around,
at times to the clappers'[30] rhythm and the chants of priests,
at times to the sound of lutes and plaintive pipes.
And how many tender, flirtatious gazelles
hunted us with their Babylonian glances!

Al-Faḍl went hunting with al-Muʿtazz one day.[31] He recalls: Al-Muʿtazz, Yūnus ibn Bughā[32] and I got separated from the rest of the company. Al-Muʿtazz complained of feeling thirsty so I said to him, 'Sire, there is a monk in this monastery whom I know. He is a good friend. And the monastery is well-appointed. Would the Commander of the Faithful like us to turn off to it?' 'Let's do that.' We came to the abbot of the monastery, who welcomed us and gave us a fine reception. He brought us cold water to drink and then invited us to dismount and spend some time with him, saying, 'You can cool off here and we will bring you the food which the monastery can offer.'

Al-Muʿtazz took to him and said, 'Let's dismount and follow him.' When we had dismounted, the superior asked me about al-Muʿtazz and Yūnus. 'They're army officers.' 'No', he retorted, 'they are two husbands of *houris* who have slipped away.'[33] 'That isn't part of your religion and beliefs.' 'It is now,' he answered, and al-Muʿtazz laughed. The abbot brought us bread and light food such as can be found in monasteries. It was very wholesome, tasty and nicely served. We ate and washed our hands, and then

[28] Mār Mārī (d. *c.* 738) was one of the earliest leaders of what became known as the Church of the East. His namesake Mārī was the disciple of Addai, who is traditionally identified as one of the seventy disciples sent out by Jesus (Luke 10:1). Addai and Mārī are regarded in the Syriac tradition as the evangelizers of Edessa and Mesopotamia.
[29] Grandson of the Caliph al-Maʾmūn, he was a cultivated man and composed poetry. He was governor of Medina in 882.
[30] In eastern Christian tradition, two pieces of wood beaten together to summon worshippers to church services.
[31] The thirteenth ʿAbbāsid caliph, he ruled from 866 to 869, when he was deposed and killed.
[32] Yūnus's father, Bughā the Younger, was a Turkish military leader who held power under two previous caliphs, al-Muntaṣir and al-Mustaʿīn. Yūnus was al-Muʿtazz's favourite.
[33] The bearing of the caliph and his favourite suggests they are more than human, like husbands of the fabled beauties who, according to the Qur'an, inhabit paradise.

al-Muʿtazz said to me, 'Ask him privately which of us two he would like to be with him and stay here?' I passed on the question, and the abbot said, 'Both of them and then some!' Al-Muʿtazz laughed so much he lent back against the wall. I said to the abbot, 'You must choose.' 'In this matter selection is perdition. God has created no mind which could distinguish between them.'

The rest of the company caught up with us, and the abbot was alarmed. Al-Muʿtazz said to him, 'By my life, let's not break off what we were doing. I'm the master of those people there, but a friend to the people here.' So we sat together for a while, and al-Muʿtazz ordered the abbot to be given 50,000 dirhams. The abbot said, 'By God, I'll only accept them on one condition.' 'What's that?' 'That the Commander of the Faithful be my guest, together with whom he likes.' Al-Muʿtazz replied, 'I grant you that.' Then we agreed on a day we would visit him as he wanted. He took utmost pains, involving his community in the preparations, and he brought young Christians who served us very well. Al-Muʿtazz was happier than I had ever seen him. He gave the abbot a great deal of money that day, and as long as he lived he regularly called on him when he passed the monastery to eat and drink there.

8

ʿAbd al-Jabbār, *Confirmation of the signs of prophethood*

Gabriel Said Reynolds,
University of Notre Dame

Abū l-Ḥasan ʿAbd al-Jabbār ibn Aḥmad al-Hamadhānī l-Asadābādī (d. 1025) was the foremost theologian of the Muʿtazilī school in the later tenth century. He was also a leading legal scholar and served as chief justice of the city of Rayy.

Born in the west of Iran, he studied in Iran and also Baṣra and Baghdad. He secured the position of judge in Rayy and became a close associate of al-Ṣāḥib ibn ʿAbbād, vizier of the powerful Buyid rulers. He attracted students from many parts of the Islamic world, though his standing with leading public figures was never secure, owing, it has been thought, to his arrogance, and when the vizier died in 995, the Buyid Emir Fakhr al-Dawla put him in prison. Although he was freed, he never re-entered public life. He lived quietly on his estates, where he died in 1025.

Tathbīt dalāʾil al-nubuwwa ('Confirmation of the signs of prophethood') has always been attributed to ʿAbd al-Jabbār. Recently, doubt has been cast on his authorship, and it could be that the weight of evidence will be seen to point to another author; for the present he will be referred to as the author. *Tathbīt*, which was completed in 995, is devoted to arguing for proofs or 'signs' which verify the Islamic claim that Muḥammad was a true prophet of God. In the course of this work, ʿAbd al-Jabbār dedicates a long section to the 'Critique of Christian origins', where he is concerned to address the arguments of Christian apologists who insist that the accusations in the Qurʾan against Christian teachings about Jesus are fundamentally wrong (arguments which would imply that the Qurʾan is not a valid revelation, and therefore that Muḥammad was not a true prophet). To this end he seeks to show in turn that the opinions of Christians regarding Christ are fundamentally unreliable because they are not faithful custodians of his teaching.

These polemical concerns lead ʿAbd al-Jabbār to construct a historical scenario meant to illustrate that Christians have deviated from the original teaching and practice of Christ (which, following traditional Muslim teachings, he insists was fundamentally like that of Muḥammad). According to the excerpt below, which is the beginning of this reconstructed account, in the days after the crucifixion (it was not Christ but another who was crucified) the followers of Christ worshipped God together with the Jews and read the true scripture of Christ (the *Injīl*). When a conflict flared up between these Christ-followers and the Jews, some of them made a deal to win the support of the pagan Romans. However, as part of the deal this group agreed to embrace certain Roman practices and to betray the practices of earlier prophets. In the conflict, the Romanizing Christ-followers lost the *Injīl* (which other faithful companions of Christ took with them as they fled from the Romans), and as a consequence they were compelled to write a new scripture, which became the historical Gospels. ʿAbd al-Jabbār insists that they refused to write this new scripture in Hebrew (which he assumes to be Christ's language) in order to hide their scheming with the pagan Romans.

This narrative – which according to some scholars preserves an authentic memory of a time when Jews and Christians worshipped together – leads into later sections where ʿAbd al-Jabbār accuses the Apostle Paul and Emperor Constantine of further corrupting the religion of Christ.

CMR 2, pp. 604–9.

This passage is from ʿAbd al-Jabbār, *Tathbīt dalāʾil al-nubuwwa*, ed. and trans. G.S. Reynolds and S.K. Samir, *Critique of Christian Origins*, Provo UT, 2010, pp. 92–6, with permission.

[The origin of the Bible]

Know that the religion of Christ and the religions of the messengers (peace be upon them)[34] were not modified and substituted all at once, but rather one portion after another, in every age and period, until the change was complete. The party of truth continually grew smaller. The party of wrong grew larger until they prevailed, and the truth died because of them.

Now, after Christ, his followers conducted their prayers and holy days with the Jews and the Israelites in one place, in their synagogues, despite the conflict between them over Christ. The Romans were ruling over them and the Christians would complain about the Jews to the Roman rulers, showing them how weak they were and asking for compassion. [The Romans] would have compassion on them. This became more frequent until the Romans said to them: 'There is an agreement between us and the Jews, that we will not change their religious practices. If you were to deviate from their religious practices and separate yourselves from them, praying to the east as we do, eating what we eat, and deeming lawful what we deem lawful, then we would aid

[34] Those among the prophets who brought divine revelations through the ages up to the coming of Muḥammad.

you and make you mightier. Then the Jews would have no way over you. You would be mightier than them.'

They said, 'We will do it.' The [Romans] said, 'Go and get your companions and your book.'

They went back to their companions, informing them of what took place between them and the Romans and demanding, 'Get the *Injīl* and get up so that we might go to [the Romans].' But [their companions] replied to them, 'You have done wretchedly! It is not permitted for us to place the *Injīl* in the hands of the unclean Romans. By agreeing with the Romans, you have left the religion. It is not permitted for us to mix with you. Rather, we must wash our hands of you and keep the *Injīl* from you.' A severe conflict ensued between them.

[The first group] returned to the Romans and said to them, 'Assist us against these companions of ours before assisting us against the Jews! Get our book from them for us.' [The companions] concealed themselves from the Romans and fled throughout the land. The Romans wrote to their agents in the regions of Mosul and the Arabian Peninsula. They were hunted down. A group of them fell [into the hands of the Romans] and was burned. Another group was killed. Those who had made a deal with the Romans gathered and consulted each other over what to adopt in place of the *Injīl*, since it had passed out of their hands. They came to the opinion that they would produce an *Injīl*, saying, 'The *Tawrāt* is only genealogies of the prophets and histories of their lives. We will construct a gospel accordingly. Let each one of us mention what he has memorised from the formulations of the *Injīl* and from what the Christians used to say about Christ.' Thus, one group wrote a gospel. Then another group came after them and wrote a gospel. They wrote a number of gospels, though much of what was in the original was left out. There were a number of them who knew many matters that were in the correct *Injīl*, which they concealed in order to establish their leadership: in [the true *Injīl*] there was no mention of the crucifixion or crucifixes. They claim that there were eighty gospels. These were continuously transcribed and abridged until only four gospels by four individuals remained. Each individual made a gospel in his time. Then another came after him and, finding it imperfect, made a gospel which according to him was more correct than the gospels of another.

Furthermore, there is no gospel in Hebrew, the language of Christ, which he and his companions spoke, the language of Abraham the close friend [of God][35] and the rest of the prophets, the language which they spoke and in which the books of God came down to these and other Israelites. God addressed them [in Hebrew], but these [Christians] abandoned it. The [Muslim] scholars have said to them, 'O Christians, your turning from the Hebrew language, the language of Christ and the prophets before him (peace be upon them) to other languages, so that no Christian recites these gospels in the Hebrew language in any of his [religious] duties, is a plot and a scheme, an attempt to avoid a scandal.' The [Muslim] people have said to them, 'The avoiding of [Hebrew]

[35] See Q 4:125.

occurred because of your first companions' attempt to camouflage their accounts, plotting to disguise the lies that they set down in writing and to cover up their plots out of desire for leadership.'

This is because the Hebrews were the People of the Book and the party of knowledge in that time. These individuals changed the language, or rather turned away from it entirely, so that the party of knowledge would not understand their teachings and their intention to cover up [their lies], lest they should be embarrassed before their teachings could become dominant and their [scheme] be completed. They turned to many languages that Christ and his companions did not speak, and which are spoken by people other than People of the Book, those who do not know the Books of God or His laws, such as the Romans, Syrians, Persians, Indians, Armenians and other foreigners. Thus, they disguised and plotted in order to cover up their shame and to achieve leadership, the object of their desire, by that small group which pursued it with religion.

9

Al-Juwaynī, *Assuaging thirst*

David Thomas, University of Birmingham

Abū l-Maʿālī ʿAbd al-Malik ibn ʿAbd Allāh al-Juwaynī is best-known as the teacher of the great Abū Ḥāmid al-Ghazālī (d. 1111), though he was a considerable theologian in his own right. He was born near Nīshāpūr, in north-eastern Iran, in 1028, and was brought up to follow the way of Ashʿarī religious thinking. He was forced to leave Nīshāpūr because of the vizier's hostility to Ashʿarī theology. For the next fifteen years he wandered through the Islamic world, spending four years in Mecca and Medina. He returned home in 1063, and under a new vizier with pro-Ashʿarī views he was given a teaching post that he occupied for the rest of his life.

Al-Juwaynī was a master of systematic theology, his major work being *Al-shāmil fī uṣūl al-dīn* ('The complete book on the principles of religion'), following Ashʿarī theological principles. He may have written *Shifāʾ al-ghalīl fī bayān mā waqaʿa fī l-Tawrāt wa-l-Injīl min al-tabdīl* ('Assuaging thirst in explanation of the substitutions that have occurred in the Torah and Gospel') in Baghdad, where he would have encountered debates between Muslims, Jews and Christians, hence sometime between 1048 and 1058. It reflects the clarity of his approach to questions of religion in the transparent way it expresses the Muslim belief that the Jewish and Christian scriptures had been subject to *tabdīl* (textual substitution or alteration), resulting in errors in their teachings and their omission of references to Muḥammad and Islam. His method is first to establish that there were circumstances in which each scripture could have been altered, and then to give examples that prove alteration did occur. Comparatively short in length, this is one of the most compelling Muslim demonstrations that the text of the Bible is no longer intact.

CMR 3, pp. 121–4.

This translation is based on M. Allard (ed. and French trans.), *Textes apologétiques de Ǧuwaini (m. 478/1085)*, Beirut, 1968.

The Qur'an clearly states openly in undisputed reports that the texts of the Torah and the Gospel include mention of the master of those who have been sent (God's blessing be upon him).[36] This is the reason that has brought scholars of Islam to talk about substitution.[37] The two groups of Christians and Jews deny this and employ arguments that are 'like a mirage in a plain, which a man parched with thirst mistakes for water until, when he comes to it, he finds it is nothing'.[38] [p. 39] [...]

[The possibility of substitution]

So we say: The Torah that is presently in the possession of the Jews is the Torah that was written by Ezra the scribe after their tribulations under Nebuchadnezzar.[39] [...] This version was written by Ezra 545 years before Christ (peace be upon him) was sent, when there was no Christian anywhere on earth. Substitution was possible at this stage because there was no concern to know about collecting together versions of the Torah dispersed through parts of the earth, [...] nor was there any prospect of individuals from the two groups agreeing together, nor was there any version of it in the possession of the Jews and Christians – it only came into the possession of the Christians after there had been substitution of it.[40]

If the one who did this was a single person, it was Ezra, and if they rank him above this, it was the one who made a copy of his copy. But substitution on his part was possible because of his desire to perpetuate his headship, and there was no talk about any impeccability[41] of his that would prevent him from deciding to commit any small or large wrongs. [p. 47] [...]

[The fact of substitution]

So we say that in the Torah that is in the possession of the Jews, Seth was born to Adam (peace be upon him) when he reached 130 years, and in the one that is in the possession of the Christians, Seth was born to him when he reached 230 years.[42] In the Torah that is in the possession of the Jews, Enosh was born to Seth when he reached 600 years, while in the one that is in the possession of the Christians, Enosh was born to Seth when he reached 700 years.[43] [p. 51] [...]

See the shamefulness and quirkiness of this difference between these two groups about a matter that is not one of those questions of opinion that differ because of

[36] According to the Qur'an, Muḥammad is referred to in both the Torah and Gospel (7:157), and by Jesus (61:6).
[37] Since the references in the Qur'an to Muḥammad are missing from the biblical books, it must follow that their original text has been changed.
[38] Q 24:39.
[39] See, e.g., Nehemiah 8:1-3.
[40] Al-Juwaynī is surmising that at this time substitution of one text for another was possible because it was before there were any collective means of ascertaining consistency between versions of the Torah.
[41] The inability to commit any sinful acts, which was a characteristic of prophets alone. There was no talk of Ezra being a prophet, so the possibility lay open of his making substitutions to the original text.
[42] Genesis 5:3. The Hebrew text, 'in the possession of the Jews', gives Adam's age at the birth of Seth as 130 years, while the Septuagint, 'in the possession of the Christians', gives it as 230 years.
[43] Genesis 5:6, giving Seth's age at the birth of Enosh as 105 years.

differences in the approaches of scholars, originating from differences in the degrees of opinions, but rather each group claims that what is in their possession is what was revealed to Moses (peace be upon him). This is the essence of substitution and alteration.[44] [pp. 55–7] [...]

Concerning the possessors of the Gospels, the debate with them comes next – and God will give help against them.

[The possibility of substitution]

Concerning their monstrous error and their lack of care for what they have been passing on, among reasonable people there is no hope of correcting it. The reason why they were brought into error in what they were transmitting was their carelessness over what must be given careful attention at times that substitution and forgetfulness can occur when transmission is oral.

Matthew declares in his Gospel that he wrote it nine years after Christ (peace be upon him) was taken up. John also states in his Gospel that he assembled it just over thirty years after the ascension of Christ (peace be upon him). Similarly, Mark declares in his Gospel that he assembled it twelve years after Christ was taken up, and similarly Luke declares in his Gospel that he wrote it twenty-two years after Christ (peace be upon him) was taken up, though some say twenty years. [pp. 57–9] [...]

[The fact of substitution]

Matthew mentions in his Gospel, and likewise Mark, [...] that when Christ was crucified, according to their claim, 'Two thieves were crucified with him, one on his right and the other on his left. Those who passed by shook their heads and said: "You who would destroy the temple and build it in three days, save yourself if you are the Son of God".'[45] Then Matthew says: 'The two thieves who had been crucified with him were shouting out and abusing him,'[46] and Mark also says: 'The two thieves who had been crucified with him were abusing him.'[47] But in the Gospel of Luke is that when Christ (peace be upon him) 'came to the place called the Skull, they crucified him there and with him two criminals, one on his right and the other on his left'.[48] Then he says: 'The leaders were mocking him and saying: "He saved others, so let him save himself if he is the Christ, the Son of God, the chosen One."[49] One of the criminals who had been crucified with him was blaspheming and saying: "If you are the Christ, save yourself and save us"; but the other answered him, reproaching him, and said to him: "Do you not fear

[44] The disagreements between the Jews and the Christians do not arise from different interpretations of the same text or opinions about it, but from factual differences in their different versions of scripture. What makes this shameful is that the revealed text itself has undergone substitution.

[45] Matthew 27:38-40; Mark 15:27-32.

[46] Matthew 27:44.

[47] Mark 15:32.

[48] Luke 23:32-3.

[49] Luke 23:35.

God? We two are under this sentence, and we are being punished as we deserve and according to what we have done. But this man, he has done nothing." Then he said to Jesus: "Remember me when you come into your kingdom." He said: "Truly, I say to you, today you will be with me in paradise"."[50]

This was the end of what he said.

Luke, the one whose words these are, makes clear in his Gospel that one of the two robbers who were crucified with him believed in him and had sympathy for him, and the other abused him and mocked him. The clear words of Matthew and Mark above are that neither of the two robbers believed in him, and that both of them abused him and mocked him. But it was a single event, and what is to be said about the two [accounts] is similar to what is said about similar instances above.[51] There can be no doubt about the contradiction between these pieces of evidence, and that those who spoke about them came long afterwards so that they said things about which they had no certainty. [pp. 75–7]

---

[50] Luke 23:29-43.

[51] I.e. that these provide evidence that the Gospels have undergone change.

10

Abū l-Qāsim al-Anṣārī, *The indispensable, on theology*

Richard Todd, University of Birmingham

In core respects a quintessential graduate of the Seljuq *madrasa* (religious school) system, Abū l-Qāsim Salmān ibn Nāṣir al-Anṣārī (d. 1118) was a Shāfiʿī jurist and Ashʿarī theologian who studied *kalām* (Islamic theology) in his native Nīshāpūr under the celebrated theologian al-Juwaynī (d. 1085). Like al-Juwaynī's most famous pupil, Abū Ḥāmid al-Ghazālī (d. 1111), he was attracted to Sufism. During his travels, which took him through Iraq, the Ḥijāz and the Levant, he is reported to have spent time in Baghdad serving the renowned Sufi master Abū l-Qāsim al-Qushayrī (d. 1074).

Though he was an avid patron of the library attached to the Niẓāmiyya *madrasa* in Nīshāpūr, al-Anṣārī (unlike al-Ghazālī) does not appear to have held a salaried teaching post, but instead earned an independent livelihood as a copyist and bookseller. By all accounts an outwardly unassuming figure who was drawn to solitude and asceticism, he also suffered from a speech impediment which, according to his contemporaries, belied a fierce intelligence. To later generations al-Anṣārī would be best known for his commentary on al-Juwaynī's *Kitāb al-irshād* ('Book of guidance') as well as for the work from which the extracts below have been taken, *Al-ghunya fī l-kalām* ('The indispensable, on theology').

In its general structure and content, the *Ghunya* is a standard compendium of Ashʿarī theology. In one section, however, al-Anṣārī turns his attention to Christian dogma, and in so doing displays, in his knowledge of relevant sources and sects, a significant level of detail, though the distinction between monophysite and dyophysite Christians becomes hazy at best. The section on Christian doctrine comes in the context of a chapter dealing with the divine attributes. Like al-Bāqillānī (d. 1013) before him, al-Anṣārī challenges the Christian assertion that the Deity may be described as a 'substance', or *jawhar*, the Perso-Arabic rendering of the Greek term *ousía* ('substance', 'essence', 'being') enshrined in the Chalcedonian creed of 451. Noticeable in his *kalām*-inflected treatment of this topic is the extent to which he appears to conceive of the term *jawhar* in a quasi-corporeal sense. In contrast to the range of entities – from corporeal individuals to immaterial causes – to which the category 'substance' is applied in Aristotelian philosophy, *jawhar* as envisaged in al-Anṣārī's theology seems all but synonymous with material bodies and is hence deemed singularly inapplicable to God.

Although al-Anṣārī's grasp of the substantive differences between Jacobites, Nestorians and Melkites seems tenuous, he recognizes nonetheless the question of Christ's being, which consisted of two natures, human and divine, as a fundamental point of contention. It is also intriguing, moreover, to see him ascribing to the Christians of the Islamic world, whether Eastern Christians or Crusaders, he does not specify, what appears to be a theoretical antecedent of the Christ-Knight motif in which the Incarnation of the divine Word is portrayed in terms of its being concealed and hence protected in the 'armour' of human nature.

CMR 5, pp. 665–7. See further:

D. Thomas, 'Christian Borrowings from Islamic Theology in the Classical Period: The Witness of al-Juwaynī and Abū l-Qāsim al-Anṣārī', *Intellectual History of the Islamicate World* 2 (2014) 125–42.

J. Thiele, 'Commonness and Derivative Work in Aš'arite Literature: A Comparison of Diyā al-Dīn al-Makkī's *Nihāyat al-Marām* and Abū al-Qāsim al-Anṣārī's *al-Ġunya fī al-Kalām*', *Mélanges – Institut dominicain d'études orientales du Caire* 32 (2017) 135–66.

The translation below is based on Abū l-Qāsim al-Anṣārī, *Al-ghunya fī l-kalām*, ed. M.H. ʿAbd al-Hādī, Cairo, 2010.

One of the doctrines professed by Christians is that the Lord – far is He above what they impute to Him – is a substance (*jawhar*). By this designation they do not mean that He may be described as possessing the characteristic properties of a substance, namely spatial location, size, susceptibility to composition, accidents, limits and finiteness, but rather that He subsists through Himself (*qā'im bi l-nafs*). When they are asked: 'Why does it follow that just because He is self-subsistent He must be a substance, especially as linguistic scholars would reject this [proposition] were it presented to them, and as no justification for its use may be found in the scriptures?,' they reply: 'Like a substance, He – glory to His transcendence – exists independently of any substrate (*maḥall*), so for that reason we refer to Him as a substance.'[52]

In response one might ask: 'What proof do you have that a substance is called a substance because it subsists by itself?' If they say, 'We have encountered no substance that is not self-subsistent,' we counter with: 'Nor will you have encountered a body (*jism*) that is not self-subsistent, so call Him a body as well; and you will have encountered no substance that is not of a definite size, so call Him that as well.'[53] Then

[52] In the Aristotelian system of thinking employed by the Christians, the category of substance does not depend on other entities in order to exist, unlike the category of accident that can only exist in a substrate. Hence, God can be called a substance.

[53] Al-Anṣārī compels the Christians to accept by the force of their own logic that God is a body, and thus physical, and also finite, characteristics that neither they nor Muslims would allow.

if they say: 'His self-subsistence does not make of Him a body,' we will say, 'His self-subsistence does not make of Him a substance either!' And nor for that matter do we encounter any accident that does not inhere in a substrate – so He is not an accident.

Now we, for our part, do not call the Eternal 'self-subsistent' just because He exists independently of any substrate. Rather, we call Him this because He is independent in an absolute sense. Moreover, Muslim scholarly consensus, which is almost tantamount to scriptural precedent, accepts the use of this designation. As for the term 'substance', however, there is neither scriptural precedent for its use nor rational proof of its legitimacy.

Christians also say that, linguistically speaking, 'substance' denotes the origin of something and that the Eternal – transcendent is He – is the origin of the hypostases, so they call Him a substance for that reason. To this we say:'[Muslim] theologians and [Arabic] linguistic scholars alike call a substance a substance because of its preciousness, not because of its being the origin of composite things. This, after all, is the reason why some stones are referred to as a *jawhar*.[54] As for the hypostases that you mention, you do not regard them as actual entities (*mawjūdāt*) but rather as properties (*khawāṣṣ*). Yet accidents, too, have properties such as colourfulness or blackness – so would you therefore call any accident in which a property exists a substance?'[55]

If they respond by saying: 'Beings are divisible into that which is precious, such as substance, and that which is base, such as accidents; and the Lord – glory to Him – is precious and therefore a substance,' we say: 'Then why do you not call Him the Precious (*al-nafīs*) as well? And besides, even if we were to accept what you say, there is no [intrinsic] preciousness in mortal bodies or buildings [for example]. But preciousness does exist in [abstract] intelligibles, for which reason it would be more appropriate to apply this term to accidents.'

[The truth] then is that a substance is called a substance precisely because of its size and corporeality. When we apply names to God – transcendent is He – scriptural authority and precedent should be observed, which is why we do not call Him the Intelligent, the Liberal, and the Astute but we do call Him the Knowing, the Munificent and the Wise.[56] [pp. 445–6] [...]

Another doctrine they profess is that the Logos (*al-kalima*) became one with Christ's body and thereby donned the chain mail of human nature. Some of them interpret this union as a mixture or intermingling, a doctrine espoused by some sects among the Jacobites and Nestorians. The Melkites for their part say that the Logos[57] permeated

---

[54] A 'jewel' or 'gem'.

[55] It would be contradictory to call accidents substances, because accidents are not self-subsistent while the term 'substance' is applied only to things that are self-subsistent.

[56] There is scriptural authority for applying the latter three names to God because they appear in the Qur'an, while the former do not.

[57] The published edition of the text gives this phrase as *al-malak māzajat*, 'the angel (masc.) permeated (fem.)'. In terms of both grammar and context, however, *al-kalima māzajat*, 'the Logos (fem.) permeated (fem.)' seems preferable.

Christ's body as wine permeates milk or water, by which they became a single thing and multiplicity became oneness. This, then, is the doctrine of the Melkites, who account for most of the Byzantines.

Now some Jacobites say that the Logos turned into flesh and blood, [but] became [only] a small part of each, even though what is meant by union [of the human and the divine] is the manifestation of divinity through human nature, like the *visible* settling (*istiwāʾ*) of the Deity upon the [divine] throne.[58] Many other sects, by contrast, hold that what is meant by union is inhabitation. They also express union as the 'donning of chain mail' (*tadarruʿ*) and see these terms as conveying the same basic meaning; for it seems they believe – both literally and metaphorically – that divinity took Christ's body as armour.

Know, therefore, that mixture, intermingling and inhabitation are attributes of bodies and so cannot possibly be conceived of as applicable to hypostases or to properties that have no independent existence. [Know too] that they have [accordingly] examined [the notion of] inhabitation and have interpreted it in the sense of the Logos inhering in Christ's body as an accident inheres in a substrate. To this, then, one might respond: 'Do you believe, therefore, in the separation of the Logos from the [divine] substance and its connection with Christ's human nature when it dwells [within it] or not?' If they answer negatively one should respond by saying: 'How then can the Logos have dwelt in Christ's human nature when it inheres in the eternal [divine] substance?' For if, as is commonly agreed, it is impossible for one and the same accident to inhere in two substrates, then it is even more inconceivable in the case of properties. Moreover, no intelligible thing may come to reside in Christ's body unless it comes into being within it or is translocated from elsewhere. Now physical translocation is impossible for intelligible things, yet they [the Christians] also hold that the Logos cannot possibly have come into being.

If, on the other hand, they accepted the separation [of the Logos], they would thereby be compelled [to accept likewise] that after the birth of Jesus – peace be upon him – the [divine] substance could no longer be [qualified as] knowing[59] and that an intrinsic attribute had separated [from the divine substance]. [pp. 447–8]

[58] The 'settling (*istiwāʾ*) of the Deity' is a reference to Qur'anic verses (7:54, 13:2, 20:5, 25:59, 32:4, 57:4) which state that God settled or sat (the verb in question, *istawā*, is ambiguous) on the throne (*al-ʿarsh*) after creating the world. Though they differed over how to interpret such verses, Muslim theologians of the Muʿtazilī and Ashʿarī schools agreed that God did not *visibly* sit on the throne, as He transcends corporeality and spatial location. Al-Anṣārī thus likens the Christian doctrine of the union of the divine Logos and Christ's human body to what he, as an Ashʿarī theologian, regards as the error of Muslim corporealists (*mujassima*) who have interpreted the Qur'anic *istawā* as the visible act of sitting, and have therefore implicitly ascribed a body and spatial location to God. He also appears to suggest that the idea that the Logos was present in only a small part of Christ's flesh and blood is an attempt to avoid the corporealist implications of the usual Christian understanding of union.

[59] According to explanations of the Trinity given by Arab Christians, it was the Logos, as the divine Word or Knowledge, that made God knowing, just as the Spirit, or Life, made God living. Therefore, if the Logos became separated from God when it united with the human Christ, God could no longer be knowing, which is logically impossible.

11

Ibn Jubayr, *Travels*

Alex Mallett, University of Waseda

Little is known about Ibn Jubayr apart from what is mentioned in his most famous work, *Riḥla* ('Travels'). He was born in 1145 in Valencia, a descendant of Muslims who had moved to al-Andalus soon after the Muslim conquest in the eighth century. He received an education in the religious sciences and became a bureaucrat in the court of Granada.

The journey he details in his *Riḥla* took place in the 1180s. He travelled east from al-Andalus, taking in Egypt, the Ḥijāz, Iraq and the Levant, before returning home. He spent some months in the Frankish kingdom of Jerusalem, one of the Crusader states, and in Sicily, a Norman possession at the time.

His work is of significance for the history of Christian-Muslim relations for two reasons. Firstly, in his accounts of the places he visited he gives details of everyday interactions between Christians and Muslims that are usually ignored in other works from the period. Secondly, since relations between the two groups he witnessed were usually fairly good, he criticizes the Muslims for living in Christian lands, and the Christians, as he sees it, for trying to seduce the Muslims into abandoning their faith by being hospitable towards them. It is likely that this rather cynical attitude resulted from his experiences back home in the Iberian Peninsula, where the Muslim population was slowly declining. The extracts presented below highlight both these perspectives.

CMR 4, pp. 159–65.

The translations below are from Ibn Jubayr, *Riḥla*, ed. W. Wright, rev. M.J. de Goeje, Leiden, 1907, repr. New York 1973, with reference to the translation by R.J.C. Broadhurst, London, 1952.

[In the Levant]

We left Tibnin[60] (may God destroy it) at dawn on a Monday. Our way was through farms and ordered villages, all the inhabitants of which were Muslims. They lived comfortably alongside the Franks (may God shield us from such temptation),[61] giving them half of their produce at harvest time and each person paying one *dīnār* and five *qīrāṭ*s. They [the Franks] do not [otherwise] bother them except for a small tax on the fruit of the trees that they [the Muslims] pay them [the Franks] as well. [pp. 301–2] [...]

[Acre] is a meeting place of ships and caravans, and a gathering place for merchants, both Muslim and Christian, from distant lands. Its roads and streets are packed full of crowds, and one's feet [sometimes] do not touch the ground. [Religious] oppression and impiety blaze, and pigs and crosses are everywhere.[62] It is filthy and dirty, and the whole place is filled with rubbish and excrement. The Franks wrested it from the hands of the Muslims in the last decade of the fifth century,[63] and Islam wept, its eyes growing swollen, because of it. This event was one of its sorrows. Its mosques were turned into churches, and its minarets became bell towers. Yet God kept clean one part of the main mosque, which remained in the hands of the Muslims as a small mosque. [p. 303] [...]

In the eastern part of the land [of Acre] is a spring known as ʿAyn al-Baqar, and it was here that God sent the cattle to Adam (may God bless and grant him salvation).[64] The opening down to this spring is via a long flight of steps. Over it is a mosque of which only its *miḥrāb*[65] remains, while the Franks have set up a *miḥrāb* of their own, to the east. The Muslims and the infidels gather there (together), each turning to their own place of worship. In the Christians' hands its greatness is preserved, and God has maintained within it a place of prayer for the Muslims. [p. 303] [...]

[In Sicily]

With regard to their king,[66] he is marvellous in his good conduct and employment of Muslims and having eunuchs as slaves, while all or most of them conceal their faith,

---

[60] In present-day Lebanon. At this time, it was part of the Latin Kingdom of Jerusalem.

[61] The Arabic term used here is *fitna*, which has a variety of meanings similar to 'temptation' (e.g. 'charm', 'attractiveness' and 'enchantment'), but it also has the meaning of 'dissension', 'strife' and 'sedition', particularly when it relates to discord within the Muslim community. Ibn Jubayr here seems to be suggesting that the Christians are stirring up 'sedition' by 'tempting' the Muslims to have close relations with them, thus enabling them to see good in Christianity and possibly convert. This whole passage carries a theme alluded to throughout Ibn Jubayr's text, which is that any good deed done by Christians towards Muslims is actually evil, as it carries the potential of tempting Muslims away from Islam.

[62] Both would be abhorrent to Muslims, pigs because pork is forbidden in the Qur'an (2:173) and crosses because the Qur'an denies the crucifixion took place (4:157).

[63] In the first decade of the twelfth century.

[64] Referring to the tradition that God revealed this spring to Adam so that he could water his cows. It is regarded by some as one of the four holiest water sources in the world.

[65] An indication, usually in the form of an alcove in the mosque wall, of the direction towards Mecca.

[66] The Norman King William II, 'the Good' (r. 1166–89).

holding fast to the law of Islam. He has great trust in the Muslims and relies on them in his affairs and his most important business, so much so that the person in charge of his kitchen is one of the Muslims, and he has a group of black Muslim slaves over whom is a commander [chosen] from among them. His viziers and chamberlains are from [the ranks of] his slaves – he has a large number of them – and they are his state officials, who are described as his most important people. With them is seen the glory of his kingdom in the splendid clothes and fine horses [they have], and there is not one of them who does not have a retinue, servants and followers. [...]

The king has [a number of Muslim] doctors and astrologers, and he is greatly concerned for them and pays much attention to them, so much so that when he is informed that a doctor or an astrologer is traversing his land, he [the king] orders him to be seized and an income to support him to be bestowed on him, so that his homeland will be forgotten (may God protect the Muslims from his temptation).[67] [...]

One of the amazing things reported about him is that he can read and write in Arabic, and his personal mark, we learnt from one of his personal slaves, is: 'Praise God, it is right to praise Him', while his father's personal mark was: 'Praise God as thanks for His blessings'. As for his slave-girls and concubines in his palace, they are all Muslims. One of the most amazing things that this slave Yahyā ibn Fityān al-Ṭirāz, who used to embroider the king's clothes with gold, told us he had heard about him was that [some of the] Frankish women from among the Christians who lived in his palace became Muslims, converted by the slave-girls. They kept this secret from the king. [...] And we were told that when a powerful earthquake struck the island this polytheist[68] ran around his palace in terror, [and as he did so] he heard nothing but supplications to God and His Prophet from his women and his slaves. Consternation overcame them when they saw him, but he said to them: 'Let everyone appeal to their (own) deity, and their religion will comfort them'. [pp. 324–6]

The Muslims of this city [Palermo] hold fast to the signs of the faith, preserving most of their mosques and performing prayers at the time the call to prayer is made, while in the areas they inhabit they live separately from the Christians. The markets are filled with them and they are the merchants of it [Palermo]. They do not gather on a Friday because the *khuṭba* is prohibited for them,[69] although on feast days they can perform the prayer with the *khuṭba* for the ʿAbbasids included in it. They have a *qāḍī* and they submit to him their legal issues, while they have a main mosque for prayers in which they gather under its lights in this blessed month.[70] As for the other mosques, they are beyond counting, and most of them are used for lessons by Qur'an teachers. However, they live separate lives from their Muslim brothers who are under

[67] Arabic: *fitna*; see n. 61 above.
[68] William's belief in the Trinity would be interpreted by Muslims as associating other beings with God, an unforgivable sin.
[69] The sermon, which customarily included prayers for the ruler as an indication of his legitimacy, would have been an understandably sensitive issue between Muslims and a Christian king.
[70] Ramaḍān 580/December 1185.

the protection of the infidels, and there is no safety for their possessions, nor their women, nor their children. [p. 332]

The Christian women of this city [Palermo] dress as Muslim women, they speak fluently, cover themselves and veil themselves when they go out; on this feast day [Christmas], they are dressed in outfits made of silk with gold, clothed in beautiful cloaks, hidden behind colourful veils and wearing gilded shoes. (Attired thus,) they display themselves in their churches – or their dens[71] – carrying all the adornments of Muslim women: jewellery, dye[72] and perfume. [p. 333]

[71] *Kunus* (sing. *kinās*, an animal's hiding-place), a pun on *kanā'is*, 'churches'.
[72] This presumably refers to henna.

12

Usāma ibn Munqidh, *The book of instructions*

Alex Mallett, University of Waseda

Usāma ibn Munqidh was one of the Banū Munqidh, the family that ruled the strategically important town of Shayzar and its hinterland in central Syria during the eleventh and early twelfth centuries. Due to a dispute over the family succession in the 1130s he took his leave of the town and went to Damascus, where he lived until 1144. During this period, he spent some time in the crusader Kingdom of Jerusalem, though he was soon forced to leave for Fāṭimid Egypt, where he became an envoy to foreign rulers, but was accused of being part of a plot against the caliph and so had to flee back to Damascus in 1154. After ten years living there, he moved to Ḥiṣn Kayfā, and the next twenty years were devoted to writing. In 1184 he was invited by Saladin back to Damascus and died there not long after in 1188.

Most of Usāma's writings are no longer extant, though a collection of poems and a book on staves (*Kitāb al-ʿaṣā*) have survived. By far his best-known work is *Kitāb al-iʿtibār* ('The book of instructions'), a collection of anecdotes that he dictated towards the end of his life, when he was almost ninety. It is sometimes referred to as an autobiography, but this is inaccurate; while it does describe events in his life, its primary goal is to describe some of the strangest things that he experienced or heard about. Thus, most of the events that are recounted are odd or noteworthy in some way, and the Franks (the Crusaders) of Syria, who are the focus of much of the work, are described as extremely odd.

The passages below well represent some of the astonishment felt by Usāma at Frankish beliefs and customs.

CMR 3, pp. 764–8.

This translation is based on Usāma ibn Munqidh, *Kitāb al-iʿtibār*, ed. P. Hitti, New York, 1930.

The oddities of the crusading Franks

The Franks (God curse them) have not one virtue out of all the virtues of men except for courage. There is no leader among them nor is anyone of high status with the exception of the knights, who are the men of opinion and the men of [legal] judgement and sentence. Once, when I was in Damascus, I brought before them [the issue that] the lord of Baniyas had taken some sheep from the forest at a time when there was a peace between us and them. I said to the king, Fulk the son of Fulk, 'This man has acted unjustly towards us, has stolen our animals at the time of lambing.' Then the king said to six or seven knights, 'Go and make a decision in this case.' Then they went out of his meeting room and kept to themselves while they deliberated until they came to a decision they all agreed upon, and then they returned to the king's meeting room. They said, 'Our verdict is that the lord of Baniyas should pay him damages equal to the amount of damage done to the sheep.' The king ordered him to pay the fine. The lord of Baniyas beseeched me, begged me and urged me until I accepted 400 dinars from him. After the knights pronounce such a verdict, neither the king nor any of the Frankish nobles are in are a position to change or revoke it. As such, the knights are very powerful among them. [pp. 64–5]

Every one of them who has recently arrived from Frankish lands is of a more uncouth disposition than those who have become acclimatized and are on intimate terms with the Muslims. Here is an example of their disposition (may God debase them). When I went to Jerusalem I went into the Aqsa mosque,[73] and to its side was a small mosque that the Franks had converted into a church. I would go into the Aqsa mosque, and inside would be [some of] the Templars, who were my friends, and they would leave that small mosque to me so that I could pray in it. One day, I entered it and [began to] give praise and start the prayer. Then, one of the Franks rushed towards me, grabbed me and turned me to face east, saying, 'Pray like this!' Some of the Templars rushed towards him, seized him and dragged him away from me. I then carried on with my prayer. But he ignored them, and continued his attack on me, grabbing me and turning me to face the east, saying, 'Pray like this!' The Templars returned, seized him and dragged him away. They apologized to me, and said, 'This is a foreigner who has only come from the lands of the Franks in the last few days. He has never seen anyone praying except towards the east.' I said, 'I have prayed enough!' I departed, astonished at [the behaviour of] that devilish man, and how his face changed, and his shaking [with anger] and what he thought when he saw the prayer [being performed] towards the south. [pp. 134–5]

I saw one of them [the Franks] come to the emir Muʿīn al-Dīn (may God have mercy upon him) who was in the Dome of the Rock. He [the Frank] said to him: 'Do you want

[73] The mosque on the Temple Mount just south of the Dome of the Rock. It had been converted into a church, and was used by the Knights Templar as their headquarters.

to see God as a child?' He replied, 'Yes'. So he led us forth until he showed us Mary with the Messiah (may peace be upon him) as a child in her lap.[74] He then said, 'This is God as a child.' Yet God is exalted much higher than what the infidels say about him. [p. 135]

They [the Franks] have absolutely no pride or jealousy. One of the men could be out walking with his wife and might meet another man. This other man might take the wife to one side and speak with her while her husband loiters nearby, waiting for her to finish the conversation. If her discussion goes on for a long time he may leave her with her interlocutor and depart! [p. 135]

Some of the Franks have become acclimatized [to the Levant] and are on intimate terms with Muslims. They are better than those recently arrived from their lands, although they are unusual and not the norm. Here is an example. I dispatched an associate to [Frankish] Antioch on business. There was in Antioch the leader Tādrus ibn al-Ṣaffī,[75] who was a friend of mine, and he was an important judge in Antioch. He said to my associate one day, 'A friend of mine, one of the Franks, has invited me. Come with me so that you can see their costume.' He said: So I set off with him and we came to the house of a knight; he was one of those old knights who had come here at the time of the first Frankish expeditions. He had been removed from the register and no longer had to fight, and in Antioch he had an estate whose income he lived off. He provided an excellent table, full of food that was very clean and outstanding. He saw me hesitate to eat and said, "Eat your fill! I do not eat Frankish food, and I have Egyptian (female) cooks and only ever eat what they cook, and pork does not enter my house." So I ate, although I did so cautiously, and then we left.' [p. 140]

---

[74] Presumably an icon in a church near the Dome of the Rock.

[75] A certain Theodoros Sophianos (P. Hitti, *An Arab-Syrian Gentleman and Warrior at the Time of the Crusades*, New York, 1929).

13

Najm al-Dīn al-Ṭūfī, *Critical commentary on the four Gospels*

Lejla Demiri, Eberhard Karl University of Tübingen

Najm al-Dīn Abū l-Rabīʿ Sulaymān ibn ʿAbd al-Qawī l-Ṭūfī (d. 1316) was a Ḥanbalī jurist, theologian, poet and man of letters. He spent most of his life in Baghdad, Damascus and Cairo, moving to Damietta and then Qūṣ in Upper Egypt, a predominantly Christian town where he apparently stayed in a Christian house. He went on pilgrimage to Mecca, spent a year in the Ḥijāz and died in Hebron in 1316.

Al-Ṭūfī wrote his *Al-taʿlīq ʿalā l-Anājīl al-arbaʿa wa-l-taʿlīq ʿalā l-Tawrāt wa-ʿalā ghayrihā min kutub al-anbiyāʾ* ('Critical commentary on the four Gospels, the Torah and other books of the prophets') in 1308. The *Taʿlīq* contains al-Ṭūfī's critical comments on the Christian scriptures, primarily on parts of the four Gospels and the books of Isaiah, Hosea, Jonah, Habakkuk, Malachi, Jeremiah, Ezekiel, Daniel and Genesis. Al-Ṭūfī aims to prove that Christian scriptures do not support Christian doctrines. In his view, biblical passages have either been misinterpreted or include textual interpolations by later generations. The *Taʿlīq* sheds light on the interreligious milieu of Mamlūk Egypt. It shows the extent of Ṭūfī's knowledge of Christian-Muslim literature and includes a number of references to his scholarly encounters with Christians.

The *Taʿlīq* is intended to serve as a guidebook for Muslims who may have been exposed to Christian criticisms of Islam. In these passages al-Ṭūfī offers a reading of the Gospel of Matthew that is compatible with the Muslim understanding of Jesus as no more than a human being and a truthful prophet of God. He interprets the biblical titles 'Lord' (*rabb*) and 'Son' (*ibn*) in reference to Jesus as honorific titles, indicating Jesus's special prophetic status in the eyes of God rather than his divinity.

CMR 4, pp. 724–31.

This translation is based on L. Demiri, *Muslim Exegesis of the Bible in Medieval Cairo: Najm al-Dīn al-Ṭūfī's (d. 716/1316) Commentary on the Christian Scriptures*, Leiden, 2013, reprinted with permission.

In [the Gospel of Matthew, Jesus says]: 'Not everyone who says [to me], "Lord, Lord", shall enter the kingdom of heaven; but he who does the will of my Father who is in the heavens. They will say to me on that day, "Lord, Lord".'[76] Thus, people often used to address him with 'Lord' and he would allow them to do so.

I say: Perhaps this is one of the things that have misled the Christians with regard to their conviction that Christ is a god. This can be addressed in a number of ways. Firstly, we have already explained earlier that there are defects and inconsistencies in the Gospel. So, this could be the case here. Secondly, if the text is authentic, their addressing Christ with lordship does not necessitate his divinity, just as it is said in common parlance: 'the lord of the house', 'the lord of the slave and of the riding animal', and the like. Thirdly, its metaphorical meaning is clearly evident, indicating that Christ is the messenger of the Lord, who commands what He has commanded and forbids what He has forbidden, so the metaphorical relationship becomes obvious. Or else it may be a case where the annexed noun (*muḍāf*) of the genitive construction is omitted, such that it had read: 'O messenger of our Lord', or 'O spirit of our Lord', and the like. In this case Christ permitted the unrestricted use of this utterance, relying on the contextual indicators (*qarā'in*) he had offered on a number of occasions, which reject the attribution of divinity to him. And God knows best.

As for his allowing people to say, 'O lord', it was because he knew they were aware he was not a god, since what they meant was only, 'O messenger of our Lord' or 'our master'. Wathīma [ibn Mūsā l-Fārisī (d. 851)] related in his *Qiṣaṣ al-anbiyā'* ['Stories of the prophets'] from Jarīr, from Qābūs, from his father, from Ibn ʿAbbās that whenever the People of the Book see a man of good appearance, they say: 'O my lord' (*yā rabbāya*), meaning 'O master' (*yā sayyid*). Also, Zakariyyā's statement [in Q 19:8], 'O my lord, how can I have a son?' is thus interpreted, indicating 'O my master', because it was Gabriel whom he addressed. [pp. 159, 161]

Among other things, there is also [Jesus's] statement in chapter 20: 'I express my gratitude to You, O my Father, Lord of the heavens and earth, for You have hidden these things from the wise and understanding and revealed them to infants. Yes, my Father, for so it was pleasing before You. All things delivered to me are of my Father. No one knows the Son, except the Father; neither does anyone know the Father, except the Son, and he to whom the Son wills to reveal Him.'[77] [p. 163]

What is clear from the context of this passage, and what precedes as well as what follows, is that the intended meaning is lordship and servanthood, not fatherhood and sonship. Also, as elucidated earlier, rational proof shows that the latter was not intended. As for what lies within the context of this saying, in his utterance, 'O my Father, Lord of the heavens and earth', the close proximity between the expressions of 'fatherhood' and 'lordship' shows that one is intended by the other.

Moreover, (Jesus) reports that his Father is the Lord of the heavens and earth. So, it should be said: It must either be the case that with His being the Lord of them both,

[76] Matthew 7:21–2.
[77] Matthew 11:25–7.

He is also the Lord of everyone within them [the heavens and earth]; or that He must be the Lord of some of them and not of others. However, the second [i.e. being the Lord of some] is invalid by consensus, while the third [i.e. not being the Lord of some others] is an act of passing arbitrary judgement and preferring one over the other without a basis for preference. We have already made clear in more than one place that the signs and wonders which appeared from Christ do not necessitate him being a god or the son of God, as (Christians) suggest. Therefore, the first [proposition] becomes necessary, namely, that God the Glorified is the Lord of the heavens and earth and of all that exists between them and within them, and Christ is part of that. Thus, he is a servant who is subject to His Lordship.

As for what precedes and follows in this chapter as well as elsewhere, by his words 'the Son of Man' and 'the Son of a human being' he means himself, as he does when saying, 'The Son of Man came eating and drinking, and they say: this is a gluttonous man and a winebibber'.[78] In his attributing to himself the sonship of humanity and the human race, there is actually a reminder that he is not a god and that he does not come from a non-human origin. He further corroborates this with his words 'eating and drinking', because eating and drinking are inseparable from urination and defecation, and these are among the characteristics of contingent existence (*ḥudūth*). However, the pre-Existent (*al-qadīm*) and whatever subsists in Him [i.e. His attributes] are far above this. There is also an allusion to this fact in the Holy Qur'an, where the Glorified says: 'The Christ, son of Mary, was no other than a messenger; messengers had passed away before him. And his mother was a virtuous woman. And they both used to eat food.'[79] Thus, He indicates by this [verse] the absence of their [Jesus's and Mary's] claim to, or their acquisition of, divinity as well as pre-existence. [pp. 165, 167]

In chapter 21 [of Matthew] there is a report from the Book of Isaiah the prophet: 'Behold! My servant (*fatā*) whom I love, and My beloved in whom My soul has taken pleasure. I shall put my Spirit upon him.'[80]

The expression 'beloved' refers neither to divinity nor to sonship. As for the expression *fatā* (young man), it clearly stands for *ʿabd* (servant) – one says *fatāya* and *fatātī*, meaning 'my male servant' and 'my female servant'. This passage also clarifies the intended meaning of (Matthew's) previously mentioned report that when (Jesus) emerged from the place of baptism [a voice out of the heavens said]: 'This is My beloved Son (*ibnī*), in whom I have taken pleasure.'[81] One may object that the expression *fatā* is ambiguous, due to its use for both 'son' (*ibn*) and 'servant' (*ʿabd*). But we respond: We have already explained, and shall continue to do so, that it is incorrect to refer to (Jesus) as 'son' except in the sense of 'servant'. Consequently, this expression [the meaning of *ibn*] determines the other [the meaning of *fatā*]. For in all scriptures, the words of God, Glorified is He, clarify one another. [p. 167]

---

[78] Matthew 11:19.
[79] Q 5:75.
[80] Matthew 12:18, quoting Isaiah 42:1.
[81] Matthew 3:17.

14

Ghāzī ibn al-Wāsiṭī, *Refutation of the* dhimmīs *and those who follow them*

Alex Mallett, University of Waseda

Ghāzī ibn al-Wāsiṭī (d. 1312) was a Muslim who worked in the administration of the Ayyūbid (r. 1174–1250) and Mamlūk (r. 1250–1517) dynasties. Little is known of his life, except that he worked in the government bureaucracy in Cairo, Aleppo and Damascus.

His tract on the *dhimmī*s, entitled *Radd ʿalā ahl al-dhimma wa-man tabiʿahum* ('Refutation of the *dhimmī*s and those who follow them'), is an attack on Christians – especially Egyptian Coptic Christians – and Jews, and contains a chronological series of anecdotes from throughout Islamic history detailing why, in his opinion, these people cannot be trusted. The work has a vicious tone throughout, something that is generally perceived as the result of al-Wāsiṭī having been held back in his career by members of these religious groups. His anti-Christian stance may, therefore, have been the result of his own thwarted ambitions in life.

CMR 4, pp. 627–9.

The translations below are based on the edition by R. Gottheil, 'An Answer to the Dhimmis', *Journal of the American Oriental Society* 41 (1921) 383–457, with reference to the translation given there.

In the days of Sultan al-Malik al-Ṣāliḥ Najm al-Dīn Ayyūb[82] – may God have mercy upon him and pardon him – one of the Muslims entered the Merchants' Market.[83] He had with him a writ regarding some money that one of the members of the army [owed him], requiring [only] what was necessary from the witnesses [i.e. signatures].

[82] The Ayyūbid sultan of Egypt, one of the descendants of Saladin, who ruled from 1240 to 1249.
[83] *Sūq al-Tujjār* in Cairo.

He encountered two Christians, who were wearing bodices and garments with loose-fitting sleeves, just the way that good Muslims[84] dress. He thought it likely that they were Muslims. He put the writ before them and they signed it, and in so doing they mocked the Muslims. This was communicated to Sultan al-Malik al-Ṣāliḥ, who ordered the Christians to be punished, be forced to wear the belt [that showed they were Christians], be made to dress distinctively and be prevented from resembling Muslims. He also ordered them to be forced down to the low and humiliating position to which God has reduced them. [p. 403] [...]

In the days of Sultan al-Malik al-Ẓāhir[85] – may God have mercy on him – [some of] the Muslims from the lands of the Tatars[86] informed him that al-Makīn ibn al-Amīd,[87] the *kātib*[88] to the army, had written to Hulagu[89] regarding the state of the Egyptian army, its soldiers and emirs. Al-Malik al-Ẓāhir seized him and intended to kill him. [...] He was detained for slightly longer than eleven years. Then his release was achieved through [the payment of] money. To secure his release the Christians' property, women and souls [i.e. lives] were taken, and no Christians or Jews remained in the land. Saʿīd al-Dawla,[90] who was in charge of the government office in Baghdad and Iraq, sought to weaken the Muslims and raise the position of the Jews. Then he sought out Arghūn[91] and poisoned him with his [own] drink after he had accumulated the wealth of Islam [for himself], raised the position of the Jews and debased Islam. For sure, the two accursed religions[92] were searching for a chance – God forbid! – to harm Islam by causing agitation. [pp. 410–11] [...]

In the days of our master, Sultan al-Malik al-Ẓāhir – may God have mercy on him – at the time when he was conquering Caesarea and Arsuf [1265], the people of Acre[93] supplied the Christians of Cairo with various people as part of a plot to set fire to the Bāṭaliyya,[94] the Farah quarter [of the city], a *waqf* of al-Ḥaram al-Sharif in Egypt and various other places, in order to trouble the heart of Sultan al-Malik al-Ẓāhir and harm the Muslims. The fire spread as far as Jurūn al-Rīf[95] in numerous places. Some friendly counsellors from the lands of the Franks[96] wrote to al-Malik al-Ẓāhir about this, so he seized the Christians and Jews of Cairo and Miṣr, gathering them all together in order

[84] The implication is that they were from the upper levels of society, since at this time a direct link was made between someone's moral conduct and their social position.
[85] The Mamlūk sultan Baybars (r. 1260–77).
[86] The Mongols.
[87] A Christian who worked in the Mamlūk administration, known as a historian who wrote an extant history of the world.
[88] A high-ranking position (usually translated as 'secretary') in the Mamlūk administration.
[89] The leader of the Mongol army who was threatening to attack the Mamlūks at this time.
[90] A Jewish administrator for the Mongols.
[91] Arghūn (r. 1284–91), the fourth Il Khān, was the Mongol ruler of Persia, Iraq and surrounding regions.
[92] Judaism, represented by Saʿīd al-Dawla, and Christianity, represented by Arghūn, who was in fact a Buddhist, but very well disposed towards Christians as his mother and several of his wives were Christians.
[93] The capital of the Crusader states at this time.
[94] A street in Cairo.
[95] It is not clear to which place this refers, though it must be in Cairo somewhere.
[96] It is unclear whether this is referring to Frankish territory in the eastern Mediterranean, or Europe.

to burn them [to death]. He himself rode along with some of the emirs in order to be at their burning, [which was to happen] at the edge of Cairo. Ibn al-Kāzarūnī al-Ṣayrafī emerged [from the condemned group] and said to the sultan, 'I beg you [in the name] of God, do not burn us together with these dogs of Christians, [who are both] your enemies and our enemies, so burn us on our own, away from them', though the sultan and the emirs laughed at Ibn al-Kāzarūnī's ridiculousness. But then [some of] the emirs approached him and requested him to fine them [instead], forgive them and not burn them. So he levied a large fine on them and appointed the emir Sayf al-Dīn Balbān al-Mahrānī to arrange with them the collection each year. [p. 411] [...]

Ghāzī ibn al-Wāsiṭī, the author of this book – may God have mercy on him! – says that it is not lawful for any of the sultans of Islam, nor any of their subordinate rulers, deputies or viziers to let the Church of Rubbish[97] that is in Jerusalem remain [standing]. This is because within it the Christians perform an act of deceit,[98] making it seem as though fire descends onto the tomb where the Christians pretend that the Messiah – peace be upon him – was buried, something that is done in order to delay [paying] the tax that is taken from them at the time of the pilgrimage. Ignorant Christians are told by the accursed patriarch that this fire is witnessed by Muslim onlookers who try to produce it [the fire] themselves. However, as the fire does not light [for the Muslims], their [the Christians'] delusion increases and they lose their intelligence, becoming even more devoted to the faith of their fathers, the unbelievers, particularly those who are born there and witness it every year. The appearance of this fire [...] is presented as a proof and [because of it] people cling to the accursed belief and religion [of Christianity]. In allowing the continuation of the place, the deputies of the sultan are supporters of the persistence of error, infidelity and heresy, and the connection to deceit. If this church is demolished and this business of the tomb and the fire ended, then the whole truth of the matter would be seen. [...] This would be a way of leading them [i.e. Christians] away from their religion. Perhaps the majority of them who had witnessed the lie of their highest-ranking member, the accursed patriarch, bishop and metropolitan, would turn to Islam. [pp. 412–13]

[97] The Church of the Resurrection/the Holy Sepulchre in Jerusalem, using the fact that the Arabic words for 'resurrection', *qiyāma*, and 'rubbish', *qumāma*, are very close in appearance to show his contempt for it.

[98] A reference to the ceremony each Easter Eve, attended by the patriarch and priests, at which fire was supposed to be kindled miraculously at Christ's tomb in the shrine known as the edicule within the Church of the Holy Sepulchre. Christians proclaimed it as miraculous, while Muslims routinely condemned it as a deception perpetrated by the Patriarch and his priests.

15

Ibn Taymiyya, *The correct answer*

Jon Hoover, University of Nottingham

Taqī l-Dīn Aḥmad ibn ʿAbd al-Ḥalīm ibn Taymiyya (d. 1328) was a traditionalist reformer and prolific theologian. He spent most of his life in Damascus. In all he wrote and did, he sought to return Islam to the pristine doctrines and practices found in the Qur'an, the Sunna of the Prophet Muḥammad, and the example of the early Muslims (*salaf*) as he understood them, and then show that these doctrines and practices accorded fully with reason.

Ibn Taymiyya wrote his *Al-Jawāb al-ṣaḥīḥ li-man baddala dīn al-Masīḥ* ('The correct answer to those who have changed the religion of Christ') in 1316 or soon thereafter to refute the Christian apologetic *Letter from the People of Cyprus*, which was a re-edition of Paul of Antioch's *Letter to a Muslim Friend. Al-jawāb al-ṣaḥīḥ* is the longest and one of the most sophisticated refutations of Christian doctrine in the Islamic tradition. It defends the universality of the Prophet Muḥammad's message, narrates how Christianity strayed from the original teachings of all the prophets, reinterprets biblical texts to accord with Islamic teachings and refutes the doctrines of the Trinity, the Incarnation and the Atonement of Christ using rational arguments. Ibn Taymiyya's express purpose in writing it is to warn Muslims against falling into the same kinds of errors that befell Christianity.

In the passage translated below, Ibn Taymiyya establishes the rational impossibility of the atonement narrative that was predominant in the early centuries of the Christian church. According to this account, Satan had rightly held human beings in bondage on account of their sins, but then God tricked Satan into crucifying the sinless man Christ, thereby forfeiting Satan's right to hold sinful humanity in captivity. Ibn Taymiyya responds that this narrative renders God weak, ignorant and unjust; God could not have left his faithful messengers of old in the clutches of Satan until he sent Christ to free them.

CMR 4, pp. 834–44. See also:

J. Hoover, *Ibn Taymiyya*, London, 2019.

This translation is based on Ibn Taymiyya, *Al-jawāb al-ṣaḥīḥ li-man baddala dīn al-Masīḥ*, ed. ʿAlī ibn Ḥasan ibn Nāṣir, ʿAbd al-ʿAzīz ibn Ibrāhīm al-ʿAskar and Ḥamdān ibn Muḥammad al-Ḥamdān, 7 vols, 2nd printing, Riyadh, 1419/1999.

Muslims have established by many proofs that [Christians] have changed the meanings of the Torah, the Gospel, the Psalms and other [scriptures] from the prophecy of the prophets, and that they have innovated a law that Christ did not bring. No one else [has brought it either], and no rational person has spoken of it. For example, they claim that all the children of Adam – including the prophets, the messengers[99] and others – were in hellfire in captivity to Satan because their forefather Adam ate from the tree, and that they were only saved from this when Christ was crucified. [vol. 2, p. 413] [...]

How is it possible for the messengers of God who were more eminent than [Adam] to be imprisoned in captivity to Satan in hell because of his sin? The father of Abraham, the friend of the All-Merciful,[100] was an unbeliever, and God did not censure [Abraham] for his [father's] sin. So, how could [God] put him in hell in captivity to Satan because of the sin of his more distant forefather Adam, even though he was a prophet? Noah lived with his people for 950 years, calling on them to worship God alone. God drowned the people of the earth when he called out [to God for help], and He preserved his progeny. So, how could he be in hell in captivity to Satan because of the sin of Adam? God spoke directly to Moses, son of ʿImrān. He manifested proofs and signs at his hands, the like of which He did not manifest at the hands of Christ. [Moses] killed someone he was not commanded to kill, and God forgave him that. His standing and honour before God are immeasurable. So, how could he be in hell in captivity to Satan?

The crucifixion was among the worst of sins, whether they crucified Christ or someone who looked like him.[101] Then what relation is there between the crucifixion and the salvation of these [messengers] from Satan? If Satan had done that with the progeny [of Adam], he would have been unjust and overstepped [his bounds]. God had the power to prevent him from treating them unjustly and indeed to punish him if he did not stop treating them unjustly. So, why did He delay in preventing him from treating them unjustly up to the time of Christ? God is the guardian of the believers, their helper and their supporter. They are His messengers whom He helped against those who showed enmity towards them. Moreover, He destroyed their enemies, who were the soldiers of Satan. How could He not have prevented Satan from treating them unjustly and casting their spirits into hell after they had died – this is only if one could imagine Satan being able to do such a thing? And how could it be possible for him to have given Satan authority to imprison His prophets and friends in hell after they had died, [after] moral obligation no longer applied to them and [after] they had become worthy of His honour, his beneficence, and His Garden by virtue of His promise and the exigency of His wise purpose?

[99] In Islamic teaching, prophets were sent by God to warn and guide various communities, while messengers were sent with revelations that were put into written form.

[100] Q 4:125.

[101] A reference to a traditional Muslim interpretation of Q 4:157, that the appearance of Jesus was put on another man (sometimes identified as Judas Iscariot), who was crucified in his place.

They may say, as they do claim, that the Lord was not able to save [His messengers] from Satan – even though He knew that he would treat them unjustly and overstep [his bounds with them] after they had died – except by tricking him through concealing Himself such that Satan would seize Him. In this is great unbelief. They have made the Lord out to be weak just as they first made Him out to be unjust. In this is contradiction that requires great ignorance on their parts and leads them to make the Lord out to be ignorant. They say that He tricked Satan [into thinking] that he was taking Him justly, just as Satan had tricked Adam with the serpent. He concealed Himself so that he [Satan] would not find out that it was the human nature of God. Unlike anyone else, the human nature of God had never committed a misdeed. Thus, Satan did not recognize his [own] misdeed when he sought to take His spirit in order to imprison Him in hell as [he had done to] everyone else who had gone before, and so Satan had it coming to him when the Lord seized him and saved the progeny [of Adam] from imprisonment to him.

With this, they make the Lord out to be ignorant, weak and unjust. Glory be to Him, and may He be highly exalted above what they say. Indeed, if He had given Satan authority over the children of Adam, as they say, there would have been no difference between the humanity of Christ and anyone else, inasmuch as all of them were children of Adam. Moreover, if one were to imagine that the humanity [of Christ] rightly defended itself against Satan – for they say that He entered hellfire and extracted the progeny of Adam from it – then let it be said that, if Satan had been given authority rightly over their imprisonment in hellfire on account of their sins along with the sin of their forefather, then it would not have been permissible to extract them on account of the humanity of Christ's freedom from sin. [Conversely], if they had been treated unjustly by Satan, it would have been necessary to have saved them before the crucifixion of the human nature [of Christ]. It would not have been permissible to delay that. For there is nothing in the mere freedom of Christ from sins that necessitates the freedom of anyone else [from sins]. [vol. 2, pp. 416–18]

Christian Arabic

Arabic-speaking Christians in the Islamic Empire

David Thomas, University of Birmingham

In the centuries after Christ, Christianity spread through the Mediterranean world and also beyond, particularly to the south and east. By the time of the Council of Chalcedon in 451, convened to resolve the problem of the relationship between the divine and human in Christ, churches were well-established in Syriac-speaking and Arabic-speaking parts of the Middle East. They maintained their own teachings about this perennial Christological problem and kept up their disagreements with the Greek-speaking church within the Roman Empire, by now centred on Constantinople as capital rather than Rome, and also with one another. When in the seventh and eighth centuries Arab Muslim armies swept through the regions where these Christians lived, they encountered no more than sporadic armed resistance, though they discovered their new Christian subjects were steadfast defenders of their beliefs and ways. Christianity under Muslim rule remained strong for hundreds of years.

Little is known about Christianity among the Arabs in the pre-Islamic period. Ecclesiastical networks with bishops, priests and churches existed from at least the fourth century. If addresses in the Qur'an to those who believe in the Trinity (Q 4:171, 5:73) and the divinity of Christ (Q 4:171, 9:30) were primarily directed at Christians in the western parts of Arabia where Muḥammad lived, there must certainly have existed communities that followed the accepted doctrines of the faith. Muslim traditions about Muḥammad knowing Ethiopian Christian traders in Mecca, about Waraqa ibn Nawfal, the Christian cousin of his wife Khadīja who explained Muḥammad's first revelatory experiences, and about Baḥīrā, the anchorite who recognized the young Muḥammad as the prophet his books told him would come, suggest that Muḥammad had more than passing acquaintance with Christians.

Christians in areas struck by the first Arab attacks may have thought they were no more than raids like those periodically conducted by bands of desert Arabs. In the years immediately after Muḥammad's death in 632, Christians learned about him as a leader with a new religious message, while their initial apprehension that the Muslims had come to stay was transformed into reality through the following years, as Arab armies established themselves in Damascus in 636, Jerusalem in 638 and Egypt in the early 640s.

In Damascus, which became the capital of the Umayyad dynasty in 661, and other urban centres, it would have been clear to Christians at an early stage that the new rulers followed their own beliefs and ways of worship. It can be imagined how Christians felt when they saw Muslims praying in their own part of the great Church of St John the Baptist, before it was converted into what is now known as the Umayyad Mosque. But outside cities the majority of Christians would have known little about them apart from the times each year when they collected taxes. On these occasions, Christians were usually made to remember their inferior status by being symbolically humiliated, in compliance with literal readings of Q 9:29, *wa-hum ṣāghirūn* ('and feel themselves subdued'), often by being slapped and forced to bow their heads.

As time progressed the measures to keep Christians and other non-Muslims under control were brought together into what became known as the *Pact of ʿUmar* (*Shurūṭ ʿUmar*), which was attributed to the second caliph ʿUmar ibn al-Khaṭṭāb (r. 634–44), though it was probably first codified around the year 800. According to its provisions, the various communities who are recognized in the Qur'an as possessors of their own scripture and named *Ahl al-kitāb* ('People of the book') were afforded legal status as *Ahl al-dhimma* ('People of the Covenant') or *dhimmīs*, in return for obeying regulations governing their conduct. These included stepping aside for Muslims in the street, not retaliating when struck by a Muslim, not employing Muslims as servants, wearing distinctive hairstyles and clothes, particularly yellow sashes around their waists, marking their houses with signs of devils on the doorposts, not displaying crosses publicly or calling service times loudly, and not building new churches or repairing damaged church buildings. These were clearly meant to remind Christians of their place, and to lead to the decline and eventual extinction of Christian communities in Islamic society. While this did not fully succeed, at least in the early centuries, the Pact played a major part in progressively segregating Christian communities from Muslim society, and it was instrumental in gaining converts who sought to avoid taxes. The rate of conversions is difficult to gauge, but from the eleventh century onwards it seems that there was a considerable decline in the numbers of Christians within the empire.

The Pact was applied more systematically under some rulers than others, and there are signs that it was not always regularly enforced. Arabic-speaking Christians certainly flourished at particular times, as medical practitioners – the personal physicians of a number of early ʿAbbasid caliphs were Christians – and translators, employed to make Greek works on science and philosophy accessible to monolingual Muslims. But even at times of relative freedom, the Pact was always in the background, discouraging real intimacy or honest respect.

Christians within the Islamic Empire, known by the Qur'anic name *Naṣārā* ('Nazarenes'), belonged to a number of separate churches, distinguished mainly by different perceptions of the relationship between Jesus's human and divine natures. The major 'sects' (*firaq*), as they were called, were three: the Melkites ('king's men'), who accepted the Christological definition of the Council of Chalcedon that had been affirmed by the Byzantine emperor (the 'king'), the Nestorians, inaccurately named after Nestorius, fifth-century Patriarch of Constantinople, and the Jacobites, named after the sixth-century Syrian bishop Jacob Baradai. For most Muslims, the differences between them and their doctrines remained of little interest.

In view of their belief that Christ was God and the climax of God's revelations to humankind, Christians could not accept Muḥammad and the Qur'an as a further stage of revelation that superseded their own. A few explained that Muḥammad had been sent to convert the pagan Arabs, but the majority condemned him as a fraud and destructively criticized what they identified as his personal failings, mainly his lust for plunder and women.

They generally dismissed the Qur'an as Muḥammad's own fabrication that incorporated misunderstood fragments from the Bible (in the Christian tradition the anchorite Baḥīrā, who according to Muslims had recognized Muḥammad as the prophet to come, became a heretic who passed on to him the mistaken Christian teachings that became part of the Qur'an).

Meetings between Christians and Muslims in the empire must have taken place regularly in the course of daily living, and exchanges about religious differences must have formed part of conversations. These could take place anywhere, though favourite settings were monasteries, which Muslims evidently enjoyed visiting. Formal debates were periodically arranged, sometimes in the presence of the caliph, when a bishop or celebrity scholar was required to defend his beliefs. The pressure created by having to maintain credibility with other Christians while not offending Muslims can be imagined, though a few Christians retaliated by circulating anonymously insulting and sometimes crude diatribes against Muḥammad.

Arabic-speaking Christian theologians appear generally to have regarded Islam and its theological elaborations as puerile, and refrained from serious engagement with them, though a few did try to explain the nature of the Trinity by employing terms from Muslim theology itself. Muslims argued that since God was utterly one, attributes necessary to His being, such as His life, knowledge and power, were intimately related to his essence (though exactly how was strongly debated). Some Christians borrowed from this theological construction to argue that the two attributes of Knowledge and Life were constitutive elements in God's being, unlike His other attributes, and were what Christians meant by the Son, as God's Word or Knowledge, and the Holy Spirit, as God's Life. But this met with little success, and for the most part Christians found that what they spoke or wrote was often at cross purposes with what Muslims found acceptable. At its core this was because the Christian perception of God as one with humankind in Christ differed so greatly from the Muslim perception of God as transcendent and beyond comparison.

Further reading

Arthur S. Tritton, *The Caliphs and Their Non-Muslim Subjects*, London, 1930 (reissued frequently).

Sidney H. Griffith, *The Beginnings of Christian Theology in Arabic. Muslim-Christian Encounters in the Early Islamic Period*, Aldershot, 2002.

Sidney H. Griffith, *The Church in the Shadow of the Mosque. Christians and Muslims in the World of Islam*, Princeton, NJ, 2008.

Sidney H. Griffith, *The Bible in Arabic. The Scriptures of the 'People of the Book' in the Language of Islam*, Princeton, NJ, 2013.

David Thomas (ed.), *Routledge Handbook on Christian-Muslim Relations*, London, 2018.

Hugh Goddard, *A History of Christian-Muslim Relations*, 2nd edition, Edinburgh, 2020.

16

Abū Rāʾiṭa l-Takrītī, *On the Incarnation*

Sandra Toenies Keating, Providence College

Ḥabīb ibn Khidma Abū Rāʾiṭa l-Takrītī (c. 770–c. 835), a Syrian Orthodox (Jacobite) theologian, is one of the first known Christians to write in Arabic. His extant writings include several *rasāʾil* (epistolary treatises) that set out responses to questions Muslims might ask about Christian doctrines. The most significant of these are the *Proof of the Christian religion*, the *First treatise 'On the Holy Trinity'* and the *Second treatise 'On the Incarnation'*. Although according to a later tradition Abū Rāʾiṭa was a bishop, there is no contemporary evidence that he was ordained.

Abū Rāʾiṭa's writings show a wide variety of strategies to convince his reader of the truth of the Christian faith. Around the turn of the ninth century, Christian scholars began to take advantage of increasing Muslim interest in Greek philosophy as a tool for explaining doctrines that seemed irrational to Muslims. They also saw the rationalist approach as an alternative to citing scriptural proof texts, which had become problematic because the Qur'an intimated that the biblical books had been altered or corrupted (*taḥrīf*). Abū Rāʾiṭa exploits this method, and is probably best known for his explanation of the Persons of the Trinity using the characteristically Muslim terminology of divine attributes (*ṣifāt*) and drawing parallels with the Islamic teaching of the Divine Names.

The excerpts below, taken from the *Second treatise 'On the Incarnation'* (*Fī l-tajassud*), reflect Abū Rāʾiṭa's adherence to the Syrian Orthodox confession, as he seeks to explain: how the infinite God could become incarnate in a limited human body; the purpose of the Incarnation; how Christ could be born, live a human life and die on the Cross, and still be truly divine; and whether Christ consented to the crucifixion. Abū Rāʾiṭa's arguments are based on analogies from nature and rules of logic, as well as references from the Bible, the Qur'an and Muslim teachings. All of these strategies became standard in Christian Arabic apologetic writings.

CMR 1, pp. 567–81.

This translation is taken from 'The second *Risāla* of Abū Rāʾiṭa al-Takrītī "On the Incarnation"', ed. S. Keating, *Defending the 'People of Truth' in the Early Islamic Period: The Christian Apologies of Abū Rāʾiṭah*, Leiden, 2006, pp. 222–97, reprinted with permission.

3. If they [the Muslims] say: 'Tell us about the Incarnation of the incarnated One. Is he an act [of God] or a part [of God]?,' it should be said to them: You have asked us about the incarnated One. Now, you are asking about an incarnated being, in which the body and the incarnation are united. [... In asking] 'Is it a part or an act?' you are speaking about the body of the incarnated One, that is His 'becoming a body'.[1] However, we say that the Incarnation of the incarnated One is something other than an act or a part; rather, it is a means to the act. [p. 225] [...]

22. If they say: 'What about the salvation you have mentioned, are you saved, unlike your opponents? We see that death is obviously upon you, just as [it affects] the rest of the peoples who are your opponents,' it should be said to them: Death is of two [kinds]. One of these is true death and the other is a metaphor, [drawn] from the expression 'true death' ([that is,] the death of sin and error), and it is a metaphor for the expression 'a separation of the spirit from the body'. Just as the body dies with the separation of the soul from it, so the soul dies separated from faith. [Through the Incarnation] we are delivered and saved from both [kinds] of death.

[We are saved] from true [death of the soul] by what He confirmed for us and taught us concerning the correct faith in God about His true predication [as one and three]. And He cast off from us the practices that were harsh and misleading for their own people, and [gave us] the work of obedience to Him in contrast to the works of the peoples, which are motivated by love of the world and immersion in it. [p. 243] [...]

24. If they say: 'Would it not have been better if He had sent someone else for the salvation and deliverance of the world, either an angel or someone from among the holy people, than to have carried it out Himself?,' it should be said to them: It would not have been better if He had entrusted it to someone other than Himself, either an angel or someone else. For just as it is necessary for Adam and his descendants to worship [God] because He created them, so it would be necessary [for them] to worship the One who had been entrusted with their deliverance and salvation, because their deliverance is the renewal of their creation, and it is impossible that someone other than the One who was entrusted with producing them should renew their creation.

To be sure, He sent [to the people] some such as Noah, Abraham, Moses, and other prophets and messengers, though each one of them was a warner to his people in his own time.[2] But all of [the people] did not follow [their prophet], they only followed him a little for a short time, then they returned to what they were before, being overpowered by error.[3] Also, these messengers were afflicted by weakness [themselves], because they were creatures, not outside the destruction [of sin], although it was not master over them as it mastered the [rest] of the people. When one of them was killed or died, he was not worthier [than the others] of the ability to [be resurrected and to] return,

[1] As a miaphysite, believing that in the Incarnation the divinity and humanity of Christ were inseparably one, Abū Rā'iṭa emphasizes the means by which God 'becomes' human, rather than a union of two natures.
[2] Cf. Q 3:33-4; 4:165; 5:19; 6:83-8.
[3] Cf. Q 23:23-50; 34:43-5.

and this led their tribe to abandon them and to scorn their commands when they did not have the power to raise themselves up after their deaths.[4] [pp. 243–5] [...]

77. If they say: 'His being killed and His crucifixion [occurred either] with His consent or through coercion. Now if it was with His consent, then it cannot be held against those who carried out His crucifixion. Rather, they deserve a reward and are entitled to the most abundant of the portions [of the reward], because they complied with His consenting [to it]. And if His being killed and His crucifixion were through coercion of Him, what god can be compelled [to do something]? Now this statement is a terrible thing!'

It should be said to them: The killing and the crucifixion, according to us [refer to] two aspects, because they are related to two [separate persons]: the one who does it and the one to whom it is done. [p. 289] [...]

79. If you say: 'He consented to what they did to Him, that is, He consented to what He suffered from them, without being compelled to it,' we say: Yes, indeed! He consented to accept this because through it He saved the world and delivered [human beings] from the error that had overpowered them, without willing their act, as we have described. [...]

81. What might you say if we asked you, similar to what you asked us about the killing [of Christ]: Does God consent to the killing of His martyrs, or does He abhor [it]? If you say: 'He has consented,' we say: Then it is not an outrage for the unbeliever who carried out the killing of the martyr, and they would deserve the most abundant reward when, with His consent, they complied in killing His martyrs. And if you say: 'He abhors [it],' we say: Certainly we [also say] He is a God [who] abhors [it]. Is not the crucifixion and killing of the body of the [same] degree in offence as insult[s] and lie[s]; all are a degradation of the one who does it and the one to whom it is done? What do you say about the one who lies about God, may He be praised? Does He consent to this [act] against Himself, or does He abhor [it]? Your answer to us in this is the answer to what you have asked us concerning the crucifixion and killing [of Christ]. [pp. 291–3]

[4] Cf. Q 14:10-13; 16:43-4; 21:7-9; 25:7-8.

17

Theodore Abū Qurra, *Some statements of Theodore, Bishop of Ḥarrān*

John Lamoreaux,
Southern Methodist University

Theodore Abū Qurra was known as the Chalcedonian bishop of Ḥarrān in the early ninth century. He is remembered today as one of the earliest Christians to write in Arabic, and to engage in sustained theological dialogue with Islam. Little is known of his life. He may have been a native of Edessa, and held the episcopal throne of Ḥarrān for a time, and he may have been deposed by the patriarch of Antioch. While it is not known when he died, a date around 830 seems not unreasonable.

Many of Theodore's Arabic works have been preserved in whole or in part. While he probably knew Greek, it is not clear that the Greek works preserved under his name are original compositions rather than translations from Arabic. He wrote on many topics, including the defence of icons and the teachings of the Council of Chalcedon, the refutation of the Jews, natural theology, the doctrine of freewill, the ecumenical councils and, above all, the refutation of Islam.

The present selection is from an unedited Arabic work by Theodore, entitled *Min qawl Thāwudūrus usquf Ḥarrān [...] ṭaʿna ʿalā l-barrāniyyīn* ('Some statements of Theodore, Bishop of Ḥarrān, [...] against the outsiders'). This is a compilation of Theodore's answers to eight theological questions, perhaps excerpted from another work or works by him. All the questions are about Muslim objections to Christianity concerning the divinity of Christ, his sufferings and death, prostration to the Cross, how death can be predicated of God and why God needed to die in order to save human beings.

Translated here is the second question, where Theodore seeks to show that God is just, even though he allowed the Virgin to die. It is one of the few places in his extant works where he provides biographical information about himself.

CMR 1, pp. 439–91.

This translation is based on *Against the outsiders*, the seventh work in the *MS Damascus, Greek Orthodox Patriarchate* 181 (formerly 1616), copied in the year 1561. On this work, see *CMR* 1, pp. 470–1.

The outsiders[5] also say to us: What do you think about a man who kills his mother?

Abū Qurra says: I and a companion were in Syria, in an extremely dolorous and wretched state, living as strangers, seeking after misery and degradation for the sake of Christ our God, who suffered all manner of terrible things for the sake of our salvation. We chanced on some people celebrating a wedding and we stayed to watch it. They sat us at the most honourable of their tables, notwithstanding that we were in a pretty wretched condition.

We then noticed that there were at our table two Muslims. One of them began to mock our fellow Christians, saying: 'Tell me, what do you think about a man who kills his mother?' The Christians tried to resist answering, lest the joy of the wedding be spoiled for them. He, however, refused to let the matter go. My companion then said to me: 'You should answer him.' I answered: 'No. If I were to do so, we would be transferred from our wretched state to one of honour, and thus depart from our customary manner of life.'

When the Muslim persisted in his obstinacy, my companion said to me: 'By God, you must answer him! If you don't, I'll become a Magian.[6] He has caused all the Christians here to fall into doubt, but you don't care.' When I realized that he was saying this out of his zeal for Christ, I praised him and turned to the questioner, and bravely and boldly said to him: 'Why don't you ask me about someone who kills his mother?' When he saw how bold I was, he knew well that I was able to answer him. Fear then came on his heart and his tongue began to tremble, and he wanted to take back his question. At this, his friend said to him: 'Why are you tongue-tied when you encounter someone who will respond to you, especially when you've been harassing everyone with your question and spoiling their meal?'

The questioner was then forced to say to me: 'Fine, I'll ask you: What do you think about someone who kills his mother?' I responded: 'The same as you think about someone who kills his friend.' He said to me: 'And who is he?' I said to him: 'That's your God.' He said to me: 'How so?'

[5] The term 'outsiders' (*barrāniyyīn*) comes from Syriac, where the *barrāyē* are the pagans, those 'outside' the people of God; cf. 1 Corinthians 5:12-13 and Colossians 4:5. Here, of course, they are Muslims.

[6] This could be no more than a cry of frustration at Abū Qurra's refusal to get involved. But since Zoroastrians believed in an ultimate source of evil as well as an ultimate source of good, the friend could be saying that if it has to be admitted that the Incarnate Son killed his own mother Christianity must include belief in a God who performs evil acts.

I said to him: 'Do you not know that Abraham was the friend of God?[7] For Him, he forsook his father and the people of his house. He emigrated from his native land and his acquaintances and he travelled about in diverse lands. With him was his wife, the most beautiful of women and a temptation to those who saw her. He travelled from one king to another, and many times they sought to kill him because of his wife. He bore all these tribulations out of obedience to God. Do you not know that a son was born to him in his old age, his consolation in this world and the joy of his heart? God then commanded him to sacrifice this son to Him, and Abraham took a knife to sacrifice the child he loved so much. Do you not know that after Abraham had so devoted himself to the love and obedience of God, God turned his attention to Abraham and killed him – according as you yourself have referred to death as "killing". Now then, if you were to see me devoted to a king, obedient to him in the same way that Abraham was obedient to God, and that king were then to kill me, would you yourself ever desire to serve him?'

He said: 'No. But tell me, is not the God of Abraham your God?' I said to him: 'Yes'. He said: 'Then you are as much at fault as I.' I said to him: 'No, the fault is yours alone, in that you're the one blaming an action the likes of which your God did. As for me, I have an escape from both this conundrum and the original conundrum.' He said: 'And what's your escape?' I said to him: 'I'll not tell you, as you didn't treat this gathering with respect.' They then pleaded with our companions, and they asked me to tell him. At this, I said to him: 'Tell me, is God not just?' He said: 'Yes'.

I then said: 'If I were a king and I were to accuse you, my father, and a close friend of one and the same crime, a crime for which all of you merited death, but I were then to remit the penalty of death for my father and my friend, would you not consider me to have contravened the limits of justice?' He said: 'Yes. And what of it?' I then said to him: 'Do you not know that God sentenced Adam and the whole of his seed to death?' He said: 'Yes'. I then said to him: 'If He were to go ahead and kill everyone but exempt those He loved, would this not void His earlier just sentence? Far be it from Him that He should contradict Himself, for otherwise He would be an object of derision! May He be exalted above that!' He then said: 'You are correct. You have put my heart at ease. May God bless you!'

[7] An allusion to Q 4:125.

18

ʿAbd al-Masīḥ al-Kindī, *Apology*

Sandra Toenies Keating, Providence College

In spite of its significant impact on European perspectives of Islam when it was translated from its original Arabic into Latin, the origins of the purported correspondence between the Muslim ʿAbd Allāh ibn Ismāʿīl al-Hāshimī and the Christian ʿAbd al-Masīḥ ibn Isḥāq al-Kindī are shrouded in mystery. Current scholarship dates it to about 830, in the reign of the Caliph al-Maʾmūn (r. 813–33), and locates it in Baghdad, but nothing is known for certain about its author(s) or the occasion of writing. The correspondence begins with a short invitation by al-Hāshimī to al-Kindī to convert to Islam, followed by al-Kindī's extensive refutation of Muḥammad, his teachings and the Qur'an, along with a summary of the Christian faith. Although al-Kindī's text is often given the title *Apology*, it is more than a defence of Christianity and includes significant and sometimes harsh polemical criticism of Islam. It has been suggested that the entire exchange may have been composed by a single Christian author to convey hypothetical responses to the Muslim call to conversion.

Al-Kindī's letter provides a unique multi-pronged attack on the legitimacy of the religion of his rulers, focusing on Muḥammad's immoral behaviour, his instruction by a Christian monk and the influence of Jews on his message, the confusion and alteration of the Qur'an following Muḥammad's death, and the consequent expansion of Muslim power through warfare. All these are explicitly contrasted with the peacefulness and moral authority of Jesus and his Apostles, and the superiority of Christian doctrine. Al-Kindī concludes that it is not surprising that no miracles are associated with Muslims, since their teachings do not follow the way of goodness and truth.

The *Apology* was one of the earliest Arabic texts about Islam, along with a version of the Qur'an, to be translated into Latin. It is found in the twelfth-century *Collectio Toletana*, the collection of Latin translations of Muslim works made in northern Spain specifically to inform European Christians about the rival faith. The Latin text, which underwent many revisions and interpolations that deviate from the original Arabic, was for several centuries the primary source of information about Islam available to many European scholars.

CMR 1, pp. 585–94.

These translations are based on *Risālat ʿAbd Allāh ibn Ismāʿīl al-Hāshimī ilā ʿAbd al-Masīḥ ibn Isḥāq al-Kindī, yadʿūhu bihā ilā l-Islām, wa-risālat al-Kindī ilā l-Hāshimī yaruddu bihā ʿalayhi wa-yadʿūhu ilā l-Naṣrāniyya*, Damascus, 2005.

Concerning the description of the Holy Trinity[8]

Now after we have clarified what are single [absolute] names and what are predicative names related to other [things],[9] we must ask you about the description of this essential property: Does it belong to [God's] essence eternally, or is it acquired by Him and He merited the attribute only later, just as He merited the attribute of Creator after He created? [...] For if it is said, just as the Almighty was described as existing, and He had no creation until after He had done the act [of creation], so it may also be said that He existed and did not have life, knowledge or wisdom until life, knowledge and wisdom began to exist in Him. Now, this is impossible to say, that God, the Powerful and Mighty, should for the blink of an eye be lacking life and knowledge. [...] For we know that the attributes of God (may His name be praised and mighty!) are of two different types: a natural, essential attribute that does not cease to describe Him, and an acquired attribute He has acquired by His own act. Those attributes that He acquired by His acts are [those] such as 'merciful', 'forgiving' and 'compassionate'. As for the revealed attributes that are natural and essential that do not cease to describe Him ('the Mighty' and 'the Powerful'), they are life and knowledge, for God does not cease to be living and knowing. Life and knowledge, therefore, are necessarily eternal.

From this it is established as true that God is One, possessing Wisdom and Spirit,[10] in three Persons subsisting by themselves, united in one divine substance. Now this is the description of the One Trinity of Persons which we worship, and this is the description that [God] Himself sanctioned, and He disclosed its secret in the books revealed in the tongues of the prophets and apostles. [pp. 39–40] [...]

Concerning those who converted to Islam

[Those who followed Muḥammad were brutish and uncivilized, living in the harsh desert and used to hunger, thirst and nakedness]. Because of this, he showed them rivers of wine and milk and fruits, and an abundance of meats and foods, [a place where they would be] sitting on beds and reclining on cushions of brocade and silk and satin, and have marriage to women who are like hidden pearls, and faithful servants and maids, and springs of flowing water, and [cool] extended shadows. [...]

Now you are aware that some of them said to each other during their war [against the Persians] when they had taken baskets containing sweets from the cupboards of

---

[8] This section has been extracted by the Christian author from Abū Rā'iṭa l-Takrītī's *Risāla on the Holy Trinity*, and summarizes many of his arguments.

[9] Al-Kindī explains this distinction in the paragraph that precedes this extract. Single, or absolute, names apply to things such as water and light that exist simply of themselves, while predicative names involve a connection, such as the predicative term knowing and its connection with knowledge: a person can be called knowing because of the knowledge she possesses. This leads into the discussion of whether God's knowledge (identified as His Word = the Son) and His life (identified as the Holy Spirit) are absolute as inherent to His being and so eternal, or predicative as related to things outside God and so existing only when those things exist.

[10] Among Christian Arabs (and their Muslim opponents) the biblical terms 'Wisdom' and 'Spirit' could be represented by the terms 'Knowledge' (= 'Word' or reason, the Son) and 'Life' (= the Spirit). Since God must necessarily have life and word, His Trinitarian character can be established on the basis of logical deduction.

the Persians and they ate and consumed their sweetness: 'By God! If we did not have a religion to fight for, we would fight for this!' [And they were successful against the Persians because God used them to punish the unjust.] [...]

Some of them profess Islam, speaking in [Arabic], but in their hearts are still the diseases of Judaism and Mazdaism.[11] For they do not know their Creator, and if one asks, 'What is the difference between yourself, and your Creator, and a beast?', they do not know and are unable to make a good distinction; they do not understand what this means or how to give answers to [the question]. They are like cattle that have strayed. [...] They do not know the truth of the religion to which they adhere and the difference from the one they belonged to before.

It is same with the idol worshippers and [... those Magians and Jews] who want to be strengthened by the power of the state and gain authority over people with influence, to extend their customs over people of honour, free people, people of goodness and knowledge, people of religion and learning, valour and virtue, dignity and nobility.

It is the same with the doubting, perfidious and criminal people who could not have committed illicit things and enjoyed the sexual freedom that God forbade if they had remained in the Christian religion, and are only [allowed] by accepting the [Islamic] doctrine.

And the same with the one who permits himself excesses of physical pleasures, of riches and the world for its own sake and its adornments, and seeking what is perishable, fleeting and mortal, abandoning and throwing away what is much more enduring and abiding, what is uninterrupted and unceasing, as it is in the Hereafter. [...]

[You know that those who have studied wisdom and philosophy, and have high morals and true belief, accept the Christian religion]; however, the one who cannot indulge or practise [ignoble and base] things can enter a religion where he can serenely have what he wants. For he is not afraid under this government, and can point to other people following the same teachings. [pp. 96–8]

Concerning the difference between Muslims and Christians

[The sound faith and peaceful actions of the disciples of Christ that I have described] are not like the story of your Associate[12] and your companions who constantly advance by killing, plundering, striking with swords, capturing children and conquering countries; they have plundered the goods of the people, [violated] their women and enslaved free people. And this situation has continued until the present. They incite the people to what is forbidden and similar [bad] morals until they learn it, so that they fabricate lies about what they should not do. This is like what ʿUmar ibn al-Khaṭṭāb[13] said: 'If someone has a neighbour who is a Nabatean[14] and he needed the price of him, he should sell him.' Many examples like this may be found in sayings and actions [of the Muslims], and this is contrary to what Simon [Peter] and Paul did, healing the sick by praying for them and raising the dead in the name of Christ our Lord. [p. 170]

---

[11] The ancient Iranian religion, also called Zoroastrianism.

[12] Muḥammad.

[13] The second caliph, and a close Companion of Muḥammad.

[14] E.g. a foreigner.

19

ʿAmmār al-Baṣrī, *Book of questions and answers*

Mark Beaumont, London School of Theology

ʿAmmār al-Baṣrī was an East Syrian diophysite (Nestorian) theologian active in the first half of the ninth century. Almost nothing is known about his life, although a little can be inferred from what is likely to be a mention of him by the tenth-century bibliophile Ibn al-Nadīm in his *Kitāb al-fihrist*, a catalogue of works written on the various disciplines practised in the early Islamic period. Among the works of the leading early-ninth-century Muʿtazilī theologian Abū l-Hudhayl al-ʿAllāf (d. *c.* 840), Ibn al-Nadīm briefly refers to a now-lost 'refutation of ʿAmmār the Christian in his reply to the Christians'.[15] This makes it probable that ʿAmmār was involved in some sort of discussions with this leading Muslim thinker, thus locating him in the mid-ninth century and possibly among the intellectual elite of the seaport city of Baṣra, where Abū l-Hudhayl lived for much of his life. Two of ʿAmmār's works are known, *Kitāb al-masāʾil wa-l-ajwiba* ('Book of questions and answers') and *Kitāb al-burhān* ('Book of the proof').

Kitāb al-masāʾil wa-l-ajwiba contains a long section on the Trinity, in the form of a series of answers to nine questions posed by an unnamed Muslim, quite probably the kind of questions raised by Abū l-Hudhayl. The first five are reproduced here in abridged form. They show that ʿAmmār was fully conversant with the kind of theological methods that Abū l-Hudhayl and Muslim scholars like him employed, and also drew on concepts from Greek philosophical thinking. He was evidently confident that the doctrine of the Trinity could be demonstrated in clear terms that any rational mind would accept. He gives no sign of defensiveness, but a clear sense of confidence and intellectual composure.

CMR 1, pp. 604–10. See further:

M. Beaumont, 'Speaking of the Triune God. Christian Defence of the Trinity in the Early Islamic Period', *Transformation* 29 (2012) 111–27.

[15] See B. Dodge (trans.), *The Fihrist of al-Nadīm, a Tenth Century Survey of Muslim Culture*, New York, 1970, vol. 1, p. 388.

M. Beaumont, ''Ammār al-Baṣrī: Ninth Century Christian Theology and Qur'anic Presuppositions', in M. Beaumont (ed.), *Arab Christians and the Qur'an from the Origins of Islam to the Medieval Period*, Leiden, 2018, 83–105.

S.L. Husseini, *Early Christian-Muslim Debate on the Unity of God*, Leiden, 2014.

W. Mikhail, ''Ammār al-Baṣrī's *Kitāb al-burhān:* A Topical and Theological Analysis of Arabic Christian Theology in the Ninth Century', Birmingham, 2013 (PhD Diss. University of Birmingham).

O. Varsanyi, *Ninth-Century Arabic Christian Apology and Polemics: A Terminological Study of 'Ammār al-Baṣrī's* Kitāb al-Masā'il wa-l-ajwiba, Piliscsaba, Hungary: The Avicenna Institute of Middle Eastern Studies, 2015.

The translation below is based on Part Three of 'Ammār's *Book of Questions and Answers*, in M. Hayek (ed.), *'Ammār al-Baṣrī. Apologie et controverses*, Beirut, 1977.

Question One: If someone who differs from us[16] asks: What is the evidence for the truth of what you claim concerning the threeness and oneness of the Creator? How can one be three or three be one?, we say: Concerning the one being three and the three being one, [...] the number one is not the number three, [...] we mean that the one eternal substance exists eternally in substantial properties that are not differentiated or separated.[17] [...] The principal substance has the attributions of life and speech; His speech is the source of His wisdom and His life is the source of His spirit. [pp. 148–50]

Question Two: If he says: We deceive ourselves with futile thinking when we affirm His existence first, then His life second, and His wisdom third. Do we not count him as three, divided and partitioned?, we say: Partition and division are not attributes of One who has no body, who exists eternally. [...] The One who created the world by His word and His spirit is necessarily one in His substance, one in His nature, and no division or partition occurs in Him. [...]

If our questioner replies to us, saying: When you say that He is living and wise, do you not believe that He is hearing, seeing, almighty, merciful, generous, kind? [...] Why do you specify three, rather than four, five, six or more attributes?,[18] We say: Do you not know the difference between the names and the attributes that belong

[16] The context shows that this questioner is a Muslim, though in this section of the work 'Ammār never says that he is.

[17] It is important to 'Ammār to establish the unity of the godhead by denying that the threeness is simply numerical. He carefully argues that the word and wisdom of God are not extra-numerical components of the one God. By choosing the term 'properties' he seeks to promote the unity of God within characteristics that are essential to Him.

[18] Muslims who debated with Christians about the Trinity regularly referred to the fact that God has multiple attributes that they regarded as essential to Him, and that it was inappropriate for Christians to separate out of this list of attributes just three.

to the essential properties of His substance? [...] The names refer to actions of God, whereas the attributes refer to properties essential to Him. [...] Only life and speech are essential properties in God. Life and speech are properties in the structure of the substance, and in the quality of the essence (*dhāt*) and the nature.[19] [pp. 152–4]

Question Three: If he says: Why does God need his speech and his spirit [...] but not hearing and sight?, our reply is: It is not possible for rational people to conceive of spirit and speech except as two substantialities (*jawhariyyān*) in the substance. [...] It is said in some of His books that God created and made by His hand or his arm, and when you explain this language you find the meaning of His arm and His hand to be His command, prohibition and will generated from His speech and spirit. [...] Whenever His speech and His spirit are mentioned, they refer to the Creator (who is to be served) without reference to all the other attributes He has.[20] [pp. 158–61]

Question Four: If he says: Why do you call these three properties three 'individuals', yet you lead the hearers of your teaching to believe that you reject three gods?, we say: We do not call them 'individuals'. [...] From our point of view, 'individual' applies only to beings with physical bodies. [...] We call them in the Syriac language three 'hypostases' (*aqānīm*). [...] A substance is like a human being, or fire and water. [...] It has power, like the speech of a human being, the heat of fire and the wetness of water. [...] It has accident, like the whiteness of snow and the blackness of tar. [...] It has a hypostasis (*qunūm*), like a servant of God such as the angel Gabriel who has his hypostasis from the nature of angels. [...] These four categories are found in everything that is imagined or experienced. [...] Two of them, 'substance' and 'hypostasis', exist without depending on anything else, and the other two, 'powers' and 'accidents', depend on something else for their existence.[21] [pp. 161–2]

Question Five: If he says: Why do you call the three hypostases Father, Son and Holy Spirit?, we say: The Apostles who were appointed and commissioned to announce the secret of the essence of the Lord of the worlds described in the glorious Gospel the account of their being sent to the nations in which [Jesus] said, 'Go and win over all

[19] 'Ammār's selection of two attributes, life and speech, gives the impression of the divine substance having two essential properties. There is a clear gap between this argument and the accepted Trinitarian formula of one essence in three hypostases. But 'Ammār has chosen to begin on ground familiar to Muslim intellectuals who at this time debated among themselves whether the names of God referred to actions of God. Abū l-Hudhayl is reported to have denied that the names did refer to actions of God, arguing that the statement 'God is knowing' must be interpreted as 'there is an act of knowing that is God' and 'there is an object that he knows' (R.M. Frank, *Beings and Their Attributes. The Teaching of the Basrian School of the Mu'tazila in the Classical Period*, Albany, NY, 1978, p. 12). Abū l-Hudhayl was concerned to defend God's unity (*tawḥīd*) by denying that there is an entity called 'knowledge' identified within God. 'Ammār, however, differed from Abū l-Hudhayl by arguing that life and speech were inherent qualities within God, without which God could not exist.

[20] Mu'tazilī thinkers tended to interpret the attributes of God metaphorically, and 'Ammār mentions this approach to the anthropomorphic language of the Bible and the Qur'an. Yet he argues that not all such statements can be treated as metaphors, since God's speech and spirit are on a different level from all other attributes of God.

[21] 'Ammār appeals to the categories into which existents were divided according to Aristotle: substance (*jawhar*), power (*quwa*) and accident (*'araḍ*), and he adds hypostasis (*qunūm*).

peoples and baptise them in the name of the Father, Son and Holy Spirit.'[22] [...] The eternal living One who speaks is Father, who has His eternal Word, and His eternal Life, the Holy Spirit.

Why do these opponents find so objectionable the meaning of the names Father, Son and Holy Spirit? If it is because they only understand 'father' and 'son' through the union of sexual intercourse, then we say to them: [...] There is no physical relationship between the properties of God's substance. In the Torah God calls Himself 'King', 'Lord' and 'wise', and human beings are also called by these names, but God's names do not have the same meaning as the human names. [pp. 164–8]

[22] Matthew 28:19.

20

The Muqaṭṭam miracle, from the Copto-Arabic *Synaxarion*

Mark Swanson, Lutheran School of Theology at Chicago

One of the best-known stories among the Copts of Egypt is the miracle of the Muqaṭṭam hills outside Cairo, set in the late tenth century, early in the Fāṭimid period. Ever since it was recorded in one of the Coptic sources of *The history of the patriarchs* (by Michael of Damrū, Bishop of Tinnīs, from the year 1051) and translated into Arabic, it has been told and retold, so that every Coptic child knows it. Today a complex of cave churches in the Muqaṭṭam hills commemorates the miracle, and artistic representations of the event may be found in a number of places, including a mosaic in the outer courtyard of the Muʿallaqa Church in Old Cairo. It is also marked in the liturgical calendar of the Coptic Orthodox Church, most notably in the three-day addition to the forty days of the Fast of the Nativity, and in the Coptic Church's *Synaxarion*, a book of short readings about the saints arranged for each day in the year, where it is part of the entry on Patriarch Abrāhām (Afrahām) ibn Zurʿa (the 62nd patriarch, r. 975–8), and is read on the day of his death, 6 *Kiyahk* (normally 15 December).

Patriarch Abrāhām's story bears witness to the practice throughout the medieval period of inter-religious debate in the presence of the Muslim ruler, and to the fact that Christians' participation in such debate could be fraught with danger, not only for the debater but for the debater's community. In the end, however, it serves as encouragement, because despite the community's lack of conventional forms of power, through its faith the power of God is revealed in such a way as to move the heart of the caliph. In later elaborations of the story the caliph actually converts to Christianity, while here he not only gives permission for the rebuilding of churches, but personally inspects and guarantees the rebuilding of the Church of St Mercurius.

CMR 4, pp. 937–45.

The Copto-Arabic *Synaxarion* has undergone (and continues to undergo) a process of elaboration since its first compilation in the thirteenth century. The translation below is representative of a form of the *Synaxarion* that stabilized in the fourteenth century. It is based on the edition of the text published by Jacques Forget, *Synaxarium Alexandrinum*, vol. 1, Beirut, 1905, pp. 136–9 (available online in the Internet Archive, https://archive.org/details/p1synaxariumalex01copt).

The sixth day of the month of Kiyahk

On this day we observe the festival commemorating the martyr Anatolius the Priest.

And on it the saint Anbā Abrāhām went to his rest. This father was one of the Christians of the East; he was a wealthy merchant who visited Egypt frequently and finally settled there. His virtues and mercy became apparent, and his reputation for righteousness and knowledge spread widely. [During a patriarchal election,] the agreement of the bishops and learned elders fell upon him, that they should advance him to be patriarch of Alexandria.

When he advanced [to this dignity], he divided all that he possessed among the poor and wretched. He cut off every evil custom from the entirety of his see: he condemned and excommunicated every [religious] head who would take anything from anyone for the sake of their advancement in the church; then he condemned whoever would take a concubine, a matter in which he was extremely severe. When those who possessed concubines heard of his condemnation, they feared God – may God be exalted – and feared [the patriarch's] condemnation. They all sent their concubines away and came to [the patriarch] and repented before him. He received their repentance and forgave them for what they had dared to do. [...]

In the time of this father, [the Fāṭimid caliph] al-Muʿizz had a vizier, a Jew who had converted to Islam. He had a Jewish friend whom he used to bring into the presence of al-Muʿizz at all hours, to converse with him. The Jew desired, by means of the vizier's standing with al-Muʿizz, that the father the patriarch should be brought to him in order to debate with him. And so this father came, accompanied by Anbā Sāwīrus ibn al-Muqaffaʿ. Al-Muʿizz commanded them to sit, and they sat. Then al-Muʿizz said to them: 'Why are you not debating?' Anbā Sāwīrus said: 'No one debates in the gathering of the Commander of the Faithful except one compared with whom the ox and donkey are more rational.' Al-Muʿizz said: 'Why is that, O bishop?' He said: 'God said by the tongue of the prophet, "The ox knows its owner, and the donkey knows the manger of its master, but Israel does not know me".'[23] The two [Christians] debated with the Jew and put him to shame. They departed, by the aid of Christ victorious and held in honour by al-Muʿizz.

[23] Isaiah 1:3.

The Jew could not bear this, nor the vizier, and after a few days the vizier came to see al-Muʿizz and said to him: 'Would you like to know, our master the sultan, that the Christians have nothing to stand on? In their Gospel it says: "If any of you has faith equivalent to a mustard seed, then if he says to this mountain 'Be moved', it will be moved!"[24] So summon the patriarch and require him to perform what his Gospel has said. If he does not perform this proof, then know that they have nothing to stand on.'

And so al-Muʿizz summoned this bishop and laid before him this speech. [The patriarch] asked him for a respite of three days, which [al-Muʿizz] granted him. When [the patriarch] had departed from him, he gathered the nearby monks and bishops, and they remained in the Muʿallaqa Church in Miṣr [Old Cairo] for three days, fasting and pleading with God to have mercy on them. At dawn after the third night, Our Lady Mary, the Mother of God, appeared to [the patriarch], and informed him of a saintly man, a tanner, and that he was the one by means of whom God would perform these miracles for him. So the father sent for and summoned that man, and took with him a company of priests and monks and all the believers, and presented themselves before al-Muʿizz, all his government, and the people of Miṣr and Cairo. The patriarch stood on one side, and al-Muʿizz and the rest of the people on the other. Then the patriarch and the believers prayed, prostrating themselves three times; with every prostration, when the father would raise his head and make the sign of the cross upon the mountain, the mountain rose up in the air before those present! Then when he bowed down, the mountain descended to its place. [It happened in this way] three times. The Muslims cried out in wonder; they were filled with great fear at the displacement of the mountain. Many people died, and pregnant women miscarried, from intense fear at the roar of the mountain. God saved this father and the people; God gave him the victory before his enemies.[25]

Al-Muʿizz summoned the patriarch, honoured him with much honour, and asked him to name a desire. He did not want to demand anything of him, but al-Muʿizz importuned him to make a demand, urging him to do so. When he had insisted upon this, [the patriarch] said to him: 'If I am required to demand something from you, then I want to rebuild the churches, especially the Church of the Martyr Mercurius in Miṣr.' [Al-Muʿizz] wrote him an order for the rebuilding of the churches and gave him much money from the treasury. [The patriarch] thanked him and prayed for him at length, and asked him to be allowed to turn down the money. Al-Muʿizz's love for the patriarch grew, because of what he saw of his piety and lack of greed for money.

Then he rode with him and stopped at the building site intended for the churches of St Mercurius. When one of the notables opposed [the caliph with respect to the building], he set one of his entourage [to supervise] until the building was completed. And that father renewed many churches, in all the provinces.

When he had completed his righteous course, he died in peace. May his prayers be with us! Amen.

---

[24] Matthew 17:20.

[25] Marco Polo also gives an account of this miracle, transferring it to a mountain between Baghdad and Mosul. See passage 74 below.

21

Elias of Nisibis and Abū l-Qāsim, *An epistolary exchange*

Michael Kuhn

In the years 1026–7, Elias of Nisibis, bishop of the Church of the East, took part in a series of live debates (*majālis*) in the town of Mayyāfāriqīn (in what is now eastern Turkey) with the Muslim Abū l-Qāsim al-Ḥusayn ibn ʿAlī l-Maghribī, vizier to the ruler Naṣr al-Dawla of the local Marwānid dynasty. They planned to publish an account of their meetings, and an exchange of letters laid the groundwork for this. The published work was known as *Kitāb al-majālis* ('Book of the sessions'), though the vizier died before he was able to see it in its final form. The exchange of letters reveals a warm bond of friendship and a sense of mutual respect between them that marks their dialogue as exceptional in the history of Muslim-Christian relations.

Elias's full exposition of the Trinity and the dual nature of Christ is expounded in Sessions 1–3. The following excerpts from the letters, expressing Elias's monotheistic confession, reveal that Abū l-Qāsim accepted his explanation of the Trinity as belief in one God and acknowledged that Christians were included within the fold of monotheism together with Muslims. This is uncharacteristic of the period, and may be the only example of an explicit admission from a medieval Muslim that Trinitarian Christians worshipped one God. The vizier displays a certain joy in discovering that the Christians of the realm are not guilty of *shirk* (association of another being with God), and expresses a warm admiration for Elias and, on a personal level, requests his assistance to overcome anxiety. In fact, the vizier died from an illness before he received Elias' reply. So he never saw the *Kitāb al-majālis* in its finished form, though as this correspondence shows, he received the preliminary record and approved heartily of them.

CMR 2, pp. 727–41.

This translation is based on Paul Sbath, *Biblothèque de manuscrits Paul Sbath,* 3 vols, Cairo, 1934, vol. 3.

[The Response from Elias]

I have considered the most excellent minister's letter, may God prolong his life. I am cognizant of what he mentions in each section, elaborated in his previous correspondence. I have contemplated it, requesting Allāh most high, to beautify the world, renew His benefits, bestow honour upon knowledge and revive His laws through the ongoing authority of his excellency.[26]

I proceed to offer a condensed response concerning each section. I will be concise, avoiding detail and protraction. As I learned from your letter concerning political leadership, elaboration exasperates ministers, kings and others in their company.

Desiring God's aid and bestowal of success, I begin by mentioning the honourable belief in one God (*tawḥīd*).

Our belief as the community of monotheistic Christians concerning the Creator, holy is His name:

He is one God. There is no God beside Him.
He has no partner (*lā sharīka lahu*) in His lordship and no peer in His divinity.
He has no equal in His eternity.
No opponent can resist Him.
No peer can contend with Him.
He is non-corporeal, non-composite, not amalgamated,
intangible, not localized, indivisible, uncontainable, not occupying space,
immutable, not confined by place, not contained in time,
eternal without beginning, eternal without end,
concealed in His essence, appearing in His actions,
matchless in his power and perfection, peerless in grandeur and honour, source of all grace, spring of all wisdom,
cause of all things from nothing,
Creator of all beings out of nothing,
Maker of all things by His command,
the Creator of all created things by His word,[27]
Knower of all things before their existence,
Discerner of mysteries before their concealment,
living, undying, unchanging never passing away,
powerful, not deviating from justice, not oppressing,
knowing not ignorant, forbearing not delaying bounty,
gentle, unhurried, bounteous not begrudging, powerful not impotent,
near to all, far from all,
answering one who calls, aiding one who hopes for Him,

---

[26] It is noticeable that in what would be regarded as the usual florid introduction to a letter, Elias is careful to avoid any attributions of God that would appear too Christian, while he also avoids anything that is characteristically Muslim. The use of the term 'Allāh' was common among both Christians and Muslims at this time.

[27] While Elias would understand this to mean the Son of God, as in John 1:1-4, the vizier could understand it to mean God's creative command, as in Q 3:47.

sufficient for one who depends upon Him,
a refuge for the one who takes refuge in Him,
Purveyor of grace if it is accepted with thanks
and Remover of it if it is accepted with unbelief,
near to the good, far from the infidels, receiver of the penitent,
enemy of the recalcitrant, God of mercy, beneficent Lord, wise Creator who created the world for His will and as He willed.
Then He commands resurrection and renewal and restoring life to those in tombs,
He rewards the good by bringing them to His mercies and the evil by making their punishment eternal,
the One who raises up, the one God, one Creator, one Lord,
who alone is worshipped, no god before Him and no creator beside Him, no lord other than Him and none to be adored but Him. [pp. 12–13]

[The response of Vizier Abū al-Qāsim al-Ḥusayn ibn ʿAlī]

In the name of Allāh, the compassionate, the merciful.

What has arrived from the excellent Bishop, may Allāh prolong his life and support him, has brought joy and benefit to the heart. As I read it, every doubt and misgiving was removed from the mind. Reflecting on his thought and discernment has prompted a pleasure beyond description.

A delegation of Qur'anic scholars was in attendance for the reading of the letter. These scholars, who profess expertise in Qur'anic exegesis, conceded the power of its argumentation. In fact, some found it difficult to countenance that a Christian was more adept in the exegetical tradition than themselves. They wondered how such a one could attain a breadth of understanding of our religion so as to respond in this fashion. How could he obtain the knowledge of these sources?

I replied that the response for which they gave thanks and offered praise demonstrates that God does not deprive those who possess knowledge of its honour. They are to be respected in the place of learning.

Now I declare to his eminence [the bishop], may God prolong his happiness, that God has removed the disdain from the monotheistic branches of Christianity that had rested upon them. Moreover, the partial understanding of Muslims is lifted from the followers of them. Contemplating this letter in the heart demonstrates the precise monotheism of Muslims to be equal with the authentic monotheism of Christians. If this is their view regarding monotheism, then all doubt and suspicion is removed from them in my mind as well as that of other Muslims. The time has come to halt deductions from their commissions, reductions in their salaries and resistance of any kind. By my life, this letter and the likes of it will spare the blood of Christians.[28] I

[28] These brief mentions of the kind of penalties that were imposed on Christians give an idea of the wider treatment of Christians as *dhimmīs*, who were subject to the *Pact of ʿUmar*. Elias's explanation that the doctrine of the Trinity is pure monotheism has enabled the vizier to categorize Christians alongside Muslims, and to remove the discriminatory measures that were against them.

believe that God most high sent the excellent Bishop, may God prolong his guidance, as mercy and virility to his nation.

As a result of this letter, the discrimination that we have observed in the Islamic invasions has grown cold in my heart, indeed, in the heart of all Muslims. We see that refraining from all crimes towards those who hold such views is correct, not mistaken.

On Christmas day, I counselled, urged and even obliged a delegation of our noblemen and distinguished servants to make their way to the place where prayer was convened. I believed that prayer with him [the bishop] led by him is purer than with someone else.

After scrutinizing all the responses of this letter, I approve of it. Indeed, its rectitude has fallen upon my heart, removing my suspicion of their [the Christians'] monotheistic faith as well as other aspects. The profession of Trinitarian monotheism has become palatable to me and I thank him for his care in its exposition. I am delighted, flying for joy because of this letter.

I would not have been delayed in my response to his excellency, if not for two reasons. The first is my lengthy contemplation of meanings expounded here. The second is a great anguish which has increased, adding worry to anxiety.[29] On the occasion of our meeting in his cell at Nisibis, he mentioned his article on the removal of grief and repelling anxiety. I am in need of a letter in this vein and request it in the hope of contemplating its gentle wisdom and consolation so as to return to my normal activity, if Allāh wills. [pp. 12–19]

[29] This anguish ('constriction of the chest') led to the vizier's death a few months later. Ironically, the vizier's attending physician was Elias' brother, who informed Elias that death was inevitable.

22

The Apocalypse of Samuel

Jos van Lent

The *Apocalypse of Samuel* is a sermon originally composed in Coptic, though surviving only in Arabic translations. It appears as a speech addressed by a seventh-century Coptic monk, Samuel of the Monastery of Qalamūn in the Fayyūm region of Egypt, to his fellow monks, and written down by his pupil Apollo. In reality, it was composed by an unknown author, probably from the same monastery but writing considerably later, possibly the mid-eleventh century. It falls into two parts: a prophetic homily with sections giving moral instruction and series of *vaticinia ex eventu* ('prophecies after the event') mainly on Arab rule, and a second part made up of eschatological prophecies.

The *Apocalypse* was written with various audiences and purposes in mind. First and most obvious is its call to monks and clergy to better fulfil their duty as educators of their flock. Probably, however, the sermon was also meant to reach a wider secondary audience of lay Copts, who received a clear message that there is no excuse – not even harassment by Muslim authorities – for violating Coptic teachings and traditions, let alone to assimilate or convert. The text thus seems to be all about authority and control, and primarily a form of Church propaganda. At the same time, however, it addresses some of its audiences' basic emotional needs: by presenting oppression as God's punishment for sin it gives meaning to suffering, while its promise of future salvation in case of repentance offers consolation and a sense of belonging.

The passages translated below bear detailed testimony to the reaction in conservative monastic circles in the Fayyūm to the impact of Muslim rule on the Christians of the region – which undermined Church authority. Concentrating on the process of cultural assimilation, in particular the Christians' abandonment of Coptic, they reflect a transitional period in the Arabization process, when Coptic was still alive but Arabic was becoming more current, even in the liturgy.

The *Apocalypse of Samuel* is of great importance as one of the few literary sources that directly deal with the language shift from Coptic to Arabic, and it also provides clues about the intricate relationship between Arabization and Islamization. Coptic is being represented here as the Egyptian Christians' sole sacred as well as ancestral language, which obviously served as an instrument for strengthening the fading boundaries between Christian and Muslim Egyptians.

CMR 2, pp. 742–52.

This translation is based on MS Vatican – Ar. 158, fols 112v-127r (1356), here 114r-124v. Words enclosed in | and | are supplied from other manuscript witnesses.

The Christians will envy them [the Hagarenes] for their deeds, and they will eat and drink with them. They will play like them, and they will revel. They will fornicate like them, and they will take for themselves concubines like them. They will defile their bodies with the dissenting and impure women of the Hagarenes, and they will lie with males like them. They will steal and curse like them. They will do wrong and they will hate one another. They will hand one another over to the merciless nations, and many idle words – which should not be said – will come out of their mouths. [fol. 114r] [...]

Truly, the Christians will turn away greatly in that time. They will neglect the affairs of God and amuse themselves with their own pursuits. In that time, their love for eating and drinking and their love for base passions will outweigh their love of God. The food halls and taverns will be attended more than God's church. They will be sitting in the streets of the markets, concerned with the matters of the world, and not at all concerned with the church. It will not stir their hearts that the passages are read, and they will escape them; even |the Gospel too, they will not hear it. On the contrary, they will only go to church at the end of the Mass. Some of them will do deeds that are not fit, because they busy themselves with their [own] things, so that| the passages |escape them|. They will go to church, they will take the Gospel, and they will inquire about the passage that was read. Then they will stand in a corner alone to read it, and in this way they will make a law for themselves.

Woe! Woe once more, my beloved children! What shall I say about those times and the magnitude of the negligence that will overtake the Christians? For in that time they will turn away much from uprightness, and they will imitate the Hagarenes in their deeds. They will call their children by their [the Muslims'] names, and they will abandon the names of the angels, the prophets, the Apostles, and the martyrs.

They will also commit another act. If I inform you of it, your hearts will be in much pain. It is that they will leave the beautiful Coptic language, in which the Holy Spirit has spoken many times through the mouths of our spiritual fathers. They will teach their children from their childhood to speak in the language of the Arabs and to take pride in it. Even the priests and the monks will dare – them too – to speak in Arabic and take pride in it, even inside the sanctuary. [fols 114v-115r] [...]

What shall I say about the laxity that will occur among the Christians? They will be eating and drinking inside the sanctuary without fear. They will forget the fear of the sanctuary, and in their opinion the sanctuary will be as nothing. The doors of the sanctuary will remain forlorn, and no subdeacon will remain at them, because they will neglect the [seven] ranks that the Church has and they will not fulfil them. You will find the people in that time seeking the orders of the priesthood, while they do not yet deserve to be Readers to read to the people.[30]

Many books from the Church will fall into disuse, because there will not remain any among them who will be interested in reading [them], since their hearts will be inclined to Arabic books. They will forget many of the martyrs in that time, because their *Live[s]* will fall into disuse, and they will not be found at all. Even if copies of the *Lives* are found – if they are read – you will find many of the people not understanding what is read, because they will not know the language.

Many churches in that time will be a ruin and empty on the eves of feasts and the eve of Sunday too, and no one will be found who will read a book during them on a pulpit, |not| even |during| the holy forty |fast days| [of Lent] that are intended for our salvation. You will not find anyone who will read to the people, and they will not be exhorted because they will have forgotten the language and will not understand what they read, or have knowledge of it.

Likewise, the Readers too will not understand, even [in] Arsinoe, the large town that belongs to the Fayyūm, or any of its provinces, where the laws of Christ are [prevalent]; those superb in their books and powerful in the knowledge of Christ, in whose mouths the Coptic language is beautiful like the sweetness of honey, diffusing from them like the fragrances of perfume, owing to the beauty of their pronunciations in Coptic. And all of them in that time will leave it. They will speak in the Arabic language and take pride in it, so that they will not be known as Christians at all, but one would think of them that they are Berbers. The rest, who remain in |Upper Egypt|, [still] knowing the Coptic language and speaking it, their fellow Christians who speak in the Arabic language will abuse and mock them. [fols 115v-116r] [...]

With this, God will become angry with them, because they will have deviated from the canons of the Church and the instruction that comes from our spiritual fathers. He will establish the Hagarenes, the Arabs, as rulers over them, and He will make them hateful to them. [f. 117v] [...]

Many Christians in that time will renounce Christ because of a short time that will pass away. Some of them will renounce Christ because of the troubles that are upon them and the fact that they did not find anyone who would teach them or console them for their troubles, so they do not have the aid of instruction. Many people will fall because of the insolence of the world by which their hearts had been bound. No one will be found who will oppose them, so they will fall. Some will fall only because of the pleasure of eating and drinking; others because of the leisure of the body and the error of sin. Thereupon, their brothers and their kinsmen will not cry over them or grieve for them. Rather, they will take pride in them, and they will eat and drink with them. Afterwards, they will envy them, imitate them, and renounce Christ like them. Woe to those who will be like this, because their place in Hell will be in darkness forever! [f. 124r-v]

---

[30] The seven ranks or orders of the Coptic miaphysite Church are: bishop, presbyter, deacon, subdeacon, reader, singer and doorkeeper.

23

Yaḥyā of Antioch on the Caliph al-Ḥākim

Paul Walker, University of Chicago

Egypt was governed by the Shīʿī Fāṭimid dynasty for over two centuries (969–1171). In this period non-Muslim citizens, Christians as well as Jews, enjoyed generally good treatment, and in some instances high officials of state were Christians, including one who held the august rank of vizier. The major exception to this picture was the reign of the sixth caliph al-Ḥākim bi-Amr Allāh (r. 996–1021), particularly his final years. Sources for his treatment of Christians derive from accounts by contemporaries, who were therefore primary witnesses if not actual eyewitnesses. On the Christian side, there is a Coptic history which focuses predominately on the career of each successive patriarch, and there is also the Melkite historian Yaḥyā ibn Saʿīd al-Anṭākī (c. 980–mid-eleventh century).

The following selection from Yaḥyā's *Tārīkh al-Anṭākī* provides a highly significant account of the worst period of anti-Christian measures set in motion by al-Ḥākim.

CMR 2, pp. 657–61.

This translation is based on the edition by ʿUmar ʿAbd al-Salām Tadmurī, *Tārīkh al-Anṭākī*, Tripoli, Lebanon, 1990, pp. 295–9.

[The fateful year according to Yaḥyā]

On Friday 8 *Rabīʿa al-ākhir* of the year 403 [27 October 1012], al-Ḥākim issued an order that the Christians and Jews, with the exception of the Khayābira,[31] were to wear black cloaks and deep-black turbans in addition to the *zunnār* and to hang from their necks wooden crosses. They were not to ride horses but to ride [on other animals] using

[31] Descendants of the Jewish tribe that had been evicted from the oasis of Khaybar at the time of Muḥammad and were thereafter considered in some accounts to have been exempted from the regulations imposed on other protected peoples.

stirrups of wood with saddles and bridles of black leather on which no ornamentation could be seen nor any evidence of silver, nor were they to employ Muslims as servants. And this rule was to be adopted in all the other districts of the kingdom. They were to wear crosses the length of which was a thumb–index finger span (*fitr*). A month later it was changed and made the length of a whole hand's span by the same [in width] (*shibr fī shibr*). Next, he ordered a census of the names of the Muslim clerks who had been dismissed and let go yet might be suitable to be employed in the bureaus and departments as replacements for the Christians. Most of his clerks, the holders of service positions and the medical doctors of his kingdom were Christian, all save a small number of them.

[31 October] The abominable offences against them multiplied along with dreadful disquieting talk. So all the Christians in Fusṭāṭ,[32] the clerks, the office holders, physicians and others, in company with their priests and clergy, gathered together and set out for his palace on Thursday 12 *Rabīʿ al-ākhir* of that same year. With uncovered heads, they walked barefoot, crying aloud, imploring him and asking for his forgiveness and pardon. For the whole length of the way, they never ceased kissing the ground until they arrived at the palace, still in that same state. He sent out to them one of his men who took from them the petition they had composed by which to plead that he would show mercy and bring an end to his evident displeasure with them. Accordingly, he sent back to them a messenger who responded favourably. Al-Ḥusayn ibn Ẓāhir al-Wazzān [the newly appointed *wāsiṭa*][33] then spoke to the elders among them in like manner in a response also conciliatory. He promised them reassurance and something to bring tranquillity to their hearts.

Feeling that their aim was achieved and the intention towards them ameliorated, they took comfort in a decree read out in their favour on the subject of their security and safety. However, on Sunday in the middle of the month of *Rabīʿ al-ākhir* of this same year [5 October 1012], they were also ordered to lengthen the crosses hanging from their necks and to make them measure a royal cubit in length and the same in width, and their spread (*fatkh*) two-thirds of a hand-span, and their thickness a finger. The purpose in this was to vex them further, especially the elite of the clerks in his bureaucracy and those in his service for whom no replacement had been found.

One of the strangest aspects of all this was that in the month of *Ṣafar* of the year 402 [September 1011], al-Ḥākim had ordered that no cross should appear in public or to be where it could be seen, and that the bells should not be rung. Crosses were taken down from churches and all traces of them were removed from the surfaces of churches and temples. And yet in this latter time he specified that crosses should be displayed in this manner. The Jews then were to wear nothing of wood along with the black *ghiyār*.[34] But subsequently a call went round stating that they were to suspend

[32] The capital of Egypt before the founding of Cairo.
[33] A quasi vizier though of lower rank.
[34] A piece of cloth or badge worn to distinguish *dhimmī*s from Muslims.

from their necks also wooden balls weighing five pounds (*raṭl*)[35] to signify the head of the calf they once worshipped.

As he menaced the Christians, they were terror-stricken, while dreadful talk and calumny against them increased. Many of the senior clerks, officials and others among the Christians adopted Islam, and a great multitude of the commoners followed their lead. A group of the Jews also converted to Islam. Vile rumours multiplied among those remaining Christians who had not converted about having their limbs cut off, about slaves and neighbours selling off their property and families, and about inquiry and warrant being set for those of the clerks and officials who had hidden and concealed themselves. The homes of a group who were in hiding were plundered and their property seized. The majority converted to Islam, many following the lead of the others in close succession. There remained of them only a small few, a handful. The streets continued for many days devoid of Christians, none to be seen.

The Jews largely held to their religion, only a tiny few among them adopting Islam. Likewise, the Christian clerks who lived in other regions also retained their faith. Except for a few, the rest of the officials of the kingdom did not convert, other than the inhabitants of Cairo, particularly those whose situation, as we have explained, allowed them to witness first-hand and in close proximity what was happening, and to verify also the evil intentions towards them in the actions of his during that period. He granted all the churches and monasteries, both old and new in Egypt and the districts of his kingdom, to the soldiery. He gave these to them, numbering in many thousands, with all their furnishings, treasure, and goods, so that they could destroy them and reduce them to rubble. All of them were demolished; a few made into mosques.

A decree was sent to the rest of his governorates to eradicate all traces of churches from the face of the earth and to remove all evidence of them. This was done: their very foundations were uprooted from the earth and, in several countries, the bones of the dead in the churches were thrown out. People burned them in the fires for the baths. They also burned copies of the scriptures and other books found in the churches. In each region those Christians in charge of affairs were made to pay the amounts due to the workers and demolishers who destroyed the churches. This happened to all of them throughout the kingdom except for the monastery once known as Isqīṭ, which is in Maryout in the district of Alexandria, now called the Monastery of Abū Maqār,[36] and the small monasteries close by. Al-Ḥākim realized that two Arab tribes, the Banū Qurra and the Banū Kilāb, defended it and that they did so because of a benefit to them from it. So he held back against his hatred for it.

He granted the churches of Qulzum,[37] the monastery of Rāya and the monastery of Mount Sinai[38] to an Arab known as Ibn Ghiyāth and instructed him to destroy the

---

[35] A *raṭl* varies in weight according to country, but in this instance it is probably 449 grams, the equivalent of a pound.

[36] The Monastery of St Macarius in the Wadi Natrun, sixty or so miles north-west of Cairo.

[37] A town located at the head of the Gulf of Suez.

[38] St Catherine's Monastery.

monastery of Mount Sinai and build in its place a mosque. This man then tore down some of the churches in Qulzum, seizing all their furnishings, and he destroyed one of two churches in the monastery of Rayā, taking away its goods and furnishings as well. Then he went on to the monastery of Mount Sinai to do likewise in accord with the instructions given him. There was at Mount Sinai at the time a man who was a scribe but preparing to be a monk there, having joined recently. He was called Ṣalmūn ibn Ibrāhīm and he was one of the notables of Egypt, of senior status and quite wise, intelligent and politically adept. This man went out to Ibn Ghiyāth, meeting him cordially and informing him that the prior and the monks would do whatever he demanded rather than trying to prevent what he had in mind. Ṣalmūn surrendered to him all the furnishings of the monastery and its treasure of gold and silver, all the while discussing this with him amiably. Ṣalmūn further explained that the destruction would be difficult for him or anyone else because the monastery was quite formidable and solidly built, and that accomplishing such a task would require an expenditure of great sums, well above what he could hope to gain from doing it. Ibn Ghiyāth then demanded a substantial payment in return for leaving off doing it, so Ṣalmūn concluded a deal with him to his satisfaction. He paid the sum and Ibn Ghiyāth departed without causing further harm.

24

Letter from the people of Cyprus

David Thomas, University of Birmingham

Sometime around the end of the twelfth or beginning of the thirteenth century, a little-known Christian monk named Paul of Antioch, who was Bishop of Sidon, composed a letter supposedly for a Muslim friend in which he recounted a probably fictitious meeting with Christian experts during a journey in Europe. These experts proceeded to demonstrate to him why, even though they had read the Qur'an, they felt no compulsion to become Muslims because their own Christian faith was confirmed by what the Qur'an taught.

Paul was unapologetic in his use – and occasional abuse – of the Qur'an, and he did not flinch from lifting verses from their contexts or making occasional changes to the text to suit his purpose. His letter evidently circulated widely and caused a reaction from at least one major Muslim scholar. At the beginning of the fourteenth century, it was edited to remove its most acerbic elements, and in its changed form it was sent to two of the leading Muslim scholars of the day, Tāqī l-Dīn Aḥmad ibn Taymiyya (1263–1328) and Shams al-Dīn Muḥammad ibn Abī Ṭālib al-Dimashqī (1256–1327), both living in or near Damascus. They each replied with two of the longest refutations written by any Muslim.

The editor of this letter, *Risāla min ahl Jazīrat Qubruṣ* ('Letter from the people of Cyprus') is completely unknown. He wrote from Cyprus, and was evidently not only proficient in Arabic but also expert in the Qur'an, which he knew well enough to be able to quote strings of related verses at will. His Christology shows that he was probably a Nestorian Christian, allowing the possibility that he was a refugee on the island from the warfare that afflicted life on the mainland. He was evidently less impulsive in his judgement than his predecessor Paul, and realized that the letter in the form he had recast it was more likely to convince by persuasion than through unpalatable interpretations of Muslim scripture. In the end, however, it achieved no greater success than Paul's.

The passage translated here is concerned with a long-standing problem for Arabic-speaking Christians who lived in the Muslim world, the representation of God as one substance and three hypostases (or Persons), Father, Son and Holy Spirit. Through his scholarly mouthpieces, the author first argues that the Christian doctrine is derived from the Bible, and that the Muslims cannot criticize it because they face a similar challenge arising from the depiction in the Qur'an of God possessing human-like qualities. He implies that both sides face their own problems over their characterizations of God arising from their scriptures, and are in no position to criticize one another. Then he argues that according to Christian doctrine, which is expressed in Greek philosophical terminology, to call God substance is to use the highest designation of Him as an independent entity, free from any need of another being. This brought Arabic-speaking Christians into difficulties, because the term they employed to translate it, *jawhar*, was used in atomistic Muslim theology to designate the fundamental component of physical matter, the building block from which everything in the visible world was made. This led to manifold misunderstanding and disagreements.

The author speaks in the first person, addressing the scholars he has supposedly met, just like Paul of Antioch in his earlier letter. The arguments in favour of the veracity of Christianity are put into their mouths.

CMR 4, pp. 769–72.

The passage below is taken from *The Letter from the people of Cyprus*, in R. Ebied and D. Thomas (eds and trans), *Muslim-Christian Polemic during the Crusades, the Letter from the People of Cyprus and Ibn Abī Ṭālib al-Dimashqī's Response*, Leiden, 2005, pp. 129–47, reprinted with permission.

I said to [the Christian scholars]: If your belief about the exalted Creator is that He is one, what has made you say 'Father, Son and Holy Spirit'? You have made those who hear think that you believe God is three composite individuals, or three gods, or three parts, and that He has a son. Someone who did not know your belief might imagine that by this you mean a son by physical intimacy and reproduction, laying you open to a charge of which you are innocent.

[The scholars] said: The Muslims as well – since their belief about the Creator, great is His might, is that He has no body, limbs or organs, nor is limited in one place – what has made them say that he has two eyes by which He sees, two hands which He spreads wide, a leg, a face which He turns in every direction, and a side, and that He comes in the darkness of clouds, so that people hearing might imagine that God the exalted has a body, limbs and organs, and that He moves from place to place in the darkness of clouds? Someone who did not know their belief might think they give a body to the Creator – indeed, people among them have believed this and taken it as their doctrine – and someone who had not verified their belief might charge them with things of which they are innocent.

I said: [The Muslims] say, The reason for our saying this, that God has two eyes, two hands, a face, leg and side, and that He comes in the darkness of clouds, is that the Qur'an speaks of it, though the intention in this is not literal. Anyone who takes it literally and believes that God has two eyes, two hands, a face, a side, limbs and organs, and that His essence moves from place to place, etc., as is involved in corporealism and anthropomorphism, we condemn him and declare him to be an unbeliever. And if we declare anyone who believes this an unbeliever, our opponents are not in a position to impose it upon us, since we do not believe it.

[The scholars] said: It is exactly the same with us. The reason we say that God is three hypostases, Father, Son and Holy Spirit, is that the Gospel speaks about it. What is meant by 'hypostases' is not composite individuals, parts and divisions and so on, as partnership and plurality entail. For the Father and Son are not the fatherhood and sonship of wedlock, procreation or reproduction. We excommunicate, curse and accuse of unbelief everyone who believes that the three hypostases are three different or coincident gods, three physical objects brought together, three separate parts, three composite individuals, accidents or powers,[39] or anything entailed by partnership, plurality, division or anthropomorphism, sonship through wedlock, intimacy, procreation, reproduction or birth from a wife, or a physical object, an angel or a creature. And if we curse and accuse of unbelief anyone who believes this, our opponents are not in any position to impose upon us what we do not believe.

Thus, if [the Muslims] force us to acknowledge polytheism and anthropomorphism on account of our teaching that God the exalted is one substance and three hypostases, Father, Son and Holy Spirit, because when taken literally this entails plurality and anthropomorphism, we in turn force them to acknowledge corporealism and anthropomorphism because of their teaching that God has two eyes, two hands, a face, a leg and a side, that his essence moves from place to place, that he was seated on the throne after not being on it,[40] and other things that literally are involved in corporealism and anthropomorphism.

[39] These terms, which would be well-known in theological and philosophical circles in the Islamic world at this time, originated in Greek philosophy, where they designated the different forms of being.

[40] Verses such as Q 7:54, 10:3 and 13:2 appear to say that God mounted the heavenly throne after He had completed the creation, the point being that this suggests movement and change in God, as well as limitation, since He is contained by the throne.

25

*The Martyrdom of Rizqallāh ibn Naba*ʿ

Mark Swanson, Lutheran School of Theology at Chicago

In all the Arabic-speaking Christian communities of the Middle East collections of stories of ancient martyrs came to be augmented with the stories of neo-martyrs, those who died while giving witness to their Christian faith in the Islamic world. The short *Martyrdom of Rizqallāh ibn Naba*ʿ that is translated here provides an example. It comes from a Melkite (Chalcedonian Orthodox) *synaxarion* in manuscript form, that is, a collection of short entries on saints and martyrs arranged for daily reading. It is probably a condensation of a longer account that would have been read at the martyr's annual commemoration.

Stories of the neo-martyrs were, of course, preserved and read by a variety of Christian communities in a number of languages (Greek, Syriac, Coptic, etc.). With regard to texts composed directly in Arabic, the Melkite Church provides some of the earliest examples, such as the eighth-century *Martyrdom of ʿAbd al-Masīḥ* (or Qays al-Ghassānī before he became a monk), or a little later the *Martyrdom of Anthony* (or Rawḥ al-Qurashī before he converted to Christianity). An early Copto-Arabic example is the (probably) tenth-century *Martyrdom of Jirjis* (or Muzāḥim before his conversion). On occasion, the original Arabic text has been lost, as is the case for the (perhaps) ninth-century *Martyrdom of Michael of Mār Saba*, preserved only in Georgian and Slavonic versions. These last two examples point to the place of Arabic in the transmission of texts: not only were texts translated from Christians' ancient languages into Arabic, but Arabic served as a source for further transmission: the *Martyrdom of Jirjis (Muzāḥim)*, like many other Copto-Arabic texts, was translated into Ethiopic; the *Martyrdom of Michael of Mār Saba*, like numerous other early Melkite texts, was translated into Georgian.

These examples mention a variety of offences that gave rise to the martyrdom. Frequently the charge was apostasy: the martyr (e.g. ʿAbd al-Masīḥ, Anthony, Jirjis) was someone who refused to recant a conversion to Christianity. In other cases (e.g. Michael), a Christian was put to death for what was considered blasphemous preaching against Islam. Sometimes the charges came together: in late-fourteenth-century Egypt, there was a wave of forty-nine voluntary martyrs during the patriarchate of Matthew I, but these were a mix of former Muslims who openly declared their Christian faith, and life-long Christians who engaged in anti-Islamic preaching.

The *Martyrdom of Rizqallāh ibn Naba'* presents a somewhat different case to these. It bears witness to the fact that throughout pre-modern times Christians often served Islamic administrations and individual Muslim grandees in a bureaucratic capacity (often as financial administrators), and that in certain times and places (e.g. in Egypt under Mamlūk rule) they came under intense pressure to convert to Islam. A number of them did, so that many of the great financial administrators of late medieval Egypt were 'Muslim Copts', converts to Islam or the children or grandchildren of converts. Others quietly removed themselves from public life (the thirteenth-century Coptic polymath and encyclopaedist Abū Shākir ibn Rāhib may be an example). Occasionally we read of someone like Rizqallāh ibn Naba', who was martyred for his faith.

The story of Rizqallāh ibn Naba' is typical in many of its plot elements: attempts by Muslims to sway the Christian by blandishments and then by threats; bold speeches in which Christ is confessed as God; a final provocative prayer; failure of attempts to destroy the martyr's body; and final burial and veneration. This particular text is interesting as a witness to the part played by Cyprus as a kind of Christian haven for Levantine Christians.

The text places the martyrdom of Rizqallāh rather vaguely 'in the days of the Muslims'. Ṭūmā Biṭār (*Al-qiddīsūn al-mansiyyūn fī l-turāth al-Anṭākī*, Beirut, 1995, pp. 268–70, notes on the text), who had access to additional copies of the *Martyrdom*, found a date (1 February 6985 in the Era of the World) and a name for the emir (Azdemur), which fit together nicely: the World Era date converts to the year 1477, and Azdemur ibn Mazīd was the Mamlūk governor in Tripoli (Lebanon) from 1475 to 1479.

CMR 5, pp. 526–8.

This translation is based on the entry for 1 Shubāṭ/February, from the unpaginated MS Dayr 'Atiya 35.

Also on this day: the struggle (*jihād*) of the newly manifest saint and martyr Rizqallāh ibn Naba', who was martyred in the days of the Muslims.

This blessed one was one of the scribes of the city of Tripoli, a senior civil servant of the emir of the municipality and privy to his private and public affairs. He was held in high honour among the elite and the common folk of the people of the city.

Owing to [the emir's] great love for him, he desired to move him away from the religion of Christ with gentleness and amiability, but [Rizqallāh] was not budged, nor did his resolve waver, and he openly declared his true faith in the presence of the emir. [The emir] was exceedingly enraged at this and ordered him to be thrown in prison. Then [the emir] sent him a group of people who were close to him to win over the martyr through personal relationships and numerous gifts, but he did not hearken to them and did not pay attention to their speech. [Rather,] he openly declared the name of Christ, without embarrassment or shame, and criticized their religion and held them in reproach.

When the emir heard this his rage and fury increased, and he considered how he might move [Rizqallāh] from his correct doctrine. So he again sent him [a delegation], which threatened him and described various punishments if he did not accede [to the emir's] desire and counselled him to deny the creed of Christ.

The martyr responded, saying: 'Do you not know that this world and its honour and splendour are to me as nothing, like a passing shadow? I reject your punishments, tortures, and threats. To me they are the easiest of things because of my love for my God and Saviour Jesus Christ, the only [-begotten] Son of God.' He discoursed with them in many words, with boldness and sagacity. When they saw that he was firm in this state, immoveable from it, [and reported this to the emir,] the tyrant immediately commanded that he should be beheaded.

They brought him outside of the city to a place called Tell al-Mushtahā. [Rizqallāh] asked the swordsman to delay a bit so that he could pray. He took off his sandals [Arabic, 'one of his garments'] and gave them to the swordsman, then he began his supplication, lifting his hands towards the east and saying: 'My God and Lord Jesus Christ, help me in this hour: accept my spirit, make me an inheritor with all your martyrs, and accept me as a pure offering in this illustrious night.' Then he bowed his neck to the swordsman without fear of martyrdom, and immediately he was beheaded and received the crown of martyrdom with the righteous ones.

Then [Satan], the hater of the good, goaded the tyrannical people into action: they gathered a lot of wood in order to burn the body of the excellent martyr. But God – may God's name be blessed – sent a cloud from heaven which poured down copious rain and hail, until the rivers flooded! Everyone who was there was overcome by the power of God; the fire was extinguished and its flame went out. Everyone who heard of the greatness of this wonder gave praise to God.

Then the believers came by night and took the body of the honoured martyr, brought it to the island of Cyprus, and gave him the most splendid of funerals, with all honour and reverence. They buried him in one of the holy sanctuaries, and he was counted among the assembly of the martyrs who wear the crown of victory in the eternal habitations of bliss.

His prayers and blessings, along with the intercession of all the saints, protect all of us and you. Amen!

Iberian Arabic

Muslims and Christians in Islamic Spain

Juan Pedro Monferrer-Sala,
University of Córdoba

Muslim armies, comprising Arabs and North African Berbers under Arab leadership, first crossed into the Iberian Peninsula in 711. Within a few years they had extended Muslim rule over most of the peninsula and continued north across the Pyrenees. A heavy defeat near Poitiers in 732 checked their progress, and they were unable to hold onto their possessions in France. The Islamic state that came into being, known as al-Andalus, occupied the whole of the peninsula with the exception of a small area in the northwest, which remained under Christian rule.

In the immediate post-conquest period, al-Andalus was part of the Umayyad Empire. Following the ʿAbbasids' overthrow of the Umayyads in 750, a surviving member of the Umayyad family fled west and came to al-Andalus in 755. He secured control, and from that time he and his descendants ruled from Córdoba as an independent Umayyad dynasty. At first, they used the secular title *amīr* ('commander'), but from 929 they styled themselves by the religious title *khalīfa* ('deputy of the Prophet'). The dynasty continued until 1031, when central rule collapsed and the country broke into petty states or Taifa kingdoms (*duwal al-ṭawāʾif*) of different sizes and power. In this situation, the Christian kings in the north of the peninsula were able to extend their territories south in what they called the *Reconquista*, until in 1085 Toledo in the middle of the country was seized from Muslim control.

Unity was restored when the recently established power of the Almoravids in Morocco was requested to help. Armies crossed to al-Andalus, and the new state was established in 1091. This lasted just over fifty years, though the country became increasingly unsettled and Christian forces from the north of the peninsula continued to gain territory. A second North-African power, the Almohads, was asked to help. They established themselves firmly at first, but by the early thirteenth century their position had grown increasingly weak. The battle of Las Navas de Tolosa in 1212, fought against a Christian army, inflicted a crushing defeat on them, and local warlords were again able to assert independence while Christian forces seized Córdoba and other major towns in the south. By the mid-thirteenth century, Iberia had come entirely under Christian control apart from the south-eastern enclave around Granada. This continued as an independent entity until 1492, when the last Muslim ruler was defeated and exiled by the Catholic Monarchs, Ferdinand and his wife Isabella.

By the time the first Muslims crossed into Iberia, Christianity, with allegiance to Rome, was firmly established in the peninsula. As in other parts of the Islamic world, Christians who came under Muslim rule, together with Jews, were recognized as *Ahl al-kitāb* ('People of the Book') as possessors of their own scriptures, and they were allowed to retain their religious practices, though many churches were taken over for use as mosques. Christians were accorded the legal status of *ahl al-dhimma* ('People of the Covenant') and came under restrictions on their conduct and relations with Muslims.

There are few signs of any compulsion to convert to Islam, or of many Christians converting in order to avoid the taxes imposed on non-Muslims. But there were great changes among Christians as they came to see the attraction of Arabic literature and the Islamic culture which it expressed. Mentions of young men preferring Arabic poetry to Latin, dressing like Muslims and even being circumcised attest to the extensive attraction of the culture introduced by the Arab rulers. However, this did not necessarily mean compromise between Christianity and Islam. As in the Islamic East, the polemical works that were written by the followers of each faith show they were unyielding in their condemnation of one another. They treated many of the same issues as their eastern counterparts: Muḥammad as a fraud and the Qur'an as inauthentic on the Christian side, and on the Muslim side the doctrines of the Trinity and Incarnation as irrational and the Bible a corrupt scripture. They often used similar arguments, which were borrowed, though the eleventh-century scholar Ibn Ḥazm of Córdoba's demonstration that the text of the Bible is corrupt by means of detailed comparisons of differences in the wording of Gospel accounts of the same story is original and one of the most impressive examples of this genre.

In works such as Ibn Ḥazm's can be seen the same combination of often considerable knowledge of the others' beliefs and hostile misunderstanding of their faith as is found in Christian and Muslim works from the Islamic heartlands. The attitudes expressed in polemical works written by followers of both faiths reinforced attitudes exhibited in society more casually and broadly to ensure that the religious other was usually identified as the opponent.

Further reading

T.E. Burman, *Religious Polemic and the Intellectual History of the Mozarabs, c. 1050–1200*, Leiden, 1994.

A. Christys, *Christians in al-Andalus, 711–1000*, Richmond, UK, 2002.

C. Aillet, *Les mozarabs. Christianisme, islamisation et arabisation en péninsule Ibérique (IXe-XIIe siècle)*, Madrid, 2010.

J.M. Safran, *Defining Boundaries in al-Andalus: Muslims, Christians and Jews in Islamic Iberia*, Ithaca, NY, 2013.

C.L. Tieszen, *Christian Identity amid Islam in Medieval Spain*, Leiden, 2013.

R. Hitchcock, *Muslim Spain Reconsidered. From 711 to 1502*, Edinburgh, 2014.

26

Ibn Ḥazm, *Judgement regarding the religions, inclinations and sects*

Camilla Adang, Tel Aviv University

Abū Muḥammad ʿAlī ibn Aḥmad ibn Saʿīd ibn Ḥazm was born in Cordoba in 994. Although he hoped to follow in the footsteps of his father, who was a vizier, he abandoned these aspirations for a life of scholarship after several stretches in prison. He is best known for his literary treatise on love in all its complexities, *Ṭawq al-ḥamāma* ('The ring of the dove'), though he is credited with some four hundred works on a wide range of topics. His critical reflection on the religious and political situation in his country made him turn to the revealed sources of Islam, which he understood in their external sense (*ẓāhir*), rejecting figurative interpretations. He regarded himself as one of the few Muslims who remained loyal to the legacy of the Prophet Muḥammad and saw it as his mission to bring people back to the original, unadulterated teachings of Islam, anchored in the Qur'an and the Sunna. In his public debates as well as in his writings he offended scholars, magistrates and rulers alike so that he became increasingly isolated, and towards the end of his life his books were publicly burned in Seville. He retired to his family's estate near Niebla, where he died in 1064.

Ibn Ḥazm's virulent polemics were not reserved for fellow-Muslims alone, but included Jews and Christians. While he objected to their growing political role in the strongest terms, his main attacks concerned their scriptures, which he regarded as having been deliberately corrupted, as a literal reading of these texts showed. This he seeks to demonstrate in his *Kitāb al-faṣl* (or *fiṣal*) *fī l-milal wa-l-ahwāʾ wa-l-niḥal* ('Judgement regarding religions, inclinations and sects') on the basis of extensive biblical quotations in surprisingly accurate Arabic translations. Among other things, he refutes the doctrines of the Trinity and Incarnation, and points to contradictions between the Gospels.

CMR 3, pp. 137–45. See further:

C. Adang, M. Fierro and S. Schmidtke (eds). *Ibn Hazm of Cordoba. The Life and Works of a Controversial Thinker*, Leiden, 2013.

This translation is based on *Kitāb al-fiṣal fī l-milal wa-l-ahwāʾ wa-l-milal*, ed. M.I. Naṣr and ʿA.R. ʿUmayra, 5 vols, Beirut, 1982.

Luke said: When dawn broke, very early on Sunday, the women proceeded to the grave carrying balm, and they found the stone pulled away from the grave; they entered it but did not find the Lord inside, so they were perplexed. Two men in white clothes stepped towards them and said to them: 'Do not look for a living person among the dead. He has risen and is not here.' So they left and told the eleven disciples and those who were with them, but they did not believe them. Peter quickly got up and rushed to the grave and only found the shroud, and he was amazed and left.

Then the Messiah appeared to two men among them who were setting out to go to a village called Emmaus, seven and a half miles away from Jerusalem, but they did not recognize him until he disappeared and left them. Immediately they went to Jerusalem and found the eleven disciples gathered with their companions, and they told them the story.

As they were discussing the matter, Jesus appeared in their midst and said: 'Peace be with you. I am he. Fear not.' But they did become fearful and were afraid that it was a devil, but he told them: 'Why are you afraid? Look at my feet and hands, I am he, for the devil has neither flesh nor bones.' Then he said: 'Have you anything to eat?.' and they brought him a piece of broiled fish and honey beverage, so he ate and left the rest to them. Then he gave them advice and left them.[1]

John, however, said: On the Sunday, Mary went to the grave early in the morning when the darkness had not yet faded, and she saw that the rock had been pulled away from the grave, and she returned to Simon Peter and the other disciple, that is, John, with this same news and she said to the two of them: 'My Lord has gone from the grave and we do not know where they have put him.' Peter and the other disciple rushed to the grave, and found the shrouds lying there; then they returned.

Mary was standing there and wept. She turned to the grave and saw two angels standing there, and they asked her: 'Who are you looking for?' She thought they were ghosts and said to [one of them]: 'My lord, if you are the one who has taken him, then tell me where you put him.' And he said to her: 'Mary!' And she turned to him and said: 'O my teacher!' And Jesus said to her: 'Do not touch me; I have not yet gone up to my Father; but go to my brothers and say to them: I am going up to my Father and yours, to my God and yours.' So she went and told them.

Then, as the disciples were gathering, Jesus came and stood in their midst and said: 'Peace be with you,' and he showed them his hands and his side. Then he [John] says that Thomas, one of the twelve disciples, was not present among them at that appearance, but when he came and they told him, he said: 'Until I see in his hands where the nails were affixed and put my finger into the place of the nails in his side, I shall not believe.' After eight days they all gathered together with the doors closed, and Jesus came and stood in their midst and said to Thomas: 'Insert your finger and look at my hands; give me your hand and I shall put it into my side, and be not an unbeliever but rather be a believer.' And Thomas said to him: 'My lord and my God!'

---

[1] Luke 24 heavily summarized.

Then he appeared before Simon Peter, Thomas, Nathanael, the two sons of Zebedee and two other disciples near the lake of Tiberias, as they were fishing in a boat on the lake.[2]

Abū Muḥammad [ibn Ḥazm] said: Marvel at this tale and at the lies and abominations it contains. For Matthew says that Mary and Mary went to the grave late Saturday evening preceding the Sunday and found that he had risen.[3] But Mark says that Mary, Mary and other persons went to the grave at dawn on Sunday and discovered that he had already risen.[4] Luke says: The women went to the grave early Sunday morning and found that he had risen, and that the darkness had not yet faded.[5]

These, now, are lies on their [the Christians'] part with regard to the time of their arrival at the grave, and with regard to the identity of those who went to the grave. Was it Mary on her own, or Mary accompanied by the other Mary? Or was it the two of them, together with additional women? [vol. 2, pp. 129–31]

At the end of the Gospel of Mark it says that the Messiah said to his disciples: Go into all the world and preach the Gospel to all creatures, and whoever believes and is baptized will be safe, and whoever does not believe will be punished. And these signs will accompany those who believe, and they are the signs they will show in my name: they will cast out demons, will speak in new languages and will take up serpents; if they drink a deadly potion it will not harm them, and they will lay their hands on the sick, who will recover.[6]

Abū Muḥammad said: in this section there are two unheard-of lies. The first one is [Jesus saying] 'Preach the gospel', which points to a gospel that was brought by the Messiah,[7] and which they do not possess now; they only possess four Gospels that differ from each other, written by four men who are known. Not one of these Gospels was written until many years and a long time after the Messiah (peace be upon him) was taken up to heaven. It is true, then, that this Gospel of which the Messiah told them that he had brought it, and which he ordered them to call the people to, has disappeared from them, for they do not know its original. Anything else is not possible.

The second is their saying that [the Messiah] promised salvation to anyone who believed in the call of the disciples, and that they would speak in languages they had not known before, and that they would cast out demons from the insane, and lay their hands on the sick who would then recover; that they would take up serpents, and that if they drank a deadly potion, it would not harm them.

Abū Muḥammad said: This is a promise whose deceitfulness is apparent and manifest. For not one of [the Christians] speaks in a language he does not know, not

[2] John 20:1-21:8, again summarized.
[3] Matthew 28:1, giving the time as 'after the sabbath, as the first day of the week was dawning'.
[4] Mark 16:1-6.
[5] Luke 24:1.
[6] Mark 16:15-18.
[7] According to Muslim beliefs based on the Qur'an (e.g. 57:27), Jesus delivered the *Injīl* from God in the same way as Muḥammad and other messengers delivered their revealed scriptures.

one of them casts out demons, not one of them lays his hands on a sick person who then recovers; not one of them takes up serpents, not one of them drinks poison and remains unharmed – they admit that John the Evangelist died by poisoning.[8] God forbid that there should come a prophet with vain, deceitful promises – how much more so a god!

Know that attributing lies to the Messiah is the easiest thing to do for the despicable people who wrote these Gospels. [vol. 2, pp. 139–40]

---

[8] According to the apocryphal *Acts of John*, he was challenged to drink poison, but this did not kill him.

27

Al-Ṭurṭūshī, *A lamp for rulers*

Maribel Fierro, Spanish National Research Council

Abū Bakr Muḥammad ibn al-Walīd al-Fihrī l-Ṭurṭūshī, known as Ibn Abī Randaqa (d. 1126), was born and studied in the Taifa kingdom of Saragossa. He left al-Andalus in 1083, travelling to Egypt, Syria and Iraq, where one of his teachers was al-Ghazālī, whose life and work had a deep influence on him. Al-Ṭurṭūshī finally settled in Fāṭimid Alexandria in 1097, where he died. From a Sunnī perspective he criticized the legal and religious innovations introduced by the Ismāʿīlī dynasty, some of which are dealt with in his *Kitāb al-ḥawādith wa-l-bidaʿ* ('Book against religious novelties and innovations'). In his *Kitāb fī taḥrīm jubn al-rūm*, he also criticized the import, sale and consumption of cheese made by the Byzantines.

Al-Ṭurṭūshī's stay in the East coincided with the First Crusade, while in al-Andalus Toledo fell into Christian hands in the year 1085. In 1086, the Almoravids were called by some of the Taifa kings to help check the Christian military advance, which they did for a time, although in 1118 Saragossa was lost forever by the Muslims. These external (Christian advance) and internal (Ismāʿīlī heresy) threats motivated al-Ṭurṭūshī's concern for the need to reform the practices and beliefs of the Muslims, as well as his views about strengthening restrictions on Jews and Christians under Muslim rule and exalting the sacredness of Jerusalem.

Sirāj al-mulūk ('A lamp for rulers'), completed in 1122, belongs to the 'mirrors for princes' genre, containing various forms of advice to the ruler about how to behave in order to ensure justice and strengthen his rule. The materials found within it relating to Christians are varied: one of the earliest preserved versions of the so-called *Pact of ʿUmar* regulating the interactions between Muslims and Christians, an anecdote on the interaction between Muslim and Christian neighbours, news about Christian military advances in al-Andalus with descriptions of battles between Muslims and Christians in the northern frontier, and discussion of the reasons for the military weakness of the Muslims in contrast to the Christians. Al-Ṭurṭūshī shows himself in favour of seeking the conversion of non-Muslims either by word or by the sword, and of not allowing the existence of any synagogue or church, old or new, in Islamic territory.

CMR 3, pp. 392–5. See further:

A. Akasoy, 'El *Sirāǧ al-mulūk* de al-Ṭurtūšī y la antropología almohade', in J. Corcó et al. (eds), *Què és l'home? Reflexions antropològiques a la Corona d'Aragó durant l'Edat Mitjana*, Barcelona, 2004, 19–40.

A. Mallett, 'Two Writings of al-Ṭurṭūshī as Evidence for Early Muslim Reactions to the Frankish Crusader Presence in the Levant', *Wiener Zeitschrift für die Kunde des Morgenlandes* 107 (2017) 153–78.

This translation is based on *Sirāj al-mulūk*, Cairo, 1319/1901.

A man endowed with intelligence and learning entered the presence of one of the caliphs and found that he was in the company of a *dhimmī* whom the caliph esteemed and kept close to him. The man said:

O king, obeyed by humankind
and love for whom is an obligatory instruction,
He, thanks to whom you are revered,
is considered a liar by this man,[9]

pointing to the *dhimmī* and saying: 'Ask him, O Prince of the Believers!' The caliph questioned him and had to concede that the man was right. Then the *dhimmī* converted to Islam.[10] [p. 61] [...]

The reason that fundamentally determined the loss of al-Andalus and its conquest by the Christians was that those Christians who lived in the frontier regions did not have a royal treasury. They collected the tribute (*jizya*)[11] from the Muslim rulers and then they went to the church. There the king distributed the money among his men with a bowl, taking for himself the same as the rest, and not even taking anything for himself in order to ensure he had soldiers at his disposal. By contrast, our rulers took the money for themselves and lost the soldiers. Thus, the Christians had reserves of soldiers and the Muslims reserves of money, and in this circumstance they vanquished us and prevailed over us. [p. 108] [...]

Ibn al-Ḥaṣṣār, the jurist from Córdoba, had a Christian neighbour who helped him when needed and from whom he benefitted. The jurist was constantly saying to him things

---

[9] The Muslim is accusing the Christian ('this man') of believing that Muḥammad ('thanks to whom you are revered') is a fraud.

[10] The same story is attributed by his biographers to al-Ṭurṭūshī and a Fāṭimid vizier.

[11] Although this tribute is paid by Muslims to Christians, al-Ṭurṭūshī refers to it by the name used for the tax paid by non-Muslims within the Islamic state.

such as: 'May God give you long life! May God take you as friend! May God give freshness to your eyes! I am pleased with what pleases you! May God bring my last day before yours!' Other than these, he never spoke any words to him. The Christian was very satisfied with this. The jurist was criticized for it, and he replied: 'When I invoke God in his favour, I do it using expressions with double meaning, and God knows my true intention. When I say "May God give you long life and take you as friend!", what I mean is that I wish God will make him live long so that he will pay the poll-tax and that He will punish him. When I say "May God give freshness to your eyes!" my intention is to say "May God paralyse your eyes so that you will be forced to watch something evil happening in front of you without being able to close your eyelids." With my words "I am pleased with what pleases you!" I am referring to being healthy, which pleases me as it pleases him. With my words "May God bring my last day before yours!", I mean that God in his mercy will fix the day that I enter paradise before he – because of his infidelity – enters hell.' [pp. 129–30] [...]

In my country, Tortosa, some military leaders narrated that in the days of Sayf al-Milla[12] they went out on a night expedition against the land of the enemy. As they were marching along they found another expedition of Christians whose intention was to do to us what we intended to do to them. They said: 'We already knew each other.' With us there were brave warriors and among them there were brave Christians. We stood facing each other for an hour and then we started fighting. The battle commenced and we fought for an hour until God bestowed on us that they fled after we had butchered them. Nearby there was a village where they had wine, and we drank until we were drunk. Then we felt like eating slices of meat, so we went to cut it from the flesh of the enemies; we put it on the fire and we ate it. The captives that were with us were terrified. When the news reached the Christians it had a huge effect on them and their hearts were filled with fear. [p. 149] [...]

Al-Muqtadir bi-Llāh ibn Hūd, king of al-Andalus,[13] left Saragossa on the frontier of al-Andalus to fight the tyrant Ramiro,[14] leader of the Christians. Both took with them great numbers of troops. The Muslims and the infidels faced each other and prepared to fight, placing themselves in combat position. The fight lasted for a long part of the day, and the Muslims had substantial losses. Al-Muqtadir grew scared and the Muslims narrowly escaped from disaster on that day. Al-Muqtadir summoned a Muslim called Saʿdāda who had no equal along the frontier in his command of war matters. Al-Muqtadir asked him. 'What do you think of this day?' He answered: 'It is a dark day, but I have a plan.' Saʿdāda then left.

He used to dress as the Christians did and spoke as they did after living near them and having much contact with them. He infiltrated the army of the infidels and made his way towards the tyrant Ramiro, finding him covered in his iron armour from feet

[12] Muqātil, ruler of Tortosa, who took the title *Sayf al-milla* (r. c. 1039–53).
[13] Abū Jaʿfar Aḥmad I ibn Sulaymān al-Muqtadir (r. 1049–82), ruler of Saragossa.
[14] Probably a nickname given to an unknown leader.

to head so that only his eyes were visible. He remained there lying in wait to catch him unsuspectingly. When the opportunity arose he threw his spear into his eyes so that Ramiro fell down on his face. Then he started crying out in the language of the Christians: 'The sultan has been killed, Christians!' News of his death spread among the army, soldiers fought among themselves and scattered, fleeing away. With God's permission victory was achieved. [pp. 155–6]

28

The Letter of al-Qūṭī

Diego R. Sarrió Cucarella, Pontifical Institute for Arabic and Islamic Studies

The *Letter of al-Qūṭī*, or 'Letter of the Goth', is the name given by scholars to a short anti-Islamic polemic in Arabic purportedly written by an unknown priest active in Toledo in the mid-1140s. The text has survived only in the refutation it occasioned, entitled *Maqāmiʿ al-ṣulbān* ('Hammers for crosses'), by the Córdoban Muslim scholar Aḥmad ibn ʿAbd al-Ṣamad al-Khazrajī (d. 1187). According to one of his early biographers, al-Khazrajī was taken prisoner in the year 540 (between 24 June 1145 and 12 June 1146) and brought to Toledo, where he remained in captivity for about two years. Most probably, his capture took place following King Alfonso VII (r. 1126–57) of León-Castile's intervention in Córdoba in the spring of 1146. It was during his sojourn in Toledo that al-Khazrajī, then in his early twenties, wrote his book of anti-Christian polemic in response to the attacks on Islam by 'a priest of Gothic descent' (*qass nasabuhu min al-Qūṭ*).

A polemical interest in Islam on the part of a Toledo churchman fits the historical context well. It suffices to recall that Peter the Venerable visited the Iberian Peninsula in 1142, where he commissioned what has come to be called the *Collectio Toletana*, the first full translation of the Qur'an into Latin along with translations of several other works documenting the 'heresy of the Saracens'. However, certain anomalies in the text preserved in al-Khazrajī's refutation have raised suspicions about its authenticity, at least in its current form, and therefore a later reworking (or translation from Latin and reworking) of the original Christian text by a Muslim writer cannot be ruled out.

After recalling the role of Jesus Christ in the divine economy of creation and redemption, the *Letter of al-Qūṭī* begins by inviting its Muslim addressee to confess the Triune God if he wishes to receive God's mercy and attain Paradise. It then proceeds to claim Qur'anic support for the Christian confession of Christ as the Son of God. The next paragraphs focus on the Incarnation and the Atonement, portraying Christ as having made satisfaction on the cross to an offended God for the sins of humankind. To deny the crucifixion is an act of unbelief by which Muslims jeopardize their own salvation. Nevertheless, they exalt Christ and there is much good in their religion. Thus, there is a chance that they may come to the full truth, as is attested by the scriptures acknowledged by Muslims. From this point onwards, the letter presents a series of arguments for the superiority of the Christian religion, as well as examples of the perceived deficiencies of Islam.

CMR 3, pp. 524–5. See further:

T.E. Burman (trans.), 'Mozarabic Refutation of Islam (c. 1140)', in O.R. Constable (ed.), *Medieval Iberia: Readings from Christian, Muslim, and Jewish Sources*, 2nd edition, Philadelphia, PA, 2012, pp. 190–4.

C.L. Tieszen, *Christian Identity amid Islam in Medieval Spain*, Leiden, 2013, pp. 212–20.

D. Potthast, *Christen und Muslime im Andalus. Andalusische Christen und ihre Literatur nach religionspolemischen Texten des zehnten bis zwölften Jahrhunderts*, Wiesbaden, 2013, pp. 533–7.

The following passage is taken from Diego R. Sarrió Cucarella, 'Corresponding across Religious Borders: the *Letter of al-Qūṭī*', *Islamochristiana* 43 (2017) 149–71.

Many of our bishops have written books discrediting your religion. [The bishops] mention your lawgiver [Muḥammad] and they describe things in such a way that we see that you [Muslims] do not follow the truth; rather, the truth is with us. And there is no benefit in [following] your religious law (*sharīʿa*) because we find that there are two kinds of religious injunctions. The first is from the Torah: 'Whoever strikes you, strike him.' The second is from the Gospel: 'Whoever strikes you on your right cheek, offer him your left one.'[15] You see that the second is superior to the first, and you will not find any other third injunction that is not already included in these two.

And what evidence is more convincing of the fact that you [Muslims] do not follow the truth than what is written in your Book: 'Marry such women as seem good to you, two, three, four'?[16] And yet God said in the Gospel that a man should not marry more than one woman, just as was [the case] with Adam and his wife.[17] And it is written in your Book that when a man divorces his wife a third time, 'it is not permitted to him to marry her after that, until she marries another husband'.[18] Yet God said in the Torah, 'Whoever divorces his wife and then wants to return to her again, she is permitted to him as long as no other man has touched her.'[19]

And it is written in your Book: 'God has bought from the believers their persons and their possessions against the gift of paradise; they fight in the way of God; they kill,

---

[15] Matthew 5:39.
[16] Q 4:3.
[17] Not a direct quote, though probably referring to Jesus's teaching in Mark 10:1-12 and Matthew 19:4-6.
[18] Q 2:230.
[19] Deuteronomy 24:4.

and are killed; that is a promise binding upon God in the Torah, and the Gospel, and the Qur'an.'[20] Yet God said in the Torah that there should be no fighting, for the slayer and the slain will both end up in hell.[21] There is nothing surprising in this because you can defend the injunctions I have mentioned from your Book by adducing the abrogation [of the previously revealed legislation], which is one of the preliminary principles at the basis of your religious law. The thing that is surprising lies only in the words of your Book which state that it is 'a promise binding upon God in the Torah and the Gospel'.[22] Yet the Torah and the Gospel state just the opposite!

There is also cause for surprise in what [your Book] says about Mary, the mother of the Messiah: 'And Mary, daughter of ʿImrān, who guarded her chastity'.[23] And in another passage it says about her: 'Sister of Aaron! Your father was not a bad man, nor was your mother a prostitute.'[24] But the mother of the Messiah was neither the sister of Aaron nor the daughter of ʿImrān. The name of her father was Joachim, and you [Muslims] have taken her to be ʿImrān's daughter, who was the sister of Moses and Aaron.[25]

And about Iblīs, [your lawgiver] has also said in your Book that God cast him to earth when he refused to worship Adam.[26] Yet God had said in the Torah that He cast Iblīs from heaven before He created Adam because he wanted to make himself the equal of God.[27] He prided himself above the angels and told them: 'I am made of fire and have no Creator. Make me, therefore, a throne upon which I will be like the Most High.' But before he had finished speaking God cast him from heaven into the disgrace of the here-below, him and all his companions who had entertained the vile notion [of setting up the throne].[28]

You [Muslims] say that in the Torah, the Gospel, the Psalms and the prophetic books there is abundant corruption, and that we have added to them and subtracted from them. But this is part and parcel of your unbelief. You have no evidence of this, nor is it written in the Book your lawgiver brought. They are just words you have made up yourselves.

If you would peruse all of our books, and [perceive] the excellent qualities we had and continue to have to this day – for among us are righteous persons who perform signs and miracles, though they do not make a display of them unless there is need of doing so; and if you could witness the descent of the light which comes to us

---

[20] Q 9:111.
[21] Rather than being a reference to a particular biblical passage, this seems to be a simplification – for polemical purposes – of the Mosaic legislation on killing.
[22] Q 9:111.
[23] Q 66:12.
[24] Q 19:28.
[25] See Exodus 15:20; Numbers 26:59; 1 Chronicles 6:3.
[26] Q 7:12; 38:76.
[27] Following Augustine, Western Christianity preferred the version of the story in which Satan's primordial transgression takes place before the creation of Adam, which is precisely al-Qūṭī's point here.
[28] The *Letter* seems to reflect here a tradition preserved in 2 Enoch 29:4-5.

every year on the night of our Great Feast[29] – you would see something amazing and unique!

You [Muslims] say that in paradise there is eating and drinking and copulation, and that all these things are mentioned in the Book your lawgiver brought.[30] All of this, which we consider to be absolutely impossible, we deny. [We believe,] however, that on the day of resurrection, we shall all be gathered together, each with his body and soul, but we shall not eat or drink.

The religion of the cross has spread throughout the earth without the sword and without coercion. Your religion triumphed on the earth by the sword and coercion, and your lawgiver fought the nations and subdued them. He is to blame for the change in our situation and for our being accused of unbelief. In his Book [it is written]: 'They are unbelievers who say, "God is the Messiah, Mary's son".'[31] The Arabs entered our towns, uprooted our homes and exposed us to dishonour. When [your lawgiver] believed in God and called people to God, God supported him. Then he fought all the nations and subdued them by his sword. But the Messiah, Mary's Son, came only as a servant and in weakness, and He did not fight anyone. He was crucified to make satisfaction for us. He is our God, our Creator, our Provider, the One Who gives us life and takes it away. He (to Whom belong might and majesty!) forgives our sins by His grace and covers us with His mercy.

[29] A reference to the miracle each year on Easter Eve of the descent of the 'holy fire' in the Church of the Holy Sepulchre in Jerusalem.
[30] E.g. Q 2:25; 76:12-22.
[31] Q 5:72.

29

Trinitizing the unity of God

Juan Pedro Monferrer-Sala, University of Córdoba

Very little is known about *Tathlīth al-Waḥdāniyya* ('Trinitizing the unity [of God]'). Its author's use of Hebrew and Aramaic in quotations from the Jewish Bible and the Talmud suggests that he was probably a Jewish convert to Christianity. He was active in the latter part of the twelfth century. His work has not survived in its original form, but as a series of fragments quoted in *Al-iʿlām bi-mā fī dīn al-Naṣārā min al-fasād wa-l-awhām wa-iẓhār maḥāsin dīn al-Islām wa-ithbāt nubuwwat nabiyyinā Muḥammad* ('Information about the corruptions and disillusions of the religion of the Christians, and a presentation of the merits of the religion of Islam and an affirmation of the prophethood of our Prophet Muḥammad') by the Cordoban Muslim scholar Abū l-Ḥasan Aḥmad ibn ʿUmar ibn Ibrāhīm ibn ʿUmar al-Anṣārī l-Qurṭubī (1182–1258).

The paragraph translated below is an example of a frank and direct debate between a Christian and a Muslim, in which the Christian evidently does not feel intimidated by the subordinate position he and other non-Muslims occupy. He certainly does not try to conceal his distaste of Islam and its claims to have superseded Christianity. He quite rationally requires the Muslim to show that the authenticity of his faith is attested not just by the Qur'an but by Christian and Jewish scripture, and he confidently shows that the authority of Muḥammad as a legislator is undermined by the moral ambiguity of his judgement about divorce. He goes on to link this to the traditional Christian rejection of Islam on the basis of the exclusion of the Arabs' (and therefore Muslims') ancestor Ishmael from the line of Abraham's successors who would inherit God's promise.

CMR 4, pp. 115–17.

This translation is based on J.P. Monferrer-Sala and P. Mantas-España, *De Córdoba a Toledo: Tathlīth al-Waḥdāniyyah ('La Trinidad de la Unidad'). Fragmentos teológicos de un judeoconverso arabizado*, Madrid, 2018, para. 13, pp. 145–8.

And you, [Muslim] sir, search in your book in 'The Family of ʿImrān': 'And He sent down the Torah and the Gospel before, as guidance for the people'.[32] So you acknowledge the Torah and the Gospel, because you draw support for your religion from the Torah just as we draw support for our religion from the books of the prophets. Know that the situation is that we accept nothing from your books.

If you state something from your book [the Qur'an], I will say to you just as your Apostle [Muḥammad] said: 'The burden of proof is upon the claimant, and the oath is upon him who denies.'[33] So you must confirm your religion from the Torah and the Gospel, both of which you acknowledge. You claim that your book comes from God. Then find confirmation [for it] from the Torah in Hebrew and from the Gospel in Latin,[34] just as you claim. For your words are: 'Muḥammad is no more than an apostle; [other] apostles passed away before him.'[35] I ask you [for this] from the book which the apostles brought, as you say, for I need only swear an oath.[36] I deny before you and we do not accept before you the sayings of the Prophet and the reported accounts from Muslim[37] in his book which says: Sufyān related to us from al-Zuhrī from Qatāda from ʿĀ'isha,[38] who said: 'Rifāʿa's wife came to the Apostle and said to him: "I was Rifāʿa's, but he divorced me. Then I married ʿAbd al-Raḥmān ibn al-Zubayr." The Apostle smiled and laughed, and said: "Do you want to return to Rifāʿa? Not until you have enjoyed his [ʿAbd al-Raḥmān's] orgasm[39] and ʿAbd al-Raḥmān ibn al-Zubayr has enjoyed your orgasm"'.

In another transmission from ʿĀ'isha, she said: 'A man pronounced the triple divorce of his wife[40] and [another] man married her but divorced her before having intercourse with her. Then her first husband wanted to (re)marry her. The Messenger was asked about this and said: "Not until the other has enjoyed her orgasm which the first has".'[41]

Understand! We do not accept prophetic sayings such as these from you, because Christ says that is not fitting for a man to divorce his wife unless she has committed fornication, and if she has committed fornication he cannot lawfully return to her.

---

[32] Q 3:3-4.

[33] The point of this Ḥadīth (recorded in Abū Bakr al-Bayhaqī, *Kitāb al-sunan al-kabīr*, no. 20604) in this argument is that it is for Muslims to demonstrate that the Qur'an is a reliable source of evidence, and it is for Christians to swear to the contrary.

[34] *ʿAjamī* is a generic term used to denote a non-Arabic language, in this case obviously Latin. It is understandable that a former Jew converted to Christianity would refer to the Torah as well as the Gospel.

[35] Q 3:144.

[36] The Christian changes the referent of the term *rasūl* ('apostle', 'messenger') from Muḥammad to the apostles of Jesus. His general argument at this point is that he will not accept evidence about the status of the Qur'an from Muḥammad but only from the scriptures written by Jesus's followers, in view of the fact that Muḥammad was clearly capable of giving the most immoral advice and judgements, as the stories that follow demonstrate.

[37] Muslim ibn Ḥajjāj (d. 875), compiler of one of the two most authoritative collections of Ḥadīths.

[38] The line of transmitters of the Ḥadīth from Muslim back to ʿĀ'isha, the wife of Muḥammad.

[39] Or 'tasted his sweet essence'.

[40] Referring to the way in which a man can divorce his wife in Islam, by pronouncing the statement 'I divorce you' three times.

[41] On these Ḥadīths, see al-Bukhārī, *Ṣaḥīḥ*, no. 2445; Muslim, *Ṣaḥīḥ*, nos. 2587–90.

'Whoever divorces his wife has made a way for her to commit adultery,' meaning he who divorces her for no reason: 'And whosoever marries a divorced woman commits adultery with her.'[42] But you say that it is not lawful for her husband to return to her unless she has committed adultery. Instead of abstaining from adultery, you order adultery. This for you is the injunction of the goat: I want to cut off the goat's tail, and if we place it on him as a beard he will move his rump towards the biting icy wind of the north and the burning heat of the dog days in the south.[43] This reply to your words is a demand for justice from you – as your Qur'an says: 'He who demands justice after being wronged commits no sin.'[44] Understand!

Then you say in your 'detailed knowledge': 'Christians seek to justify their absurdities.' But you should justify your absurdities, for you have spoken baseless lies and insults against our religion. You have uttered falsehoods about our Christ. How could you say what you do not know? How could you dare to speak? Know that if you issue insults after this, I shall send to every place a book with the text of your law and with all the statements we know are in it, which you will not be able to deny.

Understand, for you have said that Christ is worthless and insignificant, you have angered the Judge[45] against you and against all the nations on the day of resurrection. But you will find him a Judge who does not require evidence. If after this you issue insults, I shall make known to you what your family tree is so that you will know who you are.

Understand that at the start I did not wish to insult anyone, but when he sent me the first writing with insults and offences I replied to him with the answer about his mother Hagar. I did not say about her one tenth of what God has said about her in the Torah. Listen to the words of God about her and her son: 'Sarah (saw) the son of Hagar the Egyptian, whom she had borne to Abraham, and he was playing. So she said to Abraham: "Cast out this bondswoman and her son, for this bondswoman and her son shall not inherit with my son Isaac". Abraham was grieved by what she said to him about his son. Then God said to Abraham: "Do not let Sarah's words about the boy and your bondswoman be grievous to you. All that Sarah has said to you, listen to her words".'

Then Abraham said: 'This is the actual word of God to me: "He shall not inherit from you; the one who came out of your loins, he shall inherit from you".' Then God said to Abraham: 'For through Isaac shall your offspring be named.'[46]

Understand, and you shall be rightly guided, and know how God cut off the inheritance of Ishmael and his mother in accordance with his promise: 'This one shall not inherit from you.' For He said to Abraham: 'For through Isaac shall your offspring be

---

[42] Matthew 5:32; cf. 19:9. The Christian is comparing statements from Jesus and Muḥammad about divorce and finding the latter grossly inferior.

[43] In this illustration of the Christian's point, just as a goat with its tail reversed absurdly exposes its unprotected rump to cold and heat, so Muslims expose themselves to derision by requiring their wives to commit adultery.

[44] A paraphrase of Q 42:41.

[45] Used in the Qur'an as a name of God (e.g. Q 31:27; 46:2), but here, of course, used for Jesus.

[46] Genesis 21:9-12.

named' – He did not say: 'Through Ishmael shall your offspring be named'. So by night Abraham took bread and a jar of water and put it on the bondswoman's shoulder, and he put Ishmael on her neck,[47] and he sent her away with her son from inhabited lands. From him was to rise up the nation about which your Qur'an says: '[The Arabs of the desert are] the most faithless, the most hypocritical.'[48]

So understand! Peace be upon him who follows the guidance and believes in the law of Christ, the true faith. The mercy and blessings of God be with him.[49]

---

[47] Genesis 21:14.

[48] Q 9:97.

[49] If the recognizably Muslim terms 'guidance' (*hudan*), which according to Q 27:77 is a name for the Qur'an, and 'law' (*sharī'a*), and the final blessing, have any more force than as elements of formal greetings, they emphasize the Christian's attitude that since Christianity is superior to Islam, components of Islam such as these can be repurposed.

30

Al-Bājī, *Book against the Torah*

Camilla Adang, Tel Aviv University

ʿAlāʾ al-Dīn ʿAlī ibn Muḥammad al-Bājī, sometimes also called al-Maghribī, was born in 1233. His place of birth is unknown, and it is unclear whether the place name al-Bājī refers to Beja in Portugal or Beja in Tunisia. According to some, he was related to the famous Andalusī Mālikī scholar Abū l-Walīd al-Bājī (d. 1081), himself the author of a polemic against Christianity. Unlike the latter Bājī and the vast majority of scholars from the Islamic West, ʿAlāʾ al-Dīn belonged to the Shāfiʿī school. He studied law in Syria, became a specialist in legal methodology, Ḥadīth, logic, grammar and Ashʿarī theology, and was renowned for his rhetorical skills. For some time ʿAlāʾ al-Dīn acted as qadi in the town of Karak southeast of the Dead Sea, on the main route from Damascus to Cairo and Mecca, then at an unknown date he moved to Cairo, where he died in 1314, having taught some of the most important scholars of his time, such as Abū Ḥayyān al-Gharnāṭī (d. 1344) and Taqī l-Dīn al-Subkī (d. 1355). His fame was eclipsed by that of his Ḥanbalī contemporary, the controversialist Ibn Taymiyya (d. 1328).

In the unique Istanbul manuscript of his work on the Pentateuch, which aims to expose illogicalities and inconsistencies in biblical narratives, the title is given as *Kitāb ʿalā l-Tawrāt* ('Book against the Torah'). Some modern scholars have taken this to mean that it is a polemic against Judaism, whereas in fact it mainly targets Christianity. It opens with the following statement: 'I studied the Torah of Moses (peace be upon him) rendered in Arabic which the Melkite Christians possess, as they claim, and it consists of five books. Questions occurred to me about its wording, which I present in the order of their appearance.' So ʿAlāʾ al-Dīn's rendering of biblical passages follows by and large the Arabic translation ascribed to the Melkite al-Ḥārith ibn Sinān of Ḥarrān (d. before 956).

CMR 4, pp. 767–8.

This translation is based on Abū l-Ḥasan ʿAlī l-Bājī, *ʿAlā l-Tawrāt. Kitāb fī naqḍ al-Tawrāt al-Yūnāniyya*, ed. Aḥmad Ḥijāzī l-Saqqā, Paris, 2006.

The question on the fifth reading[50] from the first book, from eighteen aspects[51]

The twelfth of them: How can it be rightly said: 'Then the serpent said to the woman: "You will surely not die. Rather, God knows that on the day you eat of [the tree] your eyes will be opened, and you will be like gods, knowing good and evil"'?[52] Was the serpent, one of the creeping animals, perhaps wiser than Adam and Eve, and more knowledgeable and understanding than they of the truth of the matter and the wishes of God, despite Adam's perfect knowledge, as is stated previously: 'So God created every beast of the field and every bird of the air, and brought them to Adam to see what he would call them; and whatever name Adam gave them and called a living creature by, that was its name'?[53] Now then, how does this relate to that?

If it is objected: Perhaps the serpent said these things out of ignorance, pretending to know? I shall reply: The full text demonstrates that [the serpent] spoke out of awareness, and that Adam and Eve were the ignorant ones, as it says: 'She also gave some to her husband, who was with her, and he ate. Then the eyes of both were opened, and they knew that they were naked.'[54] Also, how can it be rightly said: '[You will be] like gods,' when at that time only one God was known, and no unbelief or polytheism existed yet, nor were there multiple objects of worship? Also, how can it be rightly said: 'You will be like gods, knowing good and evil'? Were Adam and Eve ignorant, not knowing good and evil, despite Adam's perfect knowledge, as was mentioned before, or was it the serpent that did not know [of] good and evil, not having eaten from the tree? This is what they have both said, and this is what they know, as has been stated before.[55]

If it is objected: Perhaps [the serpent] said this because the devil[56] taught it this, or it was the devil himself who spoke from between its fangs; we shall reply: These two statements contradict the apparent sense of the Torah, and besides, we ask ourselves how the serpent could speak if it was not endowed with that faculty?

The thirteenth of them: How can it be rightly said: 'The woman saw that the tree was good for food',[57] when she had not up to that moment eaten anything from that tree and did not know its taste, and whether it was good or not?

The fourteenth of them: How can it be rightly said: 'They both ate and then their eyes were opened, and they knew that they were naked'?[58] Were they perhaps blind before they ate [from the tree], or were their eyes covered, although it is said before that 'the woman saw that the tree was good for food, pleasing to the eye and beautiful

[50] The division into readings (*qirā'a*) is one of the systems used in the Coptic tradition.
[51] Numbers 12–18 are given here.
[52] Genesis 3:4-5.
[53] Genesis 2:19.
[54] Genesis 3:6-7.
[55] The use of dual forms of verbs here would seem to refer to Jews and Christians.
[56] The author uses the Qur'anic name Iblīs.
[57] Genesis 3:6.
[58] Genesis 3:6.

to behold'?[59] How does this relate to that? Were they unaware that they were naked, despite the fact that Adam possessed perfect knowledge, as was mentioned before? How does this absolute ignorance relate to that perfect knowledge?

If it is objected: Maybe what is meant is the opening of their insight, not of their eyes; I shall reply: That is an interpretation that collides with the apparent sense, besides being incorrect, for it is not fitting that the disobedient person's insight should be increased as a result of this very disobedience; rather, it should be dimmed because of it.

The fifteenth of them: How can it be rightly said: 'And they heard the sound of the Lord God walking in the garden towards evening, so Adam and his wife hid from the face of the Lord God among the trees of the garden',[60] despite the fact that God (praised and glorified is He) is too exalted to make a sound walking! And although [the Christians] hold that He incarnated Himself in Jesus (peace be upon him) when he appeared, according to their belief, they admit that He did not assume a human form in the garden. In addition, Adam knew better than to presume that he could hide from the Lord (exalted is He) among the trees of the garden. These two questions apply similarly to what is stated after that: 'He said: I heard the sound of You walking in the garden, and I was afraid because I am naked, so I hid.'[61]

The sixteenth of them: How can it be rightly said: 'But the Lord God called Adam, and said to him, "Adam, where are you?"'[62] despite the fact that He was well aware of Adam and his whereabouts. It would not have occurred to Adam [to attempt to hide from God].

The seventeenth of them: How can it be rightly said: 'Who told you that you are naked?'[63] Was Adam, in his awareness of his being naked, in need of someone to tell him that? There is no greater stupidity than this, and nothing of the kind may be imagined of Adam, nor of the most ignorant one among us.

The eighteenth of them: How can it be rightly said that when God reproached Adam saying, 'If only you had not eaten of the tree which I had forbidden you', he defended himself saying, 'The woman you made to be with me, gave me of the tree, so I ate'?[64] How could it befit Adam to justify his disobedience to God by saying that it was the woman who had given him [of the tree] and that he therefore ate. [pp. 32–4]

---

[59] Genesis 3:6.

[60] Genesis 3:8.

[61] Genesis 3:10.

[62] Genesis 3:9.

[63] Genesis 3:11. The text has 'Who told you "I am naked"?'

[64] Genesis 3:11-12.

The question about the seventh reading, from three aspects.[65] I have not found the sixth reading in the Torah.[66]

The first is: How can it be rightly said: 'The Lord God said: "Adam has become like one of us, knowing good and evil"'?[67] Does anyone endowed with reason presume that divinity can be acquired, and moreover, acquired through eating? Also, the saying 'like one of us' implies a plurality in the Lord. The Jews do not hold this, for they believe in the oneness of God.

The second: How can it be rightly said, following this: 'And now perhaps he will stretch out his hand and take of the tree of life, and eat of it, and thus live forever'?[68] The apparent sense of it is that life and death are not in the hands of God or in His power, but are caused by certain foodstuffs, and that God feared that Adam would live eternally by eating from the tree, and that He therefore expelled him from the garden. Now then, if eating the fruit of the first tree necessarily led to the knowledge of good and evil, and eating from the second tree would necessarily have led to eternal life, as follows from the apparent sense of the text, Adam would inevitably have eaten from the second tree immediately after partaking of the first one, for he now knew good and evil and thus knew that this was good, and he would not be able to abstain from it.

Also, the use of the word 'perhaps' reflects a wish on the part of the speaker [God], which is not appropriate here. Rather, the proper term would be 'I fear'. In another copy it says: 'Now he will stretch out his hand'.[69] [p. 34]

---

[65] Here, the first two aspects are translated.

[66] The author skips from the fifth to the seventh reading; his source apparently lacked the sixth reading.

[67] Genesis 3:22.

[68] Genesis 3:23.

[69] Reading *al-ān* ('now') instead of the clearly inappropriate *al-ab* ('father'); in Arabic the appearance of the two words is very similar. Al-Bājī's mention of another copy hints at the care he has taken in his examination of the Pentateuch.

Greek

Greek authors responding to Islam

Johannes Pahlitzsch, Johannes Gutenberg University of Mainz

The Muslim-Arabic conquest of Syria, Palestine and Egypt was achieved within a few decades of the death of the Prophet Muḥammad in 632. Damascus fell to the Muslims just two years later, and in 636 the Byzantines were beaten decisively in the battle of Yarmuk. In 638 the Greek Patriarch Sophronius surrendered Jerusalem to the Caliph ʿUmar, and in 642 Egypt was conquered. The loss of these provinces, in addition to concurrent Slavic migration into the Balkans, caused an existential crisis in Byzantium which in turn led to a fundamental modification of the Byzantine state. However, the Byzantine Church survived under Muslim rule with its members now called Melkites, and Greek learning continued at least until the eighth century. Accordingly, John of Damascus (d. *c.* 750), the son of an important Christian civil servant in the service of the Umayyad Caliph ʿAbd al-Malik (r. 685–705), included in his compendium of heresies (*De haeresibus*) the earliest Byzantine description of Islam, which he considered to be an Arian heresy and not a new independent religion.

After overcoming the great crises of the seventh and eighth centuries and refuting Islamic attempts to conquer the city, Byzantium was gradually able to counterbalance the power of the ʿAbbasid Caliphate in Baghdad. Thus, by the middle of the ninth century two seemingly closed societies stood face-to-face, each driven by its need to demonstrate its own distinctive ideology and identity. As a result, the dispute with the Muslims was increasingly conducted not only by force of arms but also ideologically. Theological thinking specifically about Islam developed. The Qur'an was probably translated in its entirety into Greek, enabling Nicetas of Byzantium, who lived and worked in the second half of the ninth century in Constantinople, to produce his profound refutation of Islam. But the conflict was also addressed more in hagiography, which was more accessible to a broader audience, as in the *Life* of the 42 Martyrs of Amorion, an important Byzantine stronghold in Asia Minor that was sacked by Caliph al-Muʿtaṣim (r. 833–42) in 838.

Relations between the Byzantine Empire and the Caliphate and its successors between the ninth and eleventh centuries were characterized mainly by military confrontations, the Ḥamdānid emirate of Aleppo being the most formidable adversary. In reality, however, there was a great deal of contact and interchange at different levels. Byzantine diplomatic relations and cultural exchanges with the caliphate intensified, as they did with the more or less autonomous emirates that emerged in the northern Syrian border zone as the caliphate fragmented. Further, alongside the constant raids and skirmishes across the border, personal relationships developed between the contending elites, who often shared common chivalrous ideals. The most famous example of this cross-border culture is the epic named after its hero, *Digenēs Akritēs*. Indeed the name Digenēs Akritēs says it all, referring to his origin 'of two races' (*Digenēs*), his father being a Muslim emir from Syria who abducted the daughter of a Byzantine general during a raid, eventually converted to Christianity and settled on Byzantine soil.

The re-establishment of Byzantine rule in northern Syria through the foundation of the *doukaton* ('duchy') of Antioch in 969 and the treaties concluded between the Fāṭimids and the Byzantine emperors in the eleventh century led to increased Byzantine influence and wider knowledge of Greek in Syria and Palestine. It seemed as if Byzantium was on the verge of a re-establishing itself as a major power in West Asia. The Fāṭimid rulers of Cairo acknowledged the Byzantine emperor as the 'protector' of the Orthodox Christians in the Holy Land in the 1030s. Patriarchs were now again appointed by Byzantium and were regarded by the emperors as representatives of the emperor and the Orthodox Church in the region. Numerous Byzantine pilgrims travelled in the Holy Land and took up residence in monasteries in Palestine.

However, with the Seljuk expansion in Asia Minor as a consequence of the Byzantine civil war in the 1070s and the establishment of the Crusader states in Syria and Palestine, Byzantium lost its dominant position in West Asia, this time for good. Byzantium's most important Muslim adversaries were now the invaders of Turkish origin in Asia Minor, which had to this point been the core of the empire. After a period of stability and re-conquest under the Komnenian emperors in the twelfth century, as witnessed in Nicetas Choniates' chronicle, the decline of Byzantium continued with the Latin conquest of Constantinople in 1204 and the progressing Turkish conquest of Asia Minor. West Asia became thus a very remote region for the Byzantines and one of only minor political importance. Nevertheless, generally good relations existed between Byzantium and the Mamlūk sultans of Egypt after the Byzantine re-conquest of Constantinople 1261 and the establishment of the Palaeologian dynasty.

As far as western Asia Minor and relations with the Turkish Muslims were concerned, from the end of the thirteenth century onwards Byzantium was no longer capable of fending off the attacks of various Turkish groups. Two civil wars in the 1320s and in the 1340s and 1350s crucially weakened the empire, largely through the opposing parties courting Turkish rulers in Asia Minor as allies. As a consequence of these military alliances, Turkish troops crossed over to the Balkans and soon pursued their own interests. Great parts of the Byzantine population in Thrace and Macedonia were plundered and enslaved.

In Byzantium the result of these intensified conflicts were new debates concerning Islam. Emperor Manuel II Palaeologus (r. 1392–1425) himself wrote one of the best-known refutations of Islam. In 1453 Constantinople was finally conquered by Meḥmed II and the Byzantine Empire was irretrievably lost. Byzantine culture, however, continued to exist, in particular under the Orthodox Church. Meḥmed ensured that, in the person of Gennadios Scholarios, who composed a rather accommodating rebuttal of Islam, a new Patriarch was appointed in Constantinople and soon the Orthodox Church accustomed themselves to the new situation with the sultan in part taking on the role of the emperor.

Further reading

A. Beihammer, *Byzantium and the Emergence of Muslim-Turkish Anatolia, c. 1040–1130*, Abingdon, 2019.

L. Brubaker and J. Haldon, *Byzantium in the Iconoclast Era: c. 680–850. A History*, Cambridge, 2011.

Zachary Chitwood and Johannes Pahlitzsch (eds), *Ambassadors, Artists, Theologians. Byzantine Relations with the Near East from the Ninth to the Thirteenth Centuries*, Mainz, 2019.

N. Drocourt, 'Christian-Muslim Diplomatic Relations: An Overview of the Main Sources and Themes of an Encounter [620s–1000]', in D. Thomas (ed.), *Christian-Muslim Relations. A Bibliographical History*, vol. 2, Leiden, 2010, 29–72.

Nadia Maria El Cheikh, *Byzantium Viewed by the Arabs*, Cambridge, MA, 2004.

A. Asa Eger, *The Islamic-Byzantine Frontier. Interaction and Exchange among Muslim and Christian Communities*, London, 2014.

Adel Théodore Khoury, *Apologétique byzantine contre l'islam (VIIIe–XIIIe s.)*, Altenberge, 1982.

Nevra Necipoglu, *Byzantium between the Ottomans and the Latins. Politics and Society in the Late Empire*, Cambridge, 2009.

Klaus-Peter Todt, *Dukat und griechisch-orthodoxes Patriarchat von Antiocheia in mittelbyzantinischer Zeit (969–1084)*, Mainz, 2020.

31

John of Damascus, *On heresies*, chapter 100

Manolis Ulbricht, Freie Universität Berlin

John was born in Muslim-ruled Damascus around the middle of the seventh century into a Christian family that followed the Byzantine rite (making them Melkites). His father and grandfather were both high ranking officials in the city's Muslim administration, as was John himself, being a member of the financial apparatus of the Umayyad caliphate. It was probably under the reign of the Caliph ʿUmar II (r. 717–20), who was particularly favourable towards Muslims at the expense of Christians and others, that he left his position and entered the Monastery of Mār Saba near Jerusalem, where he stayed until the end of his life. John of Damascus wrote several important works, bringing together the theological and philosophical knowledge of his time.

His main work is the 'Fount of knowledge' (*Pēgē gnōseōs*), a compendium of texts divided into three books: 'Best of Greek philosophy' (*Capita philosophica*, also called *Dialectica*), 'On heresies' (*De haeresibus*) and 'Explanation of the true faith' (*Expositio fidei*). In the second book, *De haeresibus*, John discusses various 'heresies', including under this label Christian and Jewish sects, and also ancient philosophical schools. The work may be characterized as a kind of catalogue and summary of 100 'heresies', the last of which is the *laoplanēs thrēskeia tōn Ismaēlitōn* ('the people-deceiving cult of the Ishmaelites'), Islam.

This 100th chapter of *De haeresibus* is the earliest detailed description of Islam in Byzantine literature. In it Islam is not perceived as a separate religion, but is placed among other Christian and Jewish groups.

Translated here are those passages that document John's perception of the religious and historical origins of Islam and the Prophet Muḥammad, as well as the Muslims' views about God and Christ. In addition, there are also examples of apologetic and polemical topics, such as his response to the Muslim accusation that Christianity is polytheism and that Christians worship the Cross, as well as his views about the Kaʿba in Mecca, and polygamy.

CMR 1, pp. 295–301. See further:

Joachim Braun, 'John of Damascus (died 754)', in G. Tamer, *Handbook of Qur'ānic Studies*, Berlin (forthcoming).

This translation is based on B. Kotter, *Die Schriften des Johannes von Damaskos*, vol. 4. *Liber de haeresibus. Opera polemica*, Berlin, 1981.

Finally, there is also still the people-deceiving cult of the Ishmaelites, a forerunner of the Antichrist, that is still influential to this day. It is derived from Ishmael, who was born to Abraham by Hagar. Therefore, they are called Hagarenes or Ishmaelites. However, they are called Saracens ('Sara-empty'), because Hagar said to the angel: 'Sara sent me away empty'.[1] They were idolaters and worshipped the morning star and Aphrodite, whom they also called *Khabar* in their language, which means 'the great'.

Until the time of Emperor Heraclius[2] they were apparently idolaters, but since then and until nowadays, a false prophet grew up for them, Muḥammad [Mamedh][3] by name, who, after he had made acquaintance with the Old and the New Testaments and apparently conversed with an Arian monk, created his own heresy. In order to appear to the people as evoking the fear of God, he spread the rumour that a scripture from God descended from heaven to him. [...]

He says that God is One, Creator of all things; He is neither begotten nor has He begotten.[4] He says that Christ is the Word of God and the Spirit from Him,[5] created and a servant, and that he was born to Mary, the sister of Moses and Aaron,[6] without seed. For the Word of God, he says, and the Spirit descended upon Mary,[7] and she bore Jesus, who was a prophet and a servant of God. And that the Jews sinned and wanted to crucify him, but that they had only seized a mere shadow image of him, which they crucified; but Christ himself, he says, was neither crucified nor did He die: because God took him up into heaven, because He loved him.[8] And he says furthermore that when Christ ascended to heaven, God asked him: 'Jesus, did you say: "I am the Son of God and God Himself"?' And Jesus, he says, replied: 'Have mercy with me, Lord!

---

[1] See Genesis 21:9-14, also 16:1-8.

[2] Byzantine emperor (r. 610–41) at the time Muḥammad started his prophetic career.

[3] The version of the name Muḥammad that appears throughout this chapter.

[4] A combination of the opening words of the Nicene Creed: 'We believe in one God, the Father, the Almighty, maker of heaven and earth, of all that is, seen and unseen,' and Q 112:1-3: Say, He is God, one; God, the eternal; He has not begotten nor been begotten.

[5] Q 4:171.

[6] Q 19:28.

[7] See Q 5:47 and 19:21, though this reproduces Luke 1:35.

[8] Q 4:157-8. 'They had only seized a mere shadow of him' is a free interpretation of *walākin shubbiha lahum*, 'he (or "it") was made to appear so to them'. Muslim exegetes have often understood this to mean that Jesus's appearance was put on another individual who was crucified in his place.

You know that I did not say that and that I did not show myself to be arrogant as your servant. Rather, it was the evildoers among the people who wrote that I had said such things: They invented lies against me and strayed from the right path.' And, he says, God answered him: 'I know that you did not say that.'[9] [pp. 60–1, lines 1–31]

But they call us 'polytheists' because, as they claim, we secretly place alongside God an associate god by saying that Christ is the Son of God and that he is God Himself. We answer them: 'This is what the prophets and the scripture have conveyed; and you acknowledge the prophets, as you yourselves affirm. So if we falsely claim that Christ is the Son of God, it is they who have taught and conveyed this to us.' Some of them say that we ourselves added such assertions when we interpreted the prophets; others, however, say that the Jews misled us out of hatred and wrote it down as if it came from the prophets, so that we might perish.

We in turn say to them: 'Since you yourselves say that Christ is the Word and the Spirit of God, why do you revile us as "polytheists"? For the Word and the Spirit are inseparable from the One in which they are [...]. Therefore, by wanting to avoid attaching something to God, you have mutilated Him. For it would be better for you to say that God has an associate god than to mutilate Him and secretly turn Him into a stone or a piece of wood or something inanimate. Therefore, you falsely accuse us and call us polytheists; but we call you God's mutilators.'

But they slander us as idolaters because we worship the Cross, which they even despise. We answer them: 'What now? Do you not rub a stone at your Kaʿba (*khabathan*) and kiss it reverently?'[10] Some of them say that Abraham lay with Hagar upon it, but others say that he tied his camel to it when he intended to sacrifice Isaac. But to them we answer: 'The scripture says that there was a grove-like mountain and wood from which Abraham split logs for the burnt offering, and burdened Isaac with them, and that he left the mules with the servants[11]: So where does your fairy tale come from? For there is neither wood in it, nor do asses pass through it.' They shy away from it, but still claim that it is Abraham's stone. So, we say: 'Let it be Abraham's, as you foolishly say – you are not afraid to worship it because Abraham laid upon it with his wife, or because he tied his camel to it. But you accuse us of worshipping the Cross of Christ, by which the power of the evil spirits and the aberration of the devil were destroyed.' This so-called stone is, however, the head of Aphrodite, whom they used to worship and call *Khabar*, and even today, if you look closely you can see the traces of engraving on the stone.

This Muḥammad [...] composed many absurd stories and gave each of them a name, e.g. the 'Scripture of the Woman', in which he states that a man may take four wives and as many concubines as he can, thousands even, as many as he can

[9] See Q 5:116-17.
[10] The Black Stone, set into the southeastern corner of the Kaʿba, which Muslims are required to kiss or touch as they circumambulate the Kaʿba.
[11] Genesis 22:3-13.

retain next to the four wives.[12] But if you want to divorce one, you can do that at will and take another. He ordered this for the following reason[13]: Muḥammad had a comrade named Zayd, who had a beautiful wife with whom Muḥammad had fallen in love. When they were sitting together, Muḥammad said: 'Someone, I mean God, has commanded me to marry your wife.' And he answered: 'You are the messenger: do as God has told you to do and take my wife.' [...] And in order to be able to commit adultery with her, he established the following law: 'Whoever wants to, shall dismiss his wife. But if he wants to turn to her again after her release, she shall marry someone else beforehand.'[14] [...] In the same scripture, he proclaims the following: 'Cultivate the field which God has given to you and work it with zeal, and do that and in this way'[15] – so as not to mention, as he does, all obscene things. [pp. 63–5, lines 61–113]

[12] *Sūrat al-nisā'* ('The chapter of women'), Q 4:3.
[13] This incident, referred to in Q 33:36-7, in which Muḥammad's adopted son Zayd ibn Ḥāritha divorced his wife and Muḥammad then married her, became a major topic of criticisms by Christians, who accused Muḥammad of forcing Zayd to divorce her for the sole purpose of enjoying her for himself, and by implication of uttering revelations according to his desires.
[14] Q 2:230.
[15] Q 2:223, sometimes understood as allowing anal intercourse.

32

Theophanes the Confessor, *Chronographia*

Thomas Pratsch, Johannes Gutenberg University of Mainz

Theophanes the Confessor (*c.* 760–817/18), monk and abbot of the monastery of Megas Agros in Bithynia, wrote a Byzantine world chronicle from the creation to the year 813/14. While many aspects of this *Chronographia* are still under discussion, including the authorship of certain parts, the written and oral sources, the working method used, there is no doubt that it is one of the most important historical sources for the period between the middle of the seventh century and the beginning of the ninth century in the Middle Eastern world.

The paragraph below shows open contempt for the Arabs as poor livestock farmers who live in the desert and dwell in tents, and even stronger contempt for the person of Muḥammad, who is portrayed as an extremely weak character, destitute and orphaned, and also an epileptic. He is compelled by his circumstances to enter the service of a rich and well-respected widow, who is one of his relatives, and has to use flattery to win her heart and marry her, and to keep her at his side. It emerges that his whole claim to be a prophet is based on a lie which he has invented in order to disguise his epileptic seizures. His teachings have no truth in them and do not make sense.

CMR 1, pp. 426–36.

This translation is based on *Theophanis chronographia*, ed. C. de Boor, 2 vols, Leipzig, 1883–5 (repr. Hildesheim, 1963, 1980), pp. 333–4.

In this year Mouamed [Muḥammad], the leader and false prophet of the Saracens, died after promoting his relative Aboubacharos [Abū Bakr] to his leadership. At the same time his reputation spread, and all were in fear. When he first appeared, the misled

Jews believed him to be the Messiah who was awaited by them, so that some of their leaders followed him and accepted his religion and rejected that of Moses, who had seen God. There were ten in number who did this, and they followed him until his killing.[16] But after they saw him eating camel meat, they realized that he was not the one they had believed he was. They did not know what to do, though since they were afraid of rejecting his religion, these wretched men told him wicked things about us, the Christians, and remained with him.

I think it is necessary to give an account of his descent. This man descended from a very ordinary tribe, from Ishmael, the son of Abraham. Now Nizaros,[17] a descendant of Ishmael, is held to be the father of them all. This man had two sons, Moudaros and Rabias, and Moudaros fathered Kourasos, Kaïsos, Themimes, Asandos and others whose names are unknown. These all lived in the Mardianite desert, and there they bred livestock and dwelt in tents. Further into the interior, there were also others who did not belong to their tribe but to Iktean, the so-called Amanites, that is Homerites. Some of them engaged in trade on their camels.

Since the above-mentioned Mouamed was destitute and an orphan, it seemed reasonable to him to enter the service of a wealthy woman as a hired worker who tended the camels and traded in Egypt and Palestine. She was one of his relatives, called Chadiga [Khadīja]. But after a short time, he became more audacious and more acquainted with the woman, who was a widow, and he took her to wife and thus gained her camels and her possessions. When he came to Palestine he met with Jews and Christians and grasped from them some exegetical interpretations. But he had the disease of epilepsy. When his wife realized this, she was deeply disappointed that as a noble woman she was married to such a man who was not only poor but also an epileptic. He tried to calm her, saying: 'I see a vision of a certain angel called Gabriel, and because I cannot sustain the sight of him, I become weak and fall.' Now she had a certain monk living there, who had been exiled for his heretical views, and he was a friend of hers. She told him everything, and also the name of the angel. This man wanted to please her and said to her: 'He spoke the truth, for this angel is sent to all the prophets.'[18]

She was the first who believed him after she had received the false monk's answer and proclaimed to other women of her tribe that he was a prophet. In this way, his fame spread from the women to the men, first to Aboubacharos, whom he appointed to be his successor. His heresy was spread in the region of Ethribos [Yathrib, later

[16] This word, *sphagē*, usually carries overtones of sacrifice and sacrificial slaughter, which neither Muslim nor Christian authors associate with the death of Muḥammad. The fact that Theophanes says no more about it suggests that he may not have meant by it anything more than 'death'.

[17] For the name of the tribes mentioned here, see C. Mango and R. Scott, *The Chronicle of Theophanes Confessor. Byzantine and Near-Eastern History AD 284–813*, Oxford, 1997, p. 465.

[18] This figure appears to be a combination of Waraqa ibn Nawfal, Khadīja's cousin who interpreted Muḥammad's first experience of revelation, and the Christian known as Baḥīrā or Sergius, a monk who in Christian tradition was a heretic and assisted Muḥammad with sources, and in Muslim tradition recognized him as the prophet who was to come.

renamed Medina], by war if necessary: at first secretly for ten years, then by war again for ten years, and then openly for nine years.

He taught his followers that he who kills an enemy or is killed by an enemy will enter paradise. He said that this paradise was one where the body would eat and drink and have intercourse with women, and there were rivers of wine, honey and milk, and the women were not like the ones on earth but different, and intercourse would last for a long time and provide continuous pleasure, and other things full of debauchery and foolishness, and also that people should have sympathy for one another and help those who suffered from injustice.

33

Nicetas of Byzantium, *Refutation of the Qur'an*

Manolis Ulbricht, Freie Universität Berlin

Nicetas of Byzantium was a scholar and theologian who lived and worked in Constantinople in the second half of the ninth century and probably until the beginning of the tenth century. He apparently had close ties to the Patriarchate and the imperial court. He wrote anti-heretical works against the Latin dogma of the *filioque*, the miaphysitism of the Armenians, and Islam.

Nicetas's *magnum opus* is the *Anatropē tou Koraniou* ('Refutation of the Qur'an'), which he penned around 856–63. Preserved in a single codex (Vat. gr. 681), this is one of the first Byzantine polemics that comprehensively engages not only with Islam as a new community of faith, but does so by examining very closely its scriptural text, the Qur'an. For his refutation, Nicetas quotes, at times extensively, a Greek translation of the Qur'an of unknown authorship that must already have been in existence. Its original is lost today but these fragments are remnants of the earliest known complete translation of the Qur'an, which can be called *Coranus Graecus*.

After an extensive defence of the 'Orthodox belief', Nicetas refutes selected passages of the Qur'an. His work is organized into individual *confutationes* ('confutations') that each treat one *sūra*, though *sūras* 19–114 are briefly treated together in a single *confutatio*. Nicetas concludes his work by refuting a selection of Muslim teachings, ordered according to various theological and polemical themes. The image he constructs of Islam, as well as his patterns of argument, remained influential in anti-Islamic Byzantine literature well into the thirteenth century.

Various parts of *confutatio* 1, in which Nicetas presents his methodological approach, are translated below. In them, Nicetas defines the parameters (structure, content, character) that constitute a holy scripture, as well as the characteristics by which godly, human and demonic discourse can be recognized. He establishes four categories (theology, physiology, ethics and history) into which he divides the contents of the Qur'an thematically, and levels the accusation that it plagiarizes the Old and New Testaments. Last come two polemical passages in which he treats the ritual pilgrimage to Mecca and the relation between man and woman in Islam.

CMR 1, pp. 751–6. See further:

M. Ulbricht, 'Der Islam-Diskurs bei Niketas von Byzanz. Themen und Argumentation in seinem Hauptwerk "Widerlegung des Korans" (*Ἀνατροπὴ τοῦ Κορανίου*)', *Byzantinische Zeitschrift* 114 (2021) 1351–94

This translation is based on K. Förstel, *Niketas von Byzanz. Schriften zum Islam*, Würzburg, 2000 (with German translation).

The pitiable and irrational little book of the Arab Muḥammad, which is full of all sorts of improper and loutish abominations after blaspheming against the Most High, does not preserve the compositional sequence that corresponds to generally disseminated and recognized works. For it offers neither the style of prophetic speech, nor of historical or legislative or theological exposition, nor any style whatsoever that emanates from right and rational thought; rather, it has a completely confused and disordered composition. [p. 42, lines 44–50]

All action and speech can be divided into three types: divine, human and demonic. Since the Arab does not know the first two types, namely divine and human, he is necessarily placed in the third. That he lacks human wisdom, not to speak of his lack of divine enlightenment, is evident from the following, as well as from many other signs. Human wisdom treats topics from theology, the science of natural phenomena (*physiologia*), ethics, history and similar fields, and it does this in a reasonable manner. But the author of this silly writing does not excel in either of the two ways of wisdom.

Concerning theology, he utters the godless statement according to which the Godhead is spherical, or rather, as he himself said, that God is a full sphere (*holosphyros*),[19] considering Him to be a body outright, for otherwise He could not have taken the form of a sphere. If, according to him, God is a material sphere, He will neither hear nor see, that is, with the spiritual eye; nor will He further act when, for

[19] A reference to Q 112:2, *Allāh al-ṣamad*, which is variously interpreted to mean: God the everlasting, the absolute, a refuge for all, and so on. The noun *ṣamad* can also mean something that is solid or invulnerable. Used according to this meaning, the term was translated into Greek as *holosphyros*, giving rise to the idea that the God of Muḥammad was a dense, lifeless sphere.

instance, hit by another body, but He will senselessly move mainly downwards. [...] If he calls heaven itself God, as many pagans have foolishly claimed, then our judgement, which has styled him as possessed by a demon, may also be true. Concerning the science of natural phenomena (*physiologia*), he either knows of nothing to say, or he says, if he has dared to glance at this field, that the human develops out of a leech[20] and that the sun, when it moves west, submerges itself in warm water.[21] What does he say concerning ethics? 'Conjoin with your souls'[22] and 'Be enemies to all as they are enemies to you'.[23] With respect to history (*historia*),[24] [...] how many lies does he spread in the story about Moses and even about our Lord Jesus Christ. [...] He claims the mother of Christ is the sister of Moses,[25] and that the Christians were in the desert together with Moses. [...] [p. 44, lines 72–98]

Besides, it is reassuring to know that everything he produces from the Old and from the New Scripture is distorted. [...] This, incidentally, clearly reveals his foolishness and unmasks it. [...] His own work [the Qur'an] clearly attests to his dominating fear of failing with his foolish undertaking. In almost every single chapter he demands that there shall be no doubt that he has received from God this God-offending scripture. [...] But it has escaped the camel shepherd's notice that simply preaching for and of God is not a sign of a true preacher and a true God; it is only so when the preacher is actually a preacher of a true God. [pp. 48–50, lines 164–90]

So that his cunning might become quite clear, he incites the miserable barbarians [Muslims] to worship the idol located in Baka[26] [Mecca], which he calls the object of worship (*proskynēma*) of [religious] observance (*paratērēmatos*). For he says: 'Wherever you are, turn your faces to the direction of the place of worship (*proskynētērion*) of [religious] observance (*paratērēmatos*).'[27] And he says that two barbaric names, Safa and Marwa, belong to the holy signs of God,[28] surely only of his god. And he orders the people whom he has deceived, once they have arrived at the abominable building at the site of prayer, to walk in circles around it. As we have learned from one of their people who has come over to the Christians, a stone idol sits in the middle of the house. So, the people who fulfil the instructions of this man possessed by the devil bow their miserable necks, stretch one hand out up to the idol, hold their ear with the other, and run in circles until they fall down gripped by giddiness. I believe this statue

---

[20] See Q 23:13-14.
[21] Q 18:86.
[22] Q 2:223.
[23] Q 2:194.
[24] Meaning 'biblical reports'.
[25] Q 19:28, where Mary is addressed as 'Sister of Aaron', the brother of Moses.
[26] Q 3:96, where the name appears as Bakka, understood to be identical with Mecca.
[27] Q 2:144. This translation of the term *al-masjid al-ḥarām*, referring to the sacred mosque in Mecca, indicates that the Greek translator(s) possessed deep understanding of the Arabic original. Both *masjid* and *proskynēma* or *proskynētērion* derive from verbs that mean 'to prostrate' and hence 'to worship'.
[28] Q 2:158. Al-Ṣafā and al-Marwa are the two low hills near the Kaʿba between which pilgrims hurry as part of the *ḥajj* observances.

is that well-known idol of Aphrodite, as they would probably claim themselves.[29] [p. 56, lines 311–24]

By mendaciously encouraging them to abstinence and chastity he says: 'Your women are your seed fields; go in unto your seed fields whenever you want to, and conjoin with your souls,'[30] that is: fulfil your soul's every desire. So, this life is animal-like, or rather, demonic. When he mentions the wife's divorce from the husband he says the following to the barbarians: 'If someone dismisses his wife, he should not be allowed to remarry her after her dismissal until she marries another man; and if the second dismisses her, then it is not a condemnation against them turning to each other once again.'[31] For, he says, 'These are the commandments of God.' Oh, away with the barbaric debauchery! [p. 58, lines 357–66]

---

[29] Pilgrims are enjoined to kiss or touch the Black Stone, which is set into the southeast corner of the Kaʿba, as they make each circuit of the sacred building.

[30] Q 2:223.

[31] Q 2:230.

34

Euodios the Monk, *Martyrdom of the forty-two martyrs*

Athina Kolia-Dermitzaki, National and Kapodistrian University of Athens

The *Martyrdom of the forty-two martyrs* has come down in nine versions, seven of which are dated to the ninth century, one to the tenth century, and another between the tenth and twelfth centuries. In three of the long (Z, K, M) and one abridged version (A), the author is identified as Euodios the Monk (about whom very little is known, except that he probably lived in Constantinople somewhere between the early or middle ninth to the late ninth or early tenth centuries, and was a monk in the monastery of Joseph the Hymnographer), in two others (D and E) as Sophronios, Archbishop of Cyprus (*CMR* 1, pp. 675–8), in G as Michael the Synkellos (*CMR* 1, pp. 627–31), and in the remaining two (*CMR* 1, pp. 636–8 and 639–41) he is not named. The date of the work has been placed between 855 and 887, although somewhere between the second half of the ninth and first half of the tenth centuries has also been suggested.

The work is an encomium of the forty-two officers of the Byzantine army who were captured on 15 August 838, during the sack of the city of Amorion, the capital of the Anatolian *theme*, by the ʿAbbasid Caliph al-Muʿtaṣim (r. 833–42). They were held in a dungeon in Tarsus for six years and six months with a view to making a prisoner exchange, but they were executed on 6 March 845 while negotiations were still underway. It has been suggested that the reason for this was that al-Muʿtaṣim's successor al-Wāthiq (r. 842–7) used their killing as a show of strength within the Islamic Empire in order to impose his religious policy.

The text of the *Martyrdom* begins with a long account of the expansion of the Arabs into Byzantine territory, and the miserable consequences this had for the population of the imperial provinces. This is followed by a brief (Z, K, A, though in M this is long) description of the siege and sack of Amorion, and a detailed account of the hardships suffered by the captive officers during their imprisonment and the pressures they came under to renounce their faith. Particularly significant are the debates between the prisoners and the religious representatives sent by the caliph, and the arguments used by either side.

It is from these dialogues that the passages presented here have been selected, as they constitute examples of popular Christian and Muslim polemical arguments in refutation of each other's religion.

CMR 1, pp. 844–7. See also:

A. Rigo, 'Nicetas Byzantios, la sua opera e il Monaco Evodio', in G. Fiaccadori (ed.), *In partibus Clius. Scritti in onore di Giovanni Pugliese Carratelli*, Naples, 2006, pp. 147–87.

This translation is based on the edition by V. Vasilievskij and P. Nikitin, *Skazanija o 42 amorijskix mučenikax*, St Petersburg, 1905, pp. 61–78 (version Z of the *Martyrdom*).

12. After he [al-Mu'taṣim] returned to his own territory [following the sack of Amorion], he placed the [...] commanders of the [Byzantine] troops in a dark and filthy prison, bound tightly to stocks with double and triple iron chains. After issuing an order that they were to be punished by being given only a small amount of bread and an even smaller measure of water, he placed guards and wardens so that nobody except the guards might associate with them. [...]

15. As long as their earlier bodily strength[32] remained in these most valiant men, the barbarians refrained from mentioning their faith. When, however, they observed that the prisoners were emaciated and looked like mummies, some of the connoisseurs and interpreters [of the Qur'an][33] who pretended to be devout and displayed a hypocritical humanity began coming to the prison, prompted by the commander of their nation, [...] and [...] attempted to provoke them to renounce their faith in Christ. For that fearsome lord believed that he would have gained nothing from such a great and wealthy city [Amorion] without the conversion of these saints to his own faith. [...]

16. When the saints [...] rejected this suggestion as despicable, the men who were inciting them to renounce their faith responded [... 17.]: 'Pretend that you have been circumcised and pray with the caliph[34] and, after you have received a multitude of benefactions from him, desert during combat[35] and return to your religion and your nation.' [...] But the true servants of Christ said to them: 'In other words, if the same woes that now oppress us had befallen you, would you stoop to do what you advise us to do?' They responded: 'What is more necessary than life, and a free and comfortable one at that?' [...] and immediately the Christ-loving men said: 'But we certainly will

[32] Literally, 'power of the flesh', which declines, as opposed to their spiritual resolve which remained firm.

[33] Literally, 'some of the Gnostics among them', probably the *mutakallimūn* (theological specialists).

[34] Al-Wāthiq (r. 842–7), al-Mu'taṣim's successor.

[35] Both Arabs and Byzantines used to incorporate prisoners of war and defectors into their armies, which understandably often resulted in desertions to the opposition.

not put up with accepting advice about our faith from a soul that does not stand by his own faith.'

18. After a few days, others came and used the same method as the ones before, [...] saying [19.] 'If you leave the narrow path along which the son of Mary[36] is exhorting you to walk and follow the wide and spacious road which the humane and great Prophet has promised, you will bless us for being your good counsellors and benefactors. What does our Prophet teach the infidel when he says that God can fill those who obey Him with all manner of delicacies in this world and bequeath Paradise to them in the other? [... 20.] For when God, being merciful, saw that every man who desired to follow the stern precepts of Jesus was unhappy, He sent His Prophet Muḥammad to relieve men from every burden, dispel all that sadness and promise the double enjoyment of luxuries in this life and delight in the next, and, through their faith, save those who obey Him.' [21.] As soon as those prudent men heard this nonsense, [...] they said to them: 'And this is what you consider a true and God-pleasing test, to be defeated in everything by the appetites of the flesh and submit your reason to anger and malice and various pleasures, with none of them to be defeated by wisdom or reined in by the bridle and muzzle of temperance? Living in such a way, how will a human differ from an irrational beast?' [...]

27. Being imprisoned for seven whole years, [...] they never stopped meditating upon the hymns of David[37] day and night, nor did they neglect the customary prayers, either together or individually. [... 28.] Then, while the saints were in the midst of this state of ascetic attentiveness, [... 30.] there appeared [in the prison] on the morning [of 6 March 845] an official bearing a fearfully arrogant attitude, sent by the caliph with an armed escort. [...] When the saints stood before him, he said to them: '[...] After everything, are the lords of the Romans[38] so foolish as to think that such a great and valiant nation [as the Muslims], so numerous and powerful, was created without the help of divine providence? But this inevitably attaches to those who hate God.' [32.] And the saints responded: 'That is not what we say, [...] only that your view of God is misguided. While you confess [...] that He is the Maker of all things, both the visible and invisible, you slander Him by calling Him the Creator of good and evil, truth and lies, law and lawlessness, justice and injustice, tolerance and insolence, benevolence and temerity, prudence and promiscuity, and all other such opposite forces and actions that exist.' [... 33.] The official said: 'So, what are you claiming, that there is another god who created every form of evil and sin, [...] and that there are two (gods), one good, the other evil? Then how was the world created with the two of them fighting each other?'[39] The saints replied: 'No other do we call God than

[36] Euodios sensitively makes the Muslims use the title of Jesus that is characteristically used in the Qur'an.
[37] The Psalms.
[38] The Byzantines, who considered themselves (and were considered by others) 'Romans' and their empire the 'Roman Empire'.
[39] In Q 21:22 the idea of two gods is rejected on the grounds that inevitable opposition between them would have prevented the world from being created.

Him who is good, if possible; but [we claim] that after disputing [with God] one of the angels of his own accord invented things that are contrary to our interest and to the good, and, loving them, he ended up hating God and consequently hating humankind. [...] You, therefore, have been misled by him and have attributed his evil doings to the impassable and immutable God.' [... 34.] The official said to them: 'So, will you not pray with the most faithful caliph today?' [...] The saints responded with one accord: 'We pray to the one true God that not only the caliph but also you and the entire Saracen nation will step away from the godless fallacy of Muḥammad and pray and worship the God proclaimed by the holy prophets and the apostles of Christ, not that we should abscond into darkness after abandoning the light.'

36. Therefore, he [the official] immediately ordered the armed soldiers to arrest them and tie their hands behind their backs and drag them like sheep to the place of slaughter [by the River Euphrates, near Samarra]. Indeed, a numerous crowd of Saracens and Christians flocked to the scene to witness their execution. [...]

38. Honouring each other as though they were at the emperor's table, the saints joyfully met their end, each according to the precedence of his office, without any of them displaying a sign of cowardice or hesitation.

35

Digenēs Akritēs

Elizabeth Jeffreys, University of Oxford

The anonymous epic-romance poem now generally referred to as *Digenēs Akritēs* is set on the Syrian borders that were disputed between Byzantines and Arabs. It dates from sometime in the eighth to tenth centuries, although it was probably written down in its earliest form in the mid-twelfth century; 1135 or thereabouts is a generally accepted date. Its first section describes how an Arab emir came to marry the daughter of a Byzantine general, the governor of the region, and converted to Christianity. Their child was given the 'speaking name' of Digenēs Akritēs ('the frontiersman of dual origin'), referring to his mixed-race background (he was both Byzantine and Arab, Christian and Muslim) and his future role of guarding the *akra* or borders of the Byzantine Empire.

Of the six manuscripts in which the text of the poem survives, the two oldest are G (now in the Grottaferrata monastery near Rome) and E (in the Escorial Library in Spain); the other four derive from a compilation made from them. Though they clearly retell the same narrative, the texts in G, which follows Byzantine conventions more closely, and E, which has elements of folksong, have many superficial differences of vocabulary, metrical patterning and syntax, and cannot be reconciled into a unified edition. The passages given here are taken from G (the parallel scenes in E are at lines 226–303 and 533–65).

In the first passage the emir's mother has learnt of her son's apostasy and is furious because her son has brought disgrace on his family and defamed his father's prowess. Unsurprisingly, considering the character in whose *persona* this passage is expressed, this is one of the few places in Byzantine literature where there is empathetic acceptance of the values of Islamic society. The warrior element is recognized, in, for example, the authorial listing of the military successes of the emir's father and uncle, and the resolute refusal of the emir's father to be bribed with offers of high status in terms comparable elsewhere in the work to those used of Digenēs himself. The ethical element is recognized in the reproaches of the emir's mother to her son. In the second passage, the emir has returned to his mother's home and listens to her pleas but convinces her to accept his new faith.

CMR 3, pp. 434–9.

This translation is taken from E. Jeffreys (ed. and trans.), *Digenis Akritis: The Grottaferrata and Escorial Versions*, Cambridge, 1998, reprinted with permission.

[The emir's mother pleads with her son to return to Syria and his family there]
But the emir's mother sent a letter from Syria, G 2.50
full of lamentation, reproach and blame:
'Most beloved child, how could you have forgotten your mother,
blinded my eyes and extinguished my light?
How could you renounce your kinsmen and faith and country
and become a reproach to all Syria?
We are abominated by all men
as deniers of the faith, as law-breakers,
and for not having observed well the Prophet's words.
What has happened to you, my child? How have you forgotten these things?
How could you not remember your father's deeds,
how many Romans he slew, how many he carried off as slaves?
Did he not fill prisons with generals and toparchs?[40]
Did he not plunder many of the *themes*[41] in Roman territory
and carry off beautiful high-born girls as prisoners?
Was he not pressured, like you, to become a renegade?
For when the Roman armies encircled him,
the generals swore him most terrible oaths
that he would be honoured as a *patrikios*[42] by the emperor
and become a *protostrator*,[43] if he threw down his sword.
But he kept the Prophet's commandments,
spurned renown and paid no attention to wealth,
and they hewed him limb from limb and took away his sword.
But you, not even under compulsion, have abandoned everything at once,
your faith, your kinsmen and me, your mother.
My brother, your uncle, Moursis Karoïs,

[40] A local governor.
[41] A Byzantine province, ruled over by a toparch.
[42] A high-ranking dignity in the Byzantine hierarchy of officials.
[43] 'First groom', also a high Byzantine rank in the twelfth century.

made an expedition to Smyrna, to the sea-board;
he plundered Ankyra, the city of Abydos,
Aphrike, Taranta and Hexakomia,
and when he had won these victories he returned to Syria.
You too, most miserable man, have made a campaign.
When you were about to be honoured by all Syria,
you destroyed everything for the love of a pig-eater
and you have become accursed in every mosque.
If you do not leave quickly and come to Syria,
the emirs intend to behead me,
kill your children since their father is a rebel,
and give to others your delightful girls,
who are lamenting for you and are losing patience.
My sweetest child, pity your mother:
do not send me in my old age to Hades in sorrow,
do not allow your children to be slain unjustly,
do not ignore the tears of your delightful girls
and let God in his greatness remove you from the world.
Look, I have sent you, as you see, choice horses.
Mount the chestnut, lead the black,
let the bay follow and no one will catch you.
Bring the Roman girl too, if you are upset because of her,
but if you disobey me, may you be accursed.'
Picked Arabs took the letter
and came with great speed to Roman territory.
There was a place, Lakkopetra, far from the house.
They encamped there, so as not to be seen,
and told the emir by means of their letter-carrier:
'There is moonlight shining all night, let us make our journey if you wish.'
When the emir saw his mother's letter,
he was filled greatly with the compassion a son feels for his mother,
he pitied his children and their mothers,
jealously seized him that they might embrace others.
For a former passion is never forgotten,
even though love of the girl had quite blotted it out,
for the more intense pain blots out the lesser.
And he was left wondering what to do. [...]

[The emir's mother and her household are converted to Christianity]
When they came to the tent, they immediately sat down G 3.130
and the emir's mother began to speak as follows:
'My sweetest child, light of my eyes,
and comfort of my soul in my old age,

my charming delight, my consolation,
tell me, why have you lingered, child, in Roman territory?
For when I did not see you, I no longer wished to see the light
or the gleaming sun, or to live in the world.
Do wonderful miracles happen in Roman territory,
such as are performed, my child, at the Prophet's tomb,
to which you came with me when I went to pray?
You saw a wonderful miracle, how when night fell
and there was no light, a radiance came from on high
and mystically filled the whole house with light.
You saw bears and lions, wolves with sheep,
and very many species of animals feeding together,
the one not hurting the other at all
but all waiting until the blessing at the end,
then bending the knee thus and immediately leaving.[44]
Have you seen anything more marvellous than this in Roman territory?
Do we not have the towel of Naaman,
who was emperor over the Assyrians,
and because of the number of his virtues was able to perform miracles?[45]
How have you, my child, become a renegade from all this
and spurned power and great renown?
All expected you to conquer Egypt,
but you have thwarted your own fortune,
you have destroyed everything for the sake of one Roman girl.'
While she was still wishing to say other such things,
the young man cut his mother off and spoke thus:
'I used to be well informed on all these things, mother.
And before I had a share in the light, I honoured, as if true,
things which in reality were worthy of darkness and complete destruction.
But when God in the most high,
who for my sake willingly endured poverty
and decided to clothe himself in my weakness,
was pleased to snatch me from the jaws of the wily beast
and thought me worthy of the washing of regeneration,
all these things I abandoned as nonsense and fables

[44] The miraculous presence of animals at the Prophet's tomb is not mentioned in E.

[45] Some aspects of this brief reference recall the story in 2 Kings 5:1-19 of Naaman, the army commander of the king of Aram, who is cured of his leprosy by washing in the Jordan seven times. This would account for him having a towel, though neither that nor his miracles are referred to there. It is also tempting to link the towel (*mandilin*) with the mandylion of Edessa, a cloth bearing the image of Christ, which was welcomed into Constantinople in 944 by Emperor Constantine VII Porphyrogennetos and kept in the Pharos Chapel of the Great Palace.

and leading to eternal fire;
those who revere these things are always punished.
I believe in God, Father of all.' [....]

[The emir then recites the Nicene Creed]
The emir said these things, opening the way
of blameless faith to his mother, and spoke thus:
'Mother, I am leaving once more for Roman territory,
affirming my faith in the holy Trinity,
for the world is not worth as much as one soul.
For it we gain everything but forfeit our soul,
there is no benefit at all in that hour
when God comes from heaven to judge the world.' [...]

[The emir continues with a definition of the Trinity]
Such were the emir's words, but what were his mother's?
She did not reject her child's excellent counsel
but, like fertile soil that has accepted the seed,[46]
she immediately brought forth fruit and pronounced these words:
'I believe, my child, in the Triune God through you,
and with you I will travel happily to Roman territory,
being baptised for the remission of my many faults
and acknowledging thanks that through you I have been enlightened.'

[46] A reminiscence of the Parable of the Sower (Matthew 13:8 and parallels).

36

Nicetas Choniates, *History*

Niccolò Zorzi, University of Padua

In 1180, at the end of Manuel I Comnenus's reign (1143–80), a theological controversy brought the Byzantine emperor into opposition to the patriarch of Constantinople Theodosius Boradiotes and other members of the church, including the learned Bishop Eustathius of Thessalonica. The dispute arose because of the emperor's effort to modify the formula of abjuration that converts from Islam to Christianity were required to recite, eliminating the anathema or condemnation against the definition of God that appears in Q 112: 'And furthermore, I anathematise the God of Muḥammad, of whom he says: "He is the one God, *holosphyros* [i.e. "solid", "compact", a Greek translation of the Arabic *ṣamad* in verse 2], who has neither begotten nor been begotten, and no-one has been made like him".' The controversy should be viewed within the frame of twelfth-century Seljuq–Byzantine relationships, when a succession of Turks converted to Christianity. Manuel I Comnenus's position in wanting to remove this anathema from the abjuration can be interpreted as a minority tendency, distancing itself from the Byzantine polemical tradition against Islam and acknowledging the common monotheism of Christians and Muslims in recognizing they adored one and the same God.

Nicetas Choniates adopted an attitude that was completely contrary to Manuel's attempt to find a compromise that allowed converts from Islam not to condemn directly 'their God'; he agreed with the rigid position of the clergy that was totally opposed to any concession to the notion that the Muslim God had something in common with the Christian God. In Nicetas's narrative, the emperor's initiative is described as the fruit of his sickness and madness, while Bishop Eustathius of Thessalonica, with whom Nicetas was personally acquainted, is given the role of hero.

The sources on this controversy are Nicetas Choniates's *Chronikē diēgēsis* or *Historia* ('History') book 8, which narrates events from 1118 to 1207, Nicetas's *Panoplia dogmatikē* or *Thesaurus orthodoxiae* ('The armour of doctrine') book 26, a theological work on heresies in twenty-seven chapters, published only in part, and a *tomos* (decree) issued by the synod of the Church in April 1180.

Nicetas was born in Chonai, Phrygia (Asia Minor), around 1155. He moved to Constantinople at the age of nine, where his brother Michael (*c.* 1138–1222), later metropolitan of Athens (1182), was already living. He entered the imperial bureaucracy, probably in the latter years of Manuel I Comnenus's reign, and ascended all the steps of a civil career up to the post of *Logothetēs tōn sekretōn* ('prime minister'), in the following decades. When the city was conquered by the Crusaders in 1204, Nicetas moved to Nicea and was again active in the court of Theodorus Lascaris. He died in 1217.

The text translated below is a selection taken from Nicetas's account in the *Chronikē diēgēsis*, with two insertions from the *Panoplia dogmatikè* {set within curly brackets}.

CMR 4, pp. 132–44 (Nicetas Choniates); *CMR* 3, pp. 759–63 (*Tomos*).

This translation is based on the Greek text in J.-L. van Dieten, *Nicetae Choniatae historia*, Berlin, 1975, pp. 213–20.

Near the end of his life this man [Emperor Manuel I] was also able to do what follows. Among other excommunications, the catechetical book includes the anathema against the God of Muḥammad, about whom it says: 'He has neither begotten nor been begotten,'[47] and that he is *holosphyros*. {A certain emir Chasanes – adopted by Gabras, who had the utmost power under Kilij Arslan, the sultan who currently governs the Turkish people – converted to our immaculate faith, but having heard the words of this anathema while he was being instructed, was really indignant because God the Creator of the universe was insulted by the Romans and was subjected to anathema. Therefore, Chasanes, going to the emperor – who was Manuel Comnenus – and having told him the doubts which had grown in him while he was instructed, seemed to say things that were not in disagreement with what was right.} The emperor decided to eliminate the anathematization in all the catechetical books, beginning with the one used in the Great Church [Hagia Sophia in Constantinople]. The reason was apparently a good one: he said that it was a scandal that the Agarenes [the Muslims] who converted to our pious faith should blaspheme God as such.

He therefore summoned the most great Theodosius, who at that time governed and adorned the first throne [Patriarch Theodosius Boradiotes], and among the bishops who resided in the City [Constantinople] those who excelled in learning and virtue, and made known his thought to them with verbose preambles to the issue. [...][48]

---

[47] Q 112:3.

[48] In the omitted section, the Patriarch refuses to accept the document (*tomos*) in which Manuel sets out his thoughts, and therefore the emperor presents to the synod, through an envoy, two new documents: a different version of the text that was to be approved by the synod, and a letter.

One [of the documents, i.e. the *tomos* that Manuel expected to be approved] dealt with the doctrine under discussion, which, as we have said, the emperor had submitted with the intent that the assembled bishops should affix their signatures with dispatch; in the other [document, i.e. the letter from Manuel] the emperor addressed the chief shepherd Theodosius and the synod in terms that were neither moderate nor agreeable, but criticized the opposition of the patriarch and his bishops as unreasonable. The emperor threatened to convoke a larger synod and to confer with the pope himself on the issues. 'I would be an ingrate and a fool,' he said, 'if I did not return to God, who made me emperor and is the Emperor of the universe, a small fraction of what I received from Him and did not make every effort to prevent Him, who is the true God, from being subjected to anathema.' But the listeners were so far from being intimidated by such threats that the archbishop of Thessalonica, the most learned and eloquent Eustathius, who was filled with indignation by what was being read out and could not suffer something *holosphyros* – the fabrication of a demoniacal mind – to be called true God, said: 'My brains would be in my feet and I would be wholly unworthy of this garb,' pointing to the mantle on his shoulders, 'were I to regard as true God the camel-like pederast and master and teacher of every abominable act[49] {because the fool Muḥammad, together with other absurd statements in the Saracens' book called Qur'an, allows the fools who obey it to love male love and to plough their spouses in both openings that are below the womb}.[50] The bishops were stunned by what they had heard: he had pronounced these words with a piercing voice, in the attitude of someone who is inflamed by pious zeal. Astonished, the reader of the document returned to the emperor. The emperor, perturbed by the report of what had been said, gave an able reply, commending forbearance as never before. [...][51]

On the following day, however, when the synod convened at the patriarchal residence to do what they had agreed upon (at dawn the imperial envoys had shown up to assemble the bishops in one group), they were no longer of the same mind: again they shook their heads in denial and backed out, contending that the written decree still contained certain reprehensible words which should be excised and replaced by others that would give no offence whatsoever to correct doctrine. Once again the emperor became irritated and reproached them as being evidently foolish, and having inconstant and ever-changing minds. In the end, they barely agreed to remove the anathema of Muḥammad's God from the catechetical books and to write in the anathema of Muḥammad and all his teachings.

---

[49] This passage is puzzling, as it appears to suggest that the Muslim God was to be identified with Muḥammad.
[50] It was commonplace for Christians to accuse Muslims of homosexual practices, and therefore to hold Muḥammad responsible for sanctioning them; and also on the basis of interpretations of Q 2:223 to accuse them of practising anal intercourse with their wives.
[51] In the omitted section, Manuel forgives Eustathius for his angry outburst and the synod decides to accept the decree proposed by the emperor and to sign it the following day.

37

Manuel II Palaeologus, *Dialogue with a Persian*

Miriam Salzmann and Tristan Schmidt, Johannes Gutenberg University of Mainz

Emperor Manuel II Palaeologus was born in 1350, the second son of Emperor John V. After his elder brother Andronicus died prematurely in 1385, he succeeded his father on the throne in 1391. In the same year, he was forced to follow the Ottoman sultan Bayezid I on campaign in Asia Minor. Taking up winter quarters in Ankara, he was accommodated in the house of a renowned *müderris* (teacher of Islamic theology) from Baghdad. During his stay, he engaged in extensive conversations with the *müderris* and his entourage on questions of Christian and Islamic theology, and a little later in 1392/3 he composed his *Dialogue with a Persian*, which was probably based on his diary entries of these conversations.

This highly intellectual and theologically elaborated text is characterized by a remarkably balanced and respectful depiction of the Muslim *müderris*. In the form of extensive dialogues, it addresses fundamental Christian teachings in defence against criticisms, such as the question of the Trinity, the relationship between the divine and human subjects in the person of Christ, and the redemption of humankind through Christ's Incarnation. Other passages discuss the value of Christian, Jewish and Islamic law, and the relationship between them.

In the first passage translated below, Manuel defends himself against the argument that the current military and political situation, which was very unfavourable to the Christian Byzantine Empire, demonstrates the superiority of Islam, and proves Muḥammad's prophecy that whoever refuses to comply with Islamic law will rightly suffer defeat and persecution. The second and third passages then compare Christian and Islamic law in more detail. While the *müderris* criticizes Christian law as excessively demanding and propagates Muslim law as the moderate golden mean,

We would like to thank Zachary Chitwood for his valuable comments on our translation.

Manuel focuses on God's support for the faithful and the rewards to be gained in following Christian law. Another topic discussed is the ever-recurring theme of the Christian veneration of images as set out in the fourth passage, where previously known classic arguments are exchanged by the two interlocutors.

CMR 5, pp. 314–25.

The edition used for this translation is *Manuel II. Palaiologos, Dialoge mit einem Muslim*, ed. K. Förstel, 3 vols, Würzburg, 1993, 1995, 1996.

[The significance of the Muslims' recent military victories]

4.1–2. He [the *müderris*] spoke to us as follows: [...] And you, who respect the law of Christ, and who after Muḥammad's appearance do not follow the stronger and more perfect [law] (for thus he deemed right to call the law of this lawless one and madman), rightly suffer the same as the Jews, and therefore you are persecuted by us. For the old law is good, and Christ's law is better, though Muḥammad's law is the most perfect. And, indeed, what he predicted and proclaimed directly after his appearance, namely that his [followers] would [gain] everlasting victory against those who refused to obey his law – this is coming true continuously and, so to speak, every day, and is proving clearly that he is a prophet. You, on the contrary, blaspheme against him unjustly and insult God. [...]

4.4. Despite this, after a short time I said to them [the *müderris* and those with him], smiling: [...] The fact that you are now waging war successfully against us, as providence deems appropriate, seems to be in accordance with his [Muḥammad's] pronouncements, but does not show him to be a prophet. [...] 4.12. [...] How could he appear as a prophet, when he foretold [only] normal changes that had to appear from the [expected] reversals [of fortune]? [...] 4.19. However, I think that as sensible men you should not make a faith responsible for some being unfortunate, others being fortunate. For neither are you more fortunate than all Christians nor do you always secure victory, since there are rulers in the West who entirely surpass your people with regard to good fortune. You have not infrequently suffered bad fortune, as you are not only defeated in war by us but also almost always suffer hostile afflictions from each other. [...] Therefore, you should not regard as a prophet one who appeared to foretell something about you. Indeed, neither the [predictions] concerning us have come true precisely as he foretold them to you, nor has the victory for his people, which he had announced to you. [*Dialogue* 5, vol. 1, pp. 166–78]

[Criticism and defence of Christian law]

2.2. [The *müderris* said]: It would probably not be a mistake to say that your law is good and virtuous, though it cannot be beneficial in any easy manner, just like exceedingly bitter medicines, because it is very harsh and burdensome, and therefore it is not entirely perfect. But Muḥammad's law, which is moderate in every respect, surpasses other laws because it takes the middle way and issues achievable, very gentle and benign prescriptions. [...] 2.4. Indeed, tell me, how can it be a sign of moderation to love one's enemies, to pray for them and to supply them with the necessary nourishment when they are hungry,[52] and in addition this ridiculous (if you will allow me to be frank) command to hate your parents and siblings[53] and even your own soul, and to leave also the coat to him who has taken your shirt?[54] [...] 2.5. Who is as hard as iron, as adamant and more unfeeling than stones, that he could endure all these things, suffering abuse and loving the insolent, and doing good towards someone who feels hatred towards him? [...] Who has [ever] heard of anything like this, unless we are to be requested to show great gratitude towards those who attack us in every way and will not ever be satisfied at our misfortunes? [*Dialogue* 7, vol. 1, pp. 244–6]

3.5. [Manuel said]: Now I must defend myself against these slanders. These absurd and exaggerated [commands], which, as you say, go beyond human virtue because they seem to you to be above human nature, are indeed almost superhuman, though on the other hand they are achievable as well as altogether easy for people, if they so desire. This may seem like an enigma to you, but it is completely true. That is to say, if our strength alone is considered, or rather the weakness which stems from Adam, these things might seem beyond any virtue, but if the aid and power of Him who advises us [to do this is considered, they are] not at all [impossible]. For He would not exhort us like that if He left us deprived of His help. On the contrary, God's hand invisibly supports their labours, and wherever such assistance is provided, what could [ever] seem arduous, what difficult, what could not seem easy? 3.6. Consider also the reward for these things, which is the Kingdom of God, [...] and thus those who bear this hope necessarily have to endure everything. [*Dialogue* 7, vol. 1, pp. 252–4]

[The veneration of icons]

1.1. Indeed, the veneration of painted images and sculptures did not seem to them [the Muslims] something insignificant, but rather a sign of the greatest ungodliness. [...] 1.4.[55] The Persian said: [...] But you venerate icons of mortal humans which are made of completely worthless material, and in the same way [you venerate] Christ as God.[56] Furthermore, you give the name Christ to the image of Him, and you end up paying it the highest honour because it must have come from the original. There is a risk of you making what is material a god and of there being many gods, since there are many images. [...] 1.2. Then I said to them: I have presented a sufficient defence against

[52] Matthew 5:44.
[53] Luke 14:26.
[54] Matthew 5:40.
[55] The text reads more clearly with section 1.4 placed before 1.2.
[56] As a Muslim, he would regard Christ as no more than a human prophet.

the accusation of [venerating] images, even if briefly, but now, on your account, I will make a more detailed speech about them. It must be understood that the honour given through veneration is twofold: we bestow one of them in worship; [and we bestow] the other because the thing venerated partakes of the likeness or grace of the object of worship. Worship is to be rendered to God alone, the Creator of all, and not to anything created: [this is true] not only for wood and stone, but also for the prophets and the first nature[57] after God, which I call the incorporeal powers. [...] 2.3. Therefore, we should not pay honour to [just] this or that kind of material, or to the image of just anybody, but only to those who have led a modest and prudent life and have partaken of God's grace, and to their images, since the honour [paid to] the images is rendered to the originals. The things which these [beings] have touched are all venerable through God, who alone is most venerable and is to be worshipped eternally. [*Dialogue* 20, vol. 3, pp. 57–66]

[57] Greek *physis*, referring to angelic beings.

38

The Life of George the Younger: An account of a martyr who was martyred in our time

Mirela Ivanova, University of Oxford

The anonymous *Life of George the Younger* was written sometime between 1437, the date of his martyrdom, and 1439, when Patriarch Joseph II, who is mentioned at the end of text, died. The author, probably a cleric judging from his knowledge of the Bible and digressions on David, Christ and the devil, claims he was present at the martyrdom. It is possible that the text was intended to be read out in church, though this seems unlikely as it ends with the author's appeal to George to be an intercessor for his own personal 'calamity', and it is interpolated with the first person throughout. These features would make it a rarity in liturgical hagiography.

The narrative begins with George's trip to a local Ottoman bowmaker in Adrianople (the capital of the Ottoman polity at the time) to have his bow mended. The bowmaker blasphemes against Christ, so George declares his faith openly in the market. He is arrested and, in an allusion to the arrest of Christ, he is taken to be judged by two local rulers. The second refuses to cast judgement despite the demands of religious scholars (called *tasimanioi* in the text), and after offering him many gifts to make him abandon Christ he hands him over to the crowd. They insult George and beat him and then they burn him, adding animal bones to prevent any identifiable remains being taken for relics.

The *Life* marks a shift from the thirteenth- and fourteenth-century neo-martyrdoms of Anatolians captured by raiding Turks, such as Theodore the Younger or Michael the Younger. By the fifteenth century in the Ottoman polity, Christian-Muslim interactions were not chance occurrences between raiding parties on border zones, but a feature of everyday life. As such, the *Life* is most interesting, not for what it says explicitly, but for what insights into Christian-Muslim coexistence can be gained from its moments of vagueness and silence. Thus, George is described as a Christian and a man 'of military bearing', and yet no mention is made of the fact that he was most probably serving in the Ottoman army. In addition, discussing the coming of Islam, the author is surprisingly lenient with regard to converts. He notes that 'these beasts [the Ottoman Muslims] have come because of our sins, but they [the people], not understanding these things well, became deranged in mind', i.e. converted to Islam. Rather than being evil or demonic creatures, therefore, most Christians who have gone over to Islam seem to the author to be simply confused and uneducated, lacking the knowledge of 'the many other things, as those who read know', and Islam itself is no more than another trial sent by God because of internal sins and failures within the Christian community. In fact, the martyr himself confesses to studying about Muḥammad and Islam prior to his martyrdom, and he uses the martyrdom as an opportunity formally to denounce Islam. Had he until then held both faiths at once?

Below are excerpts of some key moments in the work that lead up to the martyr's public burning.

CMR 5, pp. 375–9.

This translation is based on C.G. Patrinelēs, 'Mia anekdotē diēgēsē gia ton agnōsto neomartyra Geōrgio († 1437)', *Orthodoxos Parousia* 1 (1964) 65–74, pp. 67–9.

[…] He was brought to one of [the shops] of the Hagarene bowmakers, wanting to repair his own bow, though I fully suspect [he was also] seeking the glory which he acquired in heaven and the mortal blow against the weapon-throwing Turks. For the good martyr George the Younger was of a military bearing, as was made clear from his garments and belt, as well as his equipment, weapons and helmet, but he was of a military bearing not only literally, but also figuratively, since he was set up as a monument of victory.[58] For when [he was] there, the Hagarene bowmaker employed blasphemy against our Lord Jesus Christ, who came down for our salvation and was made flesh from the immaculate maiden in order that He might make like through like immortal.[59] […]

Hence, as the bowmaker was blaspheming, holy George the Younger was not unrestrained, though he struggled – since love endures all, according to the words of the Apostle.[60] He was filled full of anger and boldness, and he shouted in a loud and clear voice: 'The great Lord Jesus Christ, our God, alone is great, and there is no

[58] A play on the word *tropaion* which means a monument of victory in battle, but also more generally a monument in memory of something or someone.

[59] Christ became human in order to restore humanity to immortality.

[60] St Paul in 1 Corinthians 13:4-7.

end of His wisdom.[61] But yours, whom you call a prophet, holds not even the rank of a dog. Who then is like the Lord Jesus Christ, our God, who dwells in the highest [heavens] and directs affairs below?[62] One alone is holy, one is Lord, one only is to be worshipped, Jesus Christ, to the glory of God the Father. Amen.[63] Who is God alone, as our God [is]?[64] This same [God] alone is the Creator of all created things' – the noble martyr was well versed in holy scripture.

When the multitude who were nearby heard these things, for they had occurred in the marketplace, they rushed [towards him] – how do you think they rushed towards him? First, they struck him on the head, though he was not afraid, but rather without trembling, with a louder voice and resolve in his appearance, he proclaimed the things we have already related. Then, grabbing the string of the bow, they wound it around his neck, but even though they used force to hold him down, with his hands behind his back, they were not able to cause harm to the noble man – for he was also strong in his nature – but he shouted: '"What I have written I have written",[65] and I have sworn to die once in the flesh for my Lord. I am determined to seek eternal and blessed life in Him, and if you wish to kill me or lead me to the ruler I will willingly be taken to wherever is your wish.' Thus, the martyr was led in chains before one of the rulers, mouthing the blessed phrase: 'Blessed are the undefiled in the way, who walk in the law of the Lord,'[66] and continually shouting aloud: 'You see my confession, Lord, do not forsake me!' [...]

The ruler [said] to him: 'Convert, acknowledge our prophet against whom you have blasphemed, so that you may receive honour at our hands and great gifts.' But he [replied]: 'It is not for me to perish like a mortal man who does not know any sort of truth. But I acknowledge the Lord, Jesus Christ, my God and Maker, who reigns forever. For indeed, though I have misspent greatly in the world where we live, I have not abandoned the veneration and worship of the life-giving tomb of my Lord Jesus Christ; neither have I made the mistake of venerating the one whom you believe to be a prophet. But as I believe, so I proclaim in a clear voice Him who I know to be living, and who is to be worshipped and is perfect God, and I flee from this one [Muḥammad], so that I may not be condemned together with this world.'

[The ruler said:] 'Look at the multitude who are eagerly seeking you. I have nothing to say to them, but you will be a victim of the fire.' The martyr smiled and replied: 'If you become the provider of this good for me, I will be grateful to you for this great generosity, and if you now command this, I will eagerly embrace your arms.'

---

[61] Psalm 147:5.

[62] Psalm 113:5-6.

[63] The closing words of the priest's prayer that opens the Divine Liturgy of John Chrysostom.

[64] Psalm 77:13.

[65] John 19:22, Pilate's words when he refused to change the sign he had placed on Jesus's cross. George quotes them here to indicate that he will not withdraw what he has said.

[66] Psalm 119:1.

39

Gennadios Scholarios, *Questions and answers concerning our Lord Jesus Christ*

Klaus-Peter Todt, Johannes Gutenberg University of Mainz

At the end of May 1470, a soldier appeared at the Monastery of John the Baptist on Mount Menoikeus near Serres to which the former patriarch of Constantinople, Gennadios II Scholarios (1454–6), had retired in 1457. He had been sent by two high Turkish officials to fetch Scholarios for a discussion about the divinity of Christ and to escort him to where they had invited him. The venue was the camp of the two high officials and their retinue. In the discussion the first item was a proof that Jesus Christ was not just a man but God's Son and God himself (chapters 1–7), and the second (chapters 8–12) the Incarnation of Christ. Scholarios was anxious to prove that this was not only possible but essential for the redemption of humankind.

As is mentioned at the end of the text, at the beginning of chapter 12, Scholarios had already during his period of office (1454–6) given an account to Sultan Mehmed II (r. 1451–81) of the Christian faith and then written a paper for him with the title 'The only way to salvation for humankind'. At the sultan's request, Scholarios later re-worked this paper, shortened it and put it in the form of a confession of faith. Then it was translated into Ottoman Turkish by Ahmet, the judge (*qāḍī*) of Berroia (in Macedonia; in Ottoman Turkish it was known as Kara-Feriya) and submitted to Sultan Mehmed.[67] As a result of this, Turks who were interested in the teachings of Christianity regarded Scholarios as the main authority. He was also able to make the Christian faith comprehensible to Turks, not least by citing Qur'an verses on Jesus. At

[67] Tibor Halasi-Kun, 'Gennadios' confession of faith', *Archivum Ottomanicum* 12 (1987–92) 5–103 (pp. 20–30, the Ottoman Turkish text of Gennadios's confession of faith; pp. 31–41, an English translation with commentary).

the same time, he left neither the sultan nor his two partners in the dialogue in any doubt about his firm conviction that only belief in the divinity of Jesus Christ and His Incarnation could lead to salvation and the attainment of eternal bliss.

CMR 5, pp. 503–18.

This English translation, kindly made by Dr Margaret Hollis, is from a German translation based on the Greek edition, 'Demandes et réponses sur la divinité de Notre-Seigneur Jésus-Christ (1470)', in Louis Petit, Xénophon A. Siderides and Martin Jugie (eds), *Gennadiu tu Scholariu Hapanta ta heuriskomena/Oeuvres completes de Gennade Scholarios*, vol. 3. *Oeuvres polémiques – Questions théologiques. Écrits apologétiques*, Paris, 1930, 458–75.

1. Towards the end of May during the indiction[68] which was nearing its term, a soldier suddenly came to us with a strict written command which could not be put off. He led us down from this monastery to the town of Serrai and from there to the plain near the town. He brought us to two very powerful men, one younger, the other of riper years. This had been commanded by the one who sent him. When this man saw us, he first asked after our well-being with gracious benevolence; thereupon he began to question us about our faith, for this was why we had been brought to him.

He said: 'You Christians say that Christ is also God, although he was a man and born of the Virgin Mary. Explain to us the basis of this belief and the ground for this doctrine of yours about Christ.'

'Excellency', I said, 'when we Christians call our Master Jesus Christ we also name him God. For with the name of Christ he is designated as both God and man, and we will give you the reason for this if you so command. But now we will tell you why our doctrine is as it is. When we are thinking about this ourselves or when we are sharing theological statements with those of the same opinion as ourselves, we need no arguments or proofs for the divinity of Christ, since this is an absolutely true and fundamental doctrine for us. Instead, we deal with other doctrines, since it is necessary that we should follow the same teaching about Christ expressed in these statements. When it comes to those who are of a different opinion from us and who therefore contradict us, we are able through the power of the truth that is in us to answer them and to bring forward arguments and reasons for this doctrine. When they try to prove that it is impossible to demonstrate that Christ is God, we show them that it is not impossible by defeating their arguments. Then we also show that it is entirely necessary by making progress in the way.

Now, since your Excellency is not objecting to our doctrine about Christ as it is constituted, but is only asking how and why we teach that Christ is God and not just

[68] A system of dating used in the Roman Empire, in which the calendar was divided into fifteen-year periods.

man, then our answer is that we have believed through faith, that is, through the complete fulfilment of the prophecies about divinity in Christ our Lord, and we believe that our Lord Jesus Christ is both true God and true man.'

'And on what grounds'. he said, 'do you base this belief in a totally strange matter, which because of its strangeness seems to most people to be both incomprehensible and impossible?' [pp. 458–9]

3. So, after these preliminaries about the Faith have been presented, we come to your question. The basis therefore of our belief in the divinity of our Lord Jesus Christ has become the good news about him, and it is founded on the succession [of believers][69] from the first people who believed in him until those who to this day believe in him. For later generations adopt as supplement to the good news about our Lord the clear teaching about the moral excellence and wisdom of those who believed in him in earlier times. But the good news about him does not now have to be ascertained by proofs, since you do not cast any doubt on it. The Jews blasphemed against him and their descendants are still blaspheming because they are infected by an even worse failure to understand than their forebears, but this is not so for you, because you have a good opinion of him, though not as high as we Christians do. You do recognize him as a holy man, as a prophet and as the Word of God and the Spirit of God;[70] you think and proclaim many similar worthy details about him.

Now, if in your opinion all this is true with regard to his evident humanity – for greater things shall now be introduced – why is it not right to believe us and to regard it all as true without any doubting, and to regard it not just as true but as holy and inspired by God, if according to you it is logical to characterize him as Word of God and Spirit of God; if we believed in him for the reason that he himself said of himself that he is God's Son and God, that we would believe this about him and regard him as God's Son and believe that he is certainly God? The Holy Gospel reveals that he often called himself God's Son and showed that he indeed is. You also treat the Gospel with respect and reverence, and you say that those who do not follow it are far from salvation. Some common people among you raise the objection that the Gospel has been altered by additions and omissions; I am not talking about that gospel but about the true Gospel, the same as that used by us and by all Christians everywhere. That Gospel has recently been translated authentically in the new Babylon[71] and distributed from there to other parts. I think that your Excellency has been good enough to look at it.

4. 'Stop a moment,' he said, 'so that I can ask you something, and then you can finish your story. Where in the true, authentic Gospel is it written, as you say, that Christ describes himself as Son of God? And where does he call himself God?'

---

[69] In Greek *diadoche*, meaning that one generation has handed on to the next the belief in the divinity of Christ in unadulterated form; cf. art. 'Diadoche' in G.W.H. Lampe, *A Patristic Greek Lexicon*, Oxford, 1961, pp. 346–7.
[70] An allusion to Q 4:171, 'Christ Jesus the son of Mary was no more than a messenger of God, and His Word which He bestowed on Mary, and a Spirit proceeding from Him.'
[71] This may be Baghdad or Cairo. It is not always possible to decide exactly.

'First of all', I said, 'even if Christ did not say this explicitly, it was sufficient that he demonstrated this by works. That is why those who believed in him in those days took this as adequate proof, that is, proof from the works. He himself said: "If not for any other reason, then believe me for the sake of the works."[72] Thus he did not reprove those whose rational judgment was that he was God's Son by reason of his works; instead he praised and thanked them, although he was entirely accustomed to reprove them when they said something which did not seem right to him. So he reproved Peter, who advised him to stay on Mount Tabor and not to descend.[73] But when Nathaniel said: "You are the Son of God", he did not reprove him but praised him;[74] when Peter said: "You are the Christ, the Son of the living God", he did not reprove him but rather called him blessed and gave him the keys of heaven as a reward.'[75] [pp. 461–2]

[72] John 14:11.
[73] Matthew 17:4.
[74] John 1:49-51.
[75] Matthew 16:16-19.

Armenian, Syriac and Other Languages

Syriac and Armenian Christians under Muslim rule

Thomas A. Carlson, Oklahoma State University

While both Islamicists and Europeanists traditionally regarded the Arab Islamic conquests of the seventh century as a sharp and permanent rupture in historical periodization, over the last half-century scholars have increasingly realized how little and how slowly things changed with the replacement of rulers. Governments had limited reach in the medieval world, and even replacing state administration was not an overnight process for the new conquerors. In consequence, Armenian and Syriac authors were easily able to incorporate the new conquerors into earlier models of historiography, hagiography and canon law, thus providing some of the earliest, if often ambiguous, witnesses to contacts between Christians and Muslims. Contacts were mostly between elites, but some less prominent individuals had unpredictable encounters with the religious other.

The ʿAbbasid revolution in 750 shifted the caliphate's centre of gravity east from Syria and Damascus, ultimately to the new city of Baghdad, inspiring Eastern Syriac authors (so-called 'Nestorians') to write more about Islam than their counterparts further west. The vibrant intellectual culture of the capital led to deeper awareness of religious differences and to more sophisticated Christian answers to Muslim objections. It also led to increasing intellectual collaboration between Muslim and Christian elites, and deeper political connections as both Christian patriarchs and their opponents appealed to the caliph for support against their rivals. Nevertheless, the old scholarly consensus that the ʿAbbasid period saw the conversion of most Christians to Islam is yielding, in more recent scholarship, to a timeline emphasizing that Muslims remained a ruling minority to the end of the first millennium.

The decline in ʿAbbasid central authority in the later ninth century led to a revival of independent Armenian kingdoms, coinciding with a resurgence of Byzantine power as the Eastern Roman Empire recaptured territories in northern Mesopotamia and Syria. Armenians migrating to the Cilician plain on the Mediterranean coast, followed by the Turkic and Crusader invasions of the region, reconfigured the political and ethnic landscape, as well as interreligious dynamics. Armenian and Syriac authors all lamented the arrival of the new Turkic Muslims, but they were divided in their assessment of the rough-hewn Franks from western Europe who claimed to be their co-religionists. Not a few Christian leaders found it more congenial to relocate to areas under Turkic governance rather than contend with Latin ecclesiastical rivals. While modern observers often attempt to disentangle the convergence of peoples into separate histories (of Crusades, Turks, Armenians, Byzantium and Syriac Christians), the social reality was thoroughly mixed. Even as intellectual engagement deepened, the bulk of Christian-Muslim relations in the period after 1000 (if not earlier) and subsequently would not have been elite encounters but quotidian interactions with neighbours, whether neighbourly or otherwise.

The invasion of armies from the Mongol Empire founded by Genghis Khan introduced yet another variable in Muslim-Christian relations in the late medieval period. The rule of the Mongols in the thirteenth and fourteenth centuries caused untold devastation, but it also opened up new opportunities for certain Christian leaders, such as Gregory Barhebraeus, and especially the eastern Turkic Christian monks from China who became known to posterity by their ecclesiastical names Rabban Sawma and Mar Yahballaha. Some Christians hoped that a Mongol Constantine figure would convert to Christianity and reverse centuries of Islamization, and Barhebraeus revived the writing of 'secular' sciences in Syriac, in a movement described by modern scholars as the 'Syriac Renaissance'. In the event, the Mongols converted to Islam. They still provided patronage to Christian rulers, though Mongol rule did provoke widespread instability in which Christians suffered at the hands of opportunistic Muslims (and sometimes vice versa, for example during a Christian riot following the Mongol capture of Damascus in 1260).

Armenian and Syriac Christianity, and their respective literatures, survived the collapse of the Mongol Ilkhanate in the mid-fourteenth century, although the following century was evidently a very difficult time, with recurring plague, ecological disasters, and rampant political instability in the form of marauding armies and/or bandits (it is not always easy to distinguish the two in medieval sources). Despite the difficulties, some Armenian and Christian authors continued to pen treatises clarifying their relationship with the religion of their rulers, and by the late medieval period they could draw on nearly a millennium of intellectual engagement, with settled answers to many of the most pressing Islamic objections to their beliefs. These answers remained a resource for Armenian and Syriac Christians as, in the mid- to late fifteenth century, political life stabilized again under the Qaraqoyunlu Türkmen and Aqqoyunlu Türkmen, and finally under the Ottoman and Safavid Empires, which came to partition the Middle East between them.

Further reading

S. Griffith, *The Church in the Shadow of the Mosque: Christians and Muslims in the World of Islam*, Princeton, NJ, 2007.

D. Bertaina, *Christian and Muslim Dialogues: The Religious Uses of a Literary Form in the Early Islamic Middle East*, Piscataway, NJ, 2011.
S. Brock et al. (eds), *Gorgias Encyclopedic Dictionary of the Syriac Heritage*, Piscataway, NJ, 2011; https://gedsh.bethmardutho.org/
S. Dadoyan, *The Armenians in the Medieval Islamic World: Paradigms of Interaction, Seventh to Fourteenth Centuries*, 3 vols, New Brunswick, NJ, 2011–13.
M. Debié, *L'écriture de l'histoire en Syriaque: Transmissions Interculturelles et constructions identitaires entre hellénisme et islam*, Leuven, 2015.
A. Vacca, *Non-Muslim Provinces under Early Islam: Islamic Rule and Iranian Legitimacy in Armenia and Caucasian Albania*, Cambridge, 2017.
J. Tannous, *The Making of the Medieval Middle East: Religion, Society, and Simple Believers*, Princeton, NJ, 2018.

40

Sebeos the Armenian, *History of Sebeos*

Rachel Claire Dryden, University of Cambridge

Sebeos was an Armenian bishop of the mid-seventh century. The mistaken attribution of this work, known as *Patmut'iwn Sebeosi* ('History of Sebeos'), to him has stuck, though this does not detract from its importance as the longest and most substantial non-Muslim source, contemporary with events surrounding the first Arab conquests up to the year 655 (see J. Howard-Johnston, *Witnesses to a World Crisis*, p. 76). It was probably written in the 650s by an author whose knowledge of the Bible suggests he was a churchman. It details the accession and reign of the Persian Shah Khosrov II (r. 590/91–628) – hence its alternative title, *History of Khosrov* – and the war between him and the Romans (603–28), as well as the early Arab conquests. It includes brief biographical details about Muḥammad, charting his rise from merchant to preacher, and identifying the Arabs with the fourth empire symbolized by the last of the apocalyptic beasts depicted in the book of Daniel, that would trample and crush the entire earth (*Patmut'iwn Sebeosi*, p. 44, cf. Daniel 7). The third section, which relates the Arab conquests and the rise of Islam in the seventh century, remains the 'only wide-ranging, connected account to be found in a non-Muslim source written close to the events in the seventh century', without which it would be impossible to reconstruct the early history of Islam with any certainty (Howard-Johnston, *Witnesses*, p. 100).

The value of the *Patmut'iwn Sebeosi* lies not only in its content, but in its historical detail and precision. Although the work was known in the Middle Ages, the earliest manuscript, from 1568, has since disappeared, and a 1672 copy remains the earliest extant version. The absence of a colophon led to its author being identified as Sebeos when the text was first published in 1851.

CMR 1, pp. 139–44. See further:

J. Howard-Johnston, *Witnesses to a World Crisis: Historians and Histories of the Middle East in the Seventh Century*, Oxford, 2010.

This translation is taken from R.W. Thomson and J.D Howard-Johnston, *The Armenian History Attributed to Sebeos*, Liverpool, 1999, with permission.

Chapter 42

At that time a certain man from among those same sons of Ismael whose name was Mahmet, a merchant, as if by God's command appeared to them as a preacher [and] the path of truth. He taught them to recognize the God of Abraham, especially because he was learned and informed in the history of Moses.[1] Now, because the command was from on high, at a single order they all came together in unity of religion. Abandoning their vain cults, they turned to the living God who had appeared to their father Abraham. So Mahmet legislated for them: not to eat carrion, not to drink wine, not to speak falsely and not to engage in fornication. He said: 'With an oath God promised this land to Abraham and his seed after him forever;[2] [...] now you are the sons of Abraham, and God is accomplishing his promise to Abraham and his seed for you. Love sincerely only the God of Abraham, and go and seize your land which God gave to your father Abraham. No one will be able to resist you in battle, because God is with you.' [...]

All the remnants of the people of the sons of Israel gathered and united together; they formed a large army. Following that they sent messages to the Greek king [the Byzantine emperor], saying: 'God gave that land to our father Abraham as a hereditary possession and to his seed after him. We are the sons of Abraham. You have occupied our land long enough. Abandon it peacefully and we shall not come into your territory.' [...]

But the emperor did not agree. He [...] said: 'This land is mine, your lot of inheritance is the desert. Go in peace to your land.' He began to collect troops, about 70,000, [...] and ordered them to go to Arabia.[3] [...]

Then dread of [the Ismaelites] fell on all the inhabitants of the land, and they all submitted to them. [...] And in the twinkling of an eye they occupied [the land] from the edge of the sea as far as the bank of the great river Euphrates; and on the other side of the river [they occupied] Urha[4] and all the cities of Mesopotamia. [pp. 95–8]

Chapter 43

I shall also speak about the plots of the rebellious Jews, who after gaining help from the Hagarenes for a brief while, decided to rebuild the temple of Solomon. Finding the spot called Holy of Holies, they rebuilt it with base and construction as a place for their prayers. But the Ismaelites, being envious of them, expelled them from that place and called the same house of prayer their own.[5] Then the former [the Jews] built in another spot, right at the base of the temple, another place for their prayer. There they proposed their evil plot, desiring to fill Jerusalem from end to end with blood and to exterminate all the Christians from Jerusalem. [pp. 102–3]

---

[1] The Pentateuch.

[2] Genesis 17:4-8.

[3] The Roman province of Arabia, stretching from the east of the River Jordan down into the Sinai Peninsula.

[4] The ancient city of Edessa, present-day Urfa in southeastern Turkey.

[5] The Dome of the Rock.

Chapter 44

It happened in the first year of Constans king of the Greeks,[6] and in the tenth year of Yazkert king of the Persians,[7] the Persian army of 60,000 fully armed men assembled to oppose Ismael. The Ismaelites put in the field against them 40,000 armed with swords; and they joined battle with each other in the province of Media. For three days the battle continued, while the infantry of both sides diminished. [...]

However, the blessed Daniel had earlier prophesied such a disaster which befell the land. Through four beasts he indicated the four kingdoms which would arise on earth. First of all the kingdom of the West, the beast in human form, which is that of the Greeks. [...] 'And behold the second beast was like a bear, and it stood to one side', to the East; he means the Sasanian kingdom. [...] 'Now the third beast was like a leopard; there were four wings of a bird on it, and the beast had four heads.' He means the kingdom of the North, Gog and Magog and their two companions. [...] 'The fourth beast was fearful and amazing, and its teeth were of iron, and its claws of bronze. It ate and broke in pieces, and crushed the remnants under foot.' This fourth, arising from the South, is the kingdom of Ismael, just as the archangel explained: 'The fourth beast, the fourth kingdom, shall arise, which shall be greater than all [other] kingdoms; and it will consume the whole earth.'[8] [pp. 104–6]

Chapter 49

In the eleventh year of Constans the treaty between Constans and Muawiya, prince of Ismael,[9] was broken. The king of Ismael ordered all his troops to assemble in the west and to wage war against the Roman Empire, so that they might take Constantinople and exterminate that kingdom as well.

Chapter 50

'If you wish', [Muawiya] said, 'to preserve your life in safety, abandon that vain cult which you learned from childhood. Deny that Jesus and turn to the great God whom I worship, the God of our father Abraham. [...] But if you do not, that Jesus whom you call Christ, since he was unable to save himself from the Jews, how can he save you from my hands?' [...]

The king received the letter, went into the house of God, fell on his face and said: 'See, Lord, the insults which these Hagarenes have inflicted upon you. "May your pity, Lord, be upon us, as we hope in you." "Fill their faces with indignity, and they will seek your name, Lord. They will be put to shame and disquieted for ever and ever; and they will perish full of shame. They will know that your name is Lord, and you only are raised on high over all the earth."'[10]

---

[6] The Byzantine emperor Constans II (r. 641–68).
[7] Yazdegerd III (r. 632–51).
[8] Daniel 7:1-7, 23.
[9] Muʿāwiya ibn Abī Sufyān (r. 661–80), the founder of the Umayyad dynasty.
[10] Psalms 33:22, 83:16-18.

He lifted the crown from his head, stripped off his purple [robes] and put on sackcloth, sat on ashes and ordered a fast to be proclaimed in Constantinople in the manner of Nineveh.[11]

Chapter 52

Now God sent a disturbance amongst the armies of the sons of Ismael, and their unity was split. They fell into conflict amongst themselves. [...] The blood of the slaughter of immense multitudes flowed thickly among the armies of Ismael [...] until Muawiya prevailed and conquered. Having brought them into submission to himself, he rules over the possessions of the sons of Ismael and makes peace with all. [pp. 143–5]

[11] A reference to the people of the city of Nineveh, who when they heard the prophecy of doom pronounced by the prophet Jonah, repented and abandoned their former ways (Jonah 3:6-10).

41

Giwargis I, *Synodal canons*

Lev Weitz, Catholic University of America

Giwargis I was the patriarch of the Church of the East from 660/1 to 680/1. A monk and bishop in northern Iraq before his election, he served a lengthy patriarchal term that largely coincided with the rule of the first caliph of the Umayyad dynasty, Muʿāwiya (r. 661–80). Giwargis is notable for issuing some of the earliest Christian legislation intended to regulate interreligious relations in the Islamic world.

As patriarch, Giwargis convened a synod on an island in the Persian Gulf in 676. Its main purpose was to put an end to a schism between the bishops of eastern Arabia and the patriarchate, but several of its canons also address interactions with agents of the caliphal state or unlawful social practices that Giwargis associated with non-Christians. Thus, Canon 6 prohibits Christians from taking disputes to judges not sanctioned by the ecclesiastical hierarchy, most likely meaning Muslim authorities as well as powerful laymen, while Canon 19 aims to prevent laymen who have been delegated the duties of fiscal administration for the caliphate from seeking taxes from bishops. Canon 14 forbids Christian women from marrying non-Christian men, while Canon 16 emphasizes the unlawfulness of polygamy, a common practice of the Arab-Muslim ruling elite.

In his references to non-Christians, Giwargis uses the generic Syriac term *ḥanpē*, 'pagans', which could be interpreted to include Zoroastrians, Manichaeans and others in addition to Muslims. But the fact that his canons were addressed to Arabian Christians at a time when the new caliphal state was increasing in power and institutional coherence suggests that Giwargis principally had Muslims in mind when he spoke of pagan judges, pagan husbands and the pagan practice of polygamy.

CMR 1, pp. 151–3. See further:

M.P. Penn, *Envisioning Islam: Syriac Christians and the Early Muslim World*, Philadelphia, PA, 2015.

L.E. Weitz, *Between Christ and Caliph: Law, Marriage, and Christian Community in Early Islam*, Philadelphia, PA, 2018.

This translation is based on J.-B. Chabot, *Synodicon orientale ou recueil de synodes nestoriens*, Paris, 1902.

Synodal canons

6. Concerning lawsuits among Christians: that they shall take place within the church before persons chosen by the bishop with the community's agreement from among clerics and laymen; and that those matters that are to be adjudicated shall not go outside the church and [take place] before pagans or unbelievers.

Lawsuits and disputes that occur among Christians shall be adjudicated within the church and shall not go outside, like unlawful things. Rather, they shall be decided before judges chosen by the bishop with the community's agreement from among clerics known for their love of truth, fear of God, knowledge and competence in the matters [at hand]. [Christians'] cases shall not, in a different manner and according to the vehemence of their own opinion[s], go outside the church. Should something be concealed from those chosen to decide judgements, they shall bring the dispute before the bishop and they shall receive from him a solution to their difficulties. For any layman to seize for himself, on his own authority, the prerogative to decide laymen's cases without the permission of the bishop and the agreement of the community is not permissible, by the Word of our Lord, as long as no necessity [that he should do so] arises at the command of the secular rulers. [pp. 219–20] [...]

14. Concerning the fact that it is not right that Christian women should be married to pagans, strangers to the fear of God.

Women who have believed in Christ and have wanted to live the Christian life have shunned marriage to pagans with all their power, as uniting with them pushes [the women] to the wicked customs of those who are strangers to the fear of God and gives them a weak will. Christian women, therefore, should abstain entirely from living with pagans; and she who dares to transgress this has become distant from the Church and all Christian honour by the Word of our Lord. [...]

16. Concerning those who, by taking two wives, are defiled and transgress the law of Christianity.

Those who are temperate and go under the name of believers should stay away from the pagan customs of taking two wives, and warily keep themselves from condemnation by the laws. Just as they have been sanctified through the baptism of Christ and set apart from the defiled work practised by the nations, strangers to the fear of God, so God's blessing waxes strongly upon them as [they] keep the laws of the fear of His name. If there are men who, in madness, scorn this [principle] and dare to keep other women in addition to their lawful wives – whether near or far, free women or slaves, calling [them] 'concubines' or otherwise – and, when they are admonished to turn away from defiled behaviour, [either] do not obey or promise to reform but lie – men such as these have become estranged from all Christian honour by the Word of our Lord. [...]

19. Concerning the bishop and the honour due him; and that laymen who have been placed in [positions of] authority may not demand tribute from him.

The honourable position of any bishop who fulfils his office well and is skilled in his work should be distinct from [that] of his flock, in all the excellent things in which he is honoured and which he enjoys. Laymen who hold [temporal] power may not, therefore, demand from him the poll-tax or tribute as if from an unconsecrated person; for [the bishop] bears the burden of governing [those laymen] by fulfilling his office, keeping vigilance for their souls according to the pastoral rule and supporting [them in] their difficulties. Because of this, they are obligated to do him honour in this matter and not demand from him the poll-tax as [they do] from all other men. If they dare to contravene this, let them know that they are condemned to justice. [pp. 223–6]

42

Theodore bar Koni, *Scholion*, chapter 10

Ryann Elizabeth Craig, Georgetown University

Theodore bar Koni was born sometime in the mid-eighth century and died sometime in the late eighth or early ninth century. He lived in southern Iraq, between present-day Baṣra and Kufa, and was a teacher and scholar in the Church of the East. He is known for the *Scholion*, a book for teaching novices in the church at the School of Kashkar. In this he presents an apology for dyophysite (two natures) Christology based on the teachings of Theodore of Mopsuestia, the major authority in Bar Koni's Church.

Chapter (*Memrā*) 10 of the *Scholion* (c. 792/3) reflects knowledge of contemporary Christian-Muslim discourse through the common Syriac religious instruction format of a back-and-forth debate between teacher (*malpānā*) and student (*eskolyon*). Theodore never uses direct terms for Islam or Muslims, nor does he reference qur'anic passages, though he draws attention to interreligious concerns through verbal roots such as *s-h-d* (Ar. *sh-h-d*; *shahāda*, the Islamic confession of faith) and *š-l-m* (Ar. *s-l-m*; *islām* and *muslim*). His anonymous pupil serves as the Muslim counterpoint, reflecting Islamic teachings on Jesus as no more than a human messenger from God.

Bar Koni aims to illustrate that the typologies presented in the Old Testament are fulfilled in the New Testament, in response to those *ḥanpē* (non-Christians; here probably Muslims) who claim to accept the Old Testament but reject the New. In his explanation of the relationship of the Testaments, Theodore questions his student: What of the New Testament do you not agree with? This opens the discussion to the pupil's rejection of Jesus' divine sonship, through discourse on baptism, the sacraments and veneration of the Cross. Bar Koni addresses each of these objections in turn and especially draws on the *typos* (*ṭupsā*) of the Ark of the Covenant to make his case for the veneration of the Cross. His discourse on the Cross interweaves Christian discussions on images and likenesses with challenges to the public display of crosses in the Islamic world.

CMR 1, pp. 343–6.

This translation is based on A. Scher (ed.), *Theodorus bar Kōnī: Liber scholiorum* (Corpus Scriptorum Christianorum Orientalium 55), Paris, 1910, vol. 2.

On the Testaments

Teacher: Is everything that is written in both Testaments true or not?

Student: I agree with (*š-l-m*) all that is in the Old Testament because I know that there is neither addition nor subtraction in it, according to the saying of the one who handed down (*š-l-m*) this teaching to us [Muḥammad]. But I certainly do not agree with (*š-l-m*) all that is written in the New Testament because there are many things in it that are corrupted. While they were not [original], others introduced and mixed them in, causing error.

Teacher: What are those [things] from the New Testament that you do not agree with?

Student: I believe that the Messiah was born of a virgin, that he was sent by the One who gave the Law, that he will bring to pass the Resurrection and Judgement,[12] and that he is now in heaven.[13] But I am unable to call him 'Son of God', as you all blasphemously proclaim – that God has a son, that he is begotten of Him, or that he is consubstantial.

Teacher: It seems that this is what separates you from our confession; we confess that God has a Son, begotten from Him, consubstantial with Him, who is perfect like Him in everything.

Student: Truly this [belief of mine] does not permit me to believe that it might be possible that the simple and formless [God] should beget! Moreover, I do not accept (*š-l-m*) baptism, the mysteries,[14] or the [veneration of the] Cross. [pp. 235–6]

On the veneration of the Cross

Student: Why do you worship the Cross? Have you not read what God has forbidden, 'You shall not worship any image or any likeness'?[15] You who worship the Cross publicly worship creation.

Teacher: If it is because we worship the Cross that we are considered worshippers of likenesses, then let the Jews also be taken into consideration, who worshipped the wood of the Ark [of the Covenant] as well. But it is evident that it is not the *wood* that we worship; otherwise, we would not make the Cross from gold, nor from clay or plaster. But if it is from various kinds [of materials] we make each form of the Cross, it is obvious that it is not the material we worship but the Messiah, who was crucified for us, whom we worship in this type.

Student: What is the meaning of the Cross?

Teacher: The meaning of the Cross is to be an image of the death of the Messiah, who was crucified for us – although we worship this type, it is through it[16] – whose

---

[12] Cf. Q 43:61.

[13] Q 4:158.

[14] The Eucharist.

[15] Deuteronomy 5:8.

[16] Bar Koni is speaking about how the Cross is used in worship as an icon, looking to the reality behind the image.

heroic power was made known in the resurrection which he accomplished. We depict and make it [the Cross] for this purpose, and you should know that this is not an ordinary object. For all the signs of his Apostles were performed through it; otherwise, tell me, will you confess that God was in the Messiah and worked power through him – or not?

Student: I certainly do not say that God dwells in him, but that the will of God accompanied him.

Teacher: Like whom?

Student: Like Moses and like each one of the other saints.

Teacher: Then all the prophets [are messiahs]![17] What need was there for this [Messiah] when there are many messiahs? These testify (*s-h-d*) that he is superior among them; if not, by what power will he bring about the Resurrection and judge the world? For it is clear that he would not be able to judge everything unless he had surpassed those who will be judged by him. Indeed, that he is judge you too attest (*s-h-d*).

Student: And could it be that he is most excellent among the righteous ones?

Teacher: If he is more excellent than them and judges them, it is clear that God is in him since a [mere] man cannot judge spirits and bodies. And if God is in him, then likewise, it is also true that we rightly worship him and honour him as the temple and as the divine dwelling.[18]

Student: I certainly do not say that he was crucified, as this would be a dishonour for him and for us![19] For him, as the one for whom what is written down afterwards is an abuse; for us, because it is not proper that we should confess a crucified man.

Teacher: Your conscience is so very weak that it is at the same time unreflecting and incredulous! Just a little while ago, you confessed that you agree with (*š-l-m*) the Old Testament, but you have been found out as a liar regarding that! And you also strive to overthrow and conceal valuable testimony (*s-h-d*) and knowledge concerning the Law.

Student: How so?

Teacher: Behold, the holy prophets proclaimed his Passion and the whole world testifies (*s-h-d*) to it! But you boldly mock the Scriptures and the world, though God is not mocked.[20] You must know clearly that it is because he was going to be raised from the wood that he exalted it, so that by his Cross and his death, he gathered all rational minds to the wonder of his resurrection. Otherwise, tell me, what reason compelled God that by a lamb he should deliver the people from Egypt,[21] and by gazing upon the bronze serpent that Moses raised up (*z-q-p*),[22] he should heal the Hebrews from the

---

[17] Cf. Psalm 105:15; Habakkuk 3:13.

[18] Bar Koni appeals to the term *shekhinah*, used in Jewish literature to denote the settling place of the divine presence.

[19] Q 4:157-8.

[20] Galatians 6:7.

[21] Exodus 12:3-13; cf. 1 Corinthians 5:7 and John 1:29.

[22] This verbal root is used in the *Peshiṭta* for 'crucify' and 'crucifixion'.

bites of venomous snakes.[23] Now, these were allegories of the Cross of the Messiah. It is indeed the custom of God to show his strength through weak things, so that it might be known that the weakness of God is stronger than men.[24] If by these [things] God has not been diminished but exceedingly exalted, then the Cross of our Saviour does not deserve to be mocked; it is in truth the strength of God and the wisdom of God.[25] [pp. 270–2]

---

[23] Numbers 21:6–9; cf. John 3:14–15.
[24] 1 Corinthians 1:25.
[25] 1 Corinthians 1:24.

43

Dionysius of Tell Maḥrē, *Chronicle*

Marianna Mazzola, Ghent University

Patriarch of the Syrian Orthodox Church (818–45) and historian, Dionysius of Tell Maḥrē was the offshoot of a prominent Christian family from Edessa. He became a monk at the monastery of Qenneshrē, north of Mabbug, which was an important centre of Greek study in the Syriac-speaking Middle East. After the destruction of the monastery by Arab bandits, probably in 811, Dionysius moved to another monastery and eventually, in 816, to the monastery of Mor Ya'qub at Kaysum. He was elected patriarch in August 818 at a synod in Callinicum. Dionysius inherited from his predecessor Cyriacus a long-lasting conflict with a schismatic group led by Abraham, a monk of Qarṭmin, who opposed the patriarchal exclusion of the formula 'we break the heavenly bread' from the Syrian Orthodox liturgy. As a result, Dionysius had to appeal repeatedly to Muslim authorities to prevent Abraham receiving from them official recognition as patriarch.

Dionysius seems to have maintained close and continuous relations with the Muslim leaders: around 820 he obtained permission from ʿUthmān ibn Thumāma, local ruler of Syria during the fourth civil war, to rebuild his former monastery of Qenneshrē. In 824–5,[26] he travelled to Egypt to appeal to the emir ʿAbdallāh ibn Ṭāhir (r. 821/2–44) against the destruction of churches in Edessa and Ḥarrān, that had been ordered by his brother Abū Isḥāq (later caliph al-Muʿtaṣim). Besides representing his community before the caliph and his agents, Dionysius was also charged with responsibilities on behalf of the caliph. In 830 he led a diplomatic mission to mediate with a group of Coptic Christians, known as Bashmurites, who had revolted against the Muslim governor. He was certainly fluent in Arabic as he was able to converse directly with Muslim authorities, but he wrote exclusively in Syriac.

Dionysius wrote a history in sixteen books covering the years 582–842. It was divided into two parts, dealing with ecclesiastical and with secular matters, and Dionysius himself figures prominently in the narration of the ecclesiastical events of

[26] This is the date given in Dionysius' *Chronicle*, but according to Islamic sources, ʿAbdallāh ibn Ṭāhir went to Egypt in 826/7.

his time. Besides his first-hand observations, he relied on a wide range of sources in Syriac, Arabic and Greek, some of which are now lost.

A correct assessment of Dionysius's perspective on Islam is partially hindered by the fact that his *Chronicle* is not preserved independently but is known only from fragments incorporated into later chronicles, giving rise to the risk of ascribing other authors' reworkings to Dionysius's authentic material. In consequence, fragments explicitly ascribed to him, including autobiographical reports, turn out to be the most reliable sources on which the interpretation of his view of Islam can be based.

The first person narrative of Dionysius's encounter with the Caliph al-Ma'mūn (r. 813–33) in 828–9 provides an excellent example of the themes and arguments he adopted to conceptualize his ideal relationship between Christians (especially Syrian Orthodox) and their Muslim rulers. As patriarch, Dionysius had to face some internal opposition, against which he often appealed to Muslim authorities. The reason for this visit to al-Ma'mūn's court was the issuing of the edict that allowed any group of at least ten persons belonging to the same confession to appoint their own leader. Originally conceived for the Jewish community, according to Dionysius, this edict posed a serious threat to his authority and to the survival of his own Church.

Throughout the disputation, Dionysius argues for the intrinsic difference as well as the equality between ecclesiastical and caliphal authority. The establishment of the ecclesiastical hierarchy derives from the tradition of the apostolic succession and, accordingly, it does not follow the practices of political authority: the bishops elect the patriarch, and it is only then that he is confirmed by the ruler with a diploma. According to Dionysius, the political interaction between Christians and their Muslim rulers had long been regulated by the first covenants that Muḥammad or the first caliphs had made with Christians, thus providing historical legitimation to his requests.

CMR 1, pp. 622–6.

This translation is based on a fragment from Dionysius preserved in the *Chronicle* of Michael the Great, in J.B. Chabot (ed.), *Chronique de Michel le Syrien, patriarche jacobite d'Antioche (1166–1199)*, Paris, 1910, ch. 4, pp. 516–20.

In the morning I entered into his [al-Ma'mūn's] presence alone and most of the bishops remained at the door. I found him sitting on his throne with the doctors and judges of Baghdad, each one sitting according to his rank. When they had finished, I greeted him. He ordered me to sit in front of him and he told me: 'You, O patriarch, have been accused of tyranny to us because of the decree that has been issued regarding you. Because of this we have gathered the lawyers to talk with you before them.'

Then he turned towards the elders and said: 'What does it seem to you? Should we appoint governors of the Christians as long as the reign is ours or, according to the law that I have issued for them and the Jews, should they observe the good practice of being subject to us and of dwelling in peace? For they enjoy the peace that we gained with our army, since nobody forces them to change their faith or their customs. Will we be their judges when they misbehave?'

When they had heard this question and the answer that he had deceitfully implied there, they replied: 'Who else is able in judgment like you and could issue a judgment more rightful than this one?'

When I heard the verdict of the elders of Susanna[27] I did not reply, but I said to al-Ma'mūn: 'If you allow me, I would like to speak of all the mysteries of the Christians.' When he gave me permission, I said: 'Since our faith dates back to the beginning of the world through the teaching of the Messiah who saved us from idolatry after the divine economy[28] was accomplished, before ascending to heaven he called his disciples and ordered them to preach his creed by signs and wonders. These disciples attracted all men, little by little, to this confession and, since they knew that they were mortal, they thought of leaving the governance of those whom they had instructed to others before they died. They divided the habitable earth into four parts, appointed a leader for each one and called him patriarch. They established their seats in the greatest cities: Rome, Alexandria, Constantinople and Antioch. They ordained bishops, one of whom rules over every ten bishops and he is called metropolitan. When a bishop who is under (his jurisdiction) dies, they gave him the power to appoint another one in his place.

They gave the bishops power to appoint priests and deacons and the other ranks that are below them. Thanks to this, the power of the patriarch was extended to the bishops, the priests and the deacons, and whoever is ranked under the patriarch cannot revolt against him, to break one of his orders or to judge him on whatever he does unless he has a lapse of faith or he misbehaves. In this case the three [other] patriarchs gather and judge him, and this law still continues until the present, and no king from the time of the Messiah until now has changed these customs; the kings of the Arabs in particular have not done so.

Your fathers of pious memory confirmed our authority and used to give us a diploma. Even you did so at the beginning of your reign because you proceeded in justice. And now, O king, no new law should be issued for us because there is not a king wise, eloquent and magnanimous like you. As to those who complain of an insane bishop who has been deposed, the king knows that it is customary for evil men among the Christians who are deposed to make such accusations against us. Since they know that with our laws they cannot prevail, they hasten to come to you and by means of false accusers they complain of us to you, saying that we are enemies of the Muslims, that we despise your Prophet, and other absurdities worthy of death.'

[27] A reference to the story of Susanna and the Elders of the exiled Jewish community in Babylon, in Daniel 13 (found only in Roman Catholic and Orthodox versions of the Bible). The wicked elders, who have been lecherously spying on her, condemn Susanna to death on false charges.

[28] Literally 'guidance' or 'direction'. It signifies the Incarnation, life and death of Christ that brought about the salvation of the world.

When I told the story of David of Dara against George, and of the monks of Gubbo Barroyo and Abiram against Cyriacus,[29] and concluded the speech [asking him] not to accept the accusations against us, he replied: 'We have heard what [our] predecessors did with you and we also have the power to do what is suitable. But why do you Christians, more than any other religion, resist this edict?' And I replied: 'The others are also irritated: they are waiting for my speech to be delivered against this law. Our authority is different from that of the Mages[30] or the Jews: they call their leaders kings, and their authority is passed on by inheritance. They pay a tribute to their leaders, a thing that is not found at all among us.

There are three [kinds of] authorities in this world: I will call them natural, coercive and voluntary. The natural [is] like that of the father, head of the sons, or the husband, head of the wife, and in this all men are alike. The coercive [is] granted by God or established by the fear of the sword, like this worldly reign that truly belongs to you [but only] in appearance to those who take taxes and tribute, who are subject to you and offer [you] gifts, and their leader cares only about the love for money. Among us headship results from election and internal agreement, and we consider it a priesthood and not a headship. It is what you call the position of imam. Like the imam who prays first and advises on doing good actions, so the patriarch and the bishops stand at the head, pray, exhort on the law, and decree punishment for those who misbehave, not with tortures or executions as you do but with the deposition from his rank if he is a bishop or a priest, and if he is a layman we expel him from the church.

Therefore, we do not resemble the Gentiles, O king, and the harm caused to us by annulling our leadership is not about money, but it touches our faith and distances us from God. We are not interested in sharing leadership with you, but rather hope that our laws will not be damaged by allowing whoever wants to become leader'.

Then he said: 'We do not forbid you to depose someone who has misbehaved or to remove him from his rank. But we do not judge it right to expel him from the church or to forbid him to pray.'

---

29 David of Dara was Syrian Orthodox counter-patriarch in 762–4 in the time of the pontificate of George I (758–90). Abiram (Abraham, a monk of Qarṭmin) and the monks of Gubbo Barroyo, a monastery in the Syrian desert between Aleppo and Mabbug, led a revolt against the Syrian Orthodox patriarch Cyriacus (r. 793–817) and his successor Dionysius of Tell Maḥrē (r. 818–45) because of their dissenting views on the adoption of the liturgical formula 'we break the heavenly bread'.

30 Persian Zoroastrians.

44

Two excerpts from the *Life of Gabriel of Beth Qustan*

Jeanne-Nicole Mellon Saint-Laurent, Marquette University

The *Qartmin Trilogy* contains the *Lives* of three saints connected with the monastery of Qartmin, or Mor Gabriel, in present-day Ṭur ʾAbdin in southeast Turkey, an important cultural and intellectual centre for the Syrian Orthodox Church. This text probably dates to the ninth century. Below are two excerpts from the *Life* of one of these saints, Mor Gabriel of Beth Qustan (b. 593), who became abbot of the monastery of Qartmin. The story idealizes the monks of Qartmin and their way of life and features their interactions with local villagers and Arabs. The text presents Gabriel as a miracle worker and holy man who mediated for the Christians during the Arab conquest in the seventh century.

The first excerpt (*Life* 10) describes how Mor Gabriel performed miracles that inspired the conversion of an Arab. The text does not identify this Arab specifically as a Muslim, but it shows how Christian authors represented Arabs in their sacred writings. The second excerpt (*Life* 12) describes a treaty between Mor Gabriel and ʿUmar ibn al-Khaṭṭāb (r. 634–44), the second caliph, during whose reign Gabriel was Metropolitan of Dara. It is possible that Mor Gabriel met the caliph in 639 and negotiated a treaty with him about the rights and obligations of Christians under Islamic rule. Mor Gabriel's hagiography adds embellishments to the negotiation, though parts of it could be historical. It seems possible that monks in the early years after the Muslim conquests did not have to pay tribute.

CMR 1, pp. 892–7.

See also Z. Joseph, *Mor Gabriel aus Beth Qusṭan. Leben und Legende eines Syrischen Abtbischofs aus dem 7. Jahrhundert*, Hildesheim, 2010.

This English translation is reproduced with permission from Andrew Palmer, who includes the entire *Life* of Mor Gabriel as a microfiche supplement in his book *Monk and Mason on the Tigris Frontier*, Cambridge, 1990.

Chapter 10. John of the Arabs

Now, in the time of the blessed Mor Gabriel, when he was head of the abbey, there came a certain Arabian from the desert of 'Arab in the south; a rich merchant he was and of great wealth. He arrived at this abbey bringing with him a great deal of gold, and he came into this place to a certain perfect monk who was upright in [his] ways. The Arab saw the discretion of this monk and resolved that he would leave some of his gold with his saintly old friend, whether on account [of the frailty] of life [in general] or on account of the danger of the journey. Now this was God's doing! So the Arab left with the old man one thousand dinars. [...]

But when he got back to this holy abbey, he found that his friend, the old man, had been dead for a year or so. He made thorough enquiries concerning him and asked people: 'Where is my friend? He has a deposit of mine, and I want it back.' They told him, 'He has left this life.' He said to them, 'What, then, did he instruct you concerning me?' They said to him, 'He told us nothing at all about your deposit nor about you. But there is a chaste disciple of his, who will not withhold any information he may have received concerning the gold. For we know him [to be] a truthful man like his master was.' The Arab said to them, 'Come now. Show me the disciple, for I don't know him.'

Then the disciple was summoned into the assembly of the brothers, and the Arab asked the disciple about the gold. But he replied, 'I know nothing of what you say.' Then the Arab rebuked him angrily and said, 'Your master was a just and an upright man, and it was because I knew that he was God-fearing that I entrusted him with my gold. Often I tried to persuade him – begged him even – to take a little of the gold, if only one coin, or else some food or clothing – although he never yielded to such pressure – for I knew that if he were to accept anything from me, I should soon be compensated for it by his Lord. So I know now that he would not have cheated me of the gold I left with him. But as for you, you blockhead, ignoramus, of this you may be certain: if you do not return to me the deposit which your master left with you, I shall dissect you limb from limb and [I shall torment you] with brandings of fire and with cruel tortures; and do not suppose that I shall cease from this until I have extinguished your life!'

The disciple, being ignorant of this matter, was at a loss for words, so he just said, 'The Lord's will be done! He will reveal the truth.' Then the Arab took the innocent man in anger and dragged him face downwards to the ground and led him to the place where his slaves were encamped with his merchandise; there he set about him with torturing and with cruel blows all that day.

At nightfall, he chained him up with iron fetters. [...] When the day dawned, the Arab began [once more] to torture the disciple. The victim of this abuse wept bitterly from the pain of his torments. He was heard by God's bishop, Mor Gabriel, who went to the house of saints, there to pray to God concerning the gold. [At this point], the disciple looked up and saw the man of God, and he set off at a run bringing the Arab with him, and he came and found the chosen one lying face downwards above the tomb of the master of [that] disciple. When his prayer was finished, he called the Arab and said to him, 'Come over here!' And he came and stood behind him. Then the blessed one cried out aloud, '[I adjure you], O blessed Father, by the God, before whom you laboured in justice and in righteousness, tell me, where is the gold of this Arab?' No sooner had he spoken than a voice arose from within the tomb which spoke as follows, 'I, John, who fell asleep here one year ago, tell you, O chosen one of God, that the gold is still in the place where its owner himself dug a hole and placed it, without my [even] touching it. And there is no one who knows where it is except him alone.' Then the Lord cleared the mind of the Arab, and he understood what the deceased one was saying from within the tomb; and he began to ask the saintly Mor Gabriel to open up the tomb for him that his faith might be confirmed.

The blessed one did not prevent him, but rather granted his wish according to his request. So the Arab went down into the tomb and found the dead man wrapped and enveloped in a shroud, having loosened which, he gazed at him for a while. When he was sure that it was his friend, he prostrated himself upon him and kissed him, and weeping said, 'How blessed I am to have been worthy to be blessed by your holiness! From now onwards – your Lord is my witness! – I shall never leave this holy abbey nor the vicinity of your resting place, in which the dead converse and speak with the living on equal terms whenever they will. For in truth I know that there is no God except Christ,[31] to whom be glory forever!'

Then they restored the tomb to its former state; the Arab went to the place where he had buried the treasure with his own hands and found it with the seals that were on it still unbroken and whole. Immediately he freed his slaves and gave them much gold, and each of them went whither he would. His camels he left to bring grain to the abbey, but all [the rest] of his wealth he distributed in gifts to the poor, except that which he offered for the adornment of the Great Temple. And forthwith he was baptized and was given the name 'John' after his friend who had died [pp. LXVII–LXXII].

Chapter 12. Gabriel's treaty with the Arabs

Now this Mor Gabriel went to the court of the governor of the sons of Hagar, who was ʿUmar son of Khaṭṭab, in the city of Jazire. He was received with great gladness, and after a few days the blessed one petitioned the governor and received his written authority concerning the statutes and laws and orders and warnings and judgements and observances pertaining to the Christians; to churches and monasteries; and to priests and deacons, that they should not pay [poll-tax?]; and to monks that they should be exempt from tribute; and that the use of the wooden gong should not be banned, and that they might practise the chanting of anthems at the bier of a dead man when he leaves his house to be taken for burial, together with many [other] customs.[32] This prefect was pleased that the blessed one had come to see him; as for the holy man he returned to the abbey with great joy [p. LXXII].

---

[31] A possible reminiscence of the first part of the *shahāda*, the Muslim declaration of faith: 'There is no god but God'.

[32] This list of concessions overturns some of the stipulations in the *Pact of ʿUmar*, traditionally associated with the second caliph.

45

The History of the Anonymous Storyteller

Tim Greenwood, University of St Andrews

The History of the Anonymous Storyteller is a little-studied Armenian text, best known for its misidentification at the start of the twentieth century as the otherwise-missing *History* of Šapuh Bagratuni. It represents a form of historical composition which is rarely preserved, since it comprises a series of unreliable tales about well-known figures from the past, loosely woven together. Their dubious probative value as narratives should not, however, be confused with their historical potential. Even invented worlds can reveal something of the context in which they were imagined, and treating these stories as products of popular cultural expression invests them with new significance. While the characters portrayed are often creative amalgamations of two or more figures with the same names, the tales betray a remarkable geographical coherence, being focused on the eastern districts of the kingdom of Vaspurakan and regions to the east of these, including Hēr, Salmast, Marand and the city of Tabriz. The latest event alluded to is a campaign undertaken by Smbat II Bagratuni in Abkhazia in 989. There is no hint of Seljuq raiding, nor of the Byzantine annexation of Vaspurakan in 1021, establishing a late tenth- or early eleventh-century window for its composition.

The following extract derives from the first of the tales, and offers an original and divergent account of the life and career of the Prophet Muḥammad. Although containing elements of the polemical Baḥīrā legend, which is found for the first time in Armenian tradition in the *History* of T'ovma Artsruni (compiled *c.* 904), the Anonymous Storyteller also claims that Muḥammad was a Persian.[33] These and other features suggest that this story reflects a Persianate dimension, and eastern Armenia at this time affords a plausible context of production, if not origin. It is unique in medieval Armenian literature, supplying a rare glimpse of cultural interaction and fusion at a regional level.

---

[33] R.W. Thomson, 'Armenian Variations on the Baḥira Legend', *Harvard Ukrainian Studies* 3 (1979–80) 884–95.

This translation is based on Anonymous Storyteller/Pseudo-Šapuh Bagratuni, *Patmut'iwn Ananun zruc'agri karcec'eal Šapuh Bagratuni*, ed. and trans. M.H. Darbinyan-Melik'yan, Yerevan, 1971, pp. 41–7. A translation of the complete text can be found in R.W. Thomson, 'The Anonymous Story-Teller (also known as "Pseudo-Šapuh")', *Revue des Études Arméniennes* 21 (1988–9) 171–232.

[p. 41] Then the forerunner of the Antichrist appeared who is Mēhēmēt', the leader of the Muslims.[34] There was a certain man from the country of the Persians and his name was Aptṙahman ('Abd al-Raḥmān),[35] son of Abdali, son of Belmiki, from the city of Ṙueran near to the city of Ṙēy, opposite the fortress of Aspahan.[36] He fathered a son and named him Mēhēmēt' and then he fathered a daughter and named her Fat'ima, a very beautiful woman.[37] Now the son of Abdṙahman, Mahamat, was demon-possessed and driven mad by the demon day after day, and he broke out of the iron chains and bonds and was led by the demon into deserts, mountains and caves. His father spent large sums of money on doctors but to no avail and he remained in perpetual torment. And a man came to him and conversed with him, saying 'take your son to the land of the Syrians, to a man named Sargis.[38] In accordance with his faith, he will be dressed in a monk's tunic and clothed in black and he will heal your son.'

And Abdṙahman arose and took his son Mahmēt and went to the land of the Syrians and encountered the Syrian monk and they arrived at the mountain of monasteries[39] and the demon apprehended him and threw him to the ground and he raved and foamed exceedingly. And Sargis arrived and took hold of Mahmēt and lifted him up. And Abdṙahman said, 'If it is possible and you are able to heal my son, I will give you many treasures and valuable clothing and excellent horses.' And he undertook that he would cure him. And Abdṙahman left Mahmēt his son with him and went away. And the man was by faith a Nestorian, demonic and a lover of sorcery; he was particularly skilled in the demonic arts of enchantment and [p. 43] sorcery. And Mahmēt was by faith an idolator and a Magus.[40] And Sargis said to Mahmēt, 'If you believe in God and

---

[34] As Thomson observes at p. 173, n. 4, the spelling of Muḥammad is inconsistent across the text; Mahmēt is the usual form. The same applies to Aptṙahman/Abdṙahman (for 'Abd al-Raḥmān) and Fat'ima/Fatma (for Fāṭima). There may or may not be significance in these divergences.
[35] The name of Muḥammad's father is given in Muslim biographies as 'Abd Allāh.
[36] Ṙēy/Ray, now a suburb of Tehran. Aspahan/Isfahan is 300 km south, so hardly opposite.
[37] Historically, Fāṭima was Muḥammad's daughter not his sister, but her marriage to his cousin 'Alī conforms to Islamic tradition.
[38] Sargis or Sergius was one of the names by which the figure of Baḥīrā the monk was known, as was also Nestorius. In this form of the legend, he is a member of a religious community rather than an anchorite, and rather than emerging from his cell under divine inspiration to recognize the young Muḥammad, he conspires with Muḥammad to come in procession from his monastery to recognize him.
[39] The region of Ṭur 'Abdīn ('mountain of the servants of God') in southeast Turkey, known for its concentration of monasteries.
[40] Usually understood to mean a Persian Zoroastrian, a believer in ultimate powers of good and evil. The *Majūs* are mentioned in the Qur'an (22:17), and in the Muslim tradition they are consistently condemned because of their dualist beliefs.

turn from your idolatry, I shall cure you.' And he agreed and was baptized by him. And he baptized him according to the Nestorian faith. And he was healed. Mahmēt stayed with him for twenty-three years[41] and was united with Satan in his body and soul and he was instructed in the art of sorcery and he learned all the magical charms and false beliefs of Nestorius.

After this, the news reached Mahmēt, 'Your father Aptřahman has died.' And on hearing this, he wept. Sargis said, 'Do not weep because your father has died since I am going to make you greater than your father and all your clan. Now, arise and visit your father's house and return to me.' And Mahmēt arose and went to his land with two from the community of monks and reached Sumira.[42] And he discovered his dead father and his sister, the wife of Alē, his brother's son, and said 'Why, Alē, did you plunder my father's house and take all the treasures and the clothes of my father and all his possessions?'[43] And Mahmēt caused great uproar and took some part from Alē and went and returned to the land of Assyria, to the monastery of Demetrius, to the monk Sargis, and reported what had happened.[44] Sargis said, 'Do not be afraid, Mahmēt, for I am devising the means for you to become great. Now arise and go once more to your father's house and there persuade some merchants to go to the land of Egypt. And when you arrive opposite my monastery, make camp. Do not say, "I know this monastery or these places or surroundings," or that it signifies the site of your camp. And I shall take my deacons and shall approach you with torches and candles and lifting our voices to heaven. I shall terrify the Persians who will have followed you and I shall say to them, "I saw a heavenly vision concerning this young man because this one is some prophet and it is right to trust him and whatever he says will come into being".'

And Mehmēt did everything Sargis the sorcerer had instructed. And Mehmēt crossed to the land of the Persians, to the city of Sumira and he induced the merchants [p. 45] to go to the land of Egypt, to the city of Skantaria.[45] And rich and prominent men gathered and went and arrived in the land of Assyria. Now on the road, Mahmēt said, 'O wealthy Persians, we are not faithful or pious men since our idols are useless because I have heard from certain ones that God exists in heaven above the sun, who has appeared to us.' And they said, 'What are you, Mehmēt? Be quiet and don't speak about that.' But he began to describe to them the first days, from Abraham, from Noah and likewise from Adam. And they were amazed at his wisdom and said, 'O Mahmēt, from where do you speak these words and so much knowledge?' And he said, 'Wisdom, knowledge and prophecy have been given to me from above.' And

[41] The period over which Muḥammad received the revelations that were compiled into the Qur'an.

[42] Sumira/Sāmarrā in central Iraq, founded in 836.

[43] *mlk'ers*: not an Armenian word, probably based on the Arabic *milk*, 'possessions' or 'property', but with a mediaeval Armenian plural marker *er* and a classical Armenian accusative plural marker *s*, hence, following standard Armenian rules of vocalic alternation, the contraction to *mlk'*.

[44] The precise location of this monastery in the Ṭur 'Abdīn is unclear.

[45] Skantaria/Alexandria, not Cairo/Fusṭāṭ. This could suggest an awareness of traditions surrounding Alexander the Great, some of which circulated through the Alexander Romance in a wide range of languages and versions throughout the mediaeval period in Armenian, Arabic and Persian.

when they were close to the monastery, they camped there, opposite the monk's monastery in accordance with his advice.

And the monk Sargis came out at night bringing torches and candles and deacons and the monks, and coming to the spot where Mahmēt was, they surrounded him with great shouting and the merchants awoke unexpectedly and were terrified. And getting up they went to him and said to the monk, 'What is this which we have been hearing, Nestor Sargis, about this man?' And he said, 'I saw a heavenly vision about him and a great light and angels who were saying that he is a great prophet and whatever he says will be, the words of this man are true' [p. 47]. And then the merchants realized, 'The words of this man which he spoke to us when we were going along the road were correct.' And they arose and went on their way. And when they returned to their country, each to his own house, they declared that Mahmēt was a prophet. [...]

And Mahmēt began to construct the great city of Baghdad on the bank of the river Euphrates.[46] And there was hostility between Ali and Mahmēt and Ali held one side of the river and Mahmēt the other [...] warfare between Ali [and Mahmēt ...].[47] For he did not permit the performance of prophecy which Ali had. And he planned to kill Mahmēt but was unable because his sister Fatima was wife to Alē and she would not allow him to kill Mahmēt.

---

[46] Pałtad/Baghdad, founded in 762; Ebrat/Euphrates.
[47] There is a lacuna in the manuscript at this point.

46

Elias of Nisibis, *Chronography*

Anna Chrysostomides, Queen Mary University of London

Elias of Nisibis was born in Shenna, northern Iraq, sometime in the mid-tenth century. He belonged to the Church of the East and was educated near Mosul at St Michael's monastery. In his later years he was ordained as bishop of Beth Nuhadra (1002) and metropolitan of Nisibis (1008). The precise date of his death, sometime in the 1040s, is contested.

Elias was active in explaining and defending Christian teachings against the challenge of Islam. One of his best-known works is the *Kitāb al-majālis* ('The sessions'), the record of a series of debates in which he participated with the Muslim vizier Abū l-Qāsim al-Ḥusayn ibn ʿAlī l-Maghribī in the town of Mayyāfāriqīn in present-day southeastern Turkey, probably in 1026. During the course of seven sessions he succeeds, among other things, in demonstrating to the vizier's satisfaction that Christians worship one God and should be regarded as monotheists for legal purposes (see passage 21 above).

His chronicle, *Maktbānut zabnē* ('Chronography'), written in both Syriac and Arabic, covers the years 25–1018. Dated to 1019, it has two sections. The first contains a list of secular and ecclesiastical leaders, followed by short entries on politics and significant ecclesiastical events, and the second includes tables of feasts and years according to the various eastern calendars. One of its most striking features is its citations from Muslim historians writing in Arabic alongside Christians writing in Syriac. Not only was Elias unusual in listing his sources (he cites up to 60 works), but he was the first Syriac author known to employ Muslim authors without any mention of uncertainty about their dependability.

CMR 2, pp. 727–30.

This translation is based on Elias of Nisibis, *Eliae Metropolitae Nisibeni Opus Chronologicum*, ed. E.W. Brooks, Paris, 1909–10, pp. 126–30.

1 AH: The first year began on Friday 16 Tāmūz in the year 933 of the Greeks [16 July 622 CE].[48]

[Source listed: Muḥammad ibn Jarīr al-Ṭabarī, *History of the prophets and kings*]

In this year Muḥammad ibn ʿAbd Allāh, prophet of the Arabs and their first king, entered the city of Yathrib [Medina]. He reigned from Monday 8 al-Rabīʿ al-Awwal [20 September 622]. This [year] ʿAbd Allāh ibn Zubayr was born in the month of Shawwāl.[49]

2 AH: The second year began on Tuesday 5 Tāmūz of the year 934 of the Greeks [5 July 623 CE].

[Source listed: al-Ṭabarī, *History of the prophets and kings*]

In this year Muḥammad ibn ʿAbd Allāh went out to wage war with the Banū Quraysh. They met each other at a place [called] Badr and there was a battle between them on Wednesday 19 Ramaḍān. Muḥammad was victorious and took captive and killed many. All the men who were with Muḥammad were 312 [in number].

3 AH: The third year began on Sunday 27 Ḥzīrān in the year 935 of the Greeks [27 June 624 CE].

[Source listed: Isho'dnaḥ, metropolitan of Baṣra]

In this year the Jacobites, who were under the jurisdiction of Persia, assembled at the monastery of Mar Mattai in the region of Nineveh and appointed Maruta the first metropolitan of Tagrit with the consent of the Patriarch Athanasius, and ordained ten bishops under his authority. And later, following the building of Baghdad and Gezīrta, they confirmed twelve [bishops].

4 AH: The fourth year began on Thursday 13 Ḥzīrān in the year 936 of the Greeks [13 June 625 CE].

[Source listed: al-Ṭabarī, *History of the prophets and kings*]

In this year Muḥammad ibn ʿAbd Allāh made war with the Banū Nuṣayr and conquered them. They asked him to allow them to leave their dwelling-place with their camel loads and to take the rest himself. He granted them [this] and took all the horses, beasts of burden, sheep and goods that they left behind. This happened in the month of Rabīʿ I.

5 AH: The fifth year began on Monday 2 Ḥzīrān in the year 937 of the Greeks [2 June 626 CE].

[Source listed: al-Ṭabarī, *History of the prophets and kings*]

---

[48] The CE dates that are added are from L.J. Delaporte, *La chronographie d'Élie bar Šinaya, métropolitain de Nisibe*, Paris, 1910.

[49] Elias introduces each year with the Islamic calendar date (AH = *Anno Hegirae*, starting from the *hijra*, Muḥammad's migration from Mecca to Medina, in 622) and the Syrian calendar month, though he often cites important life events for famous Muslims according to months.

In this year the Jews and the Banū Quraysh made an alliance to fight against Muḥammad ibn ʿAbd Allāh. Muḥammad went out and fought them at a place called al-Khandaq. He conquered them and ʿAlī ibn Abī Ṭālib killed ʿAmr ibn ʿAdūr.[50]

6 AH: The sixth year began on Saturday 23 Iyār in the year 938 of the Greeks [23 May 627 CE].

[Source listed: Simeon, Jacobite Deacon]

In this year the Persians captured Edessa. They also arrived on the island of Rhodes and captured it.

7 AH: The seventh year began on Wednesday 11 Iyār in the year 939 of the Greeks [11 May 628 CE].

[Source listed: Isho'dnaḥ, Metropolitan of Baṣra]

In this year Khosrow, the king of the Persians, was killed, and his son Shērōē[51] ruled after him. In the beginning of his reign he ordered that Ishoʾyahb of Gdala[52] should be elected bishop of Balad and be ordained Catholicos.

8 AH: The eighth year began on Sunday 30 Nisan in the year 940 of the Greeks [30 April 629 CE].

[Source listed: al-Ṭabarī, *History of the prophets and kings*]

In this year Muḥammad ibn ʿAbd Allāh sent Zayd ibn Ḥāritha with a great army to Syria. Heraclius, King [Emperor] of the Romans, met them, accompanied by 200,000 men. He defeated the Arabs and killed Zayd ibn Ḥāritha, and with sorrow the Arabs retreated.[53]

9 AH: The ninth year began on Friday 20 Nisān in the year 941 of the Greeks [20 April 630 CE].

[Source Listed: al-Ṭabarī, *History of the prophets and kings*]

In this year Ngba[54] ibn Rūba, ruler of Eilat, came to Muḥammad ibn ʿAbd Allāh and brought him tribute. The Banū Adhkar also came to him and voluntarily gave him a tribute of 100,000 dinars. He wrote two edicts for them and for Ngba, granting all they asked from him.

10 AH: The tenth year began on Tuesday 9 Nisān in the year 942 of the Greeks [9 April 631 CE].

[Sources listed: Jacob of Edessa[55] and al-Ṭabarī, *History of the prophets and kings*]

---

[50] Otherwise known as the Battle of the Trench.

[51] Better known by his dynastic name Kavadh II (or Qobād II).

[52] Isho'yahb III.

[53] The Battle of Muʾta.

[54] This is probably a scribal error for 'Yuḥanna' ibn Rūba, as found in al-Ṭabarī; see Delaporte, *La chronographie d'Élie bar Šinaya*, p. 81.

[55] This work was presumably Jacob's *Chronology*.

In this year Athanasius, Patriarch of the Jacobites, died. And in this year Āzarmīdokht, queen of the Persians, was killed. And Hormizd reigned after her for only a few days, and the Persians drove him out of power.

11 AH: The eleventh year began on Saturday 28 Ādār in the year 943 of the Greeks [28 March 632 CE].

[Source listed: Muḥammad ibn Mūsā al-Khwārizmī, *Book of history*][56]

In this year Muḥammad ibn ʿAbd Allāh died on the Monday of the final day of Ṣafar. That same day Abū Bakr ʿAbd Allāh ibn ʿUthmān, known as al-Ṣiddīq, reigned after him. And in this year Yazdegerd ibn Shahriyar, King of the Persians, reigned. Also, in this year Fāṭima bint Muḥammad died.

12 AH: The twelfth year began on Thursday 18 Ādār in the year 944 of the Greeks [18 March 633 CE].

[Source listed: Muḥammad ibn Mūsā al-Khwārizmī, *Book of history*]

In this year Khālid ibn Walīd conquered the place of al-Yamāma. The Arabs fought with the Romans in the region of Syria.

13 AH: The thirteenth year began on Monday 7 Ādār in the year 945 of the Greeks [7 March 634 CE].

[Source listed: Muḥammad ibn Mūsā al-Khwārizmī, *Book of history*]

In this year the Arabs made war with the Romans in the region of Palestine. The Romans were defeated and many of them were killed. In this year Abū Bakr al-Ṣiddīq died. After him reigned ʿUmar ibn al-Khaṭṭāb from Monday 8 Jumādā II [8 August 634]. And in this year Abū ʿUbayd ibn Masʿūd al-Thaqafī was killed.

[56] This work is no longer extant.

47

Matthew of Edessa, *Chronicle*

Tara L. Andrews, University of Vienna

Matthew (Matt'ēos Uṙhayec'i) was an Armenian monk in the city of Edessa (present-day Şanlıurfa) in the late eleventh and early twelfth centuries. His *Zhamanakagrut'wn* ('Chronicle'), which covers the years 952–1129 (with a continuation down to 1163) is perhaps best known in the West for its account of the events of the First Crusade. But it is not merely a crusading history – rather, it contains a great deal of information pertinent to the history of the Byzantine Empire, the Kingdom of Georgia, the lost Armenian Kingdom of Ani and the nascent Kingdom of Cilicia, as well as to the Fāṭimid caliphate and the Seljuq Turkish emirates that developed in Syria and Mesopotamia during these years.

The following extract is Matthew's entry for the Armenian year 570 (1121–2). It includes an account of the Battle of Didgori in 1121, and the subsequent Georgian capture of the city of Tiflis from Seljuq control, as well as a report of a fire in Baghdad. The extract captures several features, some of them contradictory, of the perspective on Muslims that Matthew's text delivers. These include the liberal use of negative epithets for Muslim figures (Il-Ghazi as a 'murderous, insolent and evil rogue', and the mosque as 'their filthy house of assembly') and his confusion over identities and facts on the one hand ('Sadaqa the son of Dubays', referring to Dubays ibn Ṣadaqa, and Tughril Bey as the brother of Alp Arslan, when in fact they are correctly identified as uncle and nephew earlier in the text), but on the other hand the adoption of Arabic terms (Dubays as a *rafidhi*, Arabic *rāfiḍī* – a heretic or Shīʿī; Il-Ghazi as a *harami*, Arabic *ḥarāmī* – a bandit) in his account, along with a command of other details (e.g. Dubays's engagement to Il-Ghazi's daughter and his prior exploits) that suggest the Muslim world was not an entirely closed book to him – as indeed it could not have been to a resident of Edessa.

CMR 3, pp. 444–50.

This translation is based on M. Mēlik'-Adamean and N. Tēr-Mik'ayēlean (eds), *Žamanakagrut'wn Matt'ēosi Uṙhayec'woy*, Vałaršapat, 1898, pp. 348–51.

Then this thing happened in 570 of the Armenian era [19 February 1121–18 February 1122] – a certain emir from the country of Ganjak named Ghazi, a murderous, insolent and evil rogue (*harami*), shared a border with the land of the Georgians, and was friendly towards the Georgian King David [r. 1089–1125] and in submission to him. In this year he hatched an evil scheme: taking 30,000 Turkish soldiers, Ghazi entered the Georgian land, took a portion [of the people] captive and removed [them] from the Georgian land, and went and encamped in his territory.

When David the Georgian king heard this, he sent an army to the country and, coming in secret, they fell upon the Turkish army. They slaughtered 30,000 of the Turks' men and captured all their wives and children and countless flocks of sheep, together with an immense amount of booty, and they led them to the land of the Georgians.

Then the remainder of the Turkish army who had escaped the extreme danger tore their clothes and scattered ashes on their heads and, dressed in black clothes and with bare heads, went wailing to their sultan in the city of Ganjak, [p. 349] to Malik son of Tap'ar [Mahmud II, r. 1118–31], and, weeping, they raised an appeal to him about their destruction. Others reached the district of the Arab land Karmian; coming to the Emir Il-Ghazi son of Artuq [r. 1107–22],[57] they related to him with bitter weeping the losses they had sustained. In his strength and arrogance, he ordered a multitude of his troops to be assembled from all the Turkish people, from the Greek lands, as far as the east and all Karmian. He collected 150,000 soldiers, and he sent word to the southern part of the Arab lands and summoned the king of the Arabs who was called Sagha the son of Dubays [Dubays ibn Ṣadaqa, r. 1108–35], who came to him with 10,000.

This Sagha [i.e. Dubays] was a brave and warlike man; he captured the city of Baghdad and he won three battles against Tap'ar the Persian sultan [Muḥammad I, r. 1105–18], who was vanquished. He was of the *rafidhi*[58] people and a great blasphemer of Muḥammad and all his institutions. He [had] made camp with his tents in the middle of Ethiopia and in India, and at this time he had become a son-in-law to Il-Ghazi, emir of the Persians.

And in this year Il-Ghazi marched with a multitude of troops and reached the land of Ganjak, going against the land of the Georgians. Then Malik [Mahmud II], sultan of Ganjak, came with 400,000 mounted warriors; marching with a fearful multitude, they entered the Georgian land in the vicinity of the city of Tiflis at the mountain called Didgori.

When David the Georgian king, son of Bagrat, son of Georgi, heard this, he arrived to fight [p. 350] against the forces of the Turks with 40,000 men who were skilful, brave and practised in warfare. He also had other troops: 15,000 brave and choice men from the Kipchak king, and 500 men from the Alans and 100 Franks. On the 13th of the month of August, the feast of the Assumption, a Thursday, there was a violent battle

[57] This Il-Ghazi (also simply 'Ghazi' in the Armenian text) is distinct from the earlier Ghazi, whose raid was the catalyst for this episode. The names are differentiated here for clarity.

[58] From the Arabic *rāfiḍī*, 'one who rejects', often used to designate Shī'ī Muslims because they rejected the legitimacy of the first three caliphs in favour of 'Alī.

between the two mountains, so that the mountains themselves resounded from the frightful clash of the troops.

And then God's assistance came to the Georgian army. When the battle was joined, they put all the Turkish troops to flight; and on that day there was a severe and dreadful slaughter of the Turkish soldiers, and the rivers and valleys of the mountains were filled with corpses and all the rocky mountain ledges were covered with them. The number of slaughtered Turkish soldiers came to 400,000, while 30,000 men were captured and the whole surface of the fields was covered with the [bodies of the] horses and weapons of the fallen.

For eight days, the Kipchak and Georgian soldiers pursued them as far as the borders of the city of Ani. The Persian sultan Malik [Mahmud II] and Il-Ghazi returned in great disgrace to their own country having narrowly escaped, with not a hundred in a thousand [men] remaining.

In this year David, king of the Georgians, took the city of Tiflis from the Persians. He wrought fierce slaughter on the city and, impaling 500 men, brutally killed them.

In this year, in the month of August, [p. 351] fire fell from the sky and burned the chief mosque in the city of Baghdad. Tughril the Persian sultan [r. 1037–63], brother of Alp Arslan, had built this mosque; it had been built with extraordinary and marvellous craftsmanship. For when he had taken the Persian land, he had waged a great war for twenty years against the Persian nation, and finally he brought them into submission and ruled over the entire land of the Persians. Then he came to the city of Baghdad and ordered this house of prayer to be built for the Turkish nation, lest the Turkish nation enter into an Arab house of prayer. And in this year fire fell and burned the Turkish mosque, their filthy place of assembly.

48

Dionysius bar Ṣalībī, *Commentary on the Cross*

Kelli Bryant Gibson, Abilene Christian University

Dionysius (Jacob) bar Ṣalībī (d. 1171) was West Syrian bishop of Amīd and a prolific scholar. The breadth of his body of works suggests that he aimed to provide comprehensive resources for the buttressing of Syrian Orthodox doctrine. He penned apologetic works vis-à-vis other Christian denominations and other religions, including Islam. Indeed, his apology *Against the Muslims* is the longest treatise of its kind in Syriac. However, echoes of interreligious engagement are not limited to his apologetic works, and they are perhaps even more revealing when they appear in other genres.

One such text is Bar Ṣalībī's *Commentary on the Cross*, a portion of his 'sacramentary' on the rituals and implements of Christian worship. It is a short treatise, written in question-and-answer format. A central theme is the veneration of crosses: when the practice began, how it should be done, and, most importantly, that it is not idolatry. After the Arab conquests, Christians were often required to address accusations of idolatry when they mentioned the Cross, even in non-apologetic texts. Bar Ṣalībī's *Commentary on the Cross* is typical of such works in its format, appealing to figures of the Hebrew Bible cherished by Muslims and Christians alike. More striking is how Bar Ṣalībī compares Christian veneration of the Cross to Muslim reverence for Muḥammad, the Qur'an, and Mecca. In the context of the gradual numerical decline of Christianity, his casual reference to 'apostates' who break crosses is noteworthy.

CMR 3, pp. 665–70 (lacking a reference to this work).

The *Commentary on the Cross* is extant in two manuscripts, Mingana Syriac MS 215 (Birmingham, UK) and Charfeh MS 4/1 (Beirut), both of which were copied in the late nineteenth century. This translation is based on Mingana Syriac MS 215. For a full transcription and translation, see K. Bryant, 'Festal Apologetics: Syriac Treatises on the Feast of the Discovery of the Cross', Oxford, 2015 (DPhil thesis, University of Oxford).

[From Chapter 4]

But they [the Muslims] say: Why do we [Christians] worship material objects along with the sign of the cross?

We respond: 'We do not worship the materials. This is evident because we do not bow down before[59] gold, silver, stones, or other things that do not have a cross on them, but [only] those which have the mark [of the cross]. And [we do] not merely [worship] the mark, but [when] we see the sign and the cross, with the eye of the soul we perceive the crucified Christ. We worship the cross just as we eat and drink Christ by means of the bread and wine, are clothed with him in the water and oil [in baptism], and hear him in the Gospel. In this way we also worship Christ in the mark of the cross.' [...]

But they add: 'Then you *are* worshippers of material things!'

We respond: 'We do not worship gold, wood, and stones, as we have already said. Rather, in our mind we see Christ stretched upon the cross, and by adorations of the cross we worship him who was stretched upon it. In the same way, we hear his words in the gospel, even though it is written and fashioned by a person. We also eat him in the bread (that is, the Body), even though it is offered and consecrated by a person, and people bake it in an oven. We also put him on with water and oil in baptism, even though a person consecrates these things.'

The Arabs also honour Muḥammad through the Qur'an, which is honoured by them even though it is written by mere people. As for their shrine of Mecca, although they worship in it as though [worshipping] God, they also acknowledge that it was built by people, and they do not say that they worship the work of human hands. In the same way, Christians also worship Christ through the cross, although they know that the cross is the work of human hands.

If they say that it is right to reject the cross because it was fashioned by human beings, then [it would] also [be necessary] to reject the gospel and the Body and the oil which are made by human hands. [In that case,] let the Muslims[60] also reject the Qur'an and the shrine of Mecca. For people also fashioned the ark of the testimony, the tablets, the mercy seat, and the jar of manna, and, behold, they were worshipped and honoured by the Jews.[61] Again, behold, the scriptures are also fashioned from the skins of dead beasts, but because of what they signify, they are honoured.

So, therefore, [it is the same for] the cross. For just as a book is fashioned and written in a volume by a person, and a person listens to [the words][62] in it as though

---

[59] The verb 'to worship' can also mean 'to bow down'. In the Bible, Abraham performs the same action when God appears to him that Christians do towards crosses (Genesis 18:1-2). Bar Ṣalībī illustrates how the patriarchs performed physical actions (bowing down) towards physical objects while they were worshipping God. Here, when the verb is used with reference to physical objects, it is usually translated 'bowed down before', and when it is used in reference to God it is translated 'worshipped'.

[60] Bar Ṣalībī uses the word *Ṭayyoyē*, once a generic term for 'Arabs', which by his day was used synonymously with 'Muslims'.

[61] Cf. Hebrews 9:1-5.

[62] In this paragraph, the scribe has left several blank spaces to indicate deficiencies in the manuscript being copied. Here, there is a blank space of about four to five letters; this is a reasonable guess in the context.

[they come] from the mouth of God – while the construction [of the words][63] is not considered but rather the mystery hidden in them – so also [it is with] the cross [...][64] which is honoured by Christians, while with our mind's eye we see Him who was stretched upon it, and we worship him. Therefore, it is clear that we worship Christ through his cross.

[From Chapter 7]

[...] But the outsiders say, 'Because of the created materials from which the cross is fashioned, you are worshippers of created things.'[65]

Against them we say, 'Behold, when Abraham saw the likeness [of God] under the oak tree, he ran, bowed before him, and said, "My Lord, do not turn aside from your servant," even though the material of the manifestation came from various perceptible things.[66] Therefore, according to their accusation, he worshipped a created thing. Again, all of Israel bowed before the pillar of fire in the tabernacle.[67] Although they were bowing before the substance of the manifestation (that is, the pillar), [they were worshipping] God who was signified by it. Joshua and the elders also bowed before the ark, especially when Israel was routed at Ai,[68] yet Bezalel had made the ark,[69] and Moses had fashioned the tablets.[70] Solomon too bowed before an altar made by hands.[71] Likewise, the Ishmaelites[72] also bow before mosques made by hands, in the same way that we Christians also bow before the cross, yet we are not worshippers of created things. But if someone who bows before the cross worships an idol, then the Israelites who bowed before the ark worshipped idols.'

But they say, 'It is not right for you to worship the cross which has no sensation, and its physical forms are destructible and can be split.'

We say, 'Apostates do not break the power of the cross with the cross but [only] the physical material. For, behold, the ark also had no sensation, and it was worshipped by the Hebrews. The shrine of Mecca is also deprived of sensation, and it is worshipped by the Muslims. A piece of paper is not sentient, though when the name [of God] is written on it, it is worshipped. Often, the paper burns in fire, but

[63] There is a similar space in the manuscript here, but with the feminine plural pronoun suffixed to 'construction'; the feminine plural noun 'words' would make sense in the context.
[64] The scribe leaves another space here. 'To you' follows, but without the missing word(s) the original text is difficult to reconstruct. However, the gist of the passage remains clear.
[65] There is probably a play on words here. The noun 'outsider' and the adjective 'created' are spelt the same way in Syriac, and the scribe has omitted any markings that could distinguish them. Bar Ṣalībī may intend to warn his audience that those who think this way about crosses are functionally, if not literally, outsiders. The polemical bite of 'outsiders' fits the context better than 'created ones'.
[66] Genesis 18:1-3.
[67] Exodus 33:10; cf. Exodus 13:21.
[68] Joshua 7:6.
[69] Exodus 37:1.
[70] Cf. Exodus 34:1, 27-28. The tablets of the Law were kept inside the Ark of the Covenant.
[71] 1 Kings 8:54.
[72] I.e. the Muslims.

dishonour does not touch the exalted name of God which is written on it. Moses broke the tablets that God had written,[73] and it is evident that he did not break the name and the commandments of God, but the material that was in his hands (that is, the stones). If the cross is despised by enemies because of our sins or is broken by them, neither is its power broken nor its strength destroyed, but [only] the created and physical forms.' [...]

[73] Exodus 32:16, 19.

49

Gregory Barhebraeus, *Candelabrum of the sanctuaries*

Salam Rassi, University of Oxford

The following extract is taken from the *Mnōrat qudšē* ('Candelabrum of the sanctuaries') by Gregory bar ʿEbrōyō, known as Barhebraeus (d. 1285/6), *maphrian* (eastern prelate) of the Syrian Orthodox Church. The *Candelabrum* comprises twelve books (or 'bases') written in a dialectical style that is reminiscent of Islamic *kalām*, systematically approaching key issues of dogma by refuting the objections of non-Christian interlocutors, many of whom are Muslim. Like many Syriac- and Arabic-speaking Christian authors of his era, Barhebraeus was familiar with Islamic theological and philosophical systems. Indeed, parts of his *Candelabrum* and other works betray an indebtedness to Muslim thinkers, such as Ibn Sīnā (d. 1037) and Fakhr al-Dīn al-Rāzī (d. 1209/10).

In the third chapter of Base IV, Barhebraeus refutes seven 'heresies' that deny the divinity of Christ, the seventh being Islam. He addresses eight replies to objections which frequently appear in Muslim refutations of Christianity: the concept of divine unicity is irreconcilable with Christ's divinity; the doctrine of the Incarnation is at variance with biblical prophecies, in addition to Christ's own statements about his mission; Christ was no more than a prophet, as confirmed by both Christian scripture and the Qur'an; and his actions were no more miraculous than those of other prophets. In refuting each of these, Barhebraeus engages with Islamic notions of prophethood, many of which he draws from the Islamic 'proofs of prophethood' (*dalāʾil al-nubuwwa*) genre, as well as from Ḥadīths that mention Muḥammad's evidentiary miracles.

CMR 4, pp. 588–609.

This translation is based on Joseph Khoury (ed. and French trans.), *Le candélabre du sanctuaire de Gregoire Abou'l Faradj dit Barhebraeus: Quatrieme Base: de l'Incarnation*, Paris, 1964, pp. 108–21.

Part 1: Their objections

Seventh objection: They [the Muslims] say: [...] Furthermore, if it is because he performed miracles [that you believe Christ to be God], observe that Moses performed more of them and God was able to perform more of them through anyone [He chose], as Christ himself said.[74] Why not? Observe that Elisha, not only while alive but also after death, revived a corpse that touched his bones.[75] This is also more remarkable [than Christ's miracles]. Again, if it is because of the fact that he did not know sin, observe that John the Baptist, too, did not know sin and was a virgin and an ascetic in all things. If it is because he ascended to heaven, observe that Enoch and Elias, too, were lifted up and are still alive and never tasted death. And if it is because of the fact we [Muslims] say that he is the Word of God and His Spirit,[76] observe that all creatures exist by the Word of God and His Spirit.

Eighth objection: They say: Muḥammad is a prophet and messenger of God, and God said through him, 'Those who profess the Trinity truly disbelieve,'[77] and He also said, 'God is one, neither begetting nor begotten, nor is any other equal to him.'[78] That Muḥammad is a true prophet and messenger of God is known from three things. The first is the miracles he performed; the second his qualities and conduct; and the third is the fact that the ancient prophets foretold him.

Among his miracles is this Qur'an, which contains all the deeds [of the prophets] from Adam to his own time, a number of just laws and judgements, and wise sayings written in polished diction, the verses of which none of the skilled Arab poets could write or even imitate a single one. [That] such a thing as this came from the mouth of an illiterate man is a great miracle.

Also among his miracles is that he foretold future events, saying that the Romans would be defeated at the extremities of the earth[79] and he told his people that they would subjugate the east and west and prosper, and so it happened; water sprang from his fingers; the moon grew dark; a rock saluted him; the people were satisfied by a meagre amount of food; a tree trunk cried out to him [in the voice of a pregnant she-camel]; a camel complained to him; he saw a roasted sheep [for the first time after meeting God]; and the cloud that overshadowed him before he began as a prophet.

---

[74] On this familiar polemical theme, see: S. Stroumsa, 'The Signs of Prophecy: The Emergence and Early Development of a Theme in Arabic Theological Literature', *Harvard Theological Review* 78 (1985) 101–14; D. Thomas, 'The Miracles of Jesus in Early Islamic Polemic', *Journal of Semitic Studies* 39 (1994) 221–43.

[75] 2 Kings 13:21.

[76] An allusion to Q 4:171: ''Īsā son of Maryam was but a messenger of God and His word which He directed to Mary and a spirit from Him.'

[77] Paraphrase of Q. 5:73: 'They have certainly disbelieved who say, "God is a third of three".'

[78] Q 112:3-4.

[79] Compare with Q 30:2-3: 'The Romans have been defeated in the nearest land' (Barhebraeus modifies this to 'at the extremities of the earth,' *b-sawpēh d-'ar'ā*). This and the other miracles alluded to in this paragraph occur in the six canonical books of Sunnī Ḥadīth and *dalā'il al-nubuwwa* ('proofs of prophethood') works as proofs of Muḥammad's prophethood. They also occur in a Jewish critique of Islam by Ibn Kammūna (d. 1284), another likely source for Barhebraeus; see M. Perleman (trans.), *Ibn Kammūna's examination of the three faiths*, Berkeley, CA, 1971, p. 133.

Of [Muḥammad's] qualities and conduct is the fact that he never lied and never erred; he never ran away from his enemies; he was very compassionate towards his people, very generous, and was not attached to earthly possessions, since the Qurayshīs [of Mecca] promised him riches, a wife and leadership if he refrained from prophesying, but he refused; he was lofty among the lofty and gentle and humble among the meek; the ancient prophets foretold him, for God says in the Qur'an: 'Those who follow the Messenger, the unlettered prophet, whom they find written in what they have of the Torah and the Gospel.'[80] Furthermore, it says of Christ that he declared to his people: 'I am bringing you glad tidings about a messenger who will come after me. His name is Aḥmad.'[81]

Part 2: Responses to their objections

Seventh response: [...] Against [the statement] that Enoch and Elijah ascended to heaven while still alive, we say that this is not written of them. Rather, concerning Enoch it is written: 'He pleased God. Then he was no more, because God took him';[82] and concerning Elijah it is written: 'Elijah ascended to heaven in a whirlwind.'[83] It is not written that he did not die or that he would come to the end while living. In addition to these things, we say that Elijah's ascension affirms his prophethood while the ascension of Christ affirms his divinity, just as the miracles of Moses and the other prophets affirm their prophethood while the miracles of Christ affirm his divinity. For these things state [respectively] that they are prophets and he is the Messiah of God and the Son of God, as it is written in the Gospels.

Against [the statement] that because Christ is a creature of God, we [the Muslims] say that he is the Word of God and His Spirit,[84] we [the Christians] say that if your objection were correct, it would be necessary for you to call every ox, every worm, every creature great and small, clean and unclean the Word of God and His Spirit. Since this is not the case and it is you who refer to [Christ] in particular by these names, it is evident that, on this account, your book calls him the Word of God incarnate.

Eighth response: We say: Not all of you have accepted the veracity of the miracles that you have listed. For the Shīʿa among you say that [Muḥammad] performed no other miracles than the divine book that was spoken through him despite his being illiterate.[85] Thus, we say: Fakhr al-Dīn Rāzī states in his *Muḥassal*:

> We affirm his apostleship in three ways. First is the fact that he said, 'I am the Messenger of God', and his miracle, the Qur'an, has affirmed his words. Second

[80] Q 7:157. The verse continues: 'He will enjoin them to what is right and forbid them that which is wrong.'

[81] Q 61:6.

[82] Genesis 5:24.

[83] 2 Kings 2:1, 11.

[84] Q 4:171.

[85] Barhebraeus's source for this claim is uncertain. The famous Shīʿī scholar and elder contemporary of Barhebraeus, Nāṣīr al-Dīn al-Ṭūsī (d. 1274), wrote a critical commentary of al-Rāzī's *Muḥaṣṣal*, but nowhere states that Muḥammad performed no other miracles than the recitation of the Qur'an.

are his virtuous qualities and deeds. Each when taken individually does not point to his prophethood, but taken as a whole they necessarily indicate that they can only exist in prophets. This type of proof was favoured by al-Jāḥiẓ and was pleasing to al-Ghazālī in the book *Al-munqidh.* Third is that the prophets had foretold him in their heavenly books.[86]

This is why we say: If that book [the Qur'an] was a miracle, why have the best men among you not been chosen to affirm his prophethood?[87] However, that the qualities and customs that you have listed do not indicate prophethood is evident from the fact that they are present among several just kings who are not prophets. Furthermore, had the book been uttered by a Persian, Hun, or someone without interaction with literate people from other nations, then this would truly have been a miracle – just as it was truly a miracle when the apostles [of Jesus] spoke in different languages that they did not know as the Holy Spirit descended upon them like tongues of fire while assembled in the cenacle of Zion.[88]

Against [the statement] that [Muḥammad] predicted future events, saying that the Romans would be defeated and his people would be victorious, we say: All those who wish to incite their armies for battle make such promises to them. If fulfilled, they are affirmed; if not they say that their time has not yet come. And against what you have said about the Old Testament and Gospels mentioning [Muḥammad's] name, we say: You have heard this from the Qur'an and the Qur'an is affirmed by the affirmation of his prophethood. If his prophethood is, in turn, affirmed by the Qur'an, then a circularity occurs. Furthermore, if [Muḥammad's] name were mentioned in the Old Testament and Gospels, it would not be hidden from us.

[86] Fakhr al-Dīn al-Rāzī, *Muḥaṣṣal afkār al-mutaqaddimīn wa-l-muta'akhkhirīn min al-'ulamā' wa-l-ḥukamā' wa-l-mutakallimīn*, ed. Ṭāhā 'Abd al-Ra'ūf Sa'd, Beirut, 1984, p. 208. Al-Rāzī refers to Abū 'Uthman 'Amr al-Jāḥiẓ's (d. 869) *Kitāb al-ḥujja fī tathbīt al-nubuwwa* ('The book of proof about confirmation of prophethood'), which is extant only in fragments, and Abū Ḥāmid al-Ghazālī's (d. 1111) autobiographical *Al-munqidh min al-ḍalāl* ('Deliverance from error').

[87] In other words, if Muḥammad's prophethood is confirmed by his qualities and he is considered to have been an ordinary man, why, then, cannot any man who possesses these qualities also be considered a prophet?

[88] Acts 2:1-4.

50

The history of Mār Yahballāhā and Rabban Ṣawmā

Thomas A. Carlson, Oklahoma State University

This anonymous work, entitled *Tash'īthā d-Mār Yahballāhā wa-d-Rabban Ṣawmā*, is a biography of two Eastern Turkic monks who in the late thirteenth century travelled from Beijing to Baghdad. One of them was ultimately consecrated as the catholicos-patriarch, the highest office in the largest Christian denomination in Iraq, the Church of the East, and his companion and mentor travelled on to Western Europe as ambassador from the Mongol ruler of Persia to the courts of Latin Christendom. The patriarch, known as Yahballāhā III, corresponded with the papacy and enjoyed the patronage of Mongol rulers even after they converted to Islam.

The author is not identified in the text, although a plausible case has been made for Yahballāhā's successor Timothy II in the early fourteenth century. The work is best known for its account of Western Europe, but it also gives abundant information on the messy process by which the Mongol rulers of Iran adopted Islam, and how that religious transformation affected their Christian subjects.

The excerpts below concern the reign of Ghāzān Khān (r. 1295–1303), who converted to Islam in order to secure the Mongol throne while continuing to seek an alliance with the Franks against his chief enemy, the Mamlūk Sultanate in Egypt. Ghāzān is remembered in Christian sources as both a persecutor and a patron during his reign, a very different image from that given of him by the Persian historian Rashīd al-Dīn as the devout 'Padishāh of Islam'. This work chooses to blame the intense anti-Christian (and anti-Buddhist) persecution of the first eighteen months of Ghāzān's reign on the Muslim Mongol commander Nawrūz, who had acted as a kingmaker in securing Ghāzān's succession, while emphasizing the edicts and gifts given by Ghāzān himself on behalf of Christianity. Thus, for the sake of his contemporaries, the author sought to shape the narrative even of Muslim Mongol rulers in a pro-Christian direction.

This translation is based on P.G. Borbone (ed.), *Tash'īthā d-Mār Yahballāhā wa-d-Rabban Ṣawmā*, Lulu, 2010. See further:

P.G. Borbone (ed. and trans.), *The history of Mār Yahballāhā and Rabban Ṣawmā*, Hamburg, 2021.

One of the emirs who did not fear God and who was called Nawrūz was stirred up. He sent letters by the hands of messengers, and he broadcast to the four corners of the domains of this kingdom that the churches should be uprooted, the altars should be overturned, the consecrations should cease, the praises and prayer-boards should be blotted out, and the leaders of the Christians, with the leaders of the synagogues of the Jews and their nobles, should be killed.

They arrested the lord Catholicos in the [patriarchal] cell[89] which is in Marāgha on this very same night, when no one outside knew of it until dawn came. In the morning of the day, which was Monday, they entered the cell and plundered everything that was in it, whether old or new, and they did not leave a nail in the wall! In the night of the following Tuesday, which is 27 September, the Catholicos was tortured all night by those who arrested him. As for the bishops who were with him, some of them they bound naked, others abandoned their clothes and fled, others threw themselves from high places. They hung the Catholicos upside down and took a napkin, i.e. a handkerchief, and put ashes in it and bound it on his mouth. One stabbed him on his chest with a skewer, saying, 'Give up this confession of yours so that you will not perish! Convert to Islam and you will be saved.' But, weeping, he did not answer a word to him. They struck him with a rod upon his thighs and buttocks. They also brought him up to the roof of the prison, saying, 'Give us gold and we will release you! Show us your silver, reveal to us your hidden things, and lay bare your concealed things, and we will save you.' [pp. 44–5] [...]

A large mob gathered, and the people of the Arabs came with violence to destroy the great church of Mār Shallīṭā the holy martyr. They destroyed it and they took all that was in it, curtains and vestments of the service. The raging of their outcry and the storms of their shouting were all but shaking the land and its inhabitants. Perhaps the reader of this tale, because he was not in the middle of that storm, thinks that the writer is spinning a story. But what is true to say, when God calls the one who says this to witness, is that not even one of the things that happened can be spoken or written! [p. 46] [...]

But when the sun went down to Aries and the creation warmed a little, the catholicos sent one of the monks of the cell to the victorious king Ghāzān, to the place which is called Mūghān, the winter residence of the Mongol kings, so that he might bless him and make known the deeds which had happened to him. When that monk arrived at the camp, and he carefully went to see all of the emirs, they brought him in to the victorious king. The words which the lord Catholicos had told him he said in their entirety: 'Blessed is your throne, King, and let it be established forever, and let your offspring be confirmed upon it forever.' Then he asked, 'Why did the Catholicos not come to us?' The monk replied, 'Because in that confusion he was hung up and struck a lot, with his head down to the ground. From that severe pain which was brought upon him, he was not able to come to the reverence of the king. For this reason, he

[89] The residence of the Catholicos.

sent me to bless you, my lord the King. But when the victorious king shall come with peace to Tabrīz, whether he is ill or healthy, he will arrive for peace and reverence.'

God granted these words mercy in the eyes of the king, and he gave commands to the Catholicos according to custom, that the *jizya* should not be exacted from the Christians, and that none of them should abandon his confession, and that he should be the Catholicos according to custom and should conduct himself according to his rank, and have authority over his throne, and that he should grasp the rod of strength over his possession. And the command was for all the regions under the authority of all the emirs and of the armies: all that they had taken from the Catholicos or from the bishops by force they should return to them, and that whatever those people of Baghdad and their envoys who were mentioned above had taken, they should return it. He bestowed and gave as alms 5,000 dinars for his expenses, saying, 'Let these things be the sum for the Catholicos until he shall come to us.' [pp. 48–9] [...]

The king spent the night in the monastery and in that night while asleep he saw in his dream three angels who were standing above him, one of whose garments were red while the two others were shining in green clothing, and, encouraging him, they announced to him about the healing of the pains which were in his ankles.

On the morning of the day, he brought out an exalted cross of fine gold, on which were fixed very valuable precious stones, and in it was a relic of the venerated wood of the cross of our Life-giver [Christ], the one which was sent from the lord pope of the Romans to the king with honour, and the king bestowed it as a bequest on the lord Catholicos. He recounted his dream before all who were reclining (at dinner), and he confessed, 'Through the blessings of this holy house I have gained health.' He stayed that whole day, praising and magnifying the lord Catholicos. Thus he departed for the region where he was passing the summer, which is Ūghān. [pp. 61–2]

51

Grigor Tat'ewac'i, 'Against the Taǰiks', from the *Book of Questions*

Sergio La Porta, California State University, Fresno

Grigor Tat'ewac'i (1344–1409) was a monastic theologian who directed the school at the monastery of Tat'ew from 1391 to 1408. His numerous Armenian writings include sermons, commentaries and theological compendia, all composed in the question-and-answer format that was frequently used. His *magnum opus* is generally considered to be the *Girk' Harc'manc'* ('Book of questions'). Grigor divided this large work into ten volumes that systematically treat theological, exegetical and ritual questions. The book is written in simplified classical Armenian and was intended to be used by students in the monastic school system. *Girk' Harc'manc'* found an enduring place in Armenian ecclesiastical education because of its systematic approach, the broad range of its contents, and the use of tables of contents, which facilitated its use.

Vol. 1 argues against non-Christian faiths, while vol. 2 addresses Christian heresies. Tat'ewac'i's discourse against Islam is the longest of the polemics in vol. 1. It contains sixteen chapters: 1. the Muslims deny the Trinity of Persons; 2. they say good and evil are both from God; 3. they deny the Incarnation of the *Logos*; 4. they do not confess that Christ is God, but merely man and messenger; 5. they do not accept the Old and New Testaments; 6. they call Muḥammad a messenger of God; 7. they speak of physical resurrection; 8. they say angels and souls are mortal; 9. they insult the sign of the cross and holy icons; 10. they do not distinguish filthy creatures, but eat everything indiscriminately; 11. they forbid wine; 12. they wash with water every day and consider it purification; 13. they practise circumcision; 14. they have neither the old nor the new fasts; 15. they do not eat meat slaughtered by Armenians; 16. they are lawless but think themselves lawful.

Dietary practices were one of the more visible ways of differentiating people in society. While it may have been difficult to determine what someone believed, it was easy to see what they did or did not eat or drink. The regulation of these practices, therefore, constituted a significant means of constructing and defining community.

Tat'ewac'i's arguments in the passage below are meant both to defend Christians' dietary practices and also to point out contradictions within Muslim dietary practices.

CMR 5, pp. 229–38.

The translation below of chapter 10 relies upon the edition of B. Kiwlēsērean, *Islamě hay matenagrut'ean mēj*, Vienna, 1930, which is based on MS 1546 (fourteenth to fifteenth century) of the Armenian Patriarchate of St James in Jerusalem.

The tenth error of the Muslims[90]

They do not distinguish between filthy animals, but eat everything indiscriminately, except for pork.

It is to be known that God placed a variety of clean and unclean animals in natural law[91] and in the books of Moses. He placed four choices of animals in nature: first, carnivores, such as wild animals; second, gigantic, large ones, such as camels and elephants; third, lean and ugly [ones], such as insects; fourth, dangerous [ones], such as snakes, lizards and things like them. These were reckoned filthy in nature from Adam on.

God said to Noah by [His] word to bring into the ark by sevens from the clean ones and by twos from the unclean.[92] And at their leaving the ark, he sacrificed seven of the clean to God, and none from the unclean.[93] Whereas in the writing of Moses,[94] He clarified and clearly differentiated [between the animals], and moreover made a natural selection for quadrupeds: first, ruminants; second, hoofed; third, that which urinates through its bladder; fourth, horned; fifth, that which has teeth in its snout. These five [characteristics] are designated clean, but if one among them is found missing, it is unclean. Thus, the camel is a ruminant, but lacks the others; and the pig is hoofed and urinates through his bladder, but lacks the others; and the rabbit is a ruminant, but lacks the others.

As for birds: [He distinguished them as] straight-beaked, jointed, that fly in flocks, that have a membrane in their caw and that keep their talons straight after killing. These five [characteristics] indicate [a] clean [bird]. Likewise, the fish that has fins and scales is edible. Now God selected these through Moses and established the Law, and we now hold the same. But it is clear that you [Muslims] do not have a law, whether natural or rational, either scriptural or new, since you eat all animals indiscriminately.

And if they say: 'Why do you use horsehair as a sieve, and use leather?' we say: You yourselves strain the olive press with pig's hair and eat the olives, and you use horse

---

[90] In the Armenian *aylazgik'*, which literally means 'of another people'.
[91] The pre-Mosaic laws given to all humankind, as recorded in Genesis.
[92] Genesis 7:2-4.
[93] Genesis 8:20.
[94] Cf. Leviticus 11; Deuteronomy 14:1-21.

leather. And the otter, the fox, and the wolf are filthy, and the meat impure, yet you wear the skin. This is the reason that anything the artisan works is clean and useful. Likewise, the olive and the horsehair are purified by skill.

And if they say: 'Why do you eat pork?' say: For two reasons. First that it is a tradition of [our] elders, and men are accustomed to eating [it], and they do not give up the eating of pork. Second, just as the Romans [the Byzantines] and Franks eat hare and rabbit, thus also the Armenian people eat pork. But it is not necessary to eat [it]. Accordingly, it is better not to eat meat or drink wine, to maintain fasting and temperance, since this is good and acceptable to God, and not what they eat and drink.

But you, why do you eat horse? Since it has no indication of purity, it is therefore impure. And if they say: 'Our Messenger [Muḥammad] commanded us to eat it,' we say: That saying does not appear anywhere in your scripture. But he said to eat [it] only once during winter and great famine in order to live, and not to eat it all the time.[95]

Again, if Moses said the horse and camel and rabbit [are] unclean, and your Muḥammad said that they are clean, then he is against Moses and not a messenger [from God]. So, how can you accept that your scriptures descended from heaven, when you contradict the Old Law of Moses?

Again we say: As nothing differentiates sheep from goat, which is edible for us, likewise, horse and mule and donkey are not differentiated in any way, so why do you not eat them [all]? Again, since [they are] analogous to the horse, [and] the donkey and mule are forbidden,[96] so too the horse should be[97] forbidden. And if the horse is permitted,[98] why do you not make a sacrifice and an offering with a horse, as [you do] with a sheep or ox?[99]

Again, you say wine is filthy and forbidden, since it is the cause of evils. Likewise, the horse is also filthy and the cause of many evils, since war and killing and booty and raids are performed with it, on account of which one must not eat [it].

So much on this.

[95] Q 5:3, allowing forbidden foods in cases of hunger.

[96] 'forbidden', *ḥarām*.

[97] 'should be,' lit. 'is', but the argument here challenges the status of the horse as *ḥalāl*, 'permitted'. Since the horse, donkey and mule are analogous, the horse should likewise be *ḥarām*.

[98] The argument here challenges the ritual status of the horse: if it is *ḥalāl*, why is it not considered a ritually acceptable sacrificial animal like other *ḥalāl* animals?

[99] Referring to the Muslim sacrifice (here Arabic *qurbān*) of an animal at 'Īd al-aḍḥā, the second of the two major Muslim festivals.

Latin and Romance Languages

Latin and Romance writings on Islam

Graham Barrett, University of Lincoln

Running through the medieval history of Christians writing about Muslims in Latin and the Romance languages is a tension between confrontation and acculturation – a balance between denigration and investigation spanning centuries of conflict and détente.

From the perspective of western Europe, interest in the rise of Islam was at first quite desultory. Around 660 the Frankish chronicler known as 'Fredegar' reported with energy, if not accuracy, on the eventful reigns of the Eastern Roman emperors Heraclius (r. 610–41) and Constans II (641–68), when Muslim dominion spread through what had been the Roman Near East. There are otherwise only scattered notices until the mid-eighth century, when Muslim conquest of much of the Iberian Peninsula from the Visigoths in 711–14 gave rise to sustained Latin literary engagement with Islam. Even then, the focus of this output was as much inward as outward: to the substantial subject population of Christians in the south of the peninsula, and to those in the north, defeat had to be explained and reconciled to sacred history, and so they interpreted the arrival of Muslims in their midst as divine vengeance exacted for sin, with apocalyptic expectations. Drawing on a tradition originating with Jerome (d. 420), they identified these conquerors as 'Saracens', the Ishmaelites of the Old Testament who had wrongly taken the name of Abraham's free wife Sarah for their own, and the term gradually became the standard medieval Latin ethnic and religious label for all Arabs and Muslims alike.

As a 'People of the Book', Christians under Muslim rule were accorded *dhimmī* status, with guarantees of protection and some autonomy in return for obedience, subordination and payment of taxes. When social tensions inevitably led to conflict, most notoriously in the case of the martyrs of Córdoba in the mid-ninth century, Christians writing the hagiographies of those who had died for the faith reached for another age-old model, casting the Muslim rulers of al-Andalus and their agents as successors to the pagan Roman emperors in a new great age of persecution. The earliest Latin treatment of Islam as such emerged from this charged milieu of resistance to a slow but steady religious, cultural and linguistic assimilation: the polemical *Istoria de Mahomet* stands at the beginning of a long medieval tradition of scurrilous biography or anti-hagiography of Muḥammad as trickster, heresiarch and pseudo-prophet, an idol worshipped by heathens, but it also reveals a working knowledge of his life, deliberately distorted.

Muslim supremacy in the western Mediterranean had effectively been achieved by the early eighth century, reaching a climax in the later ninth with the conquest of Sicily. Raiding by 'Saracens' was a reality, overland into the Christian kingdoms and counties of northern Spain and across the Pyrenees into southern Gaul, and up along the Italian coast; encounters comprised minor skirmishes and major engagements, from the Christian defence of Tours, or Poitiers, in 732 by Charles Martel (d. 741) to the Muslim sack of Santiago de Compostela in 997 by the vizier al-Manṣūr (d. 1002). In this context, diplomacy was a necessity, and so embassies travelled back and forth across the Iberian frontier as well as between the Carolingian and Ottonian courts in Francia and those of the Umayyads in al-Andalus and the 'Abbasids in the east. To a considerable extent, the tenor of relations depends on the genre of source that is consulted: the more literary (chronicles, correspondence), the more commonly it will offer an ideological narrative of conflict, whereas the more documentary (charters, contracts), the more often it will feature a pragmatic attitude of compromise, of quiet accommodation in the name of transaction. This is not tolerance, but an instrumental approach to Muslims, whereby interest was limited to their use as discursive tools for internal Christian purposes.

The inflection point, bringing a more explicit and consistent articulation of 'holy war', came in the later eleventh century. Until that point, interreligious warfare had been messy: the ongoing Norman conquest of southern Italy came at the expense of Lombards and Byzantines as much as of Muslim rulers, and even Alfonso VI (r. 1065–1109) of Spain, who captured the old Visigothic capital of Toledo in 1085 amidst intensifying belief in a heavenly mandate of *Reconquista*, still made alliances of convenience with Muslim principalities. But against the background of the 'Peace of God' movement to constrain intra-faith warfare between Christian lords, inroads by the Seljuk Turks into Byzantine territory, and disruption of pilgrimage to the Holy Land by power struggles between the Seljuks and Fāṭimids, Pope Urban II (r. 1088–99) called the First Crusade (1096–9) to bring aid to Christians in the East. In the aftermath of victory, the Crusader states of Edessa, Antioch, Jerusalem and Tripoli established a colonial Latin presence in the east lasting until 1291. The earliest, providential histories of the 'armed pilgrimage' saw in its triumph full confirmation that the Crusaders fought as God's own knights; those who stayed on in the Levant as settlers and defenders of the Christian enclaves by necessity developed some facility in Arabic and familiarity with, even a working respect for, Muslim rituals and customs. Less of this filtered back into the Latin histories and chronicles written in contemporary western Europe, nor indeed into the Old French *chansons de geste* ('songs of deeds') composed in the new literary vernacular. These poems present the combat between Christianity and Islam in epic heroic style, telling fantastical stories of the valiant heroes of the Crusader states and, looking back, of the semi-historical Roland, tragic protagonist of Emperor Charlemagne's ill-fated foray into the Basque country in 778, now come to personify the eternal struggle against villainous Saracens.

The other theatre of Crusade was Iberia, where the Christian kingdoms campaigned intermittently against the Almoravid and Almohad regimes, successive waves of dogmatic rigorists from North Africa established in the peninsula. With the victory of Alfonso VIII (r. 1158–1214) at Las Navas de Tolosa in 1212, the balance of power shifted decisively, and by the mid-thirteenth century only Granada in the far southeast remained to 'reconquer'. Christian kings found themselves with substantial Muslim populations under their rule, and obliged by necessity observed a broadly *laissez faire* tolerance. The 'national epic' of the

Cantar de mío Cid ('Poem of the Cid'), written sometime in the latter half of the twelfth century, represents this world well: the poem transforms a mercenary who had worked with both Christians and Muslims into a quasi-Crusader of dashing exploits for king and cross, yet allows space for a 'noble Moor' character. Still more direct engagement with Islam took place at Toledo, which after its Christian conquest developed rapidly into a centre of literary translation. Here and elsewhere in Spain, southern France, and Sicily scholars translated Greek and Arabic works of philosophy and science into Latin and Castilian, a movement constituting 'the renaissance of the twelfth century', though continuing into the thirteenth, above all under the patronage of Alfonso X (r. 1252–84). At the new universities and scholastic communities of France and England, as classical logic and reason were brought into dialogue and debate with Christian tradition, theologians began to reconsider Islam not only as an object for attack but also as a logical and rational problem for study, an intellectual challenge to be met and surmounted. The most important outcome was the first translation of the Qur'an from Arabic into Latin by Robert of Ketton (*fl.* 1141–57), soon followed by other works of Islamic theology and the philosophical and scientific writings of Avicenna (d. 1037), Averroes (d. 1198) and others. Though undoubtedly the product of a polyglot society, however, this school of translation was not a reflection of 'multiculturalism' in the modern sense; insofar as it had a religious aim, the object was to provide better tools for converting Muslims to Christianity.

It is in this light that the greater, more fully realized presence of the 'matter of Islam' in later medieval Latin and Romance sources needs to be understood. Translation and study of the Qur'an and Islamic theology fed directly into the practice of mission and disputation. The mendicant orders which grew up in the early thirteenth century, the Franciscans and the Dominicans especially, practised poverty, preaching and ministry, but also travelled widely in the cause of conversion, visiting Muslim courts, settling in Muslim communities, in North Africa, the Middle East, Central Asia and beyond. As the Crusading movement faltered and finally failed, while the mythical figure of Prester John beckoned with ever greater urgency from his marvellous Christian realm in the Orient, and sensational ethnographic reports of the Far East from real and imagined travellers like Marco Polo and John Mandeville circulated in the fourteenth century, the scale and urgency of the task became more apparent. Missionaries weaponized their knowledge of Islam, and of Arabic, Persian and other major languages of the Islamic world, in oral and written disputation: formalized, often public interfaith debate intended to establish theological truth and engender conversion. The zenith of this tradition was 'the art' of Ramon Llull (d. 1315/16), a system based on first principles acceptable to Muslims and Jews, designed to lead disputants to accept the Christian revelation.

At the end of the Middle Ages, with the coming of the Ottomans and their conquest of Constantinople in 1453, two contrasting approaches to Islam gained currency across western Europe, and remained unresolved. In Spain, the fall of Granada in 1492 meant the closing of the frontier: Christian society turned in on itself, determined to root out all unbelievers in its midst, by whatever means necessary. Calls for a new 'holy war' against the Ottomans echoed this line, but were countered by arguments, most eloquently from Erasmus of Rotterdam (d. 1536), for the normalizing of relations, and prioritizing of dialogue. Even so, the goal remained conversion; such tolerance only bore its literal meaning, to endure the other, to look for the right moment and the best means to bring Muslims to accept the universal Christian truth.

Further reading

R.W. Southern, *Western Views of Islam in the Middle* Ages, Cambridge, MA, 1962.
J.V. Tolan (ed.), *Medieval Christian Perceptions of Islam: A Book of Essays*, New York, 1996.
M.R. Menocal, *The Ornament of the World: How Muslims, Jews, and Christians Created a Culture of Tolerance in Medieval Spain*, Boston, MA, 2002.
J.V. Tolan, *Saracens: Islam in the Medieval European Imagination*, New York, 2002.
R.I. Moore, *The Formation of a Persecuting Society: Authority and Deviance in Western Europe, 950–1250*, 2nd edition, Oxford, 2007.
J.V. Tolan, *Sons of Ishmael: Muslims through European Eyes in the Middle Ages*, Gainesville, FL, 2008.
M. Di Cesare, *The Pseudo-historical Image of the Prophet Muhammad in Medieval Latin Literature: A Repertory*, Berlin, 2012.
B.A. Catlos, *Muslims of Medieval Latin Christendom, c. 1050–1615*, Cambridge, 2015.
D. Nirenberg, *Communities of Violence: Persecution of Minorities in the Middle Ages*, new edition, Princeton, NJ, 2015.
J.L. Bird (ed.), *Papacy, Crusade, and Christian-Muslim Relations*, Amsterdam, 2018.
O.R. Constable, *To Live Like a Moor: Christian Perceptions of Muslim Identity in Medieval and Early Modern Spain*, ed. R. Vose, Philadelphia, PA, 2018.
I. Zaderenko, A. Montaner, and P. Mahoney (eds), *A Companion to the Poema de mío Cid*, Leiden, 2018.
J.V. Tolan, *Faces of Muhammad: Western Perceptions of the Prophet of Islam from the Middle Ages to Today*, Princeton, NJ, 2019.
L.A. Berto, *Christians and Muslims in Early Medieval Italy: Perceptions, Encounters and Clashes*, Abingdon, 2020.
E. Smelyansky (ed.), *The Intolerant Middle Ages: A Reader*, Toronto, 2020.
L.A. Berto, *Christians under the Crescent and Muslims under the Cross, c. 630–1923*, Abingdon, 2021.

Latin writings

52

History or deeds of the Franks

Roger Collins, University of Edinburgh

Historia vel gesta Francorum ('History or deeds of the Franks') is the possible title, attested in a single manuscript, of a Frankish historiographical compilation completed at an unknown location after 768 but before *c.* 800. Written under the patronage of two relatives of Charlemagne, Count Childebrand and his son Count Nibelung, it restructures and augments an earlier compilation known as the *Chronicle of Fredegar*, put together in Burgundy or Austrasia in the 660s, but it constitutes a separate work in its own right, with an entirely different manuscript tradition.

For the study of Islamic history, this concluding section of annals is of particular importance for their account of some events in western and southern France in the years between 732 and 768, especially in the 730s. As a source written for members of the Carolingian house, its narrative is highly partisan and deliberately propagandist. It presents Arab expeditions into western France in 732, culminating in the famous Battle of Poitiers, and into Provence in 737 as being the result of invitations by local rulers to assist them against the Franks. In reality, the mayor of the palace, Charles Martel, responded to appeals for help against the Muslim raids, but then took advantage of them to oust the dukes of Aquitaine and Provence and seize their territories. This was the prelude to the deposition of the ruling Merovingian dynasty and its replacement by the Carolingians in 751.

The compilers' knowledge of Muslims may have derived from the misleading information about their origin in the *Chronicle of Fredegar*, but they also had some knowledge of events that had occurred in Spain since 711. In describing the campaigns of Charles Martel, the 'Saracens' feature as standardized opponents of the hero of the narrative, being described as 'perfidious', a term favoured by Frankish historians for opponents of their rulers. In a final section of the work, relating to events in 768, an exchange of diplomatic gifts and envoys between Charles's son, King Pippin III (r. 751–68) and the *Amormuni*, meaning the ʿAbbasid caliph al-Manṣūr (r. 754–75), is described without any derogatory epithets and the caliphal ambassadors are 'escorted with much honour' to Marseille for their journey home.

CMR 1, pp. 293–4.

This translation is based on J.M. Wallace-Hadrill (ed.), *The Fourth Book of the Chronicle of Fredegar with Its Continuations*, London, 1960, revised in light of the earliest witness, MS Heidelberg, Universitätsbibliothek, Pal. lat. 864, fols 133r-134r, written in Lorsch *c.* 800.

13. At that time, Duke Eudo having withdrawn from the legal bonds of the treaty and news of this having been brought by messengers to Prince Charles [Martel], he gathered an army and crossed the River Loire. With Duke Eudo himself in flight and the land devastated by these enemies, he acquired much booty twice that year, and then returned once more to his own land. But Eudo, seeing himself defeated and derided, aroused the perfidious people of the Saracens to help against Prince Charles and the people of the Franks. Setting out with their king, by the name of Abdirama,[1] they crossed the Garonne and reached Bordeaux; having burned the churches with fire and devastated the population, they advanced to Poitiers, where the basilica of St Hilary was consumed by fire, which it is a sorrow to have to say, and then they advanced, aiming to destroy the house of the most holy Martin.[2] Against them Prince Charles fearlessly drew up his line of battle and came upon them like a mighty warrior.[3] With the help of Christ, he overthrew their efforts. He cast down their tents and hastened to grinding, crushing battle; and with their king Abdirama killed, he trampled their army; he laid it low; he fought and he won. As a victor he triumphed over enemies. [pp. 90–1]

20. Rebelling once more,[4] the mighty nation of the Ishmaelites, who now are known by the corrupt name of Saracens,[5] bore down upon the River Rhône, aided by treacherous men under the lead and deception of a certain Maurontus and his associates. Those Saracens, having gathered into a hostile force, broke into the very well-fortified and rocky city of Avignon, and with those rebels devastated the region.[6] The noble Duke Charles sent against them his brother, the illustrious Duke Childebrand, along with the other dukes and counts in offensive formation. When they were nearing that city, they set up tents, they confined both urban centre and suburbs on all sides, they besieged that most strongly fortified city, they drew up a line of battle. Then, once

[1] ʿAbd al-Raḥmān ibn ʿAbdallāh al-Ghāfiqī was governor of al-Andalus from 730 to 732.

[2] The 'house' (*domus*) referred to could be Martin's first monastery of Ligugé just south of Poitiers, rather than his basilica at Tours.

[3] The battle, whether at Poitiers or Tours, was fought on 25 October 732.

[4] From what is known of the chronology of Charles Martel's campaigns, the probable year here is 735.

[5] Why the chronicler thought 'Saracens' was a corruption of 'Ishmaelites' is not clear.

[6] The Lombard historian Paul the Deacon, writing *c.* 787–95, describes two successive Arab raids into Provence around this time, one of which was defeated by Charles Martel near Narbonne and the second of which captured Arles, leading to a planned joint expedition by Charles and the Lombard king Liutprand (r. 712–44) to expel them (*Pauli Historia Langobardorum*, ed. G. Waitz, Hanover, 1890, 6.54).

that man of war Charles had arrived, he assaulted that city, he surrounded the walls, he set up fortified camps, he tightened the siege. As at Jericho,[7] with the shout of the army and the sounding of the trumpets, with siege weapons and cords of rope they launched an attack against the walls and the defences of the buildings. Entering it they set fire to the highly fortified city, they captured the army of their enemy, killing, they slaughtered and laid low, and powerfully restored it to their control.

Thus the victor and glorious warrior, the fearless Charles crossed the Rhône with his army, he entered the land of the Goths as far as Narbonne, and he besieged that most famous city, the metropolis of Gallia Narbonensis.[8] On the River Aude he drew up a defence work to surround them in the manner of a ram;[9] there he enclosed the king of the Saracens, by the name of Athima,[10] with his following, and forts were created everywhere. Hearing this, the elders and princes of the Saracens then dwelling in Spain, having gathered an army of enemies with another king, Amormacha by name,[11] advanced together manfully against Charles and prepared for battle. Against them the aforementioned Charles the triumphant duke advanced to the palace in the valley of Corbières on the River Berre.[12] There, both sides coming together, the Saracens were defeated and laid low; perceiving that their king had been killed, they turned their backs and fled. Those who escaped, hoping to get away by naval means, swam out into the lagoon – indeed, they scrambled on top of each other in mutual destruction.[13] Soon, the Franks hurled themselves upon them in ships and with throwing weapons, and they perished suffocating in the waters.

Thus, the triumphant Franks took great spoils and loot from their enemies, they captured a multitude of prisoners and with their leader they depopulated the region of Gothia. He [Charles] burnt the most famous cities of Nîmes, Agde and Béziers, setting fire to destroy their fortifications to their foundations; he devastated their suburbs and the fortresses of that region. With the enemy host cast down, with Christ foremost in all things and at the head of the victory of salvation, he returned safely to his own region in the land of the Franks, the seat of his power. [pp. 93–5]

[7] An allusion to the Book of Joshua 6:20, though the text does not include any passages borrowed or adapted from the biblical narrative of the Israelite siege of Jericho.

[8] The former Roman province, part of the Gothic kingdom in Spain lying north of the Pyrenees. It had been conquered by the Arabs in 720, but it passed into Carolingian hands in the reign of Pippin III (r. 751–68).

[9] The meaning here is hard to determine. Previous translators have interpreted *in modum arietum* as referring to a battering ram, a possible meaning of *aries*, but this does not cohere with the preceding clause describing the creation by the besiegers of a defence work around the city.

[10] ʿAbd al-Malik ibn Qaṭan al-Fihrī, governor of al-Andalus (732–34).

[11] Possibly ʿOmar-ibn-Chaled (ʿUmar ibn Khālid), though nobody of that name appears in the sources for this period.

[12] Probably at or near Roquefort-des-Corbières in the Départment de l'Aude, roughly half-way between Narbonne and Perpignan.

[13] Probably the Étang de Leucate, which is separated from the sea by a strip of land. There is no explanation for the presence of these boats or the ones which the Franks then acquired.

53

Book of Pontiffs

Graham Barrett, University of Lincoln

The *Liber Pontificalis* ('Book of Pontiffs') is the name given to a collection of papal biographies spanning the Middle Ages. The original appears to have been assembled from primitive catalogues by a Roman priest around 530, and a second edition is dateable to about 540; compilation resumed a century later, and new lives were added during or immediately after each papacy down to the twelfth century, resuming in the fifteenth. In scope, the entries on the earliest popes are brief and often muddled, but they become longer and more informed from the fourth century, and by the eighth to ninth offer substantial eyewitness histories with developed narrative, though thereafter they are highly inconsistent.

The potted formulaic biographies of the *Liber Pontificalis* focus on the institutional history of the papacy, but notable mention is made of Muslims during the reign of Sergius II (r. 844–7) in recounting a major raid on Rome in 846, and again when describing a further, failed attempt on the city under his successor Leo IV (r. 847–55). The Aghlābid dynasty of Ifrīqiya (central North Africa) invaded Sicily in 827 and took Messina, opposite the mainland, in 842; from here these Saracens ranged up the Tyrrhenian coast towards Naples and beyond. Landing at Rome four years later, they sacked the basilicas of Saint Peter and Saint Paul, outside the protection of the Aurelian Walls, before being driven off by forces from the Lombard duchy of Spoleto and the Byzantine duchy of Naples. Leo IV began to rebuild, but in 849 news arrived of another imminent raid, as narrated in the extract translated here.

What stands out is the instrumental role played by Muslims in the develo pment of the papacy: the pope is most anxious about the real intentions of his secular Christian opposites in neighbouring states, and deploys rhetoric foreshadowing the Crusades to redirect them against a common enemy. The instrumentalism extends beyond victory, as the account closes in the first person (the papal voice?), relating how Muslim prisoners of war were put to work building the 'Leonine City': defensive works securing the Vatican from future external attack, but also providing a fortified power base for the pope against his many rivals within the city of Rome.

CMR 1, pp. 642–4. See further:

C. Gantner, 'New Visions of Community in Ninth-Century Rome: The Impact of the Saracen Threat on the Papal World View', in W. Pohl, C. Gantner and R. Payne (eds), *Visions of Community in the Post-Roman World: The West, Byzantium and the Islamic World, 300–1100*, Farnham, 2012, 403–21.

R. McKitterick, *Rome and the Invention of the Papacy: The Liber Pontificalis*, Cambridge, 2020.

This translation is based on L. Duchesne, *Le Liber Pontificalis*, ed. C. Vogel, 3 vols, Paris, 1955–7 [1886–92], vol. 2, pp. 117–19.

§105. Leo IV

47. And then, after the malevolent and grievous sacking by the Saracens, comprising every woe, which they perpetrated on the foremost head of all the churches – to wit, the Holy Roman Church – at devilish instigation, those very sons of Satan wished once more to inflict like damages as before upon the precincts of Rome and on the church of the most blessed Apostle Peter,[14] and afterwards as victors to head back to the places from which they had emerged. But as the attention and commitment of the Supreme Shepherd was shining forth and keeping watch, they were utterly unable to accomplish these ends.

48. Even so, for the faithful in the Lord justly to become more faithful and doubt not that His signs and miracles from of old have arisen anew, one must now summarize from the outset what Divine Mercy did about them praiseworthily at that time, and by what great sufferings and disasters that pestilential people was deservedly crushed and routed. As such, recalling the former profit or plunder which they had taken, a band of wicked men assembled again, with many ships besides, and they decided inexorably to come to assault the city of Rome while the twelfth indiction was current.[15] Now for many days they waited at the spot which is called Totarum,[16] adjacent to the island of Sardinia; once they had set out from it, though God was not helping them, they attempted to make for the port of Rome.[17]

49. The hostile and fiendish arrival of these men frightened the Romans more than a little. But because God Almighty has always preserved His Church inviolate, and will not cease to preserve it hereafter, He thereupon roused the hearts of (amongst others) all the Neapolitans, Amalfitans and Gaetani[18] to have no choice but bravely to

---

[14] (Old) Saint Peter's basilica.

[15] The years 848–9, according to the system based on the fifteen-year fiscal cycle of the Roman Empire.

[16] Unidentified.

[17] Portus: one of the two Roman harbours, and a bishopric.

[18] Naples, Amalfi and Gaeta: maritime republics ruled by dukes under Byzantine suzerainty.

rise and battle together with the Romans against them. And indeed, after they had promptly sortied from their own territories, these men with their ships rendezvoused in advance of the unwelcome Saracens, and abruptly made their arrival known to the most blessed Bishop Leo IV, declaring that they had come for no other object but to emerge as victors over the heathens, with the help of the Lord.

50. Only then did the reverend father instruct a number of them to come first to him in Rome, desiring particularly to learn from those men if their arrival was in peace or not. So too was it done. And amongst them then arrived the son of Sergius, master of the soldiers,[19] who had been put in charge of the army and whose name was Caesarius. Receiving them with courtesy at the Lateran Palace,[20] he [the pope] asked the reason for which they had come. They, however, testified that they had not come for anything other than what can be read written above. And the faithful Apostolic, trusting in their words, made haste before long with a great ready force of armed men to the city of Ostia,[21] and received all the Neapolitans with enormous and exceptional appreciation.

51. As soon as they caught sight of the supreme pontiff, they prostrated themselves on the ground at his feet, kissing them with reverence, and rendered thanks to the Almighty seated in heaven for having decided to dispatch so excellent a high priest to succour them. And in order to emerge better as victors over the sons of Belial,[22] they implored him sincerely to find them worthy of obtaining the body of the Lord from his holy hands. For them he sang the mass with his own mouth in the church of the blessed Aurea,[23] and they all together received communion, as has just been said, from his hands. But before these services took place, he processed with the help of Christ all the way to this church amidst hymns, litanies and special canticles, in company with the Neapolitans themselves. In it he also beseeched the Highest on bended knees, such that in response to his prayers He might deign to deliver the enemies of Christians into the hands of those standing against them. And for them too he offered this prayer with manifold tears, saying: 'God, whose right hand lifted up the blessed Apostle Peter lest he sink as he walked upon the water,[24] and set free his fellow Apostle Paul from the depths of the sea as he was shipwrecked a third time,[25] hearken favourably to us and grant for the merits of both that the arms of these your believers, as they do battle against the enemies of your holy Church, may be strengthened and fortified by your all-powerful right hand, so that your holy name may, by the triumph which they have received, become renowned amongst all the nations. Through [Our Lord Jesus Christ].'[26]

---

[19] Duke Sergius I of Naples (d. 864).

[20] The main residence of the mediaeval popes, near the Basilica of Saint John Lateran.

[21] The other Roman harbour, also a bishopric.

[22] See, e.g. Deuteronomy 13:13; 2 Corinthians 6:15.

[23] Located in Gregoriopolis, the district of Ostia fortified by Gregory IV (r. 827–44).

[24] Matthew 14:22-33.

[25] 2 Corinthians 11:25; Acts 27.

[26] Based partly on the Gelasian Collect for the Octave of the Apostles.

52. Now the next day, after the reverend prelate had returned from the aforesaid city, the allies or associates of the criminals themselves appeared along the seashore of Ostia with many ships. And the Neapolitans, in carrying out an assault, were minded to battle bravely, and even wounded a number of them; and from this start they would have achieved victory if one obstacle had not intervened too swiftly. While they were battling intently against each other, suddenly as strong and overpowering a wind as anyone can remember in these times whipped up, which dispersed both fleets immediately – yet that of the Saracens farther. They came right onto the seashore; then they were scattered as the wind was blowing and the sea surged in the gales, and once more, after a little time, they turned back with their strength shattered. For God Almighty, we firmly believe, had brought out this wind from His storehouse,[27] which totally prevented them from going forth to cause harm.

53. As to these new and numinous miracles, which the Divine Mercy of our true God has deigned in our times to reveal and present to us, though not for our merits, that [Mercy] must always be worshipped and celebrated: He allowed them to glimpse the place for which they longed and yet the power of His might drove them off still farther lest they might manage to capture it. And afterwards, not only did the deep sea relentlessly kill off many through the intercession and merits of the most blessed Peter and Paul, the Princes of the Apostles, but so also did starvation and the sword. And a great many of them, suffering across some of our islands from the privation of hunger, were eliminated by our men; the remainder, however, they took alive for the truth of the matter and as evidence of it, bringing them alive to Rome.

54. Now, lest the number of them might actually seem to have grown, the Roman nobility ordered many to be hanged on trees close by our port of Rome. We[28] in fact ordered some to live bound fast in iron, but for this purpose alone: so that they might be able to know, more clearly than light, both our hope, which we have in God, and His indescribable devotion, as well as their own despotism. And after these orders, lest they live amongst us in leisure or without hardship, we kept on directing them to carry out all our tasks, sometimes at the wall which we had begun around the church of the most blessed Apostle Peter,[29] sometimes involving the various works of the craftsmen – whatever seemed to be needed.

---

[27] Cf. Psalm 135:7.

[28] Note the use of first-person speech, perhaps drawing on papal correspondence.

[29] The Leonine Wall encircling the Vatican, built in 848–52.

54

Paschasius Radbertus, *Commentary on the Gospel of Matthew*

Charles West, University of Sheffield

Paschasius Radbertus (or Radbert) was a Frankish monk at the monastery of Corbie in the north of the kingdom of western Francia. He has recently been suspected of involvement in creating the Pseudo-Isidorian forged decretals, a massive set of letters written in the name of the early popes. But Radbert was also an accomplished theologian. Over many years he wrote a long commentary on the Gospel of Matthew, the *Expositio in Matheo*, arranged into twelve books. In glossing and explaining this biblical work, Radbert throws a great deal of light on the circumstances of his own day, around 850.

Amongst the topics which Radbert addresses in passing is Islam, providing precious evidence for Carolingian Frankish perceptions of the religion. The tone is predictably hostile, but it is surprising how well-informed Radbert is. He knows that Islam is monotheistic, that Muslims worship in mosques, and that they do not compel conversion to Islam. It is not clear how Radbert gained his knowledge, though there is some evidence for diplomatic and cultural links between al-Andalus and the West Frankish kingdom.

Below are translations of the two most relevant passages in Radbert's commentary on Matthew. The first, from Book II of his exegesis, relates to his gloss on Matthew 2, and more specifically to the rule of King Herod and his successors in Judea. Radbert notes that their rule continued until the destruction of Jerusalem in 70 AD. This he connects to an Old Testament passage, Daniel 9:27, on the desolation of the Temple: 'And there shall be in the Temple the abomination of desolation, and the desolation shall continue even to the consummation, and to the end.' Radbert suggests that the installation of a mosque in Jerusalem fulfils this prophecy. His use of the Arabo-Latin word for mosque is striking.

The second passage, from Book XI of his exegesis, relates to his gloss on the apocalyptic Matthew 24. There Jesus describes the signs of the end times: his Gospel 'shall be preached in the whole world', and his disciples will be 'hated by all peoples for my name's sake'. Radbert suggests these conditions have not yet quite been achieved, and digresses briefly but incisively on Islam.

This translation is based on *Pascasius Radbertus, Expositio in Matheo*, ed. B. Paulus, Turnhout, 1984. See further:

Hans-Werner Goetz, *Die christlich-abendländische Wahrnehmung anderer Religionen im frühen und hohen Mittelalter*, Berlin, 2013 (presents the general context, and includes some specific discussion of this passage).

Mayke de Jong and Justin Lake, *Confronting Crisis in the Carolingian Empire: Paschasius Radbertus's Funeral Oration for Wala of Corbie*, Manchester, 2020 (the best current guide in English to the author).

Sam Ottewill-Soulsby, '"Those Same Cursed Saracens": Charlemagne's Campaigns in the Iberian Peninsula as Religious Warfare', *Journal of Medieval History* 42 (2016) 405–28.

Katherine Scarfe-Beckett, *Anglo-Saxon Perceptions of the Islamic World*, Cambridge, 2003 (includes some discussion of this passage).

Matthias Tischler, 'Supposed and True Knowledge of the Qur'an in Early Medieval Latin Literature, Eighth and Ninth Centuries', *Journal of Transcultural Medieval Studies* 5 (2018) 7–54 (covers the wider context).

Book II: Herod's descendants ruled the kingdom [of Judea] in turn for a while, as the scriptures say. And no one succeeded to the priesthood in the Temple [in Jerusalem] according to the law, until the city and the Temple were levelled to the ground and destroyed along with the people. In that time, 'the victim and the sacrifice' began to fail, according to Daniel,[30] and there began to be 'the abomination of desolation'. That desolation will last, according to the prophet [Daniel], 'until the consummation and until the end'. So much so that in the place where there was once the Temple and religion, the Saracens have the temple (*phanum*)[31] of their worship in the fashion of a holy temple to profane the sanctuary, which in their language they call as they say it a 'mosque' (*myschyda*).[32] [vol. 2, pp. 145–6]

Book XI: But we are not yet 'hated by all peoples' [Matthew 24:9], some of whom the name of Christ has not yet reached. Thus in the north there are some places and peoples to whom the Gospel of Christ has not yet been preached. However, in truth, I do not know whether there is any people (*natio*) amongst them which no missionary has reached, although their fierceness may have prevented the complete acceptance of the faith of Christ. But to the west, all the islands in the whole world, as far as the British ocean, now believe [in Christianity].

[30] Daniel 9:27.

[31] A word (*fanum*) typically used for pagan temples.

[32] Evidently a transliteration of the Arabic *masjid*.

And let no one object to me that the Gospel of Christ has not reached the Saracens, who by God's permission have conquered many earthly kingdoms with their arms and now dominate almost everywhere over the Christians. It did reach them, and they accepted God's message, but they were wickedly seduced by certain pseudo-prophets, disciples of Nicholas so to speak,[33] and they established their own law for themselves from both the Old and the New Testaments. So, as if in worship of a single God, but not wishing to understand matters like us or the Jews, they perverted everything. They desire to subjugate all things to their dominion, but they do not demand that anyone should worship God, only that he should be enslaved to them.[34] As many think, perhaps the Antichrist will be received by them, since by the just judgement of God they were the first to receive the spirit of error. It is clearly written in the Apocalypse of John by whose assistance and power the Antichrist will be able to achieve so much and so many things.[35] I have written all this so that the prudent reader will understand how the mystery of evil is now at work, but it is not yet the End. [vol. 3, p. 1163]

[33] Nicholas, who is mentioned in Revelation 2:6, became associated with lack of chastity, which is possibly a veiled reference to the Islamic practice of taking more than one wife.

[34] The Latin of this important passage is unfortunately difficult to construe: *Qui dum cupiunt uniuersa suo dominio subiugari, nec querunt quem quisque Deum colat, sed ut eis tantummodo seruiatur.* The only surviving manuscript of this part of Radbert's commentary (Paris, BnF, lat. 12298, at fol. 81v) dates to the twelfth century, and contains occasional copying errors. The reading here supplies *ut* before *Deum*, 'They do not compel (*nec querunt*) anyone (*quemquisque*) to worship God' ([*ut*] *Deum colat*). An alternative interpretation could correct *querunt* to *queruntur*, 'They do not bother anyone who worships God, except only that he should be enslaved to them.' The point that conversion is not forced remains unchanged.

[35] Revelation 13:1-18.

55

Paul Alvarus, *Indiculus luminosus*

Kenneth Baxter Wolf, Pomona College

Paul Alvarus was a lay Christian scholar active in Córdoba, the capital of the Umayyad emirate of al-Andalus, in the middle of the ninth century. Like his lifelong friend Eulogius, he was an apologist for the so-called 'Córdoban martyrs', the majority of whom were executed for blasphemy, having deliberately flouted well-known proscriptions against public expressions of disrespect for Muḥammad. Such acts of defiance on the part of Christians living under Muslim rule not only rankled the Muslim leaders, but exposed deep divides within the Córdoban Christian community. While some, like Eulogius and Alvarus, lionized their executed coreligionists as martyrs of the classic Roman type, others criticized them as self-immolators whose unprovoked outbursts only complicated the long-standing working relationship between the Christian community and the Muslim authorities.

Alvarus's only contribution to the defence of these controversial new martyrs was the *Indiculus luminosus* ('The shining guide'), which he wrote in 854. The treatise is divided between an extended *apologia* on behalf of the martyrs and a commentary on parts of Daniel and Job designed to prove that Muḥammad was the Antichrist. The following selection comes from the first part. In it, Alvarus sheds light on a major split within the Córdoban Christian community as it negotiated the challenges of living within an Islamic host society. In his defence of the militancy of the spontaneous Christian blasphemers, he identifies their Christian opponents as the real problem, claiming that their passive approach to life under Islamic rule is inconsistent with the example set by Christ and the Apostles. In the process, he makes fascinating observations about the ways in which Andalusi Christians tended to mute the expression of their own Christianity in an effort to maintain a low profile. As far as he is concerned, such examples of strategic *convivencia* are rooted in fear, which stands in stark contrast to the irrepressible courage of the new martyrs. Alvarus goes so far as to argue that the Córdoban martyrs were driven by the evangelical-grounded need to preach the gospel to all corners of the earth, even suggesting that their 'mission' to the 'Ishmaelites' was the first that had ever been directed to them.

CMR 1, pp. 645–8. See further:

A. Sorber, 'Prophetic Resistance to Islam in Ninth-Century Córdoba: Paulus Alvarus and the *Indiculus Luminosus*', *Medieval Encounters* 25 (2019) 433–56.

This translation is based on Juan Gil (ed. and Spanish trans.), *Scriptores muzarabici saeculi VIII-XI*, vol. 1, Turnhout, 2020, pp. 599–601.

9. Now let us turn this section of our narrative back to the tepidness of our people and let us, in a few words, expound on the state of our own half-heartedness in order to explain that this divine judgement is just.[36] Are those of us who serve in the palace ministry at their command not plainly implicated in their errors?[37] Polluted with their stenches, they actually consider themselves splendid when they do not perform their prayers openly in the presence of the pagans;[38] when they yawn and do not safeguard their foreheads with the sign of the cross; when, their words having been put to flight, they do not publicly refer in their [the Muslims'] presence to Christ being God, calling Him the word and spirit of God[39] – as they [the Muslims] themselves assert – keeping their own [Christian] confessions in their hearts on the grounds that God examines everything.[40] When they defend Christianity not wholly but only halfway, what do they show those acting with the zeal of God except that they belong to the species of the leopard?[41] Yet we defend all these as good, declaring them not damnable but indeed most appropriate, and we neither curse nor detest those Christians who do battle against the comrades of their own faith, whether it be for the favour of the king,[42] or with an eye to expensive gifts, or in defence of the gentiles; instead we attack and defame with anathema these religious ones struggling on behalf of the true God. And we do all these things in pressing fear of an earthly king whom we maintain with unquestioning faith will not have a swift end, while we privately scorn and despise fear of the eternal king, to whom, as we rightly believe and understand, we will be dragged very soon; and we condemn as heretics and ignoramuses those who speak against their errors. Our weapons fight against us and our 'iniquity is coming down upon our own crown'.[43] Distinguished preachers, admirable chosen members of the flock, good monks and shepherds, did Christ teach us so? Did all the Apostles and

[36] Alvarus is treating the condition of the Andalusī Christian community as the result of a divine scourge, like the ones that afflicted Israel when the Jews were the chosen people.

[37] Córdoban Christians regularly served under the Muslim authorities in administrative posts, see: Eulogius, *Memoriale sanctorum* 2.2, 2.3, 3.1-2, 3.16.

[38] Here Alvarus provides valuable information about the various accommodations made by Christians working for and with the Muslims.

[39] An example of Christians conceiving of the nature of Christ as part of the Trinity using suggestive terms borrowed from Q 4.171.

[40] Alvarus is here exposing a *dhimmī* Christian strategy: publicly focusing on the commonalities between Islamic and Christian Christology while privately affirming the differences.

[41] Jeremiah 13:22-3.

[42] In this case, Muḥammad I, emir of Córdoba (r. 852–86).

[43] Psalm 7:17.

teachers teach us so? Did all those who, setting aside their lives for the sake of the truth, suffered diverse passions, teach us so?

10. I ask: Where did this new clemency that has arisen in the churches come from, this clemency that has vomited up such infernal teachings?[44] Or if you think this voice [of mine] is one of temerity, then identify the pious apostle who commanded such things. [...] Why were the prophets and Apostles sent, and why were teachers and shepherds provided, if not to fight against ignorance and to avenge all perfidy? Without such thundering preaching among the nations, how will what the Lord foretold about the future be fulfilled, to wit: 'When this gospel shall have been preached among all creatures, then will be the end'?[45] [...] Unless I am mistaken, what is rightly referred to as preaching is that which is undertaken out of necessity, just as all the Apostles did, whether it be convenient or not, even under the threat of death; and which is frequently sought out even in the case of danger, should it be present, so that nonbelievers may receive the light of the faith. He certainly did not say that every creature would accept the preaching of the gospel, rather that the preaching of the church ought to be made manifest to the whole world in general, so that, as a result of such ministry, an appropriate reward might be given to the preachers and to the despisers, a most just and eternal punishment without end. Those apostolic times were not the only ones that were to be dedicated to the preaching of the faith; in fact, the preaching of the Church is to be sowed throughout the entire world until every people and language [has the opportunity to] believe the gospel of Christ.[46] I reckon that up to the present no such preacher has appeared in the midst of this Ishmaelite people, by means of whose preaching they might be held as debtors of the faith.[47] But now these ones have fulfilled this this apostolate,[48] so to speak, this preaching of the gospel among [the Ishmaelites], and thus rendered them debtors of the faith.[49] Yet, obscured by a thick cloud of ignorance, we do not see them rushing to the mystery of the eternal gospel, and in response to those who are evangelizing justice to this people – among whom until now no one's preaching has offered a path – we insanely cry out that this is madness, not the fulfilment of that presaged prescience of the evangelizers. [...][50] We have become – oh, if only you deigned to be partners of our faith – dumb dogs unable

---

[44] That is, the 'clement' attitude towards the Muslims, a product of the *dhimmī* Christian recognition of their subordinate political status.

[45] Based on Matthew 24:14. This passage provides a biblical basis for the universal scope of Christianity. The point was not only to secure new converts, but on the Day of Judgement to hold accountable those who heard the gospel but then declined to embrace it.

[46] Alvarus is arguing for an extended apostolic age, one that would cast the neomartyrs as 'neo-apostles' and paint their Christian opponents as cowards.

[47] Alvarus was apparently unaware that Christianity was ensconced in parts of Arabia long before the rise of Muḥammad.

[48] That is, the Córdoban blasphemers.

[49] According to Eulogius, the neomartyrs who had been executed for blasphemy all sealed their fates by publicly denouncing Muḥammad *and* asserting the truth of the gospel. This is being strategically construed as a form of militant preaching.

[50] That is, the critics of the blasphemers failed to see that their actions were consistent with Christ's prediction that the gospel would ultimately be preached to everyone around the world.

to bark. The words of the most holy Jerome, that famous caretaker of the celestial library, with which he expounds on that prophecy – 'His watchmen are all blind, all dumb dogs not able to bark'[51] – are fulfilled in us: 'Dumb when it comes to speaking out against adversaries, we are rabid dogs among ourselves. Let us instead follow the ways of the Lord.'[52] But in our case the wolves that rage around the sheepfolds have carried off the voices of rebuke. In an unheard of and hitherto unseen fashion, the wolves and dogs have returned in peace.[53]

[51] Isaiah 59:10.

[52] Jerome, *Commentary on Isaiah*, 15.56.10-12.

[53] That is, the Muslims (the wolves) have silenced the Christian leaders (the dogs), thus exposing the Christian community (the flock of sheep) to danger.

56

Chronicle of Albelda

Graham Barrett, University of Lincoln

In the wake of the Muslim conquest of Iberia in 711, a number of Christian polities sprang up across the unconquered north of the Peninsula, the most consequential of which proved to be the kingdom of Asturias, founded in 718/22 and based at Oviedo. While expansion began under Alfonso II (r. 791–842), it was Alfonso III (r. 866–910) who drove the frontier most dramatically southwards, through a decisive victory over the Umayyad emir in 878. Recognizing a new centre of gravity beyond the Cantabrian mountains, his successors ruled from León.

Our principal sources for what would later be identified as the first phase of a great centuries-long *Reconquista* ('Reconquest') are three chronicles: one is transmitted in two versions under the name of Alfonso III himself, while the third, known misleadingly as the *Chronicle of Albelda*, is more a motley assemblage of historical and geographical texts and extracts, drawing heavily on the work of Isidore of Seville (d. 636). Compiled by an anonymous monk moving in the circle of the royal court, the text includes narrative sections on the Visigothic kings and on the vicissitudes of their self-proclaimed successors at Oviedo, in both combat and collaboration with the Muslims of al-Andalus, down to 883. Added onto this corpus is a supplementary set of material commonly called the *Prophetic Chronicle* and consisting of a genealogy of the 'Saracens', a polemical life of the Prophet Muḥammad, a description of the conquest, a list of the early Muslim governors and the eponymous foretelling.

The extract translated below comes from that prophecy. Through subtle and pointed rewriting of passages drawn from the book of Ezekiel, the author recasts the figure of Gog, who stands here for the Visigoths, from villain to hero and predicts his destruction of 'Ishmael' (the Saracens) after 170 years of foreordained but temporary rule over Hispania. Since the Muslim conquest is re-dated to 714, only one year remains from the date of composition of the text to the restoration of Christian rule in 884, an interesting echo of a forecast made by the ninth-century Muslim scholar ʿAbd al-Malik ibn Ḥabīb (d. 853). Scribes handled the text variously: in particular, with the passage of time they observed that the prophecy had failed to come true, and accordingly a copy dated to 974/76 from the monastery of Albelda in La Rioja updated the prediction to 270 years of rule, now expecting salvation to come in the year 984.

CMR 1, pp. 810–15.

This translation is based on J. Gil, *Chronica Hispana saeculi VIII et IX*, Turnhout, 2018, 435–84, pp. 479–84.

18. The kings of the lineage of Banū Umayya who reigned in Córdoba:

Yūsuf reigned for eleven years.

ʿAbd al-Raḥmān ibn Muʿāwiya reigned for thirty-three years.

Hishām reigned for seven years and six months.

Al-Ḥakam reigned for twenty-six years and six months.

ʿAbd al-Raḥmān reigned for thirty-two years and three months.[54] During his reign Ordoño, prince of the Christians, achieved many victories in Hispania.[55]

Muḥammad[56] saw through year thirty-two of his reign. In his time Abū Khālid, leader of his army, [. . .] was captured in the confines of Gallaecia and brought before our King Alfonso[57] in Oviedo; and many victories were realized by the Christians in Hispania.

In total, the years of the Arabs in Hispania amount to 169, and on 11 November they begin the year 170, and since the preaching of the most wicked Muḥammad in Africa there are 270 years, as of era 921 [883 CE] which is now elapsing.[58]

But we have found words to the effect that the Saracens would occupy the land of the Goths in the *Book of Destiny* by the prophet Ezekiel:[59]

'You, son of man, set your face against Ishmael,[60] and speak to him, saying, "I have given you to be the most powerful amongst the nations, I have multiplied you, I have reinforced you, and I have put a sword in your right hand and arrows in your left hand to crush the nations; and they are scattered before your face as straw before the front

[54] Yūsuf ibn ʿAbd al-Raḥmān (r. 747–56), the last governor appointed by the Umayyads of Damascus, was deposed by ʿAbd al-Raḥmān I (r. 756–88), the first independent Umayyad ruler of al-Andalus after the overthrow of the dynasty in Damascus by the ʿAbbasids. He was succeeded by Hishām (r. 788–96), al-Ḥakam I (r. 796–822) and ʿAbd al-Raḥmān II (r. 822–52).

[55] Ordoño I, king of Asturias (r. 850–66).

[56] Muḥammad I (r. 852–86).

[57] Alfonso III (r. 866–910), son and successor of Ordoño I.

[58] One manuscript adds here in the margin: 'From when the Saracens entered Hispania down to the present era 1014 [976 CE] span 262 years, and since Muḥammad the most villainous prophet down to the present era 1014 span 363.'

[59] *Liber Panticinus*: the title of this fictional book is derived from the Greek *παν-*, 'all', and *τύχe*, 'fortune'; cf. F. Montanari et al. (eds), *The Brill Dictionary of Ancient Greek*, Leiden, 2015, s.v. *παντυχία* (pantuchía), 'complete good fortune'.

[60] Ancestor of the Arabs, and therefore of the Muslims; see Ezekiel 38:2, 'Son of man, set your face against Gog'.

of a fire.[61] And you will enter the land of Gog on the ground, and you will slay Gog with your sword, and you will put your foot onto his neck, and you will make [his people] tributary slaves to you. Yet because you, [Ishmael], have forsaken the Lord your God, I shall forsake you too, and topple you,[62] and deliver you into the hand of Gog; and you will die within the bounds of Libya, and all your army by his sword. As you have done to Gog, so will he do to you; after you have mastered [his people] in slavery for 170 [or 270] seasons, Gog will repay you in turn exactly as you have done."'

19. An interpretation of this put forward by us:

'Gog', clearly, is the nation of the Goths; and as 'Ishmael' alone is written above for the whole race of Ishmaelites when it is said by the prophet, 'Set your face against Ishmael', so also is 'Gog' named for the whole nation of Goths, from whose lineage they come and from whom they have taken their name. And the same *Chronicle of the Goths* asserts that the nation of Goths came from Magog when it says: 'The nation of the Goths is very ancient, and their lineage runs down from Magog, son of Japheth;[63] they are also named after this, based on the similarity of the final syllable – that is, Gog – and *magis* [more], which they gather from the prophet Ezekiel.'[64] Indeed, the *Book of Generations* likewise asserts that the Goths come from Magog, son of Japheth, and both Gothia and Scythia are named after Magog.[65]

But the prophet also says this to Ishmael: 'You will enter the land of Gog on the ground, and you will slay Gog with your sword, and you will put your foot on his neck, and you will make [his people] tributary slaves.' We recognize that it has already been fulfilled: 'the land of Gog' clearly denotes Hispania under the rule of the Goths; and the Ishmaelites manifested themselves on account of the transgressions of the Gothic nation, and cut them down by the sword, and made them tributaries to themselves, as can readily be seen at the present time.[66]

Now the same prophet once again says to Ishmael: 'Because you have forsaken the Lord, I shall forsake you also, and deliver you into the hand of Gog, and he will repay you in turn. After you have cast them down for 170 [or 270] seasons, he will do to you as you have done to him.' Christ is our hope[67] that in the very next season, when the 170 [or 270] years from their entry into Hispania have been fulfilled, the enemy will be reduced to nothing and the peace of Christ will be restored to the Holy

[61] Cf. Exodus 15:7, from the song sung by Moses and the Israelites in thanksgiving for God's drowning of Pharaoh's hosts in the Red Sea.
[62] Cf. Ezekiel 38:4.
[63] Cf. Genesis 10:2, identifying Japheth as one of the sons of Noah.
[64] Isidore of Seville, *History of the Goths*, 1.
[65] An unknown source; drawing perhaps on Isidore of Seville, *Etymologies*, 9.2.26-7.
[66] One manuscript adds here in the margin: 'In era 1030 of Caesar [992 CE] it has been 382 years since Muḥammad preached.'
[67] This deliberately echoes the words defiantly uttered by Pelayo (r. 718–37) at the Battle of Covadonga (718/22), traditionally the first engagement in the Reconquest; see *Chronicle of Alfonso III*, 9-10.

Church (since 'seasons' are substituted for 'years'). And may Almighty God provide that as the presumption of the enemy steadily wanes the Church may ever wax to the better. Amen.

Indeed, some Saracens have themselves foretold this – that their downfall looms – by portents and signs in the stars, and they say that the kingdom of the Goths will be restored through this man, our prince;[68] and this prince, our glorious lord Alfonso,[69] is also foretold by the visions and experiences of many Christians to be on the verge of ruling over all Hispania in time very soon to come. And so, under the safeguard of divine mercy, the frontiers of the enemy have faltered day by day, and the Church of the Lord increases to the greater and better. And insofar as the honour of the name of Christ brings it to pass, the belittling disaster inflicted by the enemy accordingly wastes away.

[The enemy will] remain until 11 November, the feast-day of Saint Martin, in seven months' time, when 169 years will be complete and the year 170 begins. And, according to the prediction of the prophet Ezekiel interpreted above, when the Saracens have finished these [years], the retribution which is owing to the enemy will be nigh, and the salvation of the Christians at hand. And may Almighty God provide that, as He deigned to ransom the whole world from the power of the Devil by the blood of His son Our Lord Jesus Christ, so in the very next season He will order His Church to be set free from the yoke of the Ishmaelites – He who lives and reigns forever and ever. Amen.[70]

---

[68] Eulogius of Córdoba (d. 859) argued in his polemical *Remembrance of the saints*, 2.1.6, 2.12, that the example of the voluntary martyrs of Córdoba in the 850s had led the Muslim rulers of al-Andalus to fear for the future.

[69] King Alfonso III.

[70] These final two paragraphs are present in only one copy of the text.

57

Passion of Pelagius

Kati Ihnat, Radboud University

The *Passio Pelagii* ('Passion of Pelagius' or 'Pelayo') is a hagiographical account of the events leading up to the death of Pelagius, a boy of thirteen, when he is described as being martyred in about 925[71] by the emir (later caliph) of Córdoba, ʿAbd al-Raḥmān III (r. 912–61). The text is found in four manuscripts, each dated to the eleventh century or later. In one (El Escorial, b.I.4, f. 127r), a marginal note refers to a priest named Raguel, called the 'teacher' (*doctor*) of the text. On the basis of this note, most scholars have assumed that Raguel was the author. The ambiguity of the word *doctor* nevertheless leaves open the possibility that he did not compose it so much as copy the work or read it out in a liturgical context.[72]

The work was probably written before 967, the year in which the relics of Pelagius were moved from Córdoba to León (the end of the *Passio* still places them in the Córdoban churches of St Cyprian and St Genesius). The *Passio* was read out in a liturgical context; at least one of the manuscripts (Paris, BnF, nal 239) contains it together with the office and mass for the feast of Pelagius. The other manuscripts include it in collections of similar saints' lives, the *Passionarium Hispanicum* ('Spanish Passionary').

Although the account given in the *Passio* could be based on historical events,[73] the narrative is also shaped by a number of hagiographical conventions, as is attested by phrases shared with many late antique female martyr passions and a general similarity to them. The fact that these are female martyrs is striking, making this the first known Latin witness to the trope of homosexual advances made by Muslim men towards Christian boys, a feature for which it has attracted significant scholarly attention, and which was developed even further in the version of Hroswitha of Gandersheim (d. 973).

---

[71] A discrepancy in the date given in each manuscript has led to confusion, with Paris, BnF, nal 2179 dating his death to 925 and the others to 926.

[72] This has been argued especially by Christys, *Christians*, pp. 89–93.

[73] See J. Gil, 'La Pasión de San Pelayo', *Habis* 3 (1972) 161–202.

The extract translated below opens after a Galician bishop named Ermogius is taken captive by Andalusian troops to Córdoba, thrown in prison, then released in a hostage exchange for his ten-year-old nephew Pelagius.

CMR 2, pp. 377–80. See further:

A. Christys, *Christians in Al-Andalus, 711–1000*, Abingdon, 2002.

J.A. Bowman, 'Beauty and Passion in Tenth-Century Córdoba', in M. Kuefler (ed.), *The Boswell Thesis: Essays on Christianity, Social Tolerance, and Homosexuality*, Chicago, IL, 2006, 236–53.

M. Fierro, 'Hostages and the Dangers of Cultural Contact: Two Cases from Umayyad Córdoba', in R. Abdellatif *et al.* (eds), *Acteurs des transferts culturels en Méditerranée médiévale*, Oldenbourg, 2013, 73–83.

This translation is based on P. Riesco Chueca, *Pasionario Hispánico. Introducción, edición crítica y traducción*, Seville, 1995, pp. 310–18.

Thinking that this had all been inspired by God, the holy Pelagius lived cautiously in prison. [...] [He] became skilled in reading and quick to learn. This was his lifestyle: when he discussed in the presence of some bigmouth of another faith, this man went off rebuffed. Pelagius also preserved the purity of his body and soul in such a way that one could think he thought of nothing but his future martyrdom, since he gave such signs that he would in no way miss out on the joys of heaven. [...] Without any doubt, Christ taught him inwardly, He who had made him outwardly beautiful. This He did in order that Pelagius might honour with his physical beauty that same Master for whom he comported himself in his soul as a worthy disciple, purifying his body to prepare it as a dwelling place in which the bridegroom would soon rejoice, and out of which Pelagius, now crowned with holy blood, might join himself to Christ's embrace among the choirs of the saints, a servant worthy of the honour. Enriched with the double crown of virginity and martyrdom, Pelagius would gain a double victory over his enemy by rejecting riches and not yielding to vices; he would be so crowned by the Lord for having despised those things in which the Devil constantly rejoices.

After these praiseworthy deeds had gone on for about three and a half years, one day the servants of one of the king's pages happened to appear and, with a view to carrying out some kind of transaction, they told their lord of the remarkable beauty of holy Pelagius's face. [...] And so these foolish and unenlightened men considered sinking his beauty into the abyss of vice, he whom the Lord had promised a place at his right hand among the choirs of holy virgins. For the wretches did not understand that one cannot oppose God when one cannot even turn one's hair white or black.[74] In the meantime, the news reached the ears of the king that, even in the confines of the

[74] Cf. Matthew 5:36.

dungeons, the servant of God had remained beautiful, and this filled him with a great but unholy delight. While in the midst of celebrating a banquet, the king therefore sent his officials to bring before his own eyes the future victim for Christ. Since all things are possible for Almighty God, his orders were carried out, and they hastily dragged in the servant of God, Pelagius, with his chains in such a way that when these were cut off they clanged in the king's hall, reverberating with a terrible noise. The fools thus rejoiced to offer to a mortal king him whose soul had already been taken care of by Christ on account of his unwavering faith. Having dressed him in royal robes, they presented Pelagius before the king's gaze, whispering into the holy boy's ear that his beauty would bring him great honour.

The king soon said to him: 'Child, I shall bestow great honours on you if you consent to deny Christ and say that our prophet is the real one. Do you not see what and how many kingdoms are under our power? In addition to this, I shall add to that great quantities of gold and silver, the most sumptuous clothing, and ornaments of great value. You can have whichever you wish of these pages, who will serve you to your liking. I shall also give you palaces in which to live, horses to ride, pleasures to enjoy. I shall also release from prison whoever you ask me to, and if you like, I shall invite your parents to come to this country and I will bestow great honours on them.' The holy Pelagius, rejecting all of this and considering it contemptible, answered: 'All this you offer me, O king, is nothing, and I shall not deny Christ. I am a Christian, I was one and shall remain one, because all things come to an end and in their times all things pass,[75] but Christ, whom I worship, has no end, because he also has no beginning. For he is one single God with the Father and Holy Spirit, He who made us from nothing and has all things in his power.'

In the meantime, as the king playfully sought to place a hand on him, the holy Pelagius interrupted him: 'Hands off, dog, or do you take me to be effeminate, like your own people?' And at that moment he tore off the robes he had on and presented himself like a brave athlete in the ring, preferring to die a worthy death for Christ than to live in shame with the Devil and to foul himself with sin. Thinking that he could yet convince Pelagius, the king ordered his pages to seduce him with tempting enticements if he were to accept such royal riches by apostatizing. But Pelagius, with the help of God, stood strong and remained steadfast, proclaiming only that Christ existed and that he would always obey His commandments. Seeing that Pelagius's soul was completely resolute and resisted his pressures, and realizing that he was being condemned for his base appetites, the king became enraged and said, 'Hang him by iron hooks, and, with his limbs stretched out, raise him and lower him until he breathes his last or denies that Christ is God.'

Enduring such torment with an unwavering spirit, the holy Pelagius remained steadfast and did not refuse to suffer for Christ. Seeing Pelagius's staunch commitment, the king ordered him to be cut into pieces with a sword, limb from limb, and these to be thrown into the river.

---

[75] Ecclesiastes 3:1.

58

Gregory VII, *Register*

Guy Perry, University of Oxford

Gregory VII (r. 1073–85) was the outstanding pope of the late eleventh century. While he is most notorious for his role in the so-called Investiture Contest, he deserves to be just as well known for his part in the emergence of the crusading movement, which crystallized a decade or so after his death. The first two extracts below, taken from the surviving register of his letters under the year 1074, describe the 'proto-crusade' which he was proposing to lead so as to rescue the Byzantines from the ravages of the Seljuq Turks, with the idea that the Western army might then push on to recover Jerusalem itself. Although this expedition never took place, it is worth noting that Gregory's attitude towards the Muslims was not always so hostile. This comes across most clearly in the third extract, which seems to date from the year 1076 (see Cowdrey, *Register*, p. 493, n. 59). In this letter the pope is seeking to build on his diplomatic accord with al-Nāṣir ibn ʿAlannās, the Ḥammādid emir of north Africa. Indeed, Gregory's emphasis on how both Abrahamic faiths worship God, albeit in different ways, has a very modern ring to it. In short, this was the fiery pontiff who would do most to set the Latin world on the path which would lead to the Crusades. However, he was also capable of a much more subtle and reflective approach towards Islam.

CMR 3, pp. 182–203. See further:

C. Morris, *The Papal Monarchy. The Western Church from 1050 to 1250*, Oxford, 1989.

I. Robinson, *The Papacy, 1073–1198: Continuity and Innovation*, Cambridge, 1990.

The Papal Reform of the Eleventh Century. Lives of Pope Leo IX and Pope Gregory VII, ed. and trans. I. Robinson, Manchester, 2004.

The translation below is adapted from H.E.J. Cowdrey (trans.), *The Register of Pope Gregory VII, 1073–1085: An English Translation*, Oxford, 2002, with reference to the original Latin text.

1.49. Gregory, bishop, servant of the servants of God,[76] to all those who are willing to defend the Christian faith, greetings and Apostolic benediction.

We wish it to be known to you that [...] a race of pagans has strongly prevailed against the Christian empire,[77] and with wretched cruelty has laid waste up to the very walls of the city of Constantinople, and with tyrannical violence has seized everything. They have slaughtered many thousands of Christians like cattle.[78] Because of this, if we love God and acknowledge ourselves to be Christians, then we must grieve deeply over the pitiable plight of so great an empire, and for so great a carnage of Christians. And it is not sufficient merely to grieve over this matter, but the example of our Redeemer and the duty of fraternal charity demands that we lay down our lives for the liberation of our brothers – because, as He laid down His life for us, so too should we lay down our lives for our brethren.[79]

Know, therefore, that we, trusting in the mercy of God and in the power of His might,[80] are taking steps and making preparations [...] so that [...] with God's help we might bring assistance to the Christian empire. Therefore, through the faith in which you, through Christ, have been made one of the adopted sons of God,[81] we beseech and urge you, by the authority of the blessed Peter, prince of the Apostles, both that the wounds and blood of your brothers and the peril of the empire may inspire you with due compassion, and that, for the sake of the name of Christ, your valour may not be fruitless in bringing reinforcements to your brethren. Hence, whatever divine goodness may plant into your minds about this matter, be sure to report it to us without delay, by reliable emissaries.

Given at Rome on 1 March, in the twelfth indiction.[82] [pp. 54–5]

2.31. Gregory, bishop, servant of the servants of God, to the illustrious King Henry, greetings and Apostolic benediction.[83]

I give notice to your excellency that [...] a very great proportion of Christians from regions beyond the sea are being destroyed by pagans, an unimaginable disaster, and are daily being slaughtered like cattle, whilst the Christian people are reduced to nothing. [Some of] them have humbly sent to me and [...] have implored that I should bring help to our brothers by every means that I am able, lest, heaven forbid, the Christian religion should completely perish in our time. For my part, I have been touched by exceeding sorrow, and drawn by a longing for death itself – for I would wish to lay down my life for these people rather than, through neglecting them, command the whole world. [...]

---

[76] The standard formula at the start of papal letters.

[77] The Seljuq Turks, who had defeated the Byzantines at the battle of Manzikert in 1071. They were not pagans, in fact, but had only recently converted to Islam.

[78] While there are elements of truth here, a lot of it is 'atrocity propaganda'.

[79] 1 John 3:16.

[80] Ephesians 6:10.

[81] Romans 8:23.

[82] The year 1074.

[83] The future Holy Roman emperor Henry IV (r. 1084–1105), who was to become Gregory's greatest opponent.

I have sought to stir up Christians everywhere and incite them to this purpose: that they should seek, by defending the law, to lay down their lives for their brothers, and to show, more clearly than the light, the nobility of the children of God. By God's inspiration [...] men from Italy and beyond the Alps have accepted this challenge, and already more than 50,000[84] are making themselves ready, so that if they can have me as their leader and chief priest on the campaign they will rise up in armed force against the enemies of God, and go as far as the sepulchre of the Lord[85] under [my] leadership. [pp. 122–4]

3.21. Gregory, bishop, servant of the servants of God, to al-Nāṣir,[86] king of the province of Mauretania [...] in Africa.

Your highness sent us a letter this year, asking that we ordain the priest Servandus as a bishop according to the Christian rites. Because your request seemed right and proper, we were glad to do it. Moreover, you sent gifts to us and, out of reverence for the blessed Peter, the prince of the Apostles, and out of love for us, you have freed [various] Christians who were held captive amongst your people. Indeed, you promised that you would free other captives too. [It is] God, the Creator of all, without whom we cannot do or even think anything that is good, [who] has inspired this generosity in your heart. For Almighty God, who wants all men to be saved and that no-one should perish, approves of nothing more in us than that, after our love for Him, a man should love his fellow man, and that he should not do unto another what he would not have happen to himself.[87] In truth, such love both we and you owe more particularly to our own than to other peoples, for we believe in and confess the one God, albeit in a different way, and each day we praise and honour Him as the Creator of ages and the Ruler of the world. For, as the Apostle says, 'He is our peace, who has made both [of us] one.'[88]

What is more, many Roman nobles who are aware [...] that this grace has been granted to you by God have both admired and publicised your generosity and virtues. Among these are two of our household, Alberic and Cencius. [...] In commending them to your excellency, we wish that, for love of us and in recompense for their fidelity, you will extend to them the same love which we always desire to extend to you and all your people. For God knows that we love you [...] sincerely, to the honour of God, and that we desire your welfare and honour, both in the present life and in that which is to come. With heart and lips we beseech that God Himself will bring you, after a long continuance in this life, into the blessed bosom of the most holy patriarch Abraham. [pp. 204–5]

[84] This is a typical example of pontifical overstatement: the numbers are vastly inflated, and, in the end, little or nothing came of this enterprise.
[85] The Church of the Holy Sepulchre in Jerusalem.
[86] Al-Nāṣir ibn ʿAlannās, emir of what is now north-eastern Algeria.
[87] The 'Golden Rule': see Matthew 7:12 and Luke 6:31.
[88] Ephesians 2:14.

59

Raymond of Aguilers, *History of the Franks who captured Jerusalem*

Susan B. Edgington, Queen Mary University of London

Raymond of Aguilers participated in the First Crusade and wrote an account of it which appears to have been completed soon after 1100, although the earliest copy we have was made some thirty years later. As Raymond of Saint-Gilles's chaplain, Raymond of Aguilers had access to sound information, but his pro-Provençal bias and his enthusiasm for marvels and miracles unbalance his account. Perhaps for this reason, his *History* is the most neglected of the contemporary narratives, and there is no satisfactory edition or easily accessible translation.

Raymond's prejudices are on display in the extracts below, some of which also reveal knowledge of Islamic history and the Muslim religion, albeit grossly distorted.

CMR 3, pp. 297–300.

This translation is based on *Recueil des historiens des croisades: Historiens occidentaux*, vol. 3, Paris, 1866, pp. 231–309.

[During the siege of Antioch in 1098, the Crusaders received overtures ostensibly from the Fāṭimid caliph in Cairo (the 'king of Babylon'), but actually sent by his vizier al-Afḍal. An envoy reappeared in the spring of 1099 while the Crusaders were still in the vicinity of Antioch. The Fāṭimids had captured Jerusalem from the Turks the previous year.]

An envoy from the king of Egypt came to us there, and with the envoy he sent back to us our delegates whom he had held captive for a year. For he was undecided whether to make a treaty of friendship with us or with the Turks. We wanted to make an agreement with him on these terms: if he would give us assistance from Jerusalem or return Jerusalem to us with its lands, then we would return to him all his cities which the Turks had taken from him, when we captured them. Otherwise, if with his help we captured cities from the Turks which were not part of his kingdom, we would divide them between us. The Turks, we were told, wanted to do this for him: if he came with them to battle against us, then they would worship ʿAlī, who is of Muḥammad's kin and whom he [the caliph] worshipped,[89] they would receive money from him and would remit certain tribute, and do many other things which we know little about. He knew that there were few of us. He knew that Emperor Alexios[90] was hostile to us to the point of death. We found a letter which Emperor Alexios had written about us in the king's tents after the battle with the king of Egypt at Ascalon. Therefore, for this and other reasons the emir kept our envoys captive for a year in Cairo. Only when he heard that we had invaded his territory and laid waste villages and fields and everything, did he instruct us that two or three hundred could go to Jerusalem, worship the Lord and return. But we ridiculed his offer, putting our hope in God's mercy, and proclaimed that unless he returned Jerusalem to us unconditionally we would claim Cairo from him. [p. 277]

[As the Crusaders marched south later in 1099, they asked local Christians to advise on the best route. This provided Raymond with a digression about the Muslim occupation of Lebanon, no doubt recording atrocities as related by the Syrians, further distorted by his own prejudices.]

Certain Syrians came to us then. For there are mountains there in Lebanon where up to 60,000 Christian people live, and Christians have occupied that land and the mountains for a long time. They are called Syrians on account of the city of Tyre, which is commonly called Sur now. But when the Saracens and Turks rose to power, by God's judgement, for 400 years and more these Syrians suffered such great oppression of slavery that many of them were forced to abandon their homeland and the Christian religion. But those who, by the grace of God, rejected this course were forced to hand over their lovely little boys to be circumcised, actually made into Turks, or they were snatched from the breasts of their mothers; their fathers were killed and their mothers abused. Those races of men were fired up to such great wickedness that they overthrew God's churches and even destroyed the images of his saints. If they could not destroy them because it was too time-consuming, they dug out their eyes and shot arrows at them. All the altars were overturned. Moreover, they made mosques in the great churches. If any of those oppressed Christians wanted to have an image of God or any of His saints in his home, he would either pay a fine for it monthly or yearly, or it would be trampled in the dirt and smashed before his eyes. And what is

[89] The Fāṭimids claimed descent through ʿAlī, cousin of Muḥammad, and his wife Fāṭima, daughter of Muḥammad (hence their dynastic name). They would therefore be counted among the Shīʿa, supporters of ʿAlī and the claims made for him.

[90] The Byzantine emperor Alexios I Komnenos (r. 1081–1118).

still exceedingly hard to relate: they put the young men in brothels and bartered their sisters for wine, and worse. And even their mothers did not dare to weep openly for them or for their other sorrows. What more should we tell about these things? That race had certainly conspired against the Holy of Holies and His inheritance. [p. 288]

[Raymond gloated over the deaths of their Muslim enemies, firstly after the Crusaders had captured Antioch in 1098, and secondly when they fought a battle against the forces of Tripoli in 1099.]

It was an amusing spectacle we saw come about at last, after a long time when those who had defended Antioch against us for so long had simply not been able to escape from the city. If some of them dared to take flight, they were still unable to escape death. What happened there was quite amusing and delightful to us, for when some Turks were trying to steal away over the steep slopes which divide the southern hill from the northern, they ran into certain of our men. When they forced the Turks to retreat, the Turks were driven back at such a rate that all of them alike fell headlong. What joy there was indeed at the fallen enemy! But we grieved over the more than 300 horses that broke their necks there. [pp. 251–2]

The earth was befouled by the blood of the Moors[91] and the aqueduct was filled with their bodies. The Lord had let loose so great a fear on them that hardly any of them were able to flee after the first blows. It was indeed rather delightful to see how the stream in the aqueduct swiftly carried the headless bodies of nobles and commoners into the city. One or two of our men fell there, but we heard that up to 700 of the enemy fell. [p. 285]

[91] Originally a term applied to Muslims from the western Mediterranean and particularly North Africa, it came to include Muslims in general.

60

Guibert of Nogent, *Deeds of God through the Franks*

Beth Spacey, University of Queensland

Guibert of Nogent was a northern French Benedictine monk of Saint-Germer-de-Fly and later abbot of Nogent-sous-Coucy. The precise dates of his life are unknown, though it is likely that he was born around 1060 and died around 1125. Numerous extant works are attributed to him, including poetry, history, theology, biblical commentary, anti-Jewish polemic and criticism of the cult of relics, but he is most famous for his memoirs, known as his *Monodies*.

The *Dei gesta per Francos* ('Deeds of God through the Franks') was probably written between 1107 and 1109. It is a narrative retelling in Latin of the events of the First Crusade using the anonymous *Gesta Francorum et aliorum Hierosolimitanorum*. Guibert deliberately set out to improve upon this version, not only stylistically but, crucially, in its ability to convey the perceived spiritual significance of the Crusade as an act of divine providence. He also came across a version of Fulcher of Chartres's *Historia Hierosolymitana* later in the composition process. Guibert prefaces his narrative of the Crusade with an account of the supposed origins of Islam, comprising a polemical and derisive biography of Muḥammad, whom he calls Mathomus. By portraying Muḥammad as a profane heresiarch and Islam as a nefarious heresy, Guibert sought to rationalize and justify the Crusade and the violence against Muslims.

Translated here is part of Guibert's account of Muḥammad's life and death, leading into a summary of Turkish incursions into the Byzantine Empire in the later eleventh century.

CMR 3, pp. 329–34.

This translation is based on Guibert of Nogent. *Dei gesta per Francos*, ed. R.B.C. Huygens, Turnhout, 2002.

It is a common belief that there was a certain man who, if I portray him correctly, was called Mathomus, who at one time led them [the Muslims] away entirely from belief in the Son and the Holy Spirit, taught them to depend upon the person of the Father alone as the single God and Creator, and said that Jesus was entirely human. To define his dogma quickly: having decreed circumcision, he loosened the reins of all his shamelessness. I think that profane man was of very little antiquity, for no other reason than because I find none of the Church doctors to have written against his filthiness. Since I have learned of nowhere where his behaviour and life are written about, no one ought to be amazed if I might want to say what I have heard said in public by certain eloquent people. It is clearly pointless to discuss if these things are false or true, so long as this only considers how great that teacher may have been, whose renown for famous crimes is being propagated to such an extent. Indeed, one can safely speak wickedly about him whose malice exceeds and surpasses whatever perversities are being said. [p. 94] [...]

At this time, the darkness of this nefarious institution covered over the Christian name and still obliterates it throughout nearly the entire East, from Africa, Egypt, Ethiopia, Libya and the farthest gulfs of Spain, near us.

But it must be said by what exit this great and marvellous lawgiver was carried from our midst. Since he would often fall to the ground in a sudden epileptic seizure, by which we said above he was troubled, on one occasion it happened that, while he was walking alone, struck by this same illness, he fell, and having been discovered by pigs while twisted in suffering, he was torn to pieces to such an extent that no relics of him could be found except his ankles. Behold, just as the noble lawgiver struggled to resuscitate the Epicurean pig, which the true Stoics (that is to say, the worshippers of Christ) had slaughtered – indeed he awakens it entirely – the pig himself is exposed to be eaten by pigs, so that the master of indecency may conclude by a most obscene end, as is fitting. He rightly left behind his ankles, because he imposed the footprints of perfidy and obscenity on miserably deceived souls. Like the poet[92] we shall complete a monument to those ankles in a four-line poem 'more everlasting than bronze and loftier than the royal site of the pyramids', so that the distinguished man, already happier than every pig, might say with the same poet: 'I will not die entirely, and a great part of me will avoid Libitina.'[93]

He who has lived as a pig is chewed by the mouth of swine,
his members which are called blessed, poured from the anus of swine.
Not only the ankles but also that which the pig has poured forth in odour
may the worshipper who celebrates bring to their mouth with appropriate honour.

What if the Manichaean sect is right about cleanliness, that in all things one eats a certain part of God remains, polluted, and by the crushing of teeth and the stomach's

---

92 Horace, *Odes*, 3.30.

93 The name of the ancient Roman goddess of funerals is used as a metonym for death.

digestion part of God himself is made clean and, cleansed, is turned into angels, who are said to come forth from us in belching and windiness – how many angels do we believe the pigs fed on this flesh produced, and thence expelled by great farts?[94] But, laying aside such laughable things said in mockery of his followers, this must be made known: that they do not believe him to be God, as some estimate, but a just man and patron through whom divine laws might be delivered. They add that this man was received into heaven and only his ankles were left behind as a monument for his followers, which even now they revisit in endless veneration; truly, with fair reason they utterly despise the eating of pigs, which devoured their lord with bites.

After many generations, the error of paganism, having been fenced in, had grown strong. Then these people whom we discussed above, after a long time, spread throughout not only Palestine but also Jerusalem and the sepulchre of the Lord, and captured Armenia, Syria, and a part of Greece almost up to the sea, which is called the arm of St George. Since Antiquity, the Babylonian Empire has been the most powerful amongst all the kingdoms of the East, and it will rule in many such kingdoms. But the kingdom of the Parthians, who by name – having been corrupted – we call the Turks, is very powerful in the art of war and equestrian refinement, yet still the greatness of the land is little known. The Babylonian emperor thus captured with a great army those same provinces we have mentioned above, but in the advance of time he lost them to the rising forces of the Turks, and the Assyrians were conquered. When the Turks, vigorous in arms and making use of a skilled boldness, were threatening the empire of Constantinople and seemed about to besiege the city, the emperor of the Greeks, made to tremble by their constant menace and unremitting raids, sent a letter to France, writing to the elder Robert, count of Flanders, setting before him many reasons by which his spirit might be stirred to defend endangered Greece.[95] [pp. 98–101]

[94] Guibert refers here to the dualist cosmology of the Manichaeans.

[95] Guibert later includes an abridged version of the apocryphal letter of Alexius Comnenus to Robert of Flanders, in which the former supposedly appeals to the latter for help.

61

Book of Testaments of Lorvão

Graham Barrett, University of Lincoln

The region around the River Mondego, flowing westwards through what is today central Portugal into the Atlantic Ocean, was a frontier zone in the early Middle Ages. Under the emirate of Córdoba from the Muslim conquest of Iberia in 711, it was incorporated into the kingdom of León in 878 amidst the Christian drive southwards which established the county of Portugal. In a rare case of 'reverse reconquest', in 988 it was retaken by al-Manṣūr (d. 1002), chamberlain to the Umayyad caliph Hishām II (r. 976–1013) and power behind the throne for much of his reign. In 1064, it was conquered finally by Fernando I, king of León-Castilla (r. 1037–65).

The principal source for the history of the region in this period is the monastic cartulary (a manuscript containing copies of charters, title deeds, etc.) of Lorvão, an institution founded in the late ninth century. Known as the *Liber testamentorum* ('Book of testaments'), it was assembled around 1119 after a brief suppression of the monastery; outwardly a rough and ready effort, it transmits two short chronicles and eighty-six charters. Through these documents and the transactions recorded in them, we catch through Christian eyes precious glimpses of a landscape in which Muslims – or at least persons bearing Arab or Berber names – were deeply embedded, as much if not more so than anywhere else in the peninsula.

The three charters translated below give a flavour of this presence, and of the range of interactions which it could occasion. The first two record sales made by Muslims to the abbot of Lorvão: though normal Latin Christian diplomatic forms and language have been slightly altered to accommodate the religious sensibilities of the vendors, it is otherwise business as usual. The third text is more narrative in style, retailing the vicissitudes of some monastic property over the course of a century, and bears colourful witness to the decidedly porous boundaries existing between the two religions.

These translations are based on A.A. Nascimento, J.M. Fernández Catón, *et al.*, 'Transcripción del texto del *Liber testamentorum* – Transcrição do texto do *Liber testamentorum*', in *Liber testamentorum coenobii Laurbanensis*, 2 vols, León, 2008, vol. 2, pp. 581–717.

9. [4 December 1016–2 January 1017]

In the name of God.

This is the charter of sale which I, Zuleiman iben Giarah Aciki, have made to Abbot Dulcidius and to his brothers of the monastery of Lorvão, territory of Coimbra,[96] of all that I held in the villa[97] of Vilela. On the south side stands the mountain which they call Iben Zuleimen's, on the north side the villa of Viaster, on the east side the mountain which they call Oleaster, and on the west side Iben Zuleimen's bridge.

I have sold them broken and unbroken lands,[98] vineyards and gardens and every type of tree, roofed and unroofed dwellings,[99] ways both in and out, mountains and springs, hills and valleys and pastures, marshes and mill foundations: all this – in sound mind and full intent and complete awareness – for twenty silver coins 'of Qasim'.[100] Such has well pleased me.

None of the price remains for you to pay; and from this very day and time may it be removed from my ownership and transferred into [your] authority. But if any outrage has been perpetrated on that property, it should fall to me or those who are born of me [to make restitution]; and may the abbot together with his brothers hold what I have sold them in perpetuity.

Charter of sale made in era 407 [1016–17 CE][101] during the month of Rajab.[102]

Witnesses who were present: Acham iben Hallaz Azubeide. Abdella iben Satir Alamavi.[103] Abdella iben Zaada Alkaizi.[104] Galib iben Cidello Alamavi. Hacem iben Umar Alkazi. Humar iben Muzoud. Mahomat iben Abdelarahamen. Mahomat iben Abez Alavi. Halafac iben Zaada Alamavi. Zalama iben Nidriz Alamavi. [pp. 606–7]

10. [4 December 1016–2 January 1017]

In the name of God.

This is the charter of sale which I, Mahomat, son of Abderahmen, grandson of Harit, have made to Abbot Dulcidius of the monastery of Lorvão and to the whole congregation, of all my inheritance[105] that I held from the portion of my grandfather Abderahamen iben Abdella in the villa of Vilela, territory of Coimbra, with everything attached to it – that is, on the four sides, broken and unbroken lands, together with their dwellings[106] and all buildings.

---

[96] An important cathedral town on the River Mondego.

[97] This term encompasses everything from 'settlement' to 'farmhouse'.

[98] That is, tilled and untilled.

[99] The word *casa* normally designates 'homes', but it can also stand for agricultural 'pens' and the like.

[100] Qāsim ibn Khālid (d. 944), head of the Córdoba mint; synonymous with coinage of high quality.

[101] In Iberian charters, 'era' normally refers to the 'Spanish era', which was thirty-eight years ahead of *Anno Domini*, but here to the *hijrī* dating system, according to the Islamic lunar calendar.

[102] Fighting was traditionally forbidden in the Muslim month of Rajab.

[103] Possibly al-Umawī, of the ruling Umayyad family.

[104] Possibly al-Qays, the Arab tribal confederation.

[105] The term *hereditas* can equally denote 'property' in general.

[106] The meaning of *casal* is difficult to specify: a rural structure, but ownership, tenancy and use seem to have varied in practice.

These are the boundaries: on the one side, Iben Zuleiman's mountain, specifically, from the side along the hillock of Eyras and from Valle Kovo all the way to the spring of Garves;[107] on the other side, along the mountain which they call Otero de Rando, and from there to the bridge of Viaster, and proceeding by that brook at the plum tree all the way along to the water which runs down from the spring of Garves. All the things which I have named I have handed over in their entirety to the aforesaid abbot for forty coins of pure silver.

The abbot and the entire congregation have given it, and I have received it; none of the price remains for them to pay. And we – the abbot who has purchased and I who have sold – have done so equally on both sides with sound hearts and minds, without coercion from any person. But if any man whosoever should come to dispute this deed of mine, or if any evil whatsoever has befallen that property, and I am not able to vindicate it, I should pay you that property twice over; and let the abbot hold the aforesaid property absolutely.

Charter of sale made in era 407 [1016–17 CE] during the month of Rajab.

Witnesses: Iahia iben Farh. Iben Alhazan. Son of iben Navi. Zaada Alamavi. Halaf iben Aada Alamavi. Mozoude iben Marvan. Marvan iben Farh. Abdella iben Navi Alamavi. Abdella iben Mozoud Alkaizi.

Zuleiman iben Zaadon Alamavi. Halafac iben Zaada Alamavi. Abdella iben Abdilmalic Allahami.[108] Halafa iben Abdella. Iahia iben Zaada iben Iahie. Mahomat iben Halaf. Hamat iben Umar Almuradi. Mahomat iben Zaata. Iuzef iben Farh. [pp. 607–9]

71. [1064–5]

We make a report on the mill of Forma.

In the days of the lord Abbot Primus,[109] a master by the name of Zacarias came from Córdoba, and the council of Coimbra sent its commission [to summon] the abbot. They said to him: 'Give us the master from Córdoba who has come to you, so that he may build us bridges over our streams.' The abbot said: 'I shall go with him, for my remembrance.'[110] And the abbot came along with the master, and he set up his workshop in Alviaster. Men came from that land with their crossbeams,[111] wagons, stone and lime, and they built this bridge. They came to Coselhas and built another there. They came to the banks of Buçaco and built another there. From there they came to Forma and built another. The master said to the abbot: 'We should build mills on this bridge for the monastery, for our remembrance.' And so they did.

---

[107] Possibly al-Gharb, 'the west' (whence the modern Algarve in the south of Portugal).

[108] Al-Lakhmi (the Banu Lakhm)?

[109] Abbot of Lorvão (*c.* 966–85).

[110] The sense of this is not immediately obvious: maybe to ensure that he would be remembered in the (monastic) community for his great acts of entrepreneurship on its behalf.

[111] *Directos* (possibly 'right-angles').

Then Pelayo Halaf came and said to us that his grandfather Ezerag had built those mills. I, Arias,[112] said that the Lord Primus had built them. The lord Sisnando[113] instructed us that I, Arias, should swear an oath for them. And I swore for them.

Then his cousin Zuleiman Alafla came and sought to dispute with us, and the lord Sisnando referred us to the king. He spoke of how his grandfather was Ezerag of Condeixa, and that, when the Moors seized Coimbra,[114] Ezerag went to Farfon iben Abdella and made himself a Moor.[115] He sought [from him] thirty Moors for raiding,[116] and sent them into the woods, and said to the Christians of those villas: 'Come out, blessed people, for I have now made peace with the Moors.' They came out from the woods and reoccupied their villas, and the Moors came out from the woods, took them to Santarém, offered them for sale and obtained six bands[117] of silver for them. And [the Moors] sent them on from there to Córdoba together with Farfon's charter and their profit. Zuleiman petitioned for the mills of Forma and many other villas, and al-Manṣūr granted them.

Then the lord King Fernando came and ordered [Zuleiman Alafla] to grant us our mills. The lord Sisnando granted us our mills and our bridge and affirmed them. [pp. 700–2]

---

[112] Abbot of Lorvão (*c.* 1027–65).

[113] Sesnando Davides, lord of Coimbra (*c.* 1064–91).

[114] In 988.

[115] Ezerag converted to Islam.

[116] Original *arragaza*, which seems to represent the Arabic *al-ghāziya* (whence also *razzia*).

[117] *Haretas* ('loops, hoops, rounds, ribbons').

62

Robert of Ketton, *Prologue* and *Preface*

Robert Portass, University of Lincoln

The group of texts known as the *Collectio Toletana* ('The Toledan collection'), which was intended to explicate and refute the central tenets of Islam, was composed at the behest and under the patronage of Peter the Venerable, abbot of Cluny (1122–56). The provenance of these texts is Spanish, as the name suggests, although they were not written in Toledo but rather in a series of northern cities, perhaps concentrated in the Ebro valley. Arriving in Spain around 1141, Peter set about hiring a team of highly skilled linguists whose expertise in Latin and Arabic would allow them to perform the task in hand: foremost amongst these was Robert of Ketton (active 1141–57), an Englishman from the village of Ketton in Rutland, who by the mid-1140s had become archdeacon of Pamplona, as is attested in a letter from Peter to Bernard of Clairvaux: *Roberto Ketenensi de Anglia, qui nunc Pampilonensis ecclesiae archidiaconus est.*[118] Little is known of Robert's life, and the few clues which we possess suggest that his principal interests were in science.

The translations below are of two separate preliminary pieces, each of which attempts to explain the context and objectives underpinning the Arabic to Latin translation it accompanied. The first is of Robert's prologue (reproduced here in its entirety) to the *Chronica mendosa et ridiculosa Sarracenorum* ('Lying and laughable chronicle of the Saracens'). It forms part of a set of writings given the title *Fabule Sarracenorum* in a mid-twelfth-century manuscript that is almost certainly of Spanish origin. The *Chronica mendosa* itself is something of a mystery. It brings together a series of well-known Islamic traditions but does not seem to be a direct translation of a single extant Arabic text, and it may be a compilation of extracts or a miscellany. Its author or authors and the circumstances of its creation are far from clear. Insofar as we can tell, Robert did not distort its contents for polemical purposes: on the

[118] MS Paris, Bibliothèque de l'Arsenal, lat. 1162, fol. 4r. Robert of Ketton was for many years confused with a certain Robert of Chester (active 1145–50), but this is now thought to be a misidentification.

contrary, it was the express wish of his patron Peter of Cluny that such works should be faithfully translated into Latin in order to alert Christian intellectuals to the heretical dangers they posed.

The second translation consists of selections from Robert's preface to his translation of the Qur'an (1143), the *Lex Mahumet pseudoprophete* ('Law of the pseudo-Prophet Muḥammad'). This latter is a work of extraordinary importance, the first translation of the Qur'an into Latin.

Robert was a remarkable wordsmith and inventive paraphraser, which has sometimes led to the unjust dismissal of his translations on the grounds that they sacrifice accuracy for elegance and polemic, a position which has now been rebutted persuasively. This notwithstanding, Robert's prologue to the *Chronica mendosa* and his preface to the Qur'an, in common with all of his writings on religion, are written in 'the elevated Latin style admired in his day',[119] and are not for the faint-hearted.

CMR 4, pp. 508–19.

The first translation is based on MS Paris, Bibliothèque de l'Arsenal, lat. 1162, and the second on the edition of the *Collectio Toletana* overseen by the Swiss publisher Theodore Bibliander, *Machumetis Saracenorum principis eiusque successorum vitae ac doctrina, ipseque Alcoran*, 3 vols, Basel, 1543.

Chronica mendosa et ridiculosa Sarracenorum, Prologue [Nonsensical tales of the Saracens]

When the obligation of command and the vow of obedience coincide on both sides and in equal measure, never is the former incommoded, nor is the latter found wanting. Therefore, when the Lord Peter – a man venerated for his words, mind and work, whom the Church chose as a husband seeing within him what Christ saw in Peter[120] – thought it pleasing that the detestable history of Muḥammad, more deserving of scorn than praise, should be uncovered, I set about the task quickly and without reluctance, granted that I had already begun to mourn the Mother [Church]. For it is indeed more wholesome and appropriate to touch upon a trifling, poisonous matter than to preserve it, and better still to pass beyond the Sirens with swift, expansive advances than with numerous slow steps.[121] With his especial goodwill, having first sized up the task, I uncovered by my own hand the law of the aforementioned [Muḥammad] and brought it into the treasure chamber of the Roman tongue, in order that, its worthlessness having been recorded, the Cornerstone [Christ],[122] the most precious redemption of

[119] T.E. Burman, *Reading the Qur'ān in Latin Christendom, 1140–1560*, Philadelphia, PA, 2007, p. 35.
[120] Matthew 16:17-20.
[121] Creatures half woman and half bird that in Greek myths sang to passing ships to lure them onto the rocky shores of their island. Ships passed the island with speed.
[122] See Matthew 21:43; Ephesians 2:20.

humankind, might emit His brilliance yet further. And because He who has always known how to abolish native schisms can more conveniently and nimbly do this, He has preferred, so as to safeguard His majesty and great works, to gather up His forces and weapons, that He might strongly condemn and utterly destroy the greatest of all heresies, revealed by me, which, accepted by peoples of uncouth origin, even the Doctors of the Church have endured growing immensely and excessively for 537 years.[123] For it is manifestly pernicious that the flower of that depraved sect, by concealing a scorpion, should deceive in its efforts to entice, and by such deception kill ministers of Christian faith and law, which alone can truly and absolutely be considered law, and which – for shame! – we have so often seen happen already.

What a performance of shouts and expressions they put on! What will His heralds and ministers say in the presence of the Bridegroom, summoning all, if through either ignorance or negligence a goodly part of the human race should hear nothing of nuptials nor attend them, detained in chains of darkness or by the songs of the Sirens, and shamelessly made sport of, ignorant that His redemption has been achieved?[124] But now, with the character of the enemy cause set down by us, the Catholic community will act quickly under your command. And so that the depraved law described above – with its repeated offences and injuries, its insults often directed against Christ, our leader and Redeemer, which deny, amongst other things, that He is God and the Son of God – may be avenged in word and deed, He will drive away the wolves and the evil reptiles from his pastures, He will restore to health those who have hitherto been seduced by corrupt suggestions and have drunk from honey-sweetened poisonous nectar, and by the water of the sacred fountain He will bring them within the capacious precincts of charity in the palace of Christ. Let all those indeed who refuse to become Christian either fall into bondage, thereby to leave off their depraved works, or die before long, so that they offer no further obstruction to themselves or to others, in accordance with their sect, which affirms that struggle harms [them] more than death. [Bibliothèque de l'Arsenal, lat. 1162, fol. 5r]

[Preface to the Qur'an]

The preface of Robert the translator to Lord Peter, abbot of Cluny, concerning the book of the law of the Saracens, which they call the Qur'an: that is, the collection of teachings which the false prophet Muḥammad feigned to have been sent from heaven by the angel Gabriel.

To his Lord Peter, by divine instigation abbot of Cluny, one of his humble followers, Robert of Ketton, rejoices completely in God.

When I perceived in what ways and to what degree your soul longed for each and every good thing and thirsted to make fertile the sterile swamp of the Saracen sect,

---

[123] Robert uses the Islamic calendar: 537 H = 1142 CE.

[124] Mark 2:19-20.

to drain its well, and to utterly destroy its ramparts, I exposed its ways and points of approach most diligently, executing this task as though an infantryman, leading from the front. For who will prolong the march [into battle]? Who will not rush with the greatest speed to apprise himself of the error of the enemy and of how it was vanquished, yet also to acquire unyielding and triumphant knowledge in all areas? Yet all of Latin Christendom has heretofore been imprisoned, whether by the pernicious disadvantage of ignorance or negligence I shall not say, and has in ignorance endured its enemies' cause and not disavowed it. [...]

Therefore, I have brought stones and wood so that afterwards your most beautiful and agreeable construction may arise, buttressed and indestructible:[125] excerpting not a thing, nor altering anything pertaining to meaning save for that which could aid comprehension. I have uncovered Muḥammad's smoke to extinguish it by means of your bellows, to drain his well dry with your glass, and to bring out the kindling and heat of our fire with your shovel and the course of our wellspring by your channel. Thus law demands, for destroying the enemy's camp (nay more, his lair) and for drying up his well, that – since you are the greatest part of the world's right hand, the sharpest whetstone of religion, the most bountiful hand of charity – you reinforce the defence of your own people and sharpen your javelins in diligent fashion, such that its fountain may flow with greater force, and the bulwark of charity which you build be more extensive and capacious.

If anyone should throw accusations my way, even if perhaps justly so, on account of the worthlessness and disorder of my themes and words, I nonetheless entreat him to stop, knowing that it was never my intention to conceal poison with flowers – to gild an object that is cheap and destined for the scrap heap. This law, although deadly, in many places provides, for those who see and have been chosen, the greatest testimony and most enduring proof of the holiness and excellence of our law. This much indeed has not lain hidden from your wisdom, which compelled me, amongst other things, to put to one side my principal fields of study in astronomy and geometry. [Bibliander, *Machumetis [...] doctrina, ipseque Alcoran, Tomus primus*, pp. 7–8; at pp. 34–5 in the digitized version, https://www.e-rara.ch/bau_1/content/structure/59463]

---

[125] Peter intended to commission a refutation of Islam which was to use the translation of the Qur'an and other works in the *Collectio Toletana*.

63

Caffaro of Genoa, *History of the capture of Almería and Tortosa*

Rodrigo García-Velasco,
University of Cambridge

Caffaro di Rustico da Caschifellone (*c.* 1080–1166) was a Genoese merchant, admiral, historian and intermittent diplomat. He is best known as the original author of the *Annales Ianuenses* ('Genoese Annals'), presented by Caffaro to the Genoese consuls in 1152, and regarded as the first 'secular' urban chronicle produced in Latin Christendom.

Caffaro's *Ystoria captionis Almarie et Turtuose*, his account of the capture of the Iberian Islamic towns of Almería and Tortosa in 1147 and 1148, situates Genoese maritime activity against the backdrop of the twelfth-century Latin Crusades. Like the rest of the *Annals*, his description of these incursions is infused in a mixture of civic pride, religious zeal and economic expediency. In the following excerpt on the capture of Tortosa, Caffaro presents the local Muslims not as straw men but as real people facing tough decisions during the extended siege of their city. His precise description of Tortosa's topography and of the different factions comprising the Christian army lends a realism to his version of events. So do the concordances between his narration and the legal charters produced during the siege and eventual surrender of Tortosa to the Genoese, Crusader and Catalan-Aragonese armies.

As the *Annals* explain, the expedition against Tortosa formed part of a wider struggle for Mediterranean maritime hegemony. Tortosa's harbour controlled both the delta of the River Ebro and the route along the Mediterranean coast to Barcelona. These factors, combined with success against the significant maritime hub of Almería, explain the Genoese initiative against Tortosa. The expedition also took advantage of political turmoil in al-Andalus. The Almohads and their new brand of Islam had first crossed the Straits of Gibraltar in 1145; by 1148 the only regional ruler who resisted Almohad power resided in the *Sharq al-Andalus*, the Iberian Levant. Named as the *Rex Hispanie* ('King of Spain') in Caffaro's account, and known as the

Rey Lobo or Wolf King in Christian Iberia, Ibn Mardanīsh (d. 1172) was a skilful political operator. But when the troops gathered at the gates of Tortosa in 1148, his attention was on Almohad encroachment into his polity. As Caffaro's account insinuates, it was such political reckoning, not Christian military might, that ultimately forced the Muslims of Tortosa to surrender.

CMR 3, pp. 635–42. See further:

M. Hall and J. Phillips (trans.), *Caffaro, Genoa, and the Twelfth-Century Crusades*, London, 2013, pp. 127–36.

J.B. Williams, 'The Making of a Crusade: The Genoese Anti-Muslim Attacks in Spain, 1146–1148', *Journal of Medieval History* 23 (1997) 29–53.

A. Ubieto Arteta (ed.), *De captione Almerie et Tortuose*, Valencia, 1973.

J. Phillips, 'Caffaro of Genoa and the Motives of the Early Crusaders', in P. Ingesman (ed.), *Religion as an Agent of Change*, Leiden, 2014, 75–104.

This translation is based on the edition by L.T. Belgrano, *Annali Genovesi, di Caffaro e de suoi continuatori del MXCIX al MCCXCIII*, 14 vols, Rome, 1890–1929, vol. 1, pp. 79–89.

It is well known across the entire world that once upon a time Christians used to be seized far and wide from sea and land by the Saracens of Almería. Some of these Christians were killed, and countless were taken captive and tormented in various martyrdoms and punishments. Fearing torture, many of these Christians used to abandon the law of God and invoke the diabolical name of Muḥammad. God would not forgo vindication of such outpouring of blood. For this reason, the Genoese, forewarned and mustered by God through the Apostolic See, pledged to raise an army against the Saracens of Almería. They convened a *parlamentum*, at which six of the notables were elected consuls for the commune and four appointed for the pleas who would lead the city and army with their good sense and leadership at that time. [p. 79] [...]

Once they had approached the city [of Tortosa] from afar, they halted two miles away. They convened a *parlamentum* with the count [of Barcelona][126] and the armies, and thereupon they elected the men who would bear the Genoese standard [in battle]. [...] Once they had inspected the sectors of the city, they held a meeting amongst themselves and decided that half of the Genoese troops would be posted with a portion of the knights of the count by the citadel, which is located in the neighbourhood of the city near the river.[127] Another segment [of the army], led by the count of Barcelona and William of Montpellier, pitched tents on the mountain called Bagnare. Meanwhile, the

[126] Ramon Berenguer IV (r. 1138–62), count of Barcelona and prince of Aragón.

[127] The River Ebro.

English, together with the Knights Templar and many other foreigners, settled to the north, by the neighbourhood of Remolins next to the river.

In the meantime, part of the Genoese faction advanced towards the city without receiving orders from the leader or from the other troops armed to wage war. The Genoese did this so that the Saracens would start to appreciate their might in arms. The Saracens promptly confronted the Genoese, [fighting] on and on until the third hour; many were killed and injured on both sides. Having learned of the imprudence of their soldiers, the Genoese consuls held a *parlamentum* at once, and instructed all their men, bound by the obligation of their respective oaths, that hereafter nobody should wage war without the assent of the council and the permission of the leader. Furthermore, they also ordered the siege towers and engines to be completed and transported next to the city; and so it was done. [...] They placed a siege tower below the city, and having brought another one near the city, they destroyed all the houses and towers up to the mosque.[128] Ordering another siege tower towards the citadel, after a few days of intensified warfare they captured and destroyed forty towers.

Following this episode, the Saracens understood that they could not engage in war outside the citadel. All of them retreated into the citadel and defended it bravely with weapons and engines. At the same time, when the Genoese had realized that they would be unable to seize the citadel with the aforementioned two siege towers from that side of the city, they convened another meeting. They resolved to fill in a ditch located above Bagnare, in between it and the citadel, with wood, stones and earth without delay. [...] Having received the order, all men, both knights and foot soldiers, rich and poor, began to work collectively, presenting themselves every day for the strenuous labour which loading the ditch involved. After two parts of the ditch were full, the Genoese placed at the top a siege tower and engine with 300 soldiers standing within it. When the Saracens saw the approaching siege tower, they immediately hurled stones of 200 pounds in weight, smashing its extremity. The Genoese quickly repaired it and secured the walls of the siege tower with such sturdy rope netting that they were no longer afraid of the blows caused by the Saracen stones. [...] [pp. 85-7]

And thus, day and night, having to wage war against the Saracens mightily and on their own, [the Genoese] struck the walls of the citadel and the palace and houses with stones hurled from mangonels. Frightened by danger of death, the Saracens sent missives regarding the surrender of the city to the consuls of Genoa and the count of Barcelona. They asked for a truce of forty days, under the condition that they would send envoys to the king of Hispania and to all the Spaniards asking them to come and wage war against the Genoese.[129] If they were able to expel the Genoese through

---

[128] The great mosque of Tortosa, situated below the citadel and transformed into its cathedral after the conquest in 1148.

[129] *Ispania* here refers to al-Andalus, and *Ispanos* to Iberia's Muslim peoples; the same usage is found in contemporary charters and texts of the Crown of Aragón. The *Rex Ispanie* is Abū ʿAbd Allāh Muḥammad ibn Saʿd ibn Mardanīsh, ruler of Murcia and Valencia (r. 1147–72), rather than the Almohad Caliph ʿAbd al-Muʾmin (r. 1133–63).

fighting, then the victors would retain the city. However, if the Spaniards did not come by the aforesaid deadline, [the Saracens of Tortosa] promised to hand over the city to the Genoese. And for this reason, they placed 100 Saracens taken from the most reputed [local families] as hostages under Genoese jurisdiction.

After the forty days had passed and the Spaniards had not come to the rescue of Tortosa, the Saracens of the city, just as they had promised, flew the banners of Genoa and of the count over the citadel, and yielded the city to the Genoese and the count without hesitation. And this was accomplished in the month of December, during the two weeks of the feast of the birth of Christ, on the vigil of Saint Silvester, in the year 1148. All this accomplished, the Genoese received a third of the city, the count two-thirds. And following the triumph over the two cities of Almería and Tortosa, having offered thanks to God the Genoese returned with their whole army back to Genoa. [pp. 87–8]

64

William of Tyre, *Chronicle*

Andrew D. Buck, University College Dublin

Archbishop William of Tyre (d. *c.* 1184/5) is the most important chronicler of the four twelfth-century polities known collectively as the Latin East or the Crusader states, formed in the wake of the First Crusade (1095–9): the kingdom of Jerusalem, the principality of Antioch, and the counties of Edessa and Tripoli. Born in Jerusalem around 1130, William spent two decades in Europe, roughly 1145–65, receiving an education in the schools of Paris, Orléans and Bologna, before returning to the East. On arrival, he quickly received the patronage of King Amalric of Jerusalem (r. 1163–74), first acting as ambassador to the Byzantine court in 1168, then becoming royal chancellor in 1174 and archbishop of Tyre the year after. He even acted as tutor to Amalric's son, the future King Baldwin IV (r. 1174–85).

Alongside his religious and political duties, William was a keen author, producing several works: a now lost history of Islam known as the *Gesta orientalium principum*, an account of the Third Lateran Council (1179), and his magnum opus, the *Chronicon* ('Chronicle', otherwise known as the *Historia Ierosolymitana*, 'The history of Jerusalem'). Probably composed and edited between 1170 and the mid-1180s, this chronicle covers the history of the Crusader States from their inception through to 1184, when the text ends abruptly.

The extracts translated here, drawn from William's *Chronicon*, deal with moments of Christian-Muslim warfare or diplomacy. The first focuses on the massacre of Jerusalem's Muslim inhabitants by the forces of the First Crusade on 15 July 1099. The next passage details a battle fought between King Baldwin II of Jerusalem (r. 1118–31) and the *atabeg* (or ruler) of Mosul, Aq Sunqur al-Bursuqī, near to Muslim-held Aleppo in 1125, which includes a commentary on the nature of inter-faith warfare. The final extract details the events surrounding a diplomatic agreement made in 1167 between Amalric and the Fāṭimid Caliph al-ʿĀḍīd (r. 1160–71) at the behest of the latter's vizier, Shawar, who bears the title sultan.

CMR 3, pp. 767–77. See further:

T.S. Asbridge, 'How the Crusades Could Have Been Won: King Baldwin II of Jerusalem's Campaigns against Aleppo (1124–5) and Damascus (1129)', *Journal of Medieval Military History* 11 (2013) 73–94.

M. Köhler, *Alliances and Treaties between Frankish and Muslim Rulers in the Middle East*, trans. P. Holt and K. Hirschler, Leiden, 2013.

N. Morton, 'Perceptions of Islam in William of Tyre's *Historia*', in S.B Edgington and H.J Nicholson (eds), *Deeds Done beyond the Sea: Essays on William of Tyre, Cyprus and the Military Orders, Presented to Peter Edbury*, Abingdon, 2014, 13–24.

A.E. Zimo, 'Us and Them: Identity in William of Tyre's *Chronicon*', *Crusades* 18 (2020) 1–19.

This translation is based on R.B.C. Huygens, *Willelmi Tyrensis archiepiscopi Chronicon*, 2 vols, Turnhout, 1986.

8.20. It is certain that this [the massacre of the people of Jerusalem during the First Crusade] happened by the righteous judgement of God so that those who had profaned the Lord's sanctuary by superstitious rites, and had rendered it foreign to the faithful people, should atone for this shameful act with the loss of their own blood and pay it back by meeting with an expiatory death. Indeed, it was horrific to look upon the multitude of the slaughtered and to observe the fragments of human body parts here and there, and the staining of the bloodshed which was flowing over every surface. Not only was it difficult to look upon the bodies of the dead, with the limbs dismembered and the severed heads mutilated, but it was also as perilous to witness the victors themselves who, blood-soaked all the way from the heels of their feet to the crowns of their heads, brought horror to any who met them. Ten thousand of the enemy were said to have died within the Temple [Mount] enclosure, excepting the others, cut down throughout the city, who filled the streets and squares, and it was said that the number of these was no less. [p. 412] […]

13.16. Thus, al-Bursuqī, seeing the advance of our men and knowing for certain that they were prepared to join battle immediately, as was their way as prudent men, and seeing that he was unable to decline an honourable battle, also drew up his own forces – which were said to have numbered 15,000 horsemen – in twenty battle lines. Having ordered the cohorts on both sides, and arranged them in ranks and against those who, in their turn, were advancing against them, by custom they rushed vigorously against the enemy and each in turn inflicted unspeakable slaughter with a violent eagerness for arms, causing death in many forms.

Indeed, it is usual in conflicts of this sort for the resentment of great sacrilege and the contempt of laws to cause the provocation of hatred and the fomentation of enmity. For battle is waged differently and less vehemently between kindred of the same law and faith than between the dissolute and those holding contradictory traditions. Thus, even if no other cause for hatred exists, it is sufficient that they do not share the same articles of faith to cause continual offence and perpetual quarrels. Having joined battle, therefore, the battle lines mentioned above violently set about one another. [pp. 605–6] [...]

19.17. It pleased [Shawar], therefore, and seemed expedient to us as well, to restore the ancient pacts and to establish with inviolable stability a perpetual treaty of peace between the lord king and the caliph. [...] As the agreement pleased both sides, the lord king gave his right hand to those who had been sent by the caliph to agree the pact. However, he also sent [to Cairo] the lord Hugh of Caesarea [...] and with him certain others, in whose hand the caliph was to confirm the pact, just as it had been agreed. [...]

19.18. Having arrived at the palace [of the caliph in Cairo ...] they were led through narrow passages and places lacking in light, approaching with a great multitude of clerks, who preceded them with swords and a great din. [...]

19.19. And, having passed through many winding and devious ways [...] they were admitted into the inner part of the palace, with the sultan [Shawar] exhibiting the usual deference to his lord [the caliph] according to custom. [...] Then, the sultan, approaching with all reverence, humbly pressed kisses on the feet of the seated [caliph] and explained the cause of the arrival of the legates and the tenor of the pact [made with Amalric]. [...] At this, with a quiet cheerfulness of expression, [the caliph] responded very kindly and calmly that he was prepared to fulfil the agreement just as it had been undertaken and agreed upon by both sides. [...]

Then it was requested by our men that he should confirm this with his own hand, just as the lord king had done. At first, those who were close to him and the chamberlains who were nearby and heard this and in whose hands had been the responsibility of the royal discussions saw this as an abhorrent thing, utterly unheard of in worldly affairs. At last, though, after much deliberation and at the sultan's earnest insistence, [the caliph] extended his hand very reluctantly, albeit covered.

At this point, with the Egyptians greatly surprised and astonished that anyone might speak so freely to the highest prince, the aforementioned Hugh of Caesarea said: 'Lord, trust has no concealments, but in the midst of trust, by which princes are accustomed to be obliged to one another, everything ought to be laid bare and open, and whatsoever has been inserted into a pact by a pledge of good trust should be agreed upon with sincerity by everyone, whether to be both bound or unbound. Therefore, either you shall give your bare hand, or we shall be compelled to suppose that you have on your side something false and insincere.'

Thereupon, at length, with great reluctance and as if detracting from his own dignity, yet still smiling (which the Egyptians bore with great discomfort), he presented his bare right hand into the hand of the lord Hugh. With the same Hugh dictating the form of the pact, [the caliph], following the provisions by the syllable, called to witness that he would observe the tenor of the agreement with good faith, without deceit or evil tricks. [...] Having dismissed them, [the caliph] sent gifts to the legates as a sign of his royal liberality, which commended the prince so greatly by their magnitude and splendour that they left the presence of so great a prince delighted and joyfully returned to their own lands. [pp. 886–9]

65

Peter the Chanter, *Summa on the sacraments and spiritual advice*

Emily Corran, University College London

Peter the Chanter was a theologian who taught in Paris between *c.* 1170 and 1197. He was part of a generation of theologians who took particular interest in practical moral questions, and he was active in campaigning for moral reform: he preached against heretics and influenced the future Pope Innocent III's (r. 1198–1216) Crusade policy. This extract comes from his last work, dating from sometime after 1190, a long treatise on sacraments and spiritual advice.

The *Summa* is unfinished, surviving as a disparate set of reports of the Chanter's theology lectures given over a number of years. We do not have resolutions to all the questions raised in it, and his students' opinions are sometimes interpolated into the texts. The second half, from which this extract is taken, is a long list of moral dilemmas which might confront Christians of all kinds. Here he considers the difficult choices faced by Christian subjects of Islamic rulers. Are Christians living under Islamic rule permitted to hold services which would normally be irregular, in view of their difficult circumstances? Do Christians sin mortally if they obey a requirement to participate in prayer in an Islamic place of worship, or if, under duress, they manufacture arms for the use of Islamic armies against Christians?

In the course of discussing the dilemmas faced by Christians living under Islamic rule, the Chanter makes three points about the Islamic faith: there are no images in Islamic places of worship, there is no equivalent to Christian sacraments in the Islamic faith and therefore the role of the Islamic imam (to whom Peter refers as *princeps*, 'the leader') is simply to lead the prayer. The imam thus does not have ritual authority in the same manner as a Christian priest.

The Chanter spent the whole of his life in northern France, and therefore had no direct experience of Islam. His knowledge most likely came from polemical treatises written by Christian theologians, such as Alain of Lille's *Contra paganos*. These polemics used Islam's faith in a unified God, its lack of images, and its rejection of sacraments as a means of ridiculing the faith and undermining its status as a true religion. They characterized Islam as a heresy, that is, not a religion in its own right but a deviation from Christianity that had rejected a number of key Church doctrines.

The work is unusual in that it employs these same details about the Islamic faith as an argument for permitting Christians living in Islamic lands to pray in mosques. The Chanter's argument is that, a Christian who prays in a Muslim place of worship does not commit any formal blasphemy since Muslims worship the same God as Christians (even though they are mistaken about God's nature), they acknowledge no sacramental authority in the leader of the prayers, and there are no cultic images or other intermediaries between the individual worshipper and God. Since Islamic prayer is so simple in form, a Christian who participates does not directly take part in any deviant or heretical rites.

The final paragraph considers whether Christians sin if under duress they manufacture arms which will be used against Christians. At the Third Lateran Council (1179), Pope Alexander III (r. 1159–81) had forbidden Christians to supply arms, iron and lumber to Islamic forces. Nevertheless, there was a certain amount of ambiguity and debate about the matter. The Chanter raises this issue of culpability and duress with regard to Christian craftsmen working under Islamic rule. He does not provide an answer to the question but draws attention to this difficult moral–theological problem.

See further:

M.-T. d'Alverny, *La connaissance de l'Islam dans l'Occident médiéval*, Aldershot, 1994.

O.R. Constable, 'Clothing, Iron, and Timber: The Growth of Christian Anxiety about Islam in the Long Twelfth Century', in T.F.X. Noble and J. van Engen (eds), *European Transformations: The Long Twelfth-Century*, Notre Dame IN, 2012, 279–313.

E. Corran, *Lying and Perjury in Medieval Practical Thought: A Study in the History of Casuistry*, Oxford, 2018.

This translation is based on Petrus Cantor, *Summa de sacramentis et animae consiliis*, ed. J.-A. Dugauquier, 5 vols, Louvain, 1954–67, vol. 3/2a §219.

Many Christians live among Saracens in servitude to them, and do not dare to celebrate mass except at night. Do they sin in celebrating mass in this way?

[We reply:] I do not believe so, since their difficulty excuses them.

Saracens pray to one God and abhor idolatry to such an extent that they have no images in their temples, nor any seat,[130] nor do they make any sacrifice;[131] instead they only pray there. When it is necessary for Christians to enter the temples, and when the leader has knelt in prayer, all those with him are required to bend their knees as well;

[130] No equivalent to a bishop's throne. The Chanter is making a point about the lack of sacramental authority among Islamic religious leaders.

[131] There are no sacraments.

this is their custom. Do the Christians then sin if they pray with them, since they pray to one God like us, the same God to whom we pray?[132]

We reply: if this could take place without scandal, they would not sin.[133]

Again, they [the Christians] in their misery do not have anointed priests, nor can they have them, particularly those who are far away. But they choose someone from amongst themselves whom they obey in those matters which pertain to faith, and call him pope. He only lays his hand on the one he wishes to make a priest. Is he [truly] ordained? What is his status with regard to the substance of ordination? When this rite is administered by the bishop, at what moment can it be said that this man has first been ordained?

Moreover, almost all Christians living among the Saracens are forced to be smiths and manufacture arms for fighting against Christians. Do they commit a mortal sin in doing so? Are they required to suffer death rather than comply? It is certain that the weak are permitted to flee martyrdom as long as they do not have a flock which they are deserting.[134] But since these cannot flee, what should they do?

[132] It is relatively rare for Western Christians to emphasize the commonalities between Islam and Christianity. In a letter sent to Al-Nāṣir, emir of Mauritania, in 1076, Pope Gregory VII (r. 1073–85) expressed the view that Christians and Muslims worship the same God, but it is unclear whether the Chanter was aware of this letter.

[133] The mediaeval concept of scandal was more specific than the modern sense of the word. It was the sin of leading others into sin by example. The Chanter is saying that it is permitted for Christians to pray in this fashion as long as their actions do not lead other Christians to doubt their faith.

[134] The spiritually weak. It was acknowledged that only Christian saints would embrace martyrdom, and all other Christians were permitted to seek their own safety rather than suffer death for their faith.

66

Francis of Assisi, *Rules of the Friars Minor*

Graham Barrett, University of Lincoln

Francis of Assisi (1181/82–1226) began his life of renunciation and preaching around 1207 and founded the mendicant Order of the Friars Minor in 1209 with approval from Pope Innocent III (r. 1198–1216). Emerging from a renewed interest in forms of devout Christian life, the 'Lesser Brothers' were to live austerely on the model of Jesus and the Apostles; they were forbidden to own any property, and obliged to beg for food and to seek board from the Church while proclaiming the Gospels in the streets and ministering to the poor.

According to his hagiographer, Thomas of Celano (*c.* 1185–1265), Francis called the Rule of the Friars Minor their 'Book of Life', and it is a window into their living experience of mendicancy, inspired above all by Matthew 10:9. He first drew up the *Regula non bullata* ('Rule without a papal seal' or 'Unsealed Rule') as a working document at a chapter meeting with his fellow friars at Pentecost 1221, drawing on a decade of that experience. The text does not survive in the original, but in later and divergent forms, notably a modified version by the Franciscan reformer Angelo Clareno from 1321 to 1323. While the vision and voice remain those of Francis, the interests of others are perceptible, such as provincial ministers who wished to define their competencies. The biblical citations are traditionally ascribed to Caesar of Speyer (d. 1239).

The *Regula non bullata* contains in Chapter 16 the earliest Christian instruction for missionary activity in any religious rule, which comes in a section on living as 'evangelical men'. Francis and a 'Brother Illuminato' had visited Damietta at the mouth of the River Nile in 1219 in a failed attempt to convert al-Kāmil, the Ayyūbid sultan of Egypt (r. 1218–38), and bring an end to the Fifth Crusade (1217–21), and this experience informs his thinking here. The text recognizes mission as a calling not unlike joining the Order itself, but also its inherent danger, and it charges ministers with ensuring that only those truly capable should go forth.

Mission encompasses both Saracens (Muslims) and all others outside the Church, but whereas standard dogmatic advice for preachers was to convert by public debate or disputation, here this is decisively rejected in favour of being submissive. God's pleasure will indicate when to proclaim the Word, and the emphasis in the text on acknowledgement or confession suggests that the moment to begin was when asked if one was Christian. The concluding flurry of biblical verses appeal for the Franciscan missionary to accept the real possibility of persecution and death, drawing on Francis's own *On true and perfect joy*, which locates happiness, virtue and salvation in such patience.

As a working document the Rule continued to be revised, until Pope Honorius III (r. 1216–27) ratified the *Regula bullata* ('Rule with a papal seal' or 'Sealed Rule') by the bull *Solet annuere* ('[The Apostolic See] is accustomed to grant ... ') in 1223. This survives in the original at Assisi as well as in the Vatican Library, though there are differences between the two copies. Francis had met with his ministers at chapter that year, and the text which they agreed distils the twenty-four often-discursive chapters of the earlier Rule down to twelve terse statements shorn of almost all their biblical context. The 'missionary charter', now Chapter 12, is radically abbreviated from the earlier version and appears in a subsection on relationships with people whom the friars might meet. The emphasis is on intention, evaluation and approval of prospective missionaries, with the balance tilted in favour of the provincial ministers and greater caution in granting permission. Gone is any mention of the two ways of living among the Saracens and others, of seizing the moment for proclaiming the Word of God when it comes. In this respect, the revised Rule seems to be the result of reflection on the experience of the Franciscan protomartyrs, Berard of Carbio and his companions, who had been executed in 1220 by the 'king' of Morocco, the Almohad Caliph Yūsuf II (r. 1213–24), for preaching the Gospel and denouncing Islam.

The translations below are based on the editions of the Rules in C. Paolazzi, *Francisci Assisiensis Scripta*, Grottaferrata, 2009.

See also:

J. Hoeberichts, *Francis and Islam*, Quincy IL, 1997.

J. Tolan, *Saint Francis and the Sultan: The Curious History of a Christian-Muslim Encounter*, Oxford, 2009.

W.J. Short, 'The Rules of the Lesser Brothers', in M.W. Blastic, J.M. Hammond and J.A.W. Hellman (eds), *The Writings of Francis of Assisi: Rules, Testament, and Admonitions*, St Bonaventure, NY, 2011, pp. 17–222.

W.J. Short, 'The *Rule* and Life of the Friars Minor', in M.J.P. Robson (ed.), *The Cambridge Companion to Francis of Assisi*, Cambridge, 2011, pp. 50–67.

H.J. Grieco, 'The Rule of Saint Francis', in K. Pansters (ed.), *A Companion to Medieval Rules and Customaries*, Leiden, 2020, pp. 283–314.

The Unsealed Rule (1221)

16. On those who go amongst the Saracens and other unbelievers.

The Lord says, 'Behold, I send you forth as sheep in the midst of wolves. Be you therefore wise as serpents and harmless as doves.'[135] Wherefore let any brother who has the will by divine inspiration[136] to go amongst the Saracens and other unbelievers proceed by permission of his minister and servant. And let the minister give them permission and not speak against them if he sees that they are suited to being sent forth, for he will be obliged to render the Lord a reckoning if he has acted rashly in this or in other matters.[137]

Now, the brothers who do proceed can dwell amongst them [the Saracens and other unbelievers], spiritually speaking, in two ways. One way is not to have either quarrels or disputes, but rather to submit 'to every human creature for the sake of God',[138] while [still] confessing to being Christians.[139] The other way is, when they see that it pleases the Lord, to proclaim the Word of God, so that they [the non-Christians] may come to believe in God Almighty, Father, Son and Holy Spirit, the Creator of all things, the Redeemer and Saviour Son,[140] and so that they may be baptized and made Christians: for 'anyone who has not been reborn of the water and the Holy Spirit cannot enter into the kingdom of God'.[141] These and other things which please the Lord they can say to them and to others, for the Lord says in the Gospel: 'Everyone who will confess me before men, I shall acknowledge him also before my Father who is in the heavens.'[142] And: 'Anyone who will be ashamed of me and my utterances, the Son of Man will be ashamed of him also when He comes in His own glory and the glory of the Father and the angels.'[143]

And let all the brothers, wherever they are, keep in mind that they have dedicated themselves and given up their bodies to the Lord Jesus Christ. And for love of Him they should leave themselves exposed to the enemy,[144] both visible and invisible, for the Lord says: 'He who has lost his life on account of me will make it safe unto eternal life.'[145] 'Blessed are they who suffer persecution for the sake of righteousness, since theirs is

---

[135] Matthew 10:16.

[136] Compare *Unsealed Rule* ch. 2, where the vocation or calling to life in the Order is also 'by divine inspiration'.

[137] See Luke 16:2; compare *Unsealed Rule* ch. 4, where the minister is responsible for care of the friars' souls, and ch. 17, where his permission is required for friars to go out and preach.

[138] Titus 3:2; 2 Timothy 2:14.

[139] 1 Peter 2:13; and see *Unsealed Rule* ch. 7, which calls for friars to be 'lesser' (*minores*) and submit to all those in their household, whence the name of their Order.

[140] The words 'God Almighty and the Creator of all' would have offered doctrinal common ground to Muslim listeners, at least; not so the Trinity and the salvific Son.

[141] John 3:5.

[142] Matthew 10:32.

[143] Luke 9:26. See *Unsealed Rule* ch. 21, which enjoins friars to preach whenever they wish, with God's blessing.

[144] Not straightforwardly an injunction to be submissive, but rather, like the Apostles, to have no fear of the enemy when the time comes to proclaim the Word of God.

[145] Luke 9:24; Matthew 25:46.

the kingdom of the heavens.'[146] 'If they have persecuted me, they will persecute you also.'[147] 'If they persecute you in one city, flee into another.'[148] 'Blessed are you when men hate you, and have reviled you, and persecute you, and have expelled you, and have condemned and denounced your name as evil, and have uttered every evil against you falsely, on account of me. Rejoice on that day and jump for joy, since your reward is manifold in the heavens.'[149] 'And I say to you, my friends, do not be frightened by these, and do not fear those who kill the body and after this have nothing more they can do.'[150] 'See you, be not troubled.'[151] 'For through your patience you will possess your souls, and he who has endured even unto the end, this man will be saved.'[152]

The Sealed Rule (1223)

12. On those who go amongst the Saracens and other unbelievers.

Whoever of the brothers have the will by divine inspiration to go amongst the Saracens and other unbelievers, let them seek permission for it from their provincial ministers. But let the ministers grant permission for going to none except to those who they see are suited to being sent forth.

---

[146] Matthew 5:10.
[147] John 15:20.
[148] Matthew 10:23.
[149] Luke 6:22-23; Matthew 5:11-12.
[150] Luke 12:4; Matthew 10:28.
[151] Matthew 24:6.
[152] Luke 21:19; Matthew 10:22; 24:13.

67

Roger Bacon, *The greater work*

Amanda Power, University of Oxford

Roger Bacon (*c.* 1214–92) was an Englishman who studied and taught at the emerging universities in Oxford and Paris; he entered the Franciscan order in the 1250s. He was a prolific author, playing a significant role in the adoption of Greek and Arab thought into Latin scholarship, and is best remembered for his *Opus maius* ('The greater work'), written in the mid-1260s for Pope Clement IV (r. 1265–8). Its purpose was to urge the necessity of expanding the range of Latin competence by sponsoring study in new fields, and to apply this enhanced 'wisdom' to the practical concerns of Christendom. Bacon's evidentiary base and many of his conceptual frameworks were explicitly drawn from Muslim authors and Arabic texts. While he seems not to have travelled widely, he was unusually well-informed about distant regions through his acquaintance with William of Rubruck, a friar who had lived for several years at the heart of the Mongol Empire. Somewhat surprisingly, most of Bacon's assertions about how contemporary Muslims would think and behave were based on the anecdotes which he gleaned from William, rather than, for example, from reports by returned Crusaders. Notwithstanding his intellectual and moral admiration for Muslims, he maintained that they would find salvation only by converting to his own faith.

The sections translated below discuss the relations between the Latin West and its neighbours in terms that are equally pragmatic and idealistic. Bacon explains that both the conversion of Muslims and control over their world would be better achieved through mastery among Latin authors of the necessary languages and philosophical argumentation.

CMR 4, pp. 457–70. See further:

A. Power, *Roger Bacon and the Defence of Christendom*, Cambridge, 2012.

M.T. Abate, 'The Reorientation of Roger Bacon: Muslims, Mongols, and the Man Who Knew Everything', in A. Classen (ed.), *East Meets West in the Middle Ages and Early Modern Times: Transcultural Experiences in the Premodern World*, Berlin, 2013, 523–73.

F. Schmieder, 'Opening up the World and the Minds: The Crusades as an Engine of Change in Missionary Conceptions', in P. Ingesman (ed.), *Religion as an Agent of Change: Crusades – Reformation – Pietism*, Leiden, 2016, 105–23.

These translations are based on Roger Bacon, *Opus maius*, ed. J.H. Bridges, 3 vols, Oxford, 1897–1900, and Roger Bacon, *Moralis philosophia*, ed. E. Massa, Turin, 1953.

[On Christian responsibilities towards non-Christian peoples]

Thirdly, knowledge of languages is essential to the Latins for the conversion of unbelievers, since it is in the hands of Latins that the power of converting is placed. [...] The Greeks, Russians and many other schismatic [Christians] remain in error because the truth is not preached to them in their own language; and the same applies to Saracens, Pagans, the Tartars [Mongols] and the other unfaithful peoples through the entire world.[153] War is not effective against them, since the Church is sometimes gravely embarrassed as a consequence of the wars of Christians, as happens frequently in Outremer and especially during the most recent business, that of the lord king of France,[154] as the whole world knows. In any case, even if Christians are victorious there is no one to defend the occupied lands, nor are the unfaithful converted by these activities but killed and sent to hell. Those who survive the wars, and their sons, are more and more incited against the Christian faith as a consequence of these wars. They become infinitely estranged from the faith of Christ and stirred up to do all the harm they can to Christians. So it is that Saracens in many parts of the world, on this account, have become impossible to convert. Particularly in Outremer,[155] Prussia, and the lands near Germany, the Templars, Hospitallers and the Teutonic Knights disrupt the conversion of unfaithful peoples as a result of the wars which they are always stirring up, and because they want complete mastery of the region. [...]

Besides, it is quite obvious that the faith did not advance in this world by force, but through the simplicity of preaching. We have often heard, and we are certain of it, that many [in earlier times] made great progress through preaching – even though they had an imperfect knowledge of languages and ineffectual interpreters – and converted countless numbers to the Christian faith. Oh, how carefully we should consider this work, and how we should fear that God might hold the Latins responsible because they are neglecting languages, and as a result are neglecting the preaching of the faith.

[153] 'Unfaithful' (*infideles*): often translated 'unbelievers' or 'infidels', but the force of the word is that they are not *faithful* to their true Lord, the world's Creator; that they are rejecting the obligation of obedience taken on by *fideles*, those who are faithful.

[154] The disastrous Seventh Crusade (1248–54), during which Louis IX (r. 1226–70) was captured in Egypt and had to be ransomed.

[155] The four states set up in Syria and along the eastern Mediterranean seaboard after the First Crusade.

For Christians are few, the whole wide world is filled with unfaithful peoples, and there is no one who can reveal the truth to them.

Fourthly, [the knowledge of languages is crucial] because dealing with those who cannot be converted requires the way of wisdom much more than the struggle of war. For the unfaithful always return to their own lands, as is clear beyond the sea and on this side of it, in Prussia and the pagan lands near Germany and everywhere else. This is because Christian Crusaders, even if sometimes victorious, make their expedition and then return to their own parts, while the indigenous population remains and multiplies. In fact, the faith should first be preached by men wise in all branches of learning, who have excellent knowledge of languages or have good and trustworthy interpreters. When we see that a certain people will be resolute against us, not only should an army be prepared, but wise men must also be gathered, who must [subjugate] the unbelievers – and not temporarily, nor only some of them, but all the people who are in the vicinity of Christians, so that at least the Holy Land with Jerusalem might always remain in the possession of Christians without fear of its loss, in perpetuity. [Bridges, vol. 3, pp. 120–2]

[How to convert people to Christianity]

Concerning the conversion of the unfaithful, it seems that there are two ways in which people might be convinced about the true religion, which is Christianity alone. One is by means of miracles, which are beyond us and beyond the unfaithful – and which is a method no one could possibly rely on. The other is a method common to them and us, which (unlike miracles) is in our power, and which they will not be able to deny, because it proceeds along the paths of human reason and by the means of philosophy. Philosophy is the particular property of unfaithful peoples: we have all our philosophy from them. This arrangement exists for the greatest of all ends. It is ordered in this fashion so that we might have confirmation of our faith for our own benefit, and so that we might speak most effectually for the salvation of the unfaithful. [...]

We cannot argue our case by citing our law or the sacred authorities, because the unfaithful deny Christ the Lord and his law, and the saints. This is why we must search for another kind of reasoning, one which is common to the faithful and unfaithful alike: namely philosophy. Bear in mind that the power of philosophy in this respect is entirely consistent with the wisdom of God; indeed, it is the trace of divine wisdom with which God imbued humanity, so that humans might be roused by it to reach for divine truths. This power, this trace of wisdom: these do not belong solely to philosophy, but are common to philosophy and theology, to faithful and unfaithful alike. They are given by God and revealed to philosophers so that the human race might be prepared to receive particular divine truths. And therefore, the 'reasoning' of which I speak is not alien to the faith, nor outside its fundamentals, but has sprung from its very roots, as will be made clear in what follows.

I could put forward the truth using simple and crude methods, suitable for the ignorant multitude of the unfaithful, but doing so would not be especially advantageous, since the multitude is too imperfect and any urging towards the faith which they could understand would be too elementary, disordered and unworthy of the wise. I would rather take a more elevated approach and offer arguments for the learned to consider. This is because in every nation there are some dedicated individuals, well equipped to receive wisdom, who can be persuaded by reason so that, once they have been instructed, it becomes easier to persuade the rest through them. [Massa, pp. 195–6]

68

Riccoldo da Monte di Croce, *Letters to the Church triumphant*

Rita George-Tvrtković, Benedictine University

Riccoldo da Monte di Croce (c. 1243–1320), a Dominican missionary from Santa Maria Novella Priory in Florence, spent over a decade in Baghdad, where he learned Arabic, studied the Qur'an and engaged with local Muslims and Eastern Christians. His extant works include the *Liber peregrinationis* ('Book of pilgrimage'), *Epistole ad ecclesiam triumphantem* ('Letters to the Church triumphant'), *Ad nationes orientales* ('To the Eastern nations') and *Contra legem Sarracenorum* ('Against the law of the Saracens'), the last of which influenced European polemics for centuries.

The present selection is taken from Riccoldo's remarkable *Epistole ad ecclesiam triumphantem*, the full text of which is extant in only one manuscript. It includes a prologue, four letters addressed respectively to God, the Virgin Mary, all saints, and Patriarch Nicholas of Jerusalem and Acre's other Dominican martyrs, plus a fifth, the 'divine response'. These anguished letters include descriptions of Riccoldo's personal experiences, arguments against the Qur'an and rhetorical questions (e.g. Is the Qur'an the word of God? Were Jesus and the Apostles Muslims?). The postscripts suggest that he began composing the letters while still in Baghdad, perhaps soon after the fall of Acre in 1291, an event Riccoldo mentions frequently and is the impetus for his writing.

Translated here are excerpts from Letter Three. Riccoldo asks the saints to bring his 'impatience and hysterical grief' to the heavenly court; he is upset that his mission to the Muslims is failing and Eastern Christians are converting en masse to Islam. Stranded in Baghdad, he feels utterly abandoned by his fellow Dominicans, and by God.

CMR 4, pp. 678–91. See further:

R. George-Tvrtković, *A Christian Pilgrim in Medieval Iraq: Riccoldo da Montecroce's Encounter with Islam*, Turnhout, 2012.

I. Shagrir, 'The Fall of Acre as a Spiritual Crisis: The Letters of Riccoldo of Monte Croce', *Revue Belge de Philologie et d'Histoire* 90 (2012) 1107–20.

M.M. Bauer, *Epistole ad ecclesiam triumphantem: Herausgegeben, übersetz, und kommentiert*, Stuttgart, 2020 (German edition, translation and commentary).

The translation below is taken from R. George-Tvrtković, *A Christian Pilgrim in Medieval Iraq*, pp. 137–73, with permission (based on R. Röhricht, 'Lettres de Riccoldo de Monte-Croce', in *Archives de l'Orient latin*, vol. 2, Paris, 1884, pp. 258–96).

Letter of an afflicted soul concerning the Church militant, to the entire Church triumphant and to the celestial curia, against the blasphemy of the Qur'an.[156] [p. 276]

What should I do, poor and afflicted and left alone in the depths of the East in the midst of captives, when I hear that 30,000 Christians were killed in one day, and when I hear and see the rest deny the faith of Christ and accept the perfidy of Muḥammad because their souls are suffering and spirits are despairing? I have already sent letters about the cause of my sadness and wonder to Divine Wisdom and to His mother, and I have not received any response of comfort. Therefore, I will do as is customary for someone who endures unbearable injury in the street and who exclaims in a loud voice: 'Someone help! Someone help!' I will call out under duress; I will call out in order to know if there is someone who will respond to me. And I will turn to some of the saints with my impatient complaint.

O great, holy father Dominic, O father and founder of the Order of Preachers, you who were enflamed by the zeal of faith and piety against all kinds of heretics, you grew your beard with spiritual zeal against the Saracens. You thought that you would be able to eradicate Muslims from the West by the power of God. You wished to do so, but you were unable to. But now – when you have gone to your God, when you have become more powerful and we have such need for your protection – can you be silent? [p. 277]

O holy patriarchs! O ancient fathers of the Old Testament, why did you become Saracens and imitators of Muḥammad? Surely if the Qur'an were the word of God as the Saracens say, then I do not doubt that you would have been Saracens! For I read in the Qur'an that Abraham, Isaac, and Jacob were Saracens.[157] I also read that Noah was a Saracen, and that the Flood came because Noah personally asked everyone to become Saracens, and they refused.[158] O God, if You sent the Flood into the world because they did not wish to become Saracens, then it is not surprising that through the Saracens You have destroyed Jerusalem, Judaea, Galilee, Syria, Antioch, Tripoli and Acre! For they were Christians, and they did not wish to become Saracens.

---

[156] Most of the anti-qur'anic arguments found here in embryonic form reappear at greater length in Riccoldo's *Contra legem Sarracenorum*.

[157] E.g. Q 2:140; 3:84.

[158] Q 54:9-12.

Nor do I wish to become a Saracen. 'But where can I go from Your spirit, where can I flee from Your face,'[159] if You have decreed that the whole world should be Saracen? I certainly cannot consent to such an iniquitous law, nor can I believe that this is the law of God. Therefore, I fled from the midst of Babylon, and behold, in fleeing Babylon, I met in the desert the servants of the devil, the ministers of Muḥammad; they were Mongols in clothing, but Saracens in religion. They flogged me and beat me to make me a Saracen, but their blows and insults felt soft. Nay, love endured them as if it were a game. And certainly, if the Apostles, prophets and patriarchs became Saracens, then it would be acceptable for me to become a Saracen too! But because I did not, and do not, wish to become a Saracen, they took from me the holy habit of my [Dominican] Order, and then I took on the clothing and habit of a camel-driver, for the Saracens could make me a camel-driver, but not a Saracen![160] [pp. 283–4]

O Jesus Christ, [...] I beg You, read what he [Muḥammad] says about You, Your mother and Your Apostles! As You know, frequently when reading the Qur'an in Arabic with a heart full of utter grief and impatience, I have placed the book open upon Your altar before Your image and that of Your most holy mother and said, 'Read, read what Muḥammad says!'[161] And it seems to me that You do not wish to read. I ask, therefore, that You not disdain to hear a little of what I recount to You, and about the rest I will be silent.

I will sorrowfully tell You about one thing I have read. He says that You have explained humbly before God that You are not God, that You never said You were, and that You have never known God's thoughts. Thus I have read in Chapter Five, the chapter *al-Mā'ida*, which means 'the table', that: 'God called Jesus, son of Mary, and said to him, "Did you tell the world that you are God?" And Jesus, son of Mary, responded, "Praise to you, O God! You know everything. You know what I am thinking and I do not know what You are thinking. Far be it from me to say what is not true".'[162] Read, read, and give Muḥammad power over the Christians, as You wish! [pp. 286–7]

---

[159] Psalm 139:7.
[160] Riccoldo seems to struggle with his own Christian identity here. Given his traumatic experiences, did he ever consider converting to Islam, or is the internal dialogue merely rhetorical?
[161] Riccoldo reveals some surprising details about his personal engagement with the Qur'an: he read it in Arabic; he put it on a Christian altar in front of icons of Jesus and Mary – an act which could be considered scandalous; he begged Jesus to read it; he then recited to Christ a passage about Christ.
[162] Q 5:116.

69

Petrus Marsilius, *Letter to an apostate of the Order of Friars Minor*

Antoni Biosca i Bas, University of Alicante

Petrus Marsilius (Pere Marsili) was a Dominican, most likely born in Majorca in the late thirteenth century. He played an important role at the court of the Crown of Aragón, and acted as an ambassador of King James II to Pope Clement V. By order of this king, he wrote a Latin chronicle of his grandfather King James I, formed from the memories which he had written down in Catalan in his own work, the *Llibre dels fets* ('Book of deeds'). This chronicle is not a simple translation from the Catalan, but adds information not found elsewhere on many topics, such as Majorca and the Dominican Order.

He also wrote an *Epistola ad Abdalla, olim fratrem Andream* ('Letter to ʿAbd Allāh, formerly Brother Andrew'), in which he criticizes the conversion to Islam of a Majorcan Franciscan named Andreas or Andreu. In this short letter, an extract from the end of which is translated here, Marsilius condemns the Franciscan's conversion, stressing the terrible damage which a priest's apostasy posed to Christianity. A veiled criticism of the Franciscan strategy with regard to Islam seems to be understood, as having achieved a high number of martyrdoms and only a few conversions to Christianity. This case denounced by Marsilius was a precedent for the well-known conversion to Islam of the Majorcan Franciscan Anselm Turmeda in the fifteenth century, who recorded his own conversion in Arabic.

CMR 5, pp. 712–14. See further:

A. Biosca i Bas, 'Pere Marsili y el Islam', *Medievalia* 19 (2016) 157–73.

This translation is based on A. Biosca i Bas, Petri Marsilii opera omnia, Turnhout, 2015, pp. 447–57.

Your soul rejoiced at the desire for an end, and death awaited you as a sure reward for your affection. Nothing was difficult for you, nothing was unpleasant, nothing annoying could overcome you and you could do everything with the one who comforts you, to the point that, for you the fact of living was Jesus Christ, but dying was also an accumulation of joys, if you had been kind, if you had been pure of mind, if you had dedicated yourself to the quest for the virtues, if you had rejected worldly things, if you had sought heavenly things. You remember that all these things have been inside you, and that, I believe, you somehow delighted in these things.

O human frailty, predisposed to fall, unable to rise, scarce in virtue, fallen in vice, why do you rely on yourself? Who are you? What have you thought about yourself? Behold, you are uncertain when things happen, doubtful in decisions. You do not know with what threads your end will be closed,[163] what conclusion will be given to your work, what prize will follow your toil and fatigue, what the future day will yield, because, while you think you are standing, you are heading unknowingly towards absolute collapse.

What a surprising thing! It is an incredible thing in the Church, surprising among the peoples! You are a new disease among the clergy, and you will unleash among the believers in a terrible way a perfidious monster of religion! It happens that you, who were once Friar Andreu, of a holy and approved order, dear to God and useful to people, have become an ally of pirates and bandits, an insulter of peaceful people, a persecutor of others' properties, a despiser of obedience, an invader of poverty and, which is more serious, heaven and earth cry out against you! You have become a public renegade of the Christian faith, a counterfeiter, according to what I have heard, of Holy Scripture, a defamatory liar of the Evangelical truth and a public persecutor of the sacred name of Jesus Christ, in which the salvation of people is born and which you drank with your mother's milk from the beginning of your life. You have embraced the heretics, you join the falsehoods of the great beast,[164] you beget carnal children, who are followers of the error of the prostitute Jehanna[165] and will be devoured.

Alas, the capacity of the human mind cannot understand it! The tongue is bitten! The pen is stopped! A page is not enough to narrate the enormous gravity of such a terrible crime, when the tonsure of sacred freedom becomes a servile and shameful tress, when the crier of faith becomes an apostate, when the religious man becomes a Muslim, when the priest becomes an incestuous spouse, and when hands consecrated by God, ordained for the solemn mystery of Christ, are exposed to so many and so reprehensible, shameful and brutal abuses.

In this case, ignorance is not an excuse, because it is not caused by fear, it is not allowed by loss, nor by utility, nor pleasure, nor abundance, nor the denial of permission, nor the gift of some aspect of heritage.[166] When salvation is left aside,

---

[163] Probably a reference to the classical belief that people's destinies were woven by the three Fates.
[164] Cf. Revelation 13:1 and 11.
[165] Jehanna, possibly a woman's proper name or a reference to Gehenna, meaning Hell.
[166] Marsilius lists possible secular causes of conversion to Islam.

people abandon religion, deny faith, rush into clear embraces of unquestionable perdition: vain, frivolous, corruptible, and transitory things are put before the heavenly, enduring, incorruptible and eternal virtues of the soul.

I have exceeded the scope of a letter because of your excess. I have saddened you and I am glad that I did so. I am amazed that you persist in so much confusion and go to eternal punishment with a clear mind and with open eyes.

However, in order not to seem myself only a prosecutor of sins and [to be] a supporter of the good, if some day you are worried and you have given some thought to your salvation, I beg you, try to answer me in the way you choose; do not give up. I offer myself to you right now with all my strength – of course, always under the obedience to my order – for your total salvation, according to what you consider that I should do in this matter. I am not hiding from you what I think about you, what I want, in what good, abundant, beautiful and safe way I choose the course, how I put it ahead of all ways, decisions and remedies: everything in order that, once you have collected the shield of the faith[167] which you abandoned, I believe, because of fear, armed with the weapons created by the Holy Spirit, you come out with the passion stone of the Lord to the single combat and, having publicly confessed the truth of your crime, wash your robe, now shamefully stained by your own blood and, offering yourself to Christ for a blood sacrifice, rest with him in the courtyard of the cross, invite present and absent people wondrously to enjoy the aroma of your holocaust through your brief bodily affliction, and enter through your blood into the Holy of Holies, crowned by the happy exchange.[168] This way, he whom we now detest as a dirty and shameful servant of so much infamy will become a beloved athlete of the heavenly king, reconciled with his father, a defender of public truth, a fighter for justice and as a true penitent will be raised to praise by the Church militant and triumphant.

However, since I am not unaware that martyrdom is a very special gift from God, I invoke God, the Father of Our Lord Jesus Christ, to enlighten you, once enlightened to illuminate you, once illuminated to fortify you and once fortified to lead you to forget everything which is lost, and so, having forgotten that and been united with Christ from Heaven, for God to bring you closer to the grace of martyrdom.

---

[167] Ephesians 6:16.

[168] The exchange of his martyrdom for salvation.

70

Juan de Segovia, *Letter to the Cardinal of Saint Peter (Nicholas of Cusa)*

Anne Marie Wolf, University of Maine – Farmington

Juan de Segovia (d. 1458) was a theologian from the Iberian kingdom of Castile and a professor at the University of Salamanca before he became active at the Council of Basel, from the early 1430s until its dissolution almost two decades later. He was a tireless proponent of the Church reforms promoted by the conciliarists. From his early years, he sought to learn more about Islam, engaging Muslims in conversations about their faith while still in Castile, and later enlisting a Muslim scholar to help him produce a translation of the Qur'an which would be better than those he had seen and found wanting.

After hearing of the fall of Constantinople in 1453, he dedicated himself to persuading influential Church leaders that Christians must reject the idea of Crusade and seek peaceful conversion of the Turks instead. He proposed sending a high-level delegation to Muslim leaders, confident that this would disabuse them of their erroneous views of Christians' beliefs and thus eliminate any reason for war against Christians. The translation offered here is taken from his letter to his friend, the German theologian Nicholas of Cusa (d. 1464), finished on 2 December 1454. It follows his discussion of the delegation which he proposed and offers reasons for its benefits.

CMR 5, pp. 429–42. See further:

J.D. Mann, 'Juan de Segovia on the superiority of Christians over Muslims', in I.C. Levy, R. George-Tvrtković and D.F. Duclow (eds), *Nicholas of Cusa and Islam: Polemic and Dialogue in the Late Middle Ages*, Leiden, 2014, 145–59.

A.M. Wolf, *Juan de Segovia and the Fight for Peace: Christians and Muslims in the Fifteenth Century*, Notre Dame, IN, 2014.

This translation is based on Juan de Segovia, *Letter to Nicholas of Cusa, 2 December 1454*, Biblioteca Universitaria de Salamanca, MS 19, fols 179v-180v.

[179v] But it is not up to me to specify the character or the size of the delegation which should be sent to the Saracens regarding such a peace, of what status or pre-eminence [it should be], or [to say anything] about the number of persons or the means. The thing itself will provide that information most fully, when the greatness of the matter is considered, as well as its purpose, and to whom and from whom such a legation should go – for it would certainly be of such a character and size that, even if it could easily be destroyed, it could not be disdained, being made up of persons so impressive in their number and dignity that they would be heard even if they were not functioning as a delegation. But it is also beyond the power of my imagination even to scratch the surface of how numerous and great would be the benefits which would ensue if such an embassy were to be sent to the Saracen community on behalf of the Christian religion.

Of course, one of the chief benefits is that, by proceeding in this way, the Church would be imitating the actions of Christ, who came to preach peace to those both near and far;[169] and that, with such diligence by all parties, war against the Saracens would be justified on the part of the Christians. [...] And indeed, the master instructed his servant to go out to the highways and the fences and compel [people] to come in so that his house might be filled, having first made the command that his servants go out to the end of the roads and invite to the wedding feast whomever they found.[170] Therefore, once an overture has been made through invitation to the things which belong to peace between Christians and Saracens, it would be entirely unjustified of them both insofar as they refuse peace when they are invited to it and insofar as they themselves are bound by their own law to call for it. [...]

Furthermore, war would be justified against them all the more so, if they refused to hear of peace or to provide security so that ambassadors may be sent to them concerning the above. But this is not likely, provided they understand that the kings and princes of the Christians, along with the pope and the clergy, are in agreement on this matter, namely that peace be discussed. How this could happen can be understood by one who has read, heard and seen in what way the campaigns [180r] for the waging of war against the Saracens have been proclaimed in former times and in our own, with equal or much greater cause, because it belongs to the pope to see those things which concern the peace of Jerusalem on the authority of Christ, who gave peace to his Apostles and to their successors and left his own peace.[171] And as has been stated in the preface to this brief letter, the cardinals are the true and manifest successors of the college of the Apostles.

If indeed it should happen that, through the workings of divine clemency, the Saracens agree that a discussion of peace should occur, it will be of no small benefit for the directing of their steps into the way of peace[172] that the Saracens should perceive

---

[169] Ephesians 2:17.
[170] Luke 14:23; a justification for religious coercion dating back to Saint Augustine.
[171] John 14:27.
[172] Luke 1:79.

the great love of the Christian people for them, and once they have been conducted into their sight they should perceive how variously [the Christians] offer themselves, with reasons why they love them and wish to love them.

Whereupon, once their benevolence and their attention have been captured, it can be asked of them what on their part are the reasons for war against the Christians. If they reveal them, satisfaction can be made, or if they do not wish to reveal them, there can be pointed out to them very many reasons for having peace and love between them and the Christians. Chief amongst them is that there is such great agreement concerning divine worship: Christians believe in one God and worship only Him, [a fact] which the Saracens themselves will be compelled to believe when they listen to explanations of divine unity expounded before them with seriousness, so that they might come to see most clearly how far it is from the faith of Christians not only to believe, but even casually to suggest, that there are many gods. [...] And [they will also see] that [the Christians] know this clearly to be true, that God is one, and that it is very far – indeed, absolutely so – from their faith to believe that there are any associates and affiliates of God, and how offensive it is to divine unity to assert such a thing.

And when these Saracens understand this, even if Christians do not state it explicitly, they will need to think about their own law,[173] which in almost a hundred places inveighs against those who put forward participants in or associates or consorts of God, [and about] how they had erred for so long, thinking of Christians as worshippers of companions and associates of God.[174] And even if the Christians should keep silent about this, [the Saracens] will be able to infer that they, by their daring constancy, are in no way the unbelievers whom their law alleges them to be: worshippers of companions and associates of God. [...]

There is therefore no reason for war against these people, as if they were worshippers of many gods. For the Saracens' law enjoins them to pursue disputes and wars with discretion, saying that it is useful and just, even in months of liberty and rest,[175] to fight against those who do not call upon God as solely one, which is how they think of all Christians, who are called unbelievers throughout almost all their law.

From this indeed another infamy (no small one) can be abolished: that Christians worship their presumptuous and unworthy priests, as their [the Muslims'] law says, as if they were God.[176] It is easy to show them this, once they perceive that Christians believe God to be one and they worship only Him alone. And if Christians were to learn that such things were being done, there would be a frightful judgement of both the worshippers and of those who were worshipped throughout all of Christendom. And so, if such people are not [to be found] amongst [180v] Christians, the Saracens

[173] The Qur'an.
[174] Q 5:116.
[175] The Islamic (and pre-Islamic) sacred months when fighting was forbidden, except against infidels (Q 9:36).
[176] Q 9:31.

themselves can consequently understand that those upon whom their law places this accusation are other than the Christians.

But there is not so much an opportunity right at the beginning of the discussion of peace to address the slander against good priests, that they beg tearfully to join the Saracens. But rather, what a duty of utmost importance it is for [the Christians] to make public that the testimony – on the basis of which [the Muslims] believe their entire law to rest – is not true, namely that Christ said in the Gospel that Muḥammad, called there by name, was to come as a messenger of joy.[177] And since, to demonstrate that his name is contained in the Gospel and the Testament, they will show the latter to the Jews and the former to the Christians, [it will also be necessary] for the New Testament to be read word for word, since [they suppose that] it will be found in many a passage.

But concerning the falsification that some say was imputed to the Christians by them, with the help of God, manifold and abundant satisfaction will be made: that the Gospel was not corrupted by Christians, nor likewise the Old Testament by the Jews. But as far as protecting the innocence of Christ in this matter is concerned, I have already said that it would be a duty of greater urgency for speeches be made to the effect that Christ never asserted the coming of Muḥammad and his law. For if it is necessary for a bishop to be well regarded by those who are outside [the Christian community],[178] and Christ is indeed the shepherd and bishop of the souls of all Christians,[179] then it is certainly fitting that these [bishops] see to it that the false testimony imputed to Christ is abolished, since the bishops and priests of the Christians, whether they are good or bad, are both shamed disgracefully in the law of Muḥammad. But [this] also [applies to] all Christians, since they are considered worshippers of partners to God and therefore of many gods.[180] And what more ignominious idolatry or great infamy could there be?

I will say one thing about myself: that I was utterly amazed, even stunned as it were, when I learned of the very great quantity of infamies imputed in that law to Christ, all Christians and also their priests, because for so long the Christian people, or their leaders and teachers, have not made any effort [to challenge them].

[177] Q 61:6.
[178] 1 Timothy 3:7.
[179] 1 Peter 2:25.
[180] Q 5:116.

71

Diogo Gomes, *On the first discovery of Guinea*

Martha T. Frederiks, Utrecht University

Diogo Gomes was a fifteenth-century Portuguese merchant-explorer working in the service of Prince Henry the Navigator (d. 1460), best known for his claim to have discovered the island of Santiago, Cape Verde. Few of his biographical details are known with certainty. Estimates of his date of birth range from *c.* 1402 to 1420; he is known to have been alive in 1482 and had died by 1502. He seems to have worked in the service of Prince Henry for a substantial part of his life. During his employment with the Portuguese crown he undertook two exploratory journeys to 'Guinea' (West Africa), one in 1456 or 1457 and another some years later, with estimates ranging from 1458 and 1462. After his return to Portugal, he was appointed *almoxarife* (receiver of the royal taxes) in the town of Sintra, a post which he held until at least 1480.

Around 1482, Gomes seems to have dictated a memoir of his African ventures to the German cartographer Martin Behaim. It is uncertain in which language Behaim recorded them. These memoirs were edited – and possibly translated into Latin – by Valentim Fernandes and published in 1506 under the title *De prima iuentione Gujnee* ('On the first discovery of Guinea'), as part of an anthology of Portuguese travel reports known as the *Codex Valentim Fernandes*. Many passages in the work are obscure, possibly because they were recorded many years after the events and edited by Fernandes, who had never visited West Africa in person. The memoirs relate that during the first journey Gomes's ships travelled as far south as the Rio Grande (today known as the river Geba in Guinea Bissau). On this journey, he also explored the Gambia river up to Cantor (Kuntaur), some 240 kilometres upstream, and established links with various chiefs he met. From these contacts he was able to secure valuable information on the West African gold trade and on geographical details (such as that the river Senegal was not connected to the river Niger). During his second journey Gomes explored the land of the Barbacins, north of the Gambia river, today known as the Sine-Saloum region. It was during his second journey that he claims to have discovered Santiago Island.

Among the chiefs whom Gomes encountered during his first West African voyage was someone he calls Nomymans. The name most likely refers to the *mansa* (chief) of Niumi, an area on the north bank of the Gambia estuary. The excerpt below relates this meeting. It details that the entourage of the *mansa* included a Muslim scholar who questioned Gomes about 'the God of the Christians'; in response Gomes interrogated the Muslim scholar about Muḥammad. According to Gomes's memoirs, the *mansa* was so impressed with his exposition of the Christian faith that he dismissed the Muslim scholar, forbade any further mention of the name of Muḥammad in his domain and requested baptism.

The account suggests that in the mid-fifteenth century some African chiefs such as the Niumi *mansa* considered religious allegiance to be malleable. Their preference for either Christianity or Islam was informed not just by the beliefs and practices of these religions but also by the political and economic prospects and connections which these traditions signified.

CMR 5, pp. 596–600. See further:

M. Tymowski, *Europeans and Africans: Mutual Discoveries and First Encounters*, Leiden, 2020.

This translation is taken from G.R. Crone, *The Voyages of Cadamosto and Other Documents on Western Africa in the Second Half of the Fifteenth Century*, Farnham, 2010, pp. 97–8, with permission.

It was here that I learned the fact that all the mischief that had been done to the Christians had been done by a certain king, called Nomymans,[181] who possesses the land which lies on that promontory. I took great pains to make peace with him, and sent him many presents by his own men in his own canoes, which were going for salt to his own country.[182] This salt was plentiful there, and of a red colour. He greatly feared the Christians, on account of the injury which he had done them. I went by the river towards the ocean as far as the harbour near the mouth of the river, and many times he sent to me men and women to try me, whether I would do them any harm, but, on the contrary, I always gave them a friendly reception. When the king heard this, he came to the side of the river with a great force, and sitting down on the bank, sent for me to come to him, which I did, paying him all ceremonious respect in the best fashion I could. There was a certain bishop there of his native church,[183] who put questions to me with respect to the God of the Christians, and I answered him

[181] Most likely a corruption of the appellation Niumi *mansa*, the chief of Niumi, an area on the north bank of the Gambia estuary.
[182] Salt was a coveted commodity in early modern West Africa and an important article of trade: P.E. Lovejoy, *Salt of the Desert Sun: a History of Salt Production and Trade in the Central Sudan*, Cambridge, 1986.
[183] Christian terminology used to describe elements of Islam.

according to the intelligence which God had given me, and at last I questioned him respecting Muḥammad, in whom they believe. What I said pleased the king so much, that he ordered the bishop within three days to take his departure out of his kingdom, and springing to his feet, he declared that no one, on pain of death, should dare any more to utter the name of Muḥammad, for he believed in the one God only, and that there was no other God but He, in whom his brother, the Prince Henry, said that he believed. Calling the Infante[184] his brother, he desired that I should baptize him, and so said also all the lords of his household, and his women likewise. The king himself declared that he would have no other name than Henry, but his nobles took our names, such as Jacob, Nuiio, &c., as Christian names.[185]

I remained that night on shore with the king and his chiefs, but I did not dare to baptize them, because I was a layman. On the next day, however, I begged the king with his twelve principal chiefs and eight of his wives to come to dine with me on board the caravel, which they all did unarmed, and I gave them fowls and meat cooked after our own fashion, and wine, both white and red, as much as they pleased to drink;[186] and they said to each other that no nation was better than the Christians. Afterwards, when we were on shore, he desired that I would baptize him; but I answered that I had not received authority from the supreme pontiff.[187] I told him, however, that if he so desired, I would convey his wishes to the prince, who would send a priest to baptize them. He immediately wrote to the prince to send him a priest,[188] and someone to inform him respecting the faith, and begged the prince to send him a falcon for hunting, for he wondered greatly when I told him that the Christians carried a bird on the hand which caught other birds. He wished him also to send two rams, and sheep, and ganders and geese, and a pig, as well as two men who would know how to construct houses and make a survey [?] of his city. All these requirements I promised that the prince would fulfil. At my departure he and all his people lamented, so great was the friendship which had sprung up between him and me.

---

[184] A royal title bestowed on the sons and daughters of Portuguese monarchs who were not heirs to the throne.

[185] Gomes seems to consider Western and Christian names to be synonymous.

[186] The liberal consumption of alcohol seems to suggest that neither the *mansa* nor any Muslims in his entourage observed the Islamic prohibition against it.

[187] Here the term 'pontiff' can refer either to the primate of the Catholic Church in Portugal or to the pope in Rome.

[188] Two Portuguese missionaries were dispatched to Niumi a few years later. However, on arrival they found that the *mansa* was no longer interested in converting to Christianity: see M. Frederiks, *We Have Toiled All Night: Christianity in the Gambia, 1456–2000*, Zoetermeer, 2003, p. 165.

Romance writings

72

Old French epic poems and the *Song of Roland*

Carol Sweetenham

The Old French epic narrative poems known as *chansons de geste* present a fictional and heroicized account of past events. The combat between Islam and Christianity is a central theme, although Islam is portrayed in a luridly inaccurate stylized form. The blurring of history and fiction creates a heroic universe in which real-life Crusaders are depicted as epic heroes, and conversely epic heroes as exemplars of Crusading ethos. This is illustrated here through two texts: the *Old French Crusade Cycle* and the *Chanson de Roland* ('The Song of Roland').

The *Crusade Cycle* is a set of epics totalling up to some 40,000 lines, which takes the story of the Crusades from the legendary family history of the first king of Jerusalem, Godfrey of Bouillon, through the events of the First Crusade up to, in some manuscripts, the fall of Acre. Whilst the topic is ostensibly historical, the treatment is almost entirely fantastical, reflecting the conventions of the *chansons de geste*.

The *Chanson de Roland* is probably the best known – though atypical – Old French *chanson de geste*. The oldest version was probably written around the time of the First Crusade (1095–9) and is preserved in one manuscript generally dated to the mid-twelfth-century. The hero Roland, nephew of Charlemagne, is defeated by the Saracens at Roncesvalles in the Pyrenees. The original kernel of the story, a Basque ambush in 778, is recast as part of the eternal struggle against the Saracens, with Roland as a Crusading hero.

CMR 3, pp. 422–33, 648–52. See further:

Norman A. Daniel, *Heroes and Saracens: An Interpretation of the Chansons de Geste*, Edinburgh, 1984.

Sharon Kinoshita, *Medieval Boundaries: Rethinking Difference in Old French Literature*, Philadelphia, PA, 2006.

Catherine M. Jones, *An Introduction to the Chansons de geste*, Gainesville, FL, 2014.

The translation from the *Chanson d' Antioche* is taken from S. Edgington and C. Sweetenham, *La Chanson d' Antioche: An Old French Account of the First Crusade*, Farnham, 2011, with permission.

The translation from *La Chanson de Roland* is based on the edition by I. Short, *La Chanson de Roland*, Paris, 1990.

Chanson d' Antioche from the Old French Crusade Cycle

[The justification for launching a crusade against the Saracens]

156.[189] The Franks made their intention absolutely clear [...]: if it was the will of Jesus, in Whom they placed their trust, they would capture the Holy Sepulchre where His body rose from death, deliver Him from those who hated Him, and break down the wall and palisade of Mecca. They would drag out Mahomet and Apollin,[190] and give their gold to those who had served Jesus. Blessed be the lands that gave them birth! [p. 187]

[The Saracens throw down their image of Muḥammad when they fail in battle]

202.[191] Sansadoine[192] reacted angrily: [...] 'As far as I can see you have lost your minds. Why on earth are you worshipping this piece of wood? Let me tell you that Mohammed is not worth as much as a couple of straws. My mistake was to believe in him, and I have lost my men as a result. If you trust me, you will beat him so hard with a stick that he will never be taken for a god again.' He raised his heavy muscled fist and struck Mohammed so hard on the neck that he fell full length. Watched by a thousand of his followers, he mounted the idol's stomach. A massive outcry went up from the pagans at this, and they showered upon him long viciously sharp darts. [pp. 219–20]

[The Crusaders receive divine help in the Battle of Antioch as a manifestation of divine favour]

358. The bishop of Le Puy,[193] whom God loved and held dear, looked up an old path leading to the mountains. There he saw a company riding proudly down, so great that nobody could fail to be impressed. I am sure it must have amounted to more than half a million. They were whiter than the snow which falls at the end of February. St George was out in front at its head with the noble St Maurice, renowned as a stout warrior, and St Demetrius and St Mercurius as standard-bearers.[194] If our people had not had Jesus on their side, they would have been so terrified when they saw the lances lowered

---

[189] All references are to *laisses*, the units into which *chansons de geste* are divided.

[190] Standard names in Latin texts of this period for Saracen gods.

[191] The *topos* of Saracens rejecting their gods when they have been defeated, as Sansadoine does here, is standard in works of this kind.

[192] The Muslim son of Garsion, emir of Antioch.

[193] Adhemar, bishop of Le Puy and legate of Pope Urban II; in effect the spiritual leader of the Crusade.

[194] Byzantine warrior saints.

for the charge that they would have lost all discipline beyond hope of recovery. As it was, the bishop of Le Puy restored order: 'My lords, there is nothing to be afraid of. These forces are coming to help us. They are the angels sent by God which I told you of yesterday.' [p. 313]

Chanson de Roland

[Single combat between Archbishop Turpin and the Saracen Corsablix at the battle of Roncevalles]

95. There was a king called Corsablix, from the remote land of Barbary. He called the other Saracens to him: 'We can easily prevail in this battle, because there are very few French on the field. We need have no respect for those who are here: whatever Charlemagne may attempt, not a single one will survive.[195] Today is the day they are to meet their end.' Archbishop Turpin heard this all too clearly.[196] No man on this earth could inspire more hatred in him than Corsablix. He urged on his horse with his golden spurs and landed a blow on him with all his strength: he shattered his shield, ripped open his hauberk and plunged his great spear into the middle of his body; he thrust it right through, making the Saracen reel back, and knocked him dead in the middle of the path with the force of the blow. Glancing down at the ground, he saw the wretch sprawled in death. Unable to restrain his words, he said: 'You lied, you foul pagan. My lord Charlemagne is always ready to protect us. Our Frenchmen have no intention of running away. We shall halt every last one of your companions in their tracks; you will be forced to die a second time.' [pp. 102–4]

[The death of Roland after the Saracen attack]

176–7. The count Roland lay [dying] under a pine tree, and turned his head to look towards Spain. A string of memories came to his mind: of how many lands he had conquered in the days of his valour; of the sweet land of France; of the men of his lineage; and of his lord Charlemagne who had raised him as a child. He could not but weep and sigh at the memory of all this. But he did not want to forget his own position. He declared his sinfulness and beseeched God to have mercy on him: 'Lord of truth, You who have never lied, You who raised St Lazarus from death and rescued Daniel from the lions' den, protect my soul from all the perils I might face for the sins I committed in my life!' He offered his right glove to God in earnest of this, and St Gabriel took it from his hand. Roland bowed his head on his arm and, joining his hands, found his end. God sent down to him His angel cherubim and St Michael from the Mont-St-Michel,[197] and the holy Gabriel came with them. They carried the soul of the count to Paradise.

---

[195] The first Holy Roman emperor and, in this poem, the overlord of Roland.

[196] The archetype of the warrior bishop who fights for Christendom in a literal as well as a spiritual sense.

[197] Literally, St Michael of the Danger of the Sea, a probable reference to the treacherous tides and sandbanks around the abbey.

Roland is dead. His soul is in the keeping of God in heaven. The emperor [Charlemagne] arrives at Roncesvalles. There was not a single track or path, no bit of land as much as a yard or even a foot without a Frenchman or pagan lying across it. Charlemagne cried aloud: 'Where are you, my handsome nephew? Where are Archbishop [Turpin] and Count Oliver? Where is Gerins, and where is his companion Gerer? Where are Otto and Count Berenger, and Ivon and Ivorie whom I held in such esteem? What has become of Engelier the Gascon, Duke Samson, and the bold Anseis? Where are the venerable Gerard of Roussillon and the twelve peers whom I left here?' But all to no avail: there was no response. 'God', said the king, 'how can I not be angry with myself for failing to be there at the start of the battle!' He tore at his beard as a man in the grip of intense emotion. His noble knights wept bitterly. [pp. 168–70]

73

Ramon Llull, *The book of the Gentile and the three wise men*

Graham Barrett, University of Lincoln

Ramon Llull (*c.* 1232–1315/16) was born on the island of Majorca, just a few years after its reconquest from the Almohads by James I of Aragón (r. 1213–76). He grew up in royal circles, entered court service, married and fathered two children, but around 1263 had visions of Christ which moved him to rededicate his life to converting unbelievers. This began with learning Arabic from a Muslim slave, then took form in sustained and prodigious writing, of at least 280 works in Latin, Catalan and Arabic, ranging across theology and philosophy, law and medicine, polemics and political commentary, and didactic novels, the earliest Catalan prose compositions. Llull believed firmly in the importance of studying Arabic for success in mission, to this end establishing a Franciscan monastery at Miramar in about 1276, and lobbying the Council of Vienne (1311) to provide for university chairs in Semitic languages. He travelled constantly throughout Europe and beyond to promote his cause, and made at least three missionary trips to North Africa. He may have died on a final campaign in Tunis.

The foundation of Llull's output and understanding of mission was 'the art'. The fruit of divine revelation first enunciated in his *Ars compendiosa inveniendi veritatem* ('Succinct art of finding the truth', *c.* 1274), it was serially reworked and refined, in the face of criticism for undue Arabic influence, until his definitive *Ars generalis ultima* ('Final general art') of 1308. What he sought to articulate was the language of creation itself, based on principles amenable to Christianity, Islam and Judaism, through which 'the artist' could discover the true nature of God. An intellectual framework for conversion, when interfaith debate or disputation took place by the rules of 'the art', it would necessarily lead participants to arrive at the truth of Christianity.

The text presented here is an extract from the *Llibre del gentil i dels tres savis* ('The book of the Gentile and the three wise men'), written around 1274. It dramatizes a disputation according to 'the art'. Taken in isolation it can seem an exemplar of interfaith tolerance, but in the context of Llull's life and work this tolerance is purely strategic, serving to facilitate conversion. The three debaters – a Christian, a Muslim and a Jew – meet beside a babbling brook and there learn 'the art' from Lady

Sagacity; they then deploy its principles to demonstrate the true faith to an enquiring Gentile who has happened upon them. Each wise man seeks to prove the articles of his faith, with only the Gentile permitted to ask questions. The Muslim speaks third. His outline of Islam is unusually accurate and relatively fair, leading to the seemingly ambiguous conclusion in which the religion chosen by the Gentile is not disclosed. Yet the exchange is premised on there being only one true saving faith, and throughout the points made by the Muslim the Gentile expresses scepticism, even rejection, not least of the prophetic status of Muḥammad, forcing the Muslim to defend some of his beliefs. In this light, the text argues that Islam is irrational, and models how 'the artist' could convert unbelievers through disputation.

CMR 4, pp. 703–17. See further:

M.L. Colish, 'Ramon Lull's *Book of the Gentile and the Three Sages*: Empathy or Apology?', in K.F. Morrison and R.M. Bell (eds), *Studies on Medieval Empathies*, Turnhout, 2013, 237–53.

L. Badia, J. Santanach Suñol and A. Soler, *Ramon Llull as Vernacular Writer: Communicating a New Kind of Knowledge*, Woodbridge, 2016.

This translation is taken from A. Bonner (ed. and trans.), *Doctor Illuminatus. A Ramon Llull Reader*, Princeton, NJ, 1993, with permission.

When the Saracen saw that the time and hour had come for him to speak, he went to the spring and washed his hands, his face, his ears, his nose and his mouth; and afterwards he washed his feet and other parts of his body, as a sign of original sin and cleanliness of heart.[198] Afterwards he spread a cloth on the ground and knelt three times, touching his head to earth and kissing the ground; then, raising his heart, his hands and his eyes heavenward, he said: 'In the name of God the Merciful, the Mercifying, to whom all praise be given, since He is Lord of the world; – Him I adore and in Him I trust, for He leads us on the straight path of salvation.'[199] And the Saracen spoke many other words, as was the custom in his prayers.

After finishing his prayer, the Saracen said to the Gentile that the articles of his religion were twelve, namely: to believe in one God; Creator; Muḥammad is Prophet; the Qur'an is the law given by God; the dead man, upon being buried, is asked by the angel if Muḥammad is the messenger of God; all things will die, except God; resurrection; Muḥammad will be heeded on the Day of Judgement; we will give an accounting on the Day of Judgement; merits and faults will be weighed; all will pass along the path; the twelfth article is to believe in the existence of Paradise and Hell.[200] [pp. 140–1]

[198] The ablutions required before prayer (see Q 5:6), though there is no concept of original sin in Islam.
[199] Adapted from Q 1.
[200] This list of 'articles of faith' tallies most closely with that given by al-Ghazālī (1058–1111) in his *Iḥyā' 'ulūm al-dīn* ('The revival of the religious sciences').

[Article 12: Paradise and Hell] [...]
Question. The Gentile said to the Saracen, 'If things are as you say, then there must be filth in Paradise, for according to the natural order of things, from a man who eats and drinks and lies with women there must come forth filth and corruption, which filth is an ugly thing to see and touch and smell, and to talk about.'

Solution: The Saracen replied: 'What you say is true according to the world in which we live. But in the next world it will be just the opposite, as a result of divine influence and power, which can ordain and improve anything.'

Question. The Gentile said to the Saracen: 'As I understand it, the ultimate purpose for which man is made is to have glory in God; yet according to what you say, it would follow that man existed to have glory in the above-mentioned things. And if he did, the result would not be the purpose for which man was made; and if he did not, it would follow that in God wisdom would not accord with power, love, perfection, and this is impossible and against the conditions of the trees.'[201]

Solution. The Saracen replied, 'Man was created principally to know and love God, and it follows that, according to God's justice, perfection, men should be recompensed with the above-mentioned happiness, without which men could not be recompensed.'

Question. The Gentile said to the Saracen. 'If God is just and gives many women to a just man in Paradise, and the juster the man has been, the more women he will have to lie with, so that his glory will be greater, it therefore follows that to a woman who is juster than a man and juster than another woman, God should give her many men to lie with in Paradise, so that she may have greater glory.'

Solution. The Saracen replied, 'God has honoured man more than woman in this world, and therefore in the next world He wishes to do greater honour to him than to woman.'

Question. The Gentile said to the Saracen, 'Pray tell me is it true that all you Saracens believe you will, in Paradise, have the sort of glory you just described to me?'

Solution. The Saracen replied, saying: 'It is true that among us there are differing beliefs with respect to the glory of Paradise, for some believe it will be as I said, and this they take from a literal interpretation of the Qur'an, which is our law, of the Proverbs of Muḥammad, and of commentators' glosses on the Qur'an and the Proverbs. But there are others among us who take this glory morally and interpret it spiritually, saying that Muḥammad was speaking metaphorically to people who were backward and without understanding; and in order to inspire them with a love of God he recounted the above-mentioned glory. And therefore those who believe this say that in Paradise there will be no glory of eating or of lying with women, nor of the other things mentioned above.

---

[201] The trees in the glade represent the principles of 'the art'.

And these men are natural philosophers and great scholars, yet they are men who in some ways do not follow too well the dictates of our religion, and this is why we consider them as heretics, who have arrived at their heresy by studying logic and natural science. And therefore it has been established among us that no man dare teach logic or natural science publicly.'[202]

When the Saracen had finished talking and had recounted everything required to prove his religion, he spoke the following words to the Gentile: 'Now you have heard and understood my words, O Gentile, and the proofs I have given of the articles of our religion. And you have heard of the blessings of Paradise, which you will have everlastingly without end if you believe in our religion, which is God-given.' And when the Saracen had spoken these words, he closed his book and finished speaking, and to the two wise men he made salutation according to his custom. [pp. 159–60]

[202] See al-Ghazālī, *Tahāfut al-falāsifa* ('The incoherence of the philosophers'), which attacks philosophers such as Ibn Sīnā (*c.* 980–1037) and al-Fārābī (*c.* 872–950/51) for over-reliance on these disciplines to the disadvantage of scripture.

74

Marco Polo, *Description of the world*

Sharon Kinoshita, University of California

Marco Polo's *Devisement du monde* ('Description of the world'; misleadingly called 'The travels') was composed in 1298, at the height of Mongol power. Depicting the cities, provinces and islands of Asia and the Indian Ocean, it focuses on commodities and merchandise, interspersed with vignettes of history, local customs and marvels. Muslims are often mentioned in neutral terms; additionally, many of the 'merchants' depicted doing business in sites across Central Asia, China and numerous Indian Ocean ports were certainly Muslim.

As a foreigner in Mongol service, Marco Polo (*c.* 1254–1324) would have known many Muslims, not least his 'companion [...] Çurficar, a very wise Turk', his informant on the province of Ghinghintalas (ch. 60). The most negative portraits of Muslims occur in the miracle stories or historical episodes scattered throughout the text; the blanket condemnations they contain are perhaps attributable to Marco's co-author, the romance writer Rustichello of Pisa.

CMR 4, pp. 645–9.

This translation is taken from Marco Polo, *The Description of the World*, trans. S. Kinoshita, Indianapolis, IN, 2016, with permission.

24. The Kingdom of Mosul

In the mountains of this kingdom live people called Kurds, who are Nestorian and Jacobite Christians; some are Saracens, who worship Muḥammad.[203] They are valiant men-at-arms and bad people; and they willingly rob merchants.

---

[203] That Saracens worshipped Muḥammad is a common misconception in Latin Christian writings.

25. Baghdad

Baghdad is a very great city where the caliph of all the world's Saracens is, just as the head of all the Christians of the world is in Rome. Through the city flows a very large river, and on this river one can well reach the Indian Sea.

26. I further wish to relate to you a great marvel which occurred between Baghdad and Mosul. Truly, in the year 1275 after Christ's incarnation there was a caliph in Baghdad[204] who wished very great ill on the Christians and thought day and night about how he could make all the Christians in his land turn Saracen or, failing this, put them to death. And every day he took counsel with his habitual clerics and wise men, for all of them wished harm on the Christians. This is a truth: that all the Saracens in the world wish great harm to all the Christians of the world. Now it happened that the caliph and the sages around him found a passage [...] in a Gospel where it said that if there were a Christian who had as much faith as a mustard seed, through praying to his Lord God he could make two mountains come together.[205] When they found this they were very happy, for they said that this was the thing that would turn all the Christians into Saracens or put them to death all together.

Then the caliph sent for all the Christians – Nestorian and Jacobite – in his lands, which was a very great number. When they had come before the caliph, he showed them this Gospel and had them read it. And when they had read it, he asked if this was true. The Christians said that truly, this was the truth. [...] 'Then I will put a wager before you,' said the caliph; 'since you are so Christian, there ought to be one among you with a bit of faith. So I say to you: either you move the mountain you see there' – and he pointed to a nearby mountain – 'or I will have you all put to a bad death. For if you don't move it, you will have shown that you have no faith; I will have you all killed or you will return to our good faith, which Muhammad gave for our benefit; you will have faith and be saved. To do this, I'll give you ten days' respite, and if you haven't accomplished this by that time, I will have you all put to death.' With that, the caliph said no more and gave the Christians leave to go.[206]

30. Tabriz

It is a city where merchants doing business make great profits. They are people of little account and are very mixed in many ways: there are Nestorian and Jacobite Armenians, Georgians, Persians. There are also men who worship Muḥammad; these are the people of the city, who are called Tabrizis. [...] The Saracens of Tabriz are very bad and disloyal, for their faith, given to them by their prophet Muḥammad, commands

---

[204] In fact, the last ʿAbbasid caliph, al-Mustaʿṣim, was executed when Qubilai Khan's brother Hülegü conquered Baghdad in 1258 (erroneously reported as 1255 in ch. 25).

[205] Matthew 17:20.

[206] In the continuation of the story, chs 27–9 recount how a Christian bishop, spurred by a dream, finds a one-eyed shoemaker whose prayer successfully moves the mountain, inspiring several Saracens, including the caliph, to convert to Christianity. A similar tale is told about a tenth-century Coptic Christian patriarch and a tanner who successfully move Muqaṭṭam Mountain. See passage 20 above.

them to do all the ill they can to all people who are not of their faith, and whatever they can take from them is not regarded as a sin; for this reason they would do much ill if not for the lordship. And all the other Saracens of the world behave in this way.

166. Lesser Java

Know that this kingdom of Perlak converted to Muḥammad's law as a result of Saracen merchants who often came there by ship – only the city people; the mountain people are like animals, for I tell you in truth that they eat human flesh and all other flesh, good and bad.

176. The body of Messer St Thomas the Apostle is in the province of Maabar, in a little city; for there are few men there, nor do merchants come there since there is no merchandise which can be exported and, what is more, the place is very out of the way.[207] It is quite true that many Christians and many Saracens come here on pilgrimage: for I tell you that the Saracens of this country have great faith in him; they say that he was Saracen and that he is a great prophet, and they call him *avarian*, which means 'holy man'.

178. Ceylon

Ceylon is a big island. [...] Now it is true that on this island there is a very high mountain with cliffs so sheer that no one can climb it. [...] I tell you they say that on top of this mountain is the monument of Adam our first father. The Saracens say that this tomb is Adam's, and the idolators say that it is the monument of Sergamoni Borcan.[208]

194. Aden

Regarding the sultan [of Aden], I will [...] tell you that he did something that was very harmful to Christians: for know in all truth that when the sultan of Babylon[209] attacked the city of Acre – when he took it and did such harm to the Christians – this sultan of Aden gave some of his people to help the sultan of Babylon – a good 3,000 horsemen and a good 40,000 camels, so that it was of great profit to the Saracens and harm to the Christians. And he did this more out of the ill he wished on Christians than for the good he wished on the sultan of Babylon or for any love he bears him.[210]

---

[207] Mylapore, today a neighbourhood of Chennai (Madras) on the Coromandel coast of India.

[208] 'Sergamoni Borcan' is Sakyamuni, Gautama Buddha, plus Burkhan ('divinity'), a Mongol synonym for the Buddha.

[209] The name given to Cairo.

[210] In 1291 al-Ashraf, the Mamlūk sultan of Egypt, captured the kingdom of Acre, the last Crusader outpost on the Levantine mainland and a major centre for Latin Europe's trade in the Middle East.

75

Jean de Joinville, *Life of Saint Louis*

Huw Grange, UiT The Arctic University of Norway

In August 1248, King Louis IX of France (r. 1226–70) set sail on the first of the two disastrous Crusades which he led against Islam, numbered as the Seventh Crusade. Disembarking in Egypt, the crusaders quickly captured the port city of Damietta in June 1249. As they headed inland, however, they faced ever stiffer opposition from the Egyptian Ayyūbids. Routed at the Battle of al-Manṣūra, Louis and his men were then captured at the Battle of Fāriskūr in April 1250. Surrendering Damietta and paying an eyewatering ransom in exchange for the king's release, the Crusaders sheepishly left Egypt for Acre.

Among those accompanying Louis was Jean de Joinville (*c.* 1225–1317), a minor nobleman from Champagne who would become the king's closest confidant. Joinville began his *Vie de saint Louis* ('Life of Saint Louis') at the request of the queen of France, Joan of Navarre (1273–1305), but a dedication in the sole surviving medieval manuscript to the future King Louis X of France (r. 1314–16) suggests that the text (or perhaps an earlier manuscript) was completed after her death, in October 1309. The *Vie* is an unusual admixture of chronicle, personal memoir and hagiography (Louis was canonized in 1297). At its heart is a vivid and often frank first-hand account of the crusaders' encounters with their Muslim opponents in Egypt.

In the extract below we join Louis as he is being held captive in May 1250. Despite the recent assassination of the Ayyūbid sultan of Egypt by his own bodyguards, the Mamlūks, the deal previously struck between the Christians and Muslims is still alive. All that remains is for the negotiating parties to use their knowledge of their opponents to devise the strongest possible oaths for them to swear.

CMR 4, pp. 718–23. See further:

S. Khanmohamadi, 'Casting a "Sideways Glance" at the Crusades. The Voice of the Other in Joinville's *Vie de saint Louis*', *Exemplaria* 22 (2010) 177–99.

J.M. Elukin, 'Warrior or Saint? Joinville, Louis IX's Character, and the Challenge of the Crusade', in K.L. Jansen, G. Geltner and A.E. Lester (eds), *Center and Periphery. Studies on Power in the Medieval World in Honor of William Chester Jordan*, Leiden, 2013, 183–94.

E. Gaucher-Rémond, 'Louis IX au regard de Joinville: un saint, un monarque, un ami', in F. Laurent, L. Mathey-Maillie and M. Szkilnik (eds), *Des saints et des rois. L'hagiographie au service de l'histoire*, Colloques, Paris, 2014, 209–21.

W.C. Jordan, '"Etiam reges", Even Kings', *Speculum* 90 (2015) 613–34.

The translation below is based on N.L. Corbett (ed.), *La vie de saint Louis: le témoignage de Jehan, seigneur de Joinville. Texte du XIVe siècle*, Sherbrooke, 1977, pp. 157–9.

The oaths which the emirs were to swear to the king were formulated as follows. If they did not keep their agreement with the king, they would be held in the same opprobrium as someone who, for their sin, goes on pilgrimage to Muḥammad in Mecca bareheaded;[211] or as men who abandon their wives only to take them back afterwards. (For, according to the law of Muḥammad, a man who has forsaken his wife in this way may never have her back unless he first sees another man sleeping with her.)[212] The third oath was such that, if they did not keep their agreement with the king, they would be deemed as disgraced as a Saracen who eats pork. The king was satisfied with the wording of the emirs' oaths because Nicholas of Acre, who knew the Saracen language, said that no stronger ones could be made according to their law.

When the emirs had sworn, they had the oath which they wished the king to swear set down in writing. This had been drawn up on the advice of renegade priests who had joined their side. And it was written that if the king did not keep his agreement with the emirs, he would be held in the same opprobrium as a Christian who denies God and his Mother and is deprived of the fellowship of the Twelve Apostles and of all the saints (of both sexes). To this the king consented gladly. But the final clause of the oath was such that, if he did not keep his agreement with the emirs, he would be deemed to be as disgraced as a Christian who denies God and his law and who, in contempt of him, spits and tramples on the Cross. When the king heard this, he said that, please God, he would never make such an oath.

The emirs sent Master Nicholas, proficient in the Saracen language, to the king. This is what he said: 'My lord, after swearing exactly as you required, the emirs have taken great offence at your refusal to swear as they require. Rest assured, if you do not

[211] It was believed by almost every Western author in the Middle Ages that the tomb of Muḥammad was in Mecca not Medina.

[212] A reference to the norms of *ṭalāq*, according to which a man who has repudiated his wife three times may only take her back if she has remarried in the interim.

swear as they wish, they will have your head cut off, and the heads of all your people.' The king replied that they could do as they pleased in this regard. For he preferred to die a good Christian than to live under the wrath of God and his Mother.

The patriarch of Jerusalem,[213] an old and venerable man of eighty years, had procured a safe-conduct from the Saracens and had come to help the king secure his release. Now, the custom between Christians and Saracens is such that, when a king or a sultan dies, his envoys, whether they are travelling in pagan or Christian lands, are made prisoners and slaves. And because the sultan[214] who had granted the patriarch's safe-conduct was now dead, the patriarch was a prisoner just as we were. When the king had given his reply to the emirs, one of them said that he was acting on the patriarch's advice. He said to the other pagans, 'Trust me, I will make the king swear his oath by sending the patriarch's head flying into his lap.' The other emirs did not listen. Instead, they seized the patriarch, dragged him away from the king and bound him to a tent-pole, his hands tied so tightly behind his back that they swelled to the size of his head and blood seeped from his fingernails. The patriarch cried out to the king, 'My lord, for the love of God, you may swear in good conscience. For I will bear on my own soul any sin you commit by making it, since you truly desire to keep it.' I do not know how the oath was drawn up in the end, but the emirs were very satisfied by the words pronounced by the king and by the noblemen who were with him.

After the sultan's death, his instruments[215] were brought before the king's pavilion, and the king was told that the emirs had wanted nothing more than to make him sultan of Egypt; that was the advice which they had been given. He asked me whether I thought that he would have accepted the kingdom of Egypt if it had been offered to him. I said that he would have been mad to take it, considering these men had just murdered their lord. But he told me that he would not in fact have turned it down. I should say that nothing apparently came of this, if only because the emirs said that the king was the most steadfast Christian there was. The example they gave was that, whenever he left his lodgings, he would lie down on the ground in the shape of a cross and make the sign of the cross over his entire body. And they said that if Muḥammad had allowed such suffering to be inflicted on them they would never have had any faith in him; and that if they made the king their sultan, he would put them all to death, or else they would end up Christian.

[213] Robert of Nantes (d. 1254).

[214] Tūrānshāh had only been sultan of Egypt for a few months when he was murdered by Mamlūk rebels in May 1250. Joinville provides a graphic account.

[215] Customarily sounded before the sultan pronounced his orders.

76

John Mandeville, *Book of wonders*

Iain Macleod Higgins, University of Victoria

The *Livre des merveilles* ('Book of wonders') claims to be the work of an English knight, John Mandeville, who from 1322 until 1356 travelled as a Christian pilgrim and freelance adventurer through Constantinople to the Holy Land and beyond to India and Cathay (China). Afterwards, he purportedly set down in Old French what he could remember about the eastern world. No such John Mandeville has ever been identified, and the 'memoir' is a compilation, fusing the *Liber de quibusdam ultramarinis partibus* ('Book of certain regions beyond the Mediterranean', 1336) by William of Boldensele (d. 1338/9), a Dominican pilgrim, with the *Relatio* ('Account', 1330) by Odoric of Pordenone (d. 1331), a Franciscan missionary to India and China. On matters Islamic, the unknown compiler drew heavily on the *Tractatus de statu Sarracenorum* ('Treatise on the state of the Saracens', after 1273) by (Pseudo-)William of Tripoli.

The *Livre* itself was probably made in the later 1350s, either in England or in the French-speaking regions of north-western Europe, and it enjoyed widespread popularity for about two centuries. It survives not only in Insular and Continental French versions, but also in translation (into Czech, Danish, Dutch, English, German, Irish, Italian, Latin and Spanish). It remained popular enough that early printers issued copies in all these languages except Danish and Irish. The *Livre* takes an almost ethnographic approach to religions, viewing all but Judaism as more or less rational, and it praises pious living especially. It claims that Christians 'lost' the Holy Land to Muslims because of the latter's greater piety, that Islam is close to Christianity in many respects, and that if Christians were to reform themselves they would reconquer the Holy Land and lead Muslims to convert. The relative openness of the *Livre* to Islam and Muslims stands in sharp contrast to its attacks on Judaism and Jews.

CMR 5, pp. 147–64. See further:

I.M. Higgins (ed. and trans.), *The Book of John Mandeville with Related Texts*, Indianapolis, IN, 2011.

F. Grady, '"Machomete" and *Mandeville's Travels*', in H.A. Crocker and D.V. Smith (eds), *Medieval Literature: Criticism and Debates*, London, 2014, 266–75.

J.-P. Rubiés, 'Nature and Customs in Late Medieval Ethnography: Marco Polo and John Mandeville', in M. van der Lugt (ed.), *La nature comme source de la morale au Moyen Âge*, Florence, 2014, 189–232.

S. Khanmohamadi, *In Light of Another's Word. European Ethnography in the Middle Ages*, Philadelphia, PA, 2014.

This translation is based on Jean de Mandeville, *Le Livre des merveilles du monde*, ed. Christiane Deluz, Paris, 2000.

I dwelt with [the sultan of Egypt] as a soldier in his wars for some time against the Bedouins, and he would have married me very highly to a landed prince's daughter and given me great inheritances, had I wanted to renounce my Creator. But I had no desire to have anything that he could promise me.[216] [p. 134]

The city of Methon [Mecca] where Machomet lies[217] is [...] in the great deserts of Arabia; there his body lies most honourably in their temple that the Saracens call *Musket* [mosque]. [p. 142]

There still exists in Alexandria a beautiful church that is all white without paintings; the other churches that belonged to the Christians are also all white inside, for the pagans and the Saracens have them whitewashed to destroy the saints' images painted on the wall. [p. 162]

The tombs of the patriarchs Adam, Abraham, Isaac and Jacob are there [in Hebron] on the mountain slope [...] and above them is a beautiful crenellated church in the shape of a castle that the Saracens guard very carefully; they hold the place in great reverence because of the holy father patriarchs who lie there, and they do not allow Christians or Jews to enter unless they have the sultan's special permission; for they regard the Christians and the Jews as dogs and say that they ought not to enter so holy a place. [p. 175]

Quite close to Hebron [...] is an oak tree [...] from Abraham's time [...] called the Dry Tree. This tree is said to have been there since the beginning of the world. It was always green and leafy until Our Lord died on the cross; then it dried up. [...] Some prophecies say that a lord prince from the West will win the Promised Land with Christian help and have mass sung beneath this dry tree, and the tree will turn green again and bear leaf and fruit; through this miracle many Saracens and many Jews will be converted to the Christian law.[218] [p. 177]

---

[216] Since mediaeval Christians did serve Muslim rulers, this is a plausible claim, but the anecdote clearly mixes romance and hagiographical motifs to highlight the English knight's piety.

[217] A common mediaeval Christian error for Medina. To emphasize the historically and culturally located nature of the *Livre*'s often erroneous accounts of Islam, Muslims and the Prophet, the mediaeval names are not corrected here.

[218] This particular prophecy, one of several scattered throughout the *Livre*, fuses at least two mediaeval Christian legends.

The Saracens do not cultivate vines or drink any wine, for the books of their law that Machomet gave them – which they call Alkaron [...] prohibit them from drinking wine. For in this book Machomet curses all those who drink wine, wine [itself] and all those who sell it, because he was once accused of having killed a hermit whom he much loved through drunkenness; therefore, he cursed wine and wine-drinkers.[219] But the curses would come back on him, as David says in the Psalter: 'And his iniquity shall come down on him.'[220] The Saracens do not raise pigs nor eat any flesh of the pig at all, for they say that it is man's brother, and that it was prohibited in the Old Testament, and they consider those who eat it to be desperate.[221] [pp. 180–1]

The Saracens very greatly revere that Temple[222] and indeed say that the place is most holy, and they enter shoeless and kneel often. When my companions and I saw that, we took our shoes off and thought that we ought to do much better than the misbelievers, and we had great compunction in our hearts. [p. 201]

When Isaac was eight days old Abraham had him circumcised and Ishmael with him, who was fourteen years old. Therefore, the Jews, who are descendants of Isaac, are circumcised at eight days, and the Saracens, who are descendants of Ishmael, are circumcised at fourteen years of age.[223] [p. 228]

If you want to know a part of [Saracen] law and belief,[224] I will describe them to you according to what their book named Alkoran explains. [...] Machomet gave them this book, in which is written, amongst other things, as I have often read and seen, that the good will go to Paradise and the bad to hell, and this all Saracens believe. [p. 272]

Also, they believe in [...] the Virgin Mary and the Incarnation. [...] This book also says that Jesus was sent by God Almighty to be a mirror [...] to all men. The Alkoran also speaks about Judgement Day, [...] and [that] amongst all the prophets Jesus is the most excellent, and the closest to God, and that He made the Gospels in which there is good teaching and healthy guidance, clarity, truth, and true preaching to those who believe in God. [...] When they can get the book where the Gospels of Our Lord are written ... those who are literate say this Gospel in their prayers and they kiss it and honour it with great devotion. [pp. 273–5]

Because they come so close to our faith, they are easily converted to Christian law when one preaches to them and shows them clearly Jesus Christ's law and explains the prophecies to them. They also say that they know by the prophecies that

[219] A common Christian slander against the Prophet, probably borrowed from (Pseudo-)William's *Tractatus*. The figure of the Christian hermit, often named Baḥīrā or Sergius, appears in both Christian and Muslim biographical accounts of Muḥammad from early times.

[220] Psalm 7:17. Note how the Christian author quotes a Hebrew author accepted as a Christian prophet against the Islamic Prophet.

[221] Both the Hebrew Bible and the Qur'an prohibit the eating of pork: e.g. Leviticus 11:7-8 and Q 2:173.

[222] The Dome of the Rock in Jerusalem, converted into a church at the time of the First Crusade.

[223] Genesis 17:9-14 explains male circumcision at eight days of age as a sign of God's covenant with Abraham. There is no scripturally based practice of circumcision at fourteen in Islam, particularly not one based on Genesis.

[224] The information in this and the next two paragraphs is adapted from (Pseudo-)William; there is no evidence that 'Mandeville' read the Qur'an.

Machomet's law will fail, just like the Jews' law, [...] and that the Christian people's law will last until the world's end. [p. 276]

It often happens that a Christian becomes Saracen, either out of simple-mindedness or poverty, or out of wickedness; and the archflamens or flamens [chief priests or priests] when they receive them say *La illec ella sila Machomet Roses Alla hec*. That is in English: There is no god but One alone and Machomet [is] his prophet.[225] [p. 283]

I have seen pagans and Saracens called augurs who, when we rode out in arms somewhere against our enemies, would by the flight of the birds predict everything that we afterwards found [happened]. They did this many times and pledged their lives that it would be so. But one should not therefore put all one's faith in such things, but should always have hope in Our Lord. [p. 317]

He ['the Great Chan of Cathay'] has two hundred Christian physicians, and he has two hundred and ten Christian medics and also two hundred Saracen physicians, for they put much more faith in the work of Christians than of Saracens. [p. 396]

[225] This version of the *shahāda*, or Muslim profession of faith, comes from (Pseudo-)William's *Tractatus*. The *Livre* also borrowed (Pseudo-)William's remarkable claim that the *shahāda* was a kind of baptismal formula.

77

Juan Manuel, *Book of estates*

Anita Savo, Boston University

Don Juan Manuel (1282–1349) was recognized as one of the most powerful nobles in the kingdom of Castile. He controlled significant territories in Castile and Aragon, and was nephew to King Alfonso X of Castile (r. 1252–84), though he was never in line to inherit the throne. He held the position of *adelantado* (governor) in Murcia on the frontier between Christian Castile and the Islamic kingdom of Granada, which at that time was ruled by the Naṣrid dynasty. As a military leader, he fought in a number of battles during the Christian reconquest of lands under Islamic dominion, though he was prepared to forge an alliance with the Naṣrid king of Granada when he rebelled against his own king, Alfonso XI of Castile (r. 1312–50), during the political turbulence between 1327 and 1329.

As a writer, Juan Manuel compiled or composed works in many genres, including chronicles on the history of Spain, treatises on hunting, manuals of royal and courtly behaviour, didactic literature, poetry and rules of poetic composition, and religious treatises. The *Libro de los estados* ('Book of estates'), written *c.* 1327–30, is loosely based on the legend of Barlaam and Josaphat, a Christianized version of the life of the Buddha which circulated widely in the later Middle Ages. It consists mainly of a dialogue between the pagan Prince Johás and the Christian preacher Julio. Julio is charged with teaching the prince about the various estates, or social categories, of society and how to fulfil the responsibilities of his own estate as ruler. In the excerpts below, Julio explains the origins of Islam and the reason for wars between Christians and Muslims from an orthodox Christian perspective. He also describes the military prowess of Muslim soldiers in vivid detail, in a passage drawing upon the author's first-hand experience.

These passages illustrate Juan Manuel's ambivalence towards Iberian Muslims: while his doctrinal opposition to Islam is without question, his writings show admiration for them in secular matters such as warfare, leadership and generosity. In his most famous work, the *Libro del conde Lucanor* ('Book of Count Lucanor'), he recounts several stories which present Muslim rulers as examples worthy of imitation. The *Libro de los estados* is of special interest for the way in which its author attempts to reconcile theological arguments against Islam drawn from religious polemics with a sincere appreciation for Iberian Muslims' technological and cultural contributions to Christian society.

This translation is based on the edition published in Juan Manuel, *Libro de los estados*, ed. I.R. Macpherson and R.B. Tate, Madrid, 1991. See further:

H.T. Sturcken, *Don Juan Manuel*, New York, 1974 (a comprehensive introduction to the life and works of Juan Manuel).

A. Savo, 'The Hidden Polemic in Juan Manuel's *Libro de los estados*', *La Corónica* 44 (2016) 5–28 (posits that the *Book of estates* is unusual in defending the prerogative of lay Christians to write about and participate in religious disputations against Muslims and Jews).

M. Cossío Olavide, '*Algunos moros muy sabidores*: Virtuous Muslim kings in Examples 30 and 41 of *El conde Lucanor*', *Bulletin of Spanish Studies* 97 (2020) 127–38 (argues that Juan Manuel upholds Muslim kings as a positive example for Christian rulers in his *Book of Count Lucanor*).

Book 1, Chapter 30

A long time after Jesus Christ was crucified there came a false man named Muḥammad, and he preached in Arabia and made some foolish people believe that he was a prophet sent by God. And he preached a very lax religion which allowed the people to do whatever they wanted, wantonly and quite without reason. And so the poor people, thinking that by doing whatever they wanted they could save their souls, believed him and accepted as law the vanities he told them. And there were so many people who believed him that they conquered and took power over many lands that they still have today, which belonged to Christians who had been converted by the Apostles to the faith of Jesus Christ. And for this reason there is war between Christians and Muslims,[226] and there will be until the Christians have recovered the lands which the Muslims have taken from them by force; for if it were only for their religion or sect, there would not be war between them. For Jesus Christ never commanded Christians to kill or force anyone to take His religion, because He does not want forced service, but rather one given willingly and gladly. And good Christians believe that the reason why God allowed the Christians to receive such harm from the Muslims is to give them a reason to wage just war against them,[227] so that those who should die in battle having fulfilled the Holy Church's commandments would be martyrs, and through this martyrdom their souls would be cleansed of the sins which they committed.

---

[226] *Moros*; Juan Manuel's use of the term carries no pejorative implications, so is best translated as here. See further R. Brann, 'The Moors?', *Medieval Encounters* 15 (2009) 307–18.

[227] This notion of just war belongs to a mediaeval Christian tradition dating back to Augustine of Hippo (d. 430), in which war is considered legitimate when waged with a rightful intention, such as recovering wrongfully seized lands. Knights and nobles such as Juan Manuel understood that the Christian struggle against the Muslims in Spain was motivated not by religious belief but in response to their acquisition of lands perceived as rightfully Christian.

And the sect of the Muslims is complete nonsense in so many things and in so many ways that anyone with understanding will see that no one can be saved in it; first, because of this, and second, because it was not given by God or one of his prophets, and for this reason it is not a religion, but rather an erroneous sect in which they were placed by that bad man Muḥammad, who tricked them. [pp. 116–17]

Book 1, Chapters 75–6

My lord Prince, the warfare of Muslims is not like that of Christians, both in the waging of war and when they lay siege and attack, or are under siege or being attacked, and likewise in cavalry and raids, and in the way they move on the roads and set up camp, and in battle; in everything the one way is very different from the other.

For they wage war very masterfully, because they are often on the move and get by with very little food, and they never take foot-soldiers or mules with them, but rather each man goes on horseback, including the lords and all the others, and they carry no food other than a little bread and some figs or raisins, or some other fruit. And they carry no armour other than leather shields, and their weapons are small spears which they throw and swords with which they wound. And because they carry themselves so lightly, they can travel long distances. And when they go on an expedition, they travel as much as they can by night and by day, until they are as deep as they can be in the land they want to raid. When they invade, they invade very stealthily and very swiftly, and when they begin a raid, they raid and ravage so much land, and they know how to do this so well, that it is quite marvellous how they can raid more land and do more damage and mount a better attack with two hundred Muslim horsemen than with six hundred Christian ones.

And they do another thing which is very effective for war: however much [booty] they take, no man will take or hide any of it for himself, but instead they collect everything together for the good of the whole troop. And if one of them were to take or hide anything from the rest of the troop, each one of them would consider it such a serious lapse and fault, and it would be so condemned, that it would be comparable to a Christian who fled from battle. [...]

And in truth I tell you, lord Prince, that they are such good fighters, and know so much about war, and wage it so well, that if not for the fact that they must – and indeed do – have God against them because of the false sect they live in, and also because they are not equipped with weapons and horses in such a way that they could endure injuries or fight in combat like [Christian] knights can;[228] if it were not for these two things, I would say that there are no better fighters in the world, and none more knowledgeable about war, and none better prepared for so many conquests. [pp. 222–5]

---

[228] A reference to the Christian practice of equipping knights with heavy weapons and armour, in contrast to the Islamic style of swift, lightly armed cavalry.

78

Bertrandon de la Broquière, *Voyage to the Middle East*

Attila Bárány, University of Debrecen

Bertrandon de la Broquière (*c.* 1400–59) was 'first esquire' and counsellor to Philip the Good, duke of Burgundy (1419–67). His travels from Jerusalem through Anatolia, the Balkans and Hungary in 1431–3 were recorded in *Le voyage d'Oultremer* ('The voyage to the Middle East'), composed between 1438 and the late 1450s. The four surviving manuscripts, all held at the Bibliothèque nationale de France in Paris, were made in 1455–7.

The *Voyage* is not only a 'guide-book' for pilgrims. The overland route was chosen by Philip to obtain intelligence for a prospective Crusade against the Ottomans, and Bertrandon was to 'learn of the cities, towns, lands, rivers, mountains, access routes', and their lords. However, he was not only a spy, and beyond providing information on the Ottoman military he had an intellectual curiosity unusual for a pre-Renaissance traveller. The text is a keen narrative by an outspoken eyewitness.

Bertrandon joins pilgrims returning from Mecca. He makes every effort to become acquainted with Islam and Muḥammad. He brings home a translation of the Qur'an for his duke. Dressed in Turkish clothes, he seeks to get closer to Muslims, who share their meals and take him to the baths. He shows no aversion or bias whatsoever as he describes their prayers. Although he is moved by churches being 'now converted into mosques', he is impressed by some trustworthy Turks, and develops fraternal affection for a Mamlūk. He is concerned about the 'severe captivity' of Christians under the Turks and shocked by slave-taking excursions and the unheard-of level of obedience, he meets renegades and is moved by captives 'bursting into tears', but he is also distrustful of the unreliable Byzantines and finds the Slavs, who submit themselves and 'dare not refuse', to be double-dealing. The extracts translated below witness some of his complex interactions with Muslims.

CMR 5, pp. 443–6. See further:

A.J. Vanderjagt, 'La Broquière, Bertrandon de (c. 1400–1459)', in J.B. Friedman and K. Mossler Figg (eds), *Trade, Travel, and Exploration in the Middle Ages: An Encyclopedia*, New York, 2000, 325–6.

M. Coman, 'Experiencing Otherness. Bertrandon de la Broquière's Pilgrimage to Jerusalem (1432)', in I. Vainovski-Mihai (ed.), *New Europe College Yearbook (2007–2008)*, Bucharest, 2008, 85–120.

A. Classen, 'The Diplomat Pilgrim Bertrandon de la Broquière', in A. Classen (ed.), *East Meets West in the Middle Ages and Early Modern Times: Transcultural Experiences in the Premodern World*, Berlin, 2013, 49–56.

C. Ferlampin-Acher, 'Le Voyage d'Outremer de Bertrandon de la Broquière: récit de pèlerinage, rapport d'espionnage ou récit de voyage?', *Travaux de Littérature* 26 (2013) 11–22.

J. Svátek, 'L'idéal du souverain oriental dans le récit de Bertrandon de la Broquière', *Publications du Centre Européen d'Études Bourguignonnes* 56 (2016) 61–72.

B. Stojkovski, 'Bertrandon de la Broquière on Byzantium and Serbia. Richness and Decline in the Age of the Ottoman Conquest of the Balkans', in E. Juhász (ed.), *Byzanz und das Abendland V. Studia Byzantino-Occidentalia 2017*, Budapest, 2018, pp. 115–31.

M. Rossabi, 'Introduction', in *A Mission to the Medieval Middle East: Travels of Bertrandon de la Broquière to Jerusalem and Constantinople*, trans. T. Johnes, London, 2019, pp. vii–xvii.

The passages below are translated from the original French edition by S. Cappellini, 'The Voyage d'Oultre Mer by Bertrandon de la Broquière (1432–1433): An Enlightened Journey in the World of the Levant', Baltimore, MD, 1999 (2 vols, PhD thesis, Johns Hopkins University).

[The treatment of pilgrims]

Desert Arabs [...] have authority to escort pilgrims [...]. [The Great Interpreter][229] asked our name, surname and age and recorded it in writing, with physiognomic[230] [descriptions], whether we had any traces of wounds [...], our heights and appearance. A copy [...] is sent to [...] Cairo [...] for the safety of pilgrims so that the Arabs do not detain any. [p. 481]

[I had to] dress like Saracens; the sultan authorized the Franks to [wear] Saracen clothes for their safety. [p. 495]

Pilgrims are often maltreated [...]; we would have been harmed if [the governor] had not attended us kindly [...]. He wanted to do us due justice. [...] We appealed to him [...] as we had disputes with some guides. [p. 483]

[In Hebron] Abraham, Isaac and Jacob [...] are buried in a mosque. [...] We had wanted to get in, but our interpreters would only dare to take us in at night. [...] No

---

[229] The *grant trucheman* (Arabic *tarjumān*, Turkish *tercüman*), a senior official in Mamlūk Egypt.

[230] French *les philosomies.*

Christian dares to enter their mosques on pain of death or having to renounce [his] faith. [p. 482]

In the desert we stayed in a *khan*, [...] built through charity so that travellers could find shelter. [p. 482]

No Christian [...] dares to ride a horse in cities.[231] [In Damascus ...] I was wearing a wide felt hat, which is unusual [...], and a Saracen knocked it off my head. [...] It is useless to quarrel with them: they [are] wicked and of low intellect. [...] One should not seem weak, nor show that one is afraid, [...] or rich, because they are covetous and hardly ever contented. [...] Christians are much hated here. [...] I was wrongly arrested [as] I came on pilgrimage; [the governor] allowed me to leave. [...] A guide carried my Turkish clothes outside; no Christian dares to wear white headdress in the city. [pp. 490, 493, 495, 512]

[Muḥammad and the Qur'an]

The Qur'an is the law which Muḥammad, the false prophet, left to the Saracens. [... They] claim that after they have once been to Mecca, they can do nothing for which they can be damned. There must be seven hundred thousand pilgrims every year. [A renegade slave] often kept me company [...]. I asked him between us about Muḥammad. When Judgement Day comes, Muḥammad will let [...] people into Paradise as he pleases. [pp. 502–4]

So much was said about Muḥammad that [...] I asked a priest. [...] He knew well their entire Qur'an. I begged him [...] to provide me in writing what he knew. [p. 505]

[Ablutions and prayers]

They wash their hands, faces, and all their noses, mouths and ears, and take off their shoes, [...] turn their faces towards the south, raise two fingers of each hand, kneel down and kiss the ground, and repeat this three times. [p. 516]

[Wine]

[Some Turks] pursued me [... to] get wine in secret; [...] it is forbidden by their law. If [...] a Frank gave wine, he would be reprimanded. [...] To have a pretext [...] they made haste to seize [me]. [p. 519]

[The sultan's] greatest pleasure is drinking. [...] A Moor came to preach [...] that those who drink wine violate the commandments of the Prophet and are not good Saracens. He threw him into prison. [p. 588]

[Bertrandon's relations with his hosts]

The Arab [guide] kept me in good company, which they do not usually do with Christians. [...] He had me stay in one of their tents. [...] They saw that I was ill, [...] cured me in

[231] Following the regulation in the *Pact of ʿUmar*.

their own way, kneaded and pinched me. [...] They did not take anything from me, nor did me any harm, though they could have done so. [p. 485]

I found [the chief of the caravan] full of honesty, more than I would have [done ...] among many Christians. [p. 506]

[The Turks] were making much effort to teach me to speak [the language]. [p. 509]

They did not bother me but were pleased when [...] I was saying my paternosters,[232] which seemed marvellous to them. [In their prayers] they sit in a circle, sway their bodies and heads, and sing wildly.[233] [p. 528]

[At] baths [...] I did not dare to undress. [...] They gave me their clothes [...]; I found myself closer to them. They are charitable towards each other and have a solid faith. [p. 529]

When a poor man passed by, they called him over to eat with us, which we would not do. [p. 529]

[The Mamlūk companion]

[The] Mamlūk [...] took me along, out of benevolence. [...] Two Turkmen [wanted] to kill me, since I was a Christian and unworthy [of] their company. The Mamlūk replied that it would be wrong and a sin against their law because I had eaten [...] with them. God made Christians like Saracens. [... He] had so many good things for me [...], he did for me as for himself, [... he was] a man not of our faith. [...] He warned me to beware of Saracens: some [are] as bad as the Franks. [pp. 513–15, 546]

[Slaves]

It is distressing [to see] Christians [...] being sold [and the] hardships they suffer. [They had] chains coiled up around their necks. [...] I feel great pity for a [...] woman [...] whom a renegade [...] had captured [...] and considered his wife. [...] She began to cry pitifully [but] had not yet renounced our faith. [pp. 554–5, 601, 605]

---

[232] Saying his prayers, the Paternoster being the Lord's Prayer.

[233] Evidently *dhikr* ('remembrance') ceremonies, rather than the formal prayers recited five times each day. This form of invocation, typical of Sufi orders, is intended to induce a trance-like state in which the worshipper achieves heightened awareness of God.

79

Hernando de Talavera, *Instruction from the Archbishop of Granada*

Anita Savo, Boston University

Fray Hernando de Talavera (*c.* 1430–1507) was a priest in the Hieronymite Order (an enclosed religious order following the example of St Jerome), best known as the confessor and counsellor to Queen Isabel of Castile (r. 1474–1504), and for a time to her husband King Fernando of Aragon (r. 1479–1516). Probably born into a family of *converso* origin, he studied theology at the University of Salamanca and was ordained to the priesthood in 1460. In 1486 he became bishop of Ávila, where his experience with local Jewish and Mudéjar communities may have helped him earn his position as the first archbishop of Granada after the Islamic kingdom's capitulation to Isabella and Fernando, the Catholic Monarchs, in 1492.

Hernando de Talavera was doctrinally committed to eradicating Islam, and favoured the means of evangelization through individual persuasion, which he sought to achieve by commissioning Arabic translations of the catechism and encouraging his priests to learn Arabic. This stood in stark contrast to the forced conversions implemented by his rival, Francisco Jiménez de Cisneros, archbishop of Toledo, upon his arrival in Granada in 1499. In 1506 the Inquisition brought charges of 'Judaizing' against Talavera and his family, but Pope Julius II dismissed them in April 1507, shortly before the friar's death on May 14.

Among Talavera's catechetical works is the *Instrucción del Arzobispo de Granada* ('Instruction from the Archbishop of Granada'), also known as the *Memorial y tabla de ordenaciones dirigidas por Talavera para la comunidad morisca de Granada* ('Memorandum and list of ordinances given by Talavera to the Morisco community of Granada'). This brief treatise is addressed to the residents of the Albaicín neighbourhood, who had rebelled against Cisneros's policy of forced conversions for a three-day period in December 1499, but ultimately submitted to mass baptism. Modern historians use the term *Moriscos* for these converted Muslims who remained in Spain, but during Talavera's time the word referred to Muslims and Islamic practices. In his treatise of *c.* 1500, Talavera demonstrates a two-pronged approach to integrating his newly converted parishioners into Christian society, instructing them in religious rites such as the sacraments and also recommending customs such as sartorial and culinary practices.

While Talavera's modern reputation is as a relatively tolerant religious leader with a sincere appreciation for Islamic texts, the *Instrucción* reveals his draconian policy of exacting the absolute submission of Morisco subjects to the religious, political and cultural hegemony of the Catholic Monarchs. Talavera fits the mould of Christian clerics and scholars whose deep knowledge of Islam remained firmly in service of their orthodox position against it.

CMR 6, pp. 60–6. See further:

M. García Arenal, 'Granada as a New Jerusalem: The Conversion of a City', in G. Marcocci et al. (eds), *Space and Conversion in Global Perspective*, Leiden, 2014, 15–43.

M.D. Johnston, 'Hernando de Talavera on Conduct: Cultural Hegemony in Post-Conquest Granada', *Confluencia* 30 (2015) 11–22.

This translation is based on the edition published in M.A. Ladero Quesada, *Granada después de la conquista. Repobladores y mudéjares*, 2nd edition, Granada, 1993, pp. 545–8.

IHS.[234]

Dearly beloved in Our Lord, good residents of the Albaicín: I have seen your petition, and it pleases me very much to see the great care which you place in knowing about and doing what good Christians are obliged to do. I have failed to visit you as frequently as I did at the beginning, because many concerns and time constraints have impeded me; moreover, having provided such good vicars as I have, my presence was not needed at first. But now that time permits and the situation requires it, I will emend this with the help of Our Lord, even though my cares continue to grow. But so that you all have a complete account and reminder of what I have told you, I have written this summary of what I wish you to uphold.

First, you shall forget all Morisco ceremonies and practices, including prayers, fasting, holidays, celebrations, births, weddings, bathing, burial preparations and all other such things.

You shall know – and make sure your wives and sons and daughters, big and small, know – how to make the sign of the cross, and bless yourselves, and enter and be in the church, and take holy water there; and say the Pater Noster, the Ave Maria and the Creed; and worship Our Lord during Holy Mass, and worship the Holy Cross, and make due reverence to all images there.[235]

---

[234] The first three letters of the name of Jesus in Greek.

[235] The emphasis on images (*imágenes*) both here and in the section on church conduct suggests a concern that the recent converts should demonstrate their willingness to worship saints and their figural images, practices considered idolatrous in Islam.

You shall be sure to confess and take Communion, and have your wives and all those of your households do the same.

You shall be sure that your children are baptized within eight days, or before if you see that it is necessary.

You shall be sure that they are confirmed as soon as possible.

When they get sick, have them receive the sacraments of Confession and Communion and, if they are near death, Extreme Unction.

Have them make their last will and testament and pious bequests as Catholic Christians, and let them and you be buried in blessed cemeteries near your churches, just as born Christians do.

Have them marry at the hand of the clergy, and when they do, they shall receive their marriage blessings in the church in what the Christians call a veiling ceremony.[236]

You shall have confraternities like the ones Christians have, to which you can turn for help in life and death.

You shall observe and ensure the proper observance of Sundays and feast days; and on these holy days you and those of your households will attend High Mass and Vespers, either in your parish, in the Church of San Salvador, or in the main church of this city.[237]

On working days during the week, you shall all go to church in the afternoon to pray and take holy water, so that God will have mercy on you in all that you do and in your work, and if you are able to hear Mass in the afternoon, that would be best.

You shall send your children to the churches to learn how to read and sing, or at the very least to learn the prayers mentioned above.

Those who know how to read shall carry with you all the books in Arabic which will be given to you containing prayers and Psalms and this memorandum, and pray with them in church.

You and those of your household shall fast according to the fasts of the Christians, following how they do them and how they should be done.

Whenever people go to take Communion [outside the church], you shall accompany the body of Our Lord until returning to the church.[238]

Those who are able shall be present to bury your dead and attend their masses and vigils.

You shall have one or two hospitals dedicated to treating and consoling those who are poor and ill and in need, and these hospitals shall be maintained by alms which are given and collected amongst yourselves.

You shall have in your homes, in decorous and clean places, some images of Our Lord, or the Holy Cross, or Our Lady the Virgin Mary, or some male or female saint.

---

236 This refers to the traditional Castilian veiling ceremony, in which typically the bride's head was veiled and the priest draped a white and purple cord over the shoulders of the couple.

237 Like most parish churches in Granada at this time, the Church of San Salvador in the Albaicín (today called Iglesia del Salvador) was a converted mosque.

238 Christians were expected to accompany the priest carrying the host at least to the end of the street, while Muslims and Jews were required either to kneel with heads bowed or to vacate the street.

Near that image you shall hang the blessed candle which is blessed for you on the Day of Our Lady who is called Santa María Candelaria, and on the other side the blessed palm which is blessed on Palm Sunday. All this pertains to the service of Our Lord God and the good keeping of our Holy Catholic Faith.

But so that your company does not cause any scandal to born Christians, and so they do not think that you still keep the sect of Muḥammad in your hearts, you must conform in every way to the good and honest company of good and honest Christian men and women: in your dress, footwear and grooming;[239] in your diet, eating practices and in preparing food as Christians usually prepare it; in the way you walk and give and take; and most of all in the way you talk, forgetting the Arabic language as much as you can, letting it be forgotten and not allowing it to be spoken in your homes.

And because some people will require some kind of coercion to uphold the things that have been mentioned, and because the excommunication which I could impose is both very dangerous and not much feared among you, it is necessary that you and I together entreat our lord and lady, the king and queen, to impose penalties against those who do not obey and executors to enforce them.

[239] The word *afeytar* typically denoted beard grooming but could also refer to haircuts, hair styling and makeup.

Table of themes

Theme	Passage number
apostasy	25, 33, 34, 57, 69
Biblical predictions of Muḥammad	4, 6, 9, 70
Christian morals	11, 12, 41, 65
Christian preaching	66, 67, 68, 70, 73, 79
Christian and Muslim coexistence	3, 62, 65, 76
conversion to Islam	23, 27, 34, 35, 63, 67, 68, 71, 73, 76, 79
corruption of the Bible	8, 9, 13, 15, 26, 28, 39, 42, 70
divorce	28, 29, 31, 33, 75
God as substance	5, 10, 18, 19, 24
Hagar	29, 31
heretical monk	31, 32, 44, 76
homosexual practices	22, 36, 57, 59
Ishmael	4, 31, 40, 76
Islam as a Christian heresy	31, 54, 60, 62, 65, 77
Jews	3, 8, 14, 20, 31, 32, 37, 40
martyrdom	25, 34, 38, 55, 57, 63, 65, 66
miracles	20, 25, 28, 39, 43, 44, 49, 67, 74
Muḥammad	31, 32, 40, 46, 60, 76, 77
as an epileptic	32, 44, 60
worship of	72, 73, 74
Pact of ʿUmar	2, 3, 14, 21, 23, 44, 78
poll-tax	1, 27, 41, 44, 50, 52
polygamy	31, 41
Trinity	5, 10, 18, 19, 24, 31, 35
veneration of images	37, 46, 79
veneration of the Cross	31, 42, 48, 50, 79
Virgin Mary	17, 20, 28, 31, 33, 76

Glossary

ʿAbbasids	the second major Islamic dynasty, 750–1258
abrogation (*naskh*)	cancelling of one verse or whole scripture by another
Agarenes	*see* Hagarenes
AH (*Anno hegirae*)	the Muslim lunar dating system starting from 622 CE, the year of the *hijra* (Muḥammad's migration)
Ahl al-dhimma	*see* People of the Covenant
Ahl al-kitāb	*see* People of the Book
Al-Andalus	the Islamic state in the south of the Iberian Peninsula
Armenian	the language used by Christians in north-eastern parts of the Islamic Empire
Ashʿariyya	a Muslim theological school named after Abū l-Ḥasan al-Ashʿarī (d. 935) that advocated the use of reason to defend Qur'an-based teachings
Ayyūbids	a dynasty that ruled Egypt and Syria, 1169–*c.* 1260
Byzantine Empire	the continuing Roman Empire after the capital was moved to Constantinople in the early fourth century; it was overthrown by the Ottoman Turks in 1453
c.	*circa* or 'about'
caliph (*khalīfa*)	deputy or representative of the Prophet, the title of the ruler of the Islamic Empire
Catholicos	the title of the senior bishop of some Eastern Churches
Chalcedon	Church Council convened in 451, which defined the relationship between the divine and human natures in Christ
Church of the East	one of the denominations that rejected the teaching of Chalcedon, holding that Christ's divine and human natures were distinct; it was one of the three major denominations within the Islamic Empire, known (inaccurately) as the *Nasṭūriyya*, followers of Nestorius
CMR	*Christian-Muslim Relations, a Bibliographical History*, Leiden, 2009-, a comprehensive history of the known works on Christian-Muslim relations from throughout the world; vols 1–5 cover the years 600–1500

Commander of the Faithful *or* Believers (*amīr al-mu'minīn*)	a title of the caliph
Conversos	originally Muslims who remained in Spain under Christian rule, later Spanish Muslim converts to Christianity
convivencia, 'coexistence'	the supposed harmonious existence between Muslims and Christians in Islamic Spain
Coptic Orthodox Church	the main Christian denomination in Egypt, distinguished by its miaphysite Christology
corruption (*taḥrīf*)	usually of the Torah or Gospel, alteration either by misinterpretation or change to the actual text
dhāt	*see* essence
dhimmīs	*see* People of the Covenant
dīnār	the main unit of currency in the Arab Islamic world
diophysites	Christians who hold that in the person of Christ the divine and human natures remained distinct; known in the Islamic Empire as Nestorians
divine nature (*lāhūt*)	one of the two natures that united in Christ
East Syriac Church	*see* Church of the East
Eastern Roman Empire	*see* Byzantine Empire
emir (*amīr*)	commander, prince
essence (*dhāt*)	the actual being of God
Fāṭimids	the Shī'a caliphate in Egypt, 909–1171, claiming descent from the Prophet's daughter Fāṭima
Franks (*Ifranj*)	Europeans, usually crusaders from Western Europe who from the late eleventh century onwards sought to reclaim the Christian holy places
Ḥadīth (simplified here to Hadith)	the collected sayings of Muḥammad, accepted alongside the Qur'an as an authoritative basis of *sharī'a*
Hagarenes	Arabs or Muslims as descendants of Abraham through his servant Hagar, distinguished from Jews and Christians as descendants through his wife Sarah
hagiography	idealised biography, particularly of a saint
ḥalāl	items, particularly foodstuffs, and actions permitted under Islamic law
ḥarām	items, particularly foodstuffs, and actions forbidden under Islamic law
ḥulūl	*see* inhabitation
human nature (*nāsūt*)	one of the two natures that united in Christ

imam (*imām*)	a political or religious leader, often a leader in congregational prayer or religious teacher
inhabitation (*ḥulūl*)	the indwelling of the divine Word in the person of Christ
Injīl	according to the Qur'an a single revelation given to Jesus that was later either corrupted or lost
Ishmaelites	Arabs and Muslims as descendants of Abraham's son Ishmael
ittiḥād (union)	the uniting of the divine and human in Christ
Jacobites (*Ya'qūbiyya*)	churches following the teachings of Jacob Baradeus, distinguished by their miaphysite Christology
jawhar	usually a technical term used in *kalām*; in Christian usage, the substance of God; in Muslim usage, a unit of physical bodies
jihād	'striving in the way of God', usually referring to armed struggle to propagate or defend the faith and community of Islam
jizya	*see* poll-tax
kalām (discourse)	the form of speculative theology that was employed by Arabic-speaking Muslims and Christians in the early Islamic era; it was used both to defend religious teachings and to demonstrate their rational coherence
khalīfa	*see* caliph
lāhūt	*see* divine nature
majlis (pl. *majālis*)	a formal debating session
Mamlūks	the 'slave' dynasty that ruled in Egypt and Syria, 1250–1517
Melkites	Christians who accepted the Christology of the Council of Chalcedon, that the divine and human natures in Christ were united but retained their individual identities; known to Arabic-speaking Muslims as *Malkiyya*, they were one of the three major denominations in the Islamic Empire
miaphysites	Christians who hold that the divine and human in Christ united into a single nature
monophysites	another term for miaphysites
Moors, *Moros*	the term for Muslims habitually used by Spanish-speaking Christians
Moriscos	originally Muslims living in Spain under Christian rule, later Spanish Muslims who converted (outwardly at least) to Christianity
mutakallim (pl. *mutakallimūn*)	Arabic-speaking Muslim and Christian practitioners of *kalām*; roughly equivalent to 'theologian'
Mu'tazila	a school of *kalām* that prioritized the use of reason in theological enquiry, flourishing mainly in the ninth and tenth centuries

Naṣārā ('Nazarenes')	the term for Christians in the Qur'an and Islam
naskh	*see* abrogation
nāsūt	*see* human nature
Nestorians (*Nasṭūriyya*)	*see* Church of the East
Ottomans	a Muslim Turkish tribe that settled in north-west Anatolia, it became prominent in the thirteenth century, capturing Constantinople in 1453 and establishing an empire that lasted into the twentieth century
Pact of ʿUmar (*Shurūṭ ʿUmar*)	regulations attributed to the second caliph ʿUmar ibn al-Khaṭṭāb that governed relations between Muslims and non-Muslims in the Islamic Empire
People of the Book (*Ahl al-kitāb*)	Jews, Christians and other communities named in the Qur'an as recipients of revealed scriptures
People of the Covenant (*Ahl al-dhimma* or *dhimmīs*)	communities that had received revealed scriptures, given protection in the Islamic state in return for payment of the poll tax
poll-tax (*jizya*)	a tax levied by Muslim authorities on non-Muslims
Qurʾān (simplified here as Qur'an and abbreviated to Q)	the Holy Book of Islam, believed to have been revealed to Muḥammad between 610 and 632
renegade (*renegado*)	used in Spain and elsewhere for a Christian who had converted to Islam
reconquista	the gradual process by which Christian armies in Spain won territory from Muslim rule
risāla (pl. *rasāʾil*)	letter or treatise
Saracens	used in Christian works to refer to Muslim Arabs or to any Muslims
Seljuks	Turkish tribes from Central Asia, branches of which ruled in Iraq, Syria and other parts of the Islamic Empire in the eleventh and twelfth centuries
sharīʿa	the body of legal teachings based on Qur'an and Hadith that provides a legal and moral 'path' for Muslim life
Shīʿa Muslims	followers of Muḥammad's cousin and son-in-law ʿAlī and a number of his descendants, who for them are inspired teachers; one of the main divisions in Islam
shirk	association of another being with God
sīra	a biography of Muḥammad, usually referring to the eighth-century work by Ibn Isḥāq

substance (*jawhar*)	used by Arabic-speaking Christians for the element common to the three Persons of the Trinity, but by Muslims for a unit of physical matter
sultan (*sulṭān*)	a title for the person with actual power in an Islamic state
Sunna	the sayings, actions and signs of approval of Muḥammad, forming a comprehensive example for Muslim conduct
Sunnī Muslims	Muslims who follow the example of the Prophet as recorded in his *Sunna*; the largest division in Islam
Syriac	a major language in the Middle East in pre-Islamic times, in the early Islamic period it was mainly spoken by Christians in northern Syria and Mesopotamia
Syriac Orthodox Church	known to Arabic-speaking Muslims as the *Yāʿqubiyya* after the sixth-century bishop Jacob Baradeus, it rejected the Chalcedonian teaching about Christ, holding a miaphysite Christology; one of the three major Christian denominations in the Islamic world
taḥrīf	*see* textual corruption
Tawrāt	according to the Qur'an the revelation given to Moses, believed by Muslims to have suffered corruption in transmission
Umayyads	the first major dynasty of Islam, 661–750
vizier (*wazīr*)	the senior minister under a caliph or sultan
waqf	an inalienable financial endowment made for a religious purpose such as maintenance of a mosque or school
West Syriac Church	*see* Syriac Orthodox Church
Yaʿqūbiyya	*see* Jacobites
Zabūr	the name in the Qur'an for the Psalms of David
Zoroastrians	dualists who believed in two supreme opposing forces, following the ancient Iranian teacher Zoroaster
zunnār	a belt or sash worn by Christians, Jews and Zoroastrians in Islamic society, which became the most distinctive sign of the *dhimmī* status

Index

'Abbasid dynasty 1, 9, 12, 13, 23, 28, 35, 51, 68, 105, 129, 169, 218, 300
'Abd al-Jabbār al-Hamadhānī 37–40
'Abd al-Masīḥ al-Kindī 76–8
'Abd al-Raḥmān III, Spanish Umayyad caliph 239–41
Abraham, patriarch 31, 39, 63, 71, 75, 119, 121–2, 133, 134, 137, 173, 174, 192, 203, 217, 244, 279, 306, 307, 313
Abū l-Hudhayl al-'Allāf 79
Abū 'Īsā l-Warrāq 27–9
Abū l-Qāsim 'Alī al-Maghribī 86–9, 194
Abū Rā'iṭa, Ḥabīb ibn Khidma 70–2
Adam, first human 14, 31, 42, 50, 63, 64, 71, 75, 116, 117, 124–6, 157, 192, 206, 213, 301, 306
Aden 301
'Against the law of the Saracens' 278, 279
'Against the Muslims' 201
'Against the Tajiks' 212–14
Agarenes. *See* Hagarenes 91, 92, 133, 153, 160, 173, 174
Ahl al-dhimma 10, 68, 106
Alain of Lille 267
Albelda', 'Chronicle of 235–8
Alfonso III, Spanish king 235, 236, 238
'Alī al-Ṭabarī 23–6
'Alī ibn Abī Ṭālib, cousin and son-in-law of Muḥammad 21, 22, 192, 193, 196, 246
Almohad dynasty 105, 218, 259, 260, 271, 295
Almoravid dynasty 105, 111, 218
'Ammār al-Baṣrī 79–82
Anatropē tou Koraniou 139–42
Annales Ianuenses 259
al-Anṣārī, Abū l-Qāsim 45–8
anthropomorphism 29, 98–9
The Apocalypse of Samuel 90–2
Apollin, Saracen idol 292
'Apology' ('Abd al-Masīḥ al-Kindī) 76–8
Aristotle 19, 20, 46, 81
The armour of doctrine 152
Ars compendiosa inveniendi veritatem 295
Ars generalis ultima 295
'Assuaging Thirst' 41–4
atonement 62–4, 102, 118
Averroes (Ibn Rushd) 219
Avicenna (Ibn Sīnā) 205, 219
Ayyūbid dynasty 59, 302

Baghdad 9, 10, 19, 27, 37, 41, 45, 56, 60, 76, 129, 155, 164, 169, 184, 193, 195, 198, 199, 200, 219, 21, 278, 300
Baḥīrā (Sergius or Sargis), heretical monk 4, 67, 69, 76, 133, 137, 190, 191–3, 219, 307
Baldwin II, king of Jerusalem 263
Barhebraeus, Gregory 170, 205–8
Barlaam and Josaphat, legend of 309
Bertrandon de la Broquière 312–15
'Best of Greek philosophy' 132
'Book of certain regions beyond the Mediterranean' 305
'Book of Count Lucanor' 309
'Book of Deeds' 281
'Book of Estates' 311–13
'The book of the Gentile and the Three Wise Men' 295–298
'Book of Guidance' 45
'The Book of Instructions' 53–5
'Book of Monasteries' 34–6
'Book of Pilgrimage' 78
'Book of Pontiffs' 224–7
'Book of the Proof' 79
'The Book of Religion and Empire' 23–6
'Book of the Sessions' 86–9
'Book of Testaments' of Lorvão 251–4
'Book against the Torah' 123–6
'Book of Wonders' 307–10

Caffaro of Genoa 259–62
Cairo 9, 34, 56, 59, 60, 61, 83, 85, 95, 123, 130, 176, 246, 265, 301, 313
'Candelabrum of the Sanctuaries' 205–8
Cantar de mío Cid 219
Capita philosophica 132
Ceylon 301
Chalcedon, Council of 45, 67, 68, 73
Chanson d'Antioche 291–3
Chanson de Roland 291–4
Charlemagne, Holy Roman Emperor 294
Charles Martel 221, 222–3, 218
Chronica mendosa et ridiculosa Sarracenorum 255–8
'Chronicle' (Dionysius of Tell Maḥrē) 183–6
'Chronicle' (Matthew of Edessa) 198–200
'Chronicle' (William of Tyre) 263–6
'Chronicle of Albelda' 235–8
'Chronicle of Fredegar' 221
Chronicon (William of Tyre) 263–6
Chronikē diēgēsis 152–4
Chronographia 136–8
'Chronography' 194–7
Church of the Holy Sepulchre 61, 118, 244, 250, 264, 292
Cid, Cantar de mío 219
Codex Valentim Fernandes 288
Collectio Toletana 76, 115, 255, 258
'Commentary on the Cross' 201–4
'Commentary on the Gospel of Matthew' 228–30
'The complete book on the principles of religion' 41
'Confirmation of the signs of prophethood' 37–40
Constans II, Byzantine emperor 174, 217
Constantine the Great, Roman emperor 38, 170
Constantine VI, Byzantine emperor 12
Constantinople 9, 67, 129, 130, 139, 143, 150, 153, 174, 175, 185, 243, 250
  fall of 217, 284
Contra legem Sarracenorum 278, 279
Contra paganos 267
conversion 271–3, 274–7
  to Christianity 17, 50, 83, 100–1, 119, 130, 147, 149–50, 152, 153–4, 187, 219, 270, 271, 272–3, 274, 275–7, 284, 289, 290, 295–6, 300, 305, 306, 307, 310, 316–17, 317–19
  to Islam 11, 12, 15, 21, 23, 51, 68, 76, 77–8, 84, 90, 95, 101, 106, 111, 112, 144, 160, 161, 170, 209, 210, 228, 278 280, 281–3, 301, 308
Coranus Graecus 139
Córdoba 9, 105, 107, 112, 115, 231, 232, 236, 239, 240, 253, 254
'The correct answer to those who have changed the religion of Christ' 62–4
corruption of the Bible (*taḥrīf*) 3, 4, 10, 12, 38–40, 41–4, 56–8, 70, 106–10, 117, 180, 287
'Critical commentary on the four Gospels, the Torah and other books of the prophets' 56–8
cross, veneration of the 73, 132, 134, 179, 180–2, 201–4, 211
Crusader states 49, 60, 130, 218, 263
Crusades and crusaders 3, 46, 153, 169, 170, 218, 219, 224, 242, 259, 270, 274, 275, 276, 284, 291–4, 302–4, 312

dalāʾil al-nubuwwa (proofs of prophethood) 23, 37–40, 205, 206, 208
Damascus 9, 53, 54, 56, 59, 62, 67, 97, 123, 129, 132, 169, 170, 314
David, king of Georgia 199–200, 307
David, psalmist 25–6, 30–3, 145, 159
De haeresibus 132–5
'Deeds of God through the Franks' 248–50
'Deeds of the Franks and of others going to Jerusalem' 248
Dei gesta per Francos 248–50
'Description of the world' 301–3
Devisement du monde 301–3
dhimmīs 10, 59, 68, 88, 94, 112, 217, 232, 233
'Dialogue with a Persian' 155–8
Digenēs Akritēs 130, 147–51
al-Dimashqī, Muḥammad ibn Abī Ṭālib 2, 97
al-dīn wa-l-dawla, Kitāb 23–6
Diogo Gomes 288–90
Dionysius bar Ṣalībī 201–4
Dionysius of Tell Maḥrē 183–6
divine substance 28, 45–8, 77, 80–2, 97, 98, 99
divorce 116, 119, 120–1, 135, 142, 303
al-diyārāt, Kitāb 34–6
Dome of the Rock 54, 173, 229, 307

Elias, prophet 206
Elias of Nisibis 86–9, 194–7

Elisha, prophet 206
Enoch/Enosh, scriptural character 32, 42, 206, 207
Epistola ad Abdalla, olim fratrem Andream 281–3
An epistolary exchange 86–9
Epistole ad ecclesiam triumphantem 278–80
Estados, Libro de los 311–13
Eulogius 231, 232, 233, 238
'Explanation of the true faith' 132
Expositio fidei 132
Expositio in Matheo 228–30
Ezra, scriptural character 42

Fabule Sarracenorum 255
Fakhr al-Dīn al-Rāzī 205, 207–8
Fātima, Muḥammad's daughter 191, 193, 197
Fāṭimid dynasty 53, 93, 111, 130, 198, 218, 245, 246
Firdaws al-ḥikma 23
First Crusade 111, 198, 218, 245–7, 248, 263, 264–6, 275, 307
'On the first discovery of Guinea' 288–90
First treatise 'On the Holy Trinity' 70
foodstuffs, clean and unclean 35, 55, 77, 212–14, 303, 319
'Fount of knowledge' 132
Francis of Assisi 270–3
Franks 50, 51, 53, 54–5, 60, 170, 199, 209, 214, 217, 221–3, 245–7, 248–50, 292, 313, 314, 315
Fredegar', 'Chronicle of 217, 221
Fulcher of Chartres 248

Gennadios Scholarios, patriarch of Constantinople 130, 162–5
Genoa 259–62
gentil i dels tres savis, Llibre del 295–8
Gesta Francorum et aliorum Hierosolimitanorum 248
Gesta orientalium principum 263
al-Ghazālī, Abū Ḥāmid 41, 45, 111, 208, 296, 298
Ghāzān Khan, Mongol ruler 209
Ghāzī ibn al-Wāsiṭī 59–61
Al-ghunya fī l-kalām 45–8
Girk' Harc'manc' 212–14
Giwargis I 176–8
God as a sphere 140–1, 152, 153, 154
Gog and Magog 174, 235, 237
Granada 10, 105, 218, 219, 316–19
'The greater work' 274–7
Gregory Barhebraeus 170, 205–8
Gregory VII, pope 242–4, 269
Grigor Tat'ewac'i 212–14
Guibert of Nogent 248–50
Gujnee, De prima iuentione 288–90

De haeresibus 132–5
Hagar, Abraham's handmaid 121, 122, 133, 134, 189
Hagarenes 91, 92, 133, 153, 160, 173, 174
al-Ḥākim bi-Amr Allāh, Fāṭimid caliph 11, 93–6
'Hammers for crosses' 115
Hārūn al-Rashīd, 'Abbasid caliph 12, 13
al-Ḥawādith wa-l-bida', Kitāb 111
Henry the Navigator, Prince 288, 290
Heraclius, Byzantine emperor 133, 196, 210
'On heresies' 132–5
Hernando de Talavera 316–19
Historia Francorum qui ceperunt Iherusalem 245–7
Historia Hierosolymitana (Fulcher of Chartres) 248
Historia Ierosolymitana (William of Tyre) 263–6
Historia vel gesta Francorum 221–3
'History' (Nicetas Choniates) 152–4
'The History of the Anonymous Storyteller' 190–3
'History of the capture of Almería and Tortosa' 259–62
'History of the Franks who captured Jerusalem' 245–7
'History of Khosrov' 172–5
'The history of Mār Yahballāhā and Rabban Ṣawmā' 209–11
'The history of the patriarchs' 83
'History of Sebeos' 172–5
'History or deeds of the Franks' 221–3
holosphyros, God as 140–1, 152, 153, 154
holy fire, miracle of the 61, 117–18
homosexual practices 91, 154, 239–41, 246, 269

Hugh of Caesarea 265
hypostases, divine 28–9, 47, 48, 81, 97, 99

Iblīs (Satan) 117, 124
Ibn Ḥazm 106, 107–10
Ibn Jubayr 49–52
Ibn al-Layth 12–15
Ibn Sīnā 205, 219
Ibn Taymiyya 62–4, 97, 123
'On the Incarnation' (Abū Rā'iṭa) 70–2
Incarnation of Christ 4, 12, 27, 46, 62, 70–2, 106, 108, 155, 162, 163, 185, 205, 212, 307
Al-i'lām bi-mā fī dīn al-Naṣārā min al-fasād wa-l-awhām 119
Incarnation of Christ 3, 12, 27, 46, 62, 70–2, 106, 107, 115, 155, 162, 163, 185, 205, 212, 300, 307
Indiculus luminosus 231–4
'Information about the corruptions and disillusions of the religion of the Christians' 119
'The indispensable, on theology' 45–8
Injīl (Gospel) 3, 10, 38–40, 109
Innocent III, pope 267, 270
Instrucción del Arzobispo de Granada 316–19
'Instruction from the Archbishop of Granada' 316–19
al-irshād, Kitāb 45
Isaac, son of Abraham 121, 134, 279, 306, 307, 313
Ishmael/Ismā'īl, son of Abraham, and Ishmaelites 24, 25, 119, 121–2, 133, 137, 173, 194, 203, 217, 222, 231, 233, 235, 236, 237, 238, 307
Islamic Psalms of David 30–3
Istoria de Mahomet 217
al-i'tibār, Kitāb 53–5

Jacobites 27, 46, 47, 48, 68, 70, 195, 196, 197, 299, 300
al-Jāḥiẓ, Abū 'Uthmān 19–22, 208
James I, king of Aragon 281, 295
Java 301
Al-Jawāb al-ṣaḥīḥ li-man baddala dīn al-Masīḥ 62–4
Jawhar 28, 45–8, 77, 80–2, 97, 98, 99. *See also* divine substance
Jean de Joinville 302–4
Jerome, saint and scholar 217, 234, 316
Jerusalem 49, 50, 54, 61, 67, 108, 111, 129, 173, 218, 228, 229, 242, 245–7, 250, 263, 264, 276, 279, 285, 291, 304, 312
Jesus Christ 1, 2, 3, 4, 24, 30, 32, 37, 44, 48, 56, 57, 58, 68, 76, 81, 102, 108, 109, 115, 121, 125, 133, 141, 145, 160, 161, 162–5, 174, 228–9, 238, 249, 270, 272, 278, 280, 282, 292, 307, 310, 317
  prophet of Islam 1, 3, 10, 42, 145, 179
  not crucified (Q 4:157) 10, 50, 63, 133, 181
  thieves crucified with him 43–4
Jews 1, 10, 12, 20, 21, 23, 27, 38–9, 41, 42–3, 59, 60, 73, 76, 78, 84–5, 93, 94, 95, 106, 107, 111, 119, 124, 126, 132, 133, 134, 137, 155, 156, 164, 173, 174, 180, 184–5, 186, 196, 202, 210, 219, 230, 248, 287, 306, 307, 308, 318
jihād 13
jihād (Christian) 101
jizya 12, 13, 14, 16, 112, 211. *See* also poll-tax
John the Baptist 68, 206
John of Damascus 129, 132–5
John Mandeville 219, 305–8
Juan Manuel 309–11
Juan de Segovia 284–7
'Judgement regarding the religions, inclinations and sects' 107–10
al-Juwaynī, Abū l-Ma'ālī 41–4, 45

Ka'ba 132, 134, 141, 202, 203, 292
Khadīja, wife of Muḥammad 67, 137
Khozrov II, Persian shah 172
al-Kindī, 'Abd al-Masīḥ 76–8
Kitāb al-'aṣā 53
Kitāb al-burhān 79
Kitāb al-dīn wa-l-dawla 23–6
Kitāb al-diyārāt 34–6
Kitāb al-faṣl (or fiṣal) fī l-milal wa-l-ahwā' wa-l-niḥal 107–10
Kitāb al-fihrist 79
Kitāb al-ḥawādith wa-l-bida' 111
Kitāb al-irshād 45
Kitāb al-i'tibār 53–5

Kitāb al-majālis 86–9
Kitāb fī taḥrīm jubn al-rūm 111
Kitāb ʿalā l-Tawrāt 123–6

'A lamp for rulers' 111–14
'Law of the pseudo-Prophet Muḥammad' 255–8
'Letter to ʿAbd Allāh, formerly Brother Andrew' 281–3
'Letter to an apostate of the Order of Friars Minor' 281–3
'Letter to the Cardinal of Saint Peter' 284–7
'Letters to the Church triumphant' 278–80
'The Letter of Ibn al-Layth' 12–15
'Letter to a Muslim Friend' 62
'Letter from the people of Cyprus' 97–9
'The Letter of al-Qūṭī' 115–18
Lex Mahumet pseudoprophete 255–8
Leo IV, pope 224, 225–7
Liber peregrinationis 78
Liber Pontificalis 224–7
Liber de quibusdam ultramarinis partibus 305
Liber testamentorum (Lorvão) 251–4
Libro del conde Lucanor 309
Libro de los estados 311–13
'Life of Gabriel of Beth Qustan' 187–9
'The Life of George the Younger' 159–61
'Life of Saint Louis' 302–4
Livre des merveilles 305–8
Llibre del gentil i dels tres savis 295–8
Llibre dels fets 281
Logos 47–8, 212
Louis IX, king of France 275, 302–4
'Lying and laughable chronicle of the Saracens' 255–8

al-Maghribī, Abū l-Qāsim al-Ḥusayn ibn ʿAlī 86–9
Magi, Zoroastrians 27, 74, 78, 176, 186, 191
Mahomet, Saracen idol 292
al-majālis, Kitāb 86–9
Maktbānut zabnē 194–7
Mamlūk companion 312, 315
Mamlūk dynasty 56, 59, 101, 130, 209, 302
al-Maʾmūn, ʿAbbasid caliph 19, 76, 184–5
Manichaeism 20, 21, 176, 249–50
Manuel I Comnenus, Byzantine emperor 152, 153–4
Manuel II Palaeologus, Byzantine emperor 130, 155–8
Maqālāt al-nās wa-ikhtilāfihim 27
Maqāmiʿ al-ṣulbān 115
Marco Polo 85, 219, 299–301
marriage, Muslim-Christian 177, 317
martyrdom 72, 129, 144–6, 159–61, 180–2, 217, 231, 239–40, 260, 269, 283, 310
'Martyrdom of ʿAbd al-Masīḥ' 100
'Martyrdom of the forty-two martyrs' 143–6
'Martyrdom of Jirjis' 100
'Martyrdom of Michael of Mār Saba' 100
'The Martyrdom of Rizqallāh ibn Nabaʿ' 100–2
martyrs of Córdoba 217, 238
Mary Magdalene 108, 109
Mary, Virgin 2, 55, 58, 74, 85, 117, 133, 163, 278, 280, 307, 318
Matthew of Edessa 198–200
Mecca 25, 41, 50, 56, 67, 123, 132, 140, 141, 195, 201, 202, 203, 207, 292, 303, 306, 312, 314
Medina 9, 41, 138, 195, 303, 306
Mehmed II, Ottoman sultan 130, 162
Melkites 27, 28, 46, 47–8, 68, 93, 100, 123, 129, 132
'Memorandum and list of ordinances given by Talavera to the Morisco community of Granada' 316–19
Memorial y tabla de ordenaciones dirigidas por Talavera para la comunidad morisca de Granada 316–19
Merveilles, Livre des 305–8
Min qawl Thāwudūrus usquf Ḥarrān [...] ṭaʿna ʿalā l-barrāniyyīn 73–5
miracle of Muqaṭṭam 83–5
miracles of Jesus 12, 206
miracles of Muḥammad 23, 150, 205, 206, 207–8
miracles of prophets and holy men 117, 187, 206, 207, 225, 227, 276, 292, 296, 306
Mnōrat qudšē 205–8
Moses 24, 25, 32, 43, 63, 71, 117, 123, 133, 137, 141, 173, 181, 203, 204, 206, 207, 213–14
Muʿāwiya, Umayyad caliph 174–5
Muḥammad, Prophet 1, 2, 3, 4, 9, 10, 12, 21, 37, 67, 68–9, 107, 116, 120, 129,

132, 133–5, 136–8, 145, 152, 153, 155, 156, 157, 160, 172, 180, 184, 190, 191–3, 195, 196, 201, 202, 205, 206–8, 212, 214, 231, 235, 236–8, 248, 249–50, 256, 258, 260, 279, 280, 287, 289, 290, 296, 297, 299, 300, 301, 303, 304, 307, 310–11, 312, 314, 319
false prophet 3, 37, 76, 78, 106, 112, 119, 136, 140, 146, 154, 161, 191–3, 199, 206–8, 217, 236, 310
foretold in the Bible 3, 10, 12, 23–6, 31–2, 41, 42, 206, 208, 236–7, 287
al-Muʿizz, Fāṭimid caliph 84–5
the Muqaṭṭam miracle 83–5
Mūsā (Moses) 24, 25, 32, 43, 63, 71, 117, 123, 133, 137, 141, 173, 181, 203, 204, 206, 207, 213–14
al-Muʿtaṣim, ʿAbbasid caliph 143, 144–6, 183
al-Mutawakkil, ʿAbbasid caliph 11, 19, 23
Muʿtazila 19, 27, 37, 48, 79, 81
Monodies 248
al-Muʿtazz, ʿAbbasid caliph 35–6

al-Nāṣir ibn ʿAlannās, Ḥammādid emir 242, 244
Nestorians 23, 27, 46, 47, 68, 79, 97, 169, 191, 192, 299, 300
Nicetas of Byzantium 129, 139–42
Nicholas of Cusa 284–7
Noah 63, 71, 192, 213, 279
'Nomymans', West African ruler 289–90

Old French epic poems 291–4
'On the first discovery of Guinea' 288–90
'On heresies' 132–5
'On the Incarnation' 70–2
'The opinions of people and the differences between them' 27
Opus maius 274–7
Ottoman dynasty 9, 155, 159, 170, 219, 312

Pact of ʿUmar 1, 10, 16–18, 21, 68, 88, 93–4, 111, 189, 314
Panoplia dogmatikē 152
Paradise 35, 44, 113, 115, 116, 118, 138, 145, 293, 296, 297–8, 307, 314
Paschasius Radbertus 228–30
Passio Pelagii 239–41
'Passion of Pelagius' 239–41
Patmut'iwn Sebeosi 172–5
Paul, Apostle 38, 78, 224, 226, 227
Paul Alvarus 231–4
Paul of Antioch 62, 97–8
Pēgē gnōseōs 132
People of the Book (*Ahl al-kitāb*) 1, 10, 32, 40, 57, 68, 106, 217
Peter, Apostle 78, 108, 109, 165, 225, 226, 227, 243, 244, 256
Peter the Chanter 267–9
Peter the Venerable 115, 255, 256, 257
Petrus Marsilius 281–3
pigs and pork 18, 50, 55, 149, 213, 249–50, 290, 303, 307
'Poem of the Cid' 219
Poitiers, battle of 105, 218, 221, 222–3
poll-tax (*jizya*) 12, 21, 113, 178
De prima iuentione Gujnee 288–90
'Proof of the Christian Religion' 70
proofs of prophethood (*dalāʾil al-nubuwwa*) 23, 37–40, 205, 206, 208
property, divine (*khāṣṣa*) 28–9, 47, 77
Prophetic Chronicle 235, 236–8
Psalms 10, 24, 30–3, 63, 117, 145, 307, 318

Q 4:157 10, 50, 63, 133, 181
Q 4:171 2, 10, 67, 133, 164, 206, 207, 232
'Questions and answers concerning our Lord Jesus Christ' 162–5

Radd ʿalā ahl al-dhimma wa-man tabiʿahum (Ghāzī ibn al-Wāṣitī) 59–61
Al-radd ʿalā l-Naṣārā (ʿAlī l-Ṭabarī) 23
Fī l-radd ʿalā l-Nasārā (al-Jāḥiẓ) 19–22
Al-radd ʿalā l-thalāth firaq min al-Naṣārā 27–9
Ramon Llull 295–8
Raymond of Aguilers 245–7
'In rebuttal of the Christians' (al-Jāḥiẓ) 19–22
Reconquista 105, 218, 235
'Refutation of the Christians' (ʿAlī l-Ṭabarī) 23
'Refutation of the dhimmīs and those who follow them' (Ghāzī ibn al-Wāṣitī) 59–61

'Refutation of the Qur'an' 139–42
'The refutation of the three sects of the Christians' 27–9
'Register' (Pope Gregory VII) 242–4
Regula bullata and *Regula non bullata* 270–3
remarriage in Islam 116, 120, 135, 143
Riccoldo da Monte de Croce 278–80
Riḥla (Ibn Jubayr) 49–52
'The ring of the dove' 107
Risāla (ʿAbd al-Masīḥ al-Kindī) 76–8
Risāla min ahl Jazīrat Qubruṣ 97–9
Risālat Abī l-Rabīʿ Muḥammad ibn al-Layth 12–15
Robert of Ketton 219, 255–8
Roger Bacon 274–7
Roncevalles 293
'Rules of the Friars Minor' 270–3

St Peter's basilica 225–6
Samuel of Qalamūn 90–2
Saracens 115, 133, 136, 146, 154, 217, 218, 221, 222–3, 225–7, 229, 230, 235, 236, 238, 246, 255, 256–7, 260, 261–2, 269, 271, 272–3, 275, 279–80, 285–7, 291, 292–3, 293–4, 296–8, 299–301, 303, 304, 306–8, 313–15
Sargis or Sergius (Baḥīrā), heretical monk 4, 67, 69, 76, 133, 137, 190, 191–3, 219, 307
Satan 31, 62–4, 102, 117, 192, 225
Scholion 179–82
Sebeos the Armenian 172–5
Seljuk dynasty 130, 218
Sergius II, pope 224
Sergius (Baḥīrā) 4, 67, 69, 76, 133, 137, 190, 191–3, 219, 307
al-Shābushtī, ʿAlī ibn Muḥammad 34–6
Al-shāmil fī uṣūl al-dīn 41
Shifāʾ al-ghalīl 41–4
'The shining guide' 231–4
Shurūṭ ʿUmar (Pact of ʿUmar) 1, 10, 16–18, 21, 68, 88, 111, 189, 314
Sirāj al-mulūk 111–14
sister of Aaron and Moses (Q 19:28) 117, 133, 141
'Some statements of Theodore, Bishop of Ḥarrān [...] against the outsiders' 73–5
Spanish Umayyads 105, 218, 231, 235, 236
Summa de sacramentis et animae consiliis 267–9
'Summa on the sacraments and spiritual advice' 267–9
Synodal canons (Giwargis I) 176–8

Tabriz 190, 211, 300–1
Fī l-tajassud 70–2
Al-taʿlīq ʿalā l-Anājīl al-arbaʿa wa-l-taʿlīq ʿalā l-Tawrāh wa-ʿalā ghayrihā min kutub al-anbiyāʾ 56–8
Tārīkh al-Anṭākī 93–6
Tashʿītha d-Mār Yahballāhā wa-d-Rabban Ṣawmā 209–11
Tathbīt dalāʾil al-nubuwwa 37–40
Tathlīth al-Waḥdāniyya 119–22
Ṭawq al-ḥamāma 107
Tawrāt (Torah) 3, 10, 20, 24, 25, 31, 39, 41, 42–3, 56, 63, 82, 116, 117, 120, 123–6, 207
ʿalā l-Tawrāt, Kitāb 123–6
Testamentorum, Liber 251–4
Thāwudūrus usquf Ḥarrān [...] ṭaʿna ʿalā l-barrāniyyīn, Min qawl 73–5
Theodore Abū Qurra 73–5
Theodore bar Koni 179–82
Theophanes the Confessor 136–8
Thesaurus orthodoxiae 152
The Toledan Collection 76, 115, 255, 258
Torah 3, 10, 20, 24, 25, 31, 39, 41, 42, 56, 63, 82, 116, 117, 120, 123–6, 207
Tractatus de statu Sarracenorum 305
'Travels' (Ibn Jubayr) 49–52
'Treatise on the state of the Saracens' 305
'Trinitizing the unity of God' 119–22
Trinity 3, 4, 12, 27–9, 48, 51, 62, 67, 69, 70–2, 77, 79–82, 86–9, 99, 106, 107, 119–22, 151, 155, 206, 212, 232
al-Ṭūfī, Najm al-Dīn 56–8
Turks 9, 130, 152, 153, 159, 160, 162, 169, 170, 198–200, 218, 242, 245–6, 247, 248, 250, 284, 299, 312, 314, 315
al-Ṭurṭūshī 111–14

ʿUmar ibn al-Khaṭṭāb 1, 16, 17, 68, 78, 187, 197
Umayyad dynasty 9, 10, 20, 67, 105, 132, 176

Urban II, pope 218, 292
Usāma ibn Munqidh 53–5

veneration of the cross 73, 132, 134, 179, 180–2, 201–4, 211
Vie de saint Louis 302–4
'Voyage to the Middle East' 312–15
Le voyage d'Oultremer 312–15

Waraqa ibn Nawfal 67, 137
al-Warrāq, Abū ʿĪsā 27–9
al-Wāthiq, ʿAbbasid caliph 23, 143, 144
William II, Norman king of Sicily 50–1
William of Rubruck 274
William of Tyre 263–6
wine 48, 58, 77, 113, 138, 173, 202, 212, 214, 247, 290, 307, 314
Wonders', 'Book of 305–8, 50

Yaḥyā al-Anṭākī 93–6
Ystoria captionis Almarie et Turtuose 259–62

Zabūr. *See* Psalms
Zayd ibn Ḥāritha 21, 22, 135, 196, 246
Zhamanakagrut'iwn 198–200
Zoroastrians, Magi 27, 74, 78, 176, 186, 191
zunnār 18, 21, 60, 68, 93

www.ingramcontent.com/pod-product-compliance
Lightning Source LLC
Chambersburg PA
CBHW082144230426
43672CB00015B/2841
* 9 7 8 1 3 5 0 2 1 4 0 9 5 *